Youth Movements and Elections in Eastern Europe

At the turn of the twenty-first century, a tide of nonviolent youth movements swept across Eastern Europe. Young people demanded political change in repressive political regimes that emerged since the collapse of communism. The Serbian social movement Otpor ("Resistance") played a vital role in bringing down Slobodan Milosevic in 2000. Inspired by Otpor's example, similar challenger organizations were formed in the former Soviet republics. The youth movements, however, differed in the extent to which they could mobilize citizens against the authoritarian governments on the eve of national elections. This book argues that the movement's tactics and state countermoves explain, in no small degree, divergent social movement outcomes. Using data from semistructured interviews with former movement participants, public opinion polls, government publications, nongovernmental organizations' reports, and newspaper articles, this book traces state-movement interactions in five post-communist states: Azerbaijan, Belarus, Georgia, Serbia, and Ukraine.

Olena Nikolayenko is Associate Professor of Political Science at Fordham University and an Associate at the Davis Center for Russian and Eurasian Studies, Harvard University. She received her Ph.D. in political science from the University of Toronto and held visiting appointments at the Center on Democracy, Development, and the Rule of Law, Stanford University; the Davis Center for Russian and Eurasian Studies, Harvard University; the Princeton Institute for International and Regional Studies, Princeton University; and the Department of Sociology, the National University of Kyiv–Mohyla Academy, Ukraine. Her research was supported by the International Center on Nonviolent Conflict and the Social Sciences and Humanities Research Council of Canada.

Cambridge Studies in Contentious Politics

Rina Agarwala, *Informal Labor, Formal Politics, and Dignified Discontent in India*
Ronald Aminzade, *Race, Nation, and Citizenship in Post-Colonial Africa: The Case of Tanzania*
Ronald Aminzade et al., *Silence and Voice in the Study of Contentious Politics*
Javier Auyero, *Routine Politics and Violence in Argentina: The Gray Zone of State Power*
Phillip M. Ayoub, *When States Come Out: Europe's Sexual Minorities and the Politics of Visibility*
Amrita Basu, *Violent Conjunctures in Democratic India*
W. Lance Bennett and Alexandra Segerberg, *The Logic of Connective Action: Digital Media and the Personalization of Contentious Politics*
Nancy Bermeo and Deborah J. Yashar, *Parties, Movements, and Democracy in the Developing World*
Clifford Bob, *The Global Right Wing and the Clash of World Politics*
Clifford Bob, *The Marketing of Rebellion: Insurgents, Media, and International Activism*
Charles Brockett, *Political Movements and Violence in Central America*
Marisa von Bülow, *Building Transnational Networks: Civil Society and the Politics of Trade in the Americas*
Valerie Bunce and Sharon Wolchik, *Defeating Authoritarian Leaders in Postcommunist Countries*
Lars-Erik Cederman, Kristian Skrede Gleditsch, and Halvard Buhaug, *Inequality, Grievances, and Civil War*

(*continued after index*)

Youth Movements and Elections in Eastern Europe

OLENA NIKOLAYENKO
Fordham University

CAMBRIDGE
UNIVERSITY PRESS

CAMBRIDGE
UNIVERSITY PRESS

University Printing House, Cambridge CB2 8BS, United Kingdom

One Liberty Plaza, 20th Floor, New York, NY 10006, USA

477 Williamstown Road, Port Melbourne, VIC 3207, Australia

314-321, 3rd Floor, Plot 3, Splendor Forum, Jasola District Centre, New Delhi - 110025, India

79 Anson Road, #06-04/06, Singapore 079906

Cambridge University Press is part of the University of Cambridge.

It furthers the University's mission by disseminating knowledge in the pursuit of education, learning and research at the highest international levels of excellence.

www.cambridge.org
Information on this title: www.cambridge.org/9781108404143
DOI: 10.1017/9781108241809

First published 2017
First paperback edition 2020

A catalogue record for this publication is available from the British Library

ISBN 978-1-108-41673-3 Hardback
ISBN 978-1-108-40414-3 Paperback

To my sons, Anvar and Sanjar

Contents

Tables

Acknowledgments

This book would not have been possible without the support of many people and institutions. First and foremost, I am deeply indebted to the social movement participants and civic activists who were willing to share with me their insights into civil resistance and tell their stories. I have profound respect for their courage and determination to stand up against authoritarian governments at the risk of their physical, psychological, and financial well-being. No matter how much they succeeded in bringing down the regime, they left an indelible mark on their societies and stimulated further debate over the organization of civil resistance in the region. My critical remarks regarding tactical missteps of some youth movements are meant to provide some food for thought for a new cohort of youth activists and do not diminish the significance of the defunct challenger organizations in demanding political change. Most interviewees are identified by their real names. I use pseudonyms for those who preferred to conceal their identity and/or continue to reside in countries with a high level of state repression. I am thankful to the Belgrade-based Center for Applied Nonviolent Action and Strategies (CANVAS) and in particular Srdja Popovic and Sinisa Sikman for their support of my research in Serbia. I also thank Imke Hansen, Ivan Marovic, Tamara Martsenyuk, Giorgi Meladze, Vitali Silitski, Charles Szrom, and Steve York for facilitating my fieldwork in Eastern Europe.

A number of institutions shaped my thinking about state-movement interactions in a nondemocratic setting. The graduate program at the University of Toronto provided me with solid training in the discipline and brought me in contact with many outstanding scholars. My thanks go to Jeffrey Kopstein, Neil Nevitte, Susan Solomon, Peter Solomon, and Lucan Way for advancing my understanding of comparative politics and supporting my research endeavors on the linkage between youth and politics in Eastern Europe. As a postdoctoral fellow at Stanford University's Center on Democracy, Development, and the Rule of Law, I found an intellectually stimulating environment for the development of my research project. In particular, the workshop "Political Sociology, Social Movements, and Collective Action" in the Department of Sociology and the Comparative Politics Workshop in the Department of Political Science provided superb venues for a productive exchange of ideas on social science research. I am thankful to Doug McAdam and Michael McFaul for their mentorship and Larry Diamond, Karen Long Jusko, Susan Olzak, Paolo Parigi, and Andrew Walder for their helpful feedback on my work. At a later stage in my research project, the Princeton Institute for International and Regional Studies at Princeton University provided an intellectually invigorating setting for drafting a book-length manuscript. In particular, I am grateful to Mark Beissinger for his immense support of my research project in so many different ways. I also thank the Caucasus Research Resource Centers (Azerbaijan), the Liberty Institute (Georgia), the Department of Sociology at the National University of Kyiv–Mohyla Academy (Ukraine), and the Centre for Political Studies and Public Opinion Research at the Institute of Social Sciences (Serbia) for warm receptions during my visit to the region. Finally, the Department of Political Science at Fordham University offered a collegial environment for completing this research project. I am especially thankful to Jeff Cohen for his sage advice on academic publishing.

On the completion of data collection, I greatly benefited from the feedback I received at the pre-ASA workshop, "Making Connections: Movements and Research in a Global Context," the Politics and Protest Workshop held at the CUNY Graduate Center, and the manuscript-development workshop held at the Leitner Center for International Law and Justice, Fordham Law School. Some findings from this research were also presented at the Canadian Institute of Ukrainian Studies, University of Alberta; the Center for Russian, East European, and Eurasian Studies, Stanford University; the Institute of Slavic, East European, and Eurasian Studies, University of California–Berkeley; the Kokkalis Program on Southeastern and East-Central Europe, Harvard University; the National University of Kyiv–Mohyla Academy, Ukraine; the Social Sciences Research Center (WZB) Berlin, Germany; the Ukrainian Catholic University, Ukraine; the Kennan Institute, Woodrow Wilson International Center for Scholars; and annual meetings of the American Political Science Association, the American Sociological Association, the Association for Slavic, East European, and Eurasian Studies, and the Association for the Study of Nationalities. I thank participants and in particular Robyn Angley, Maciej Bartkowski, Marije Elvira Boekkooi, Valerie Bunce, Jeff Goodwin, Henry Hale, Valerii Khmelko, Lester Kurtz, David Marples, Sharon Erickson Nepstad, Tsveta Petrova, Blair Ruble, Kurt Schock, Fredrik M. Sjoberg, Marlene Spoerri, Mark Thompson, and Sharon Wolchik for their insightful comments.

This research was supported by the Social Sciences and Humanities Research Council of Canada (SSHRC postdoctoral fellowship); the Center on

Democracy, Development, and the Rule of Law, Stanford University; the First Year Faculty Research Grant, Fordham University; and the International Center on Nonviolent Conflict (manuscript-development grant).

As an author, I was fortunate to work with an extraordinary editorial, production, and marketing team at Cambridge University Press. I thank Lewis Bateman for expressing initial interest in the book project and Robert Dreesen for deftly taking it over and efficiently handling the review process. I am also thankful to the series editors and anonymous reviewers for their constructive criticism of my work.

Last but not least, I thank my family for their steady support of my research endeavors. Words are not enough to express my gratitude to my spouse for his love and encouragement throughout my academic career. I dedicate this book to my sons, Anvar and Sanjar, who frequently insisted on a respite from my working on the computer and joyfully brought me to Astoria Park or a nearby playground. I hope that my children's generation will live in a freer world.

COPYRIGHT ACKNOWLEDGMENTS

1

Introduction

At the turn of the twenty-first century, there has been a spectacular rise of nonviolent youth movements in Eastern Europe.[1] Young people called for free and fair elections to bring about political change in repressive political regimes that had emerged since the collapse of communism. In 2000, the Serbian social movement *Otpor* ("Resistance"), formed by a small group of students from the University of Belgrade, recruited thousands of young people and propelled electoral defeat of the incumbent president. Within three months of Slobodan Milosevic's downfall, the youth movement *Zubr* ("Bison") was set up in Belarus to press for political change during the 2001 presidential election. Similarly, the youth movement *Kmara* ("Enough") was established in the Republic of Georgia to challenge the current regime during the 2003 parliamentary election. This tide of youth activism continued with the emergence of two Ukrainian youth movements with the same name – *Pora* ("It's Time") – on the eve of the 2004 presidential election. The following year, the youth movements *Maqam* ("It's Time"), *Yeni Fikir* ("New Thinking"), and *Yokh* ("No") called for free and fair elections in Azerbaijan. Never before have post-communist youth mobilized against the regime on such a grand scale.

A striking feature of these youth movements was the adoption of similar strategies regarding the timing of mass mobilization, the content of movement claims, and the repertoire of contention. Almost all the youth movements were formed during an election year. In anticipation of vote rigging, youth activists campaigned for free and fair elections and targeted the incumbent president as a stumbling block to democratization. Another common attribute of the youth movements was the use of nonviolent methods. The cross-national diffusion of ideas explains, to a large degree, cross-movement similarities.[2]

[1] The term "Eastern Europe" is here loosely applied to refer to the whole post-communist region, including Southeastern Europe and the South Caucasus.

[2] On the cross-national diffusion of ideas, see Arias-King, Fredo. 2007. "Orange People: A Brief History of Transnational Liberation Networks in East Central Europe." *Demokratizatsiya: Journal of Post-Soviet Democratization* 15(1): 29–71; Beissinger, Mark. 2007. "Structure and

Since post-communist youth shared similar political values and faced a similar set of institutional constraints on political participation, the attribution of similarity provided a basis for the adoption of Otpor's tactics.[3]

Some youth movements, however, were more successful than others in mobilizing young people against the regime. Thousands of youngsters joined Otpor to wage a nonviolent struggle against the incumbent. Similarly, thousands of young Ukrainians challenged the power of the ruling elite through nonviolent action in 2004. Compared with Pora, Zubr mobilized a smaller number of youth during the 2001 presidential elections. Likewise, the Azerbaijani youth groups Maqam, Yeni Fikir, and Yokh recruited a smaller fraction of the youth population than Georgia's Kmara on the eve of the parliamentary elections.

A central argument of this book is that tactical interactions between social movements and incumbent governments explain, in part, the level of youth mobilization against the regime. Tactical interaction is "an ongoing process ... in which insurgents and opponents seek, in chess-like fashion, to offset the moves of the other."[4] On the one hand, the social movement seeks to attain its goals through the deployment of innovative tactics. On the other hand, the movement's adversary tries to devise savvy countermobilization tactics. The level of youth mobilization is affected by the extent to which the social movement and the incumbent government deploy innovative tactics and counteract each other's action. Here innovation does not imply the generation of absolutely novel ideas. The novelty of protest tactics or state countermoves in a particular context might be sufficient to catch an opponent by surprise and gain a strategic advantage.

This study further contends that learning is vital to the development of effective tactics. The analysis focuses on two learning mechanisms: participation in previous protest campaigns and the cross-national diffusion of ideas. The underlying assumption is that both civic activists and the ruling elite can draw lessons from earlier episodes of contention. Movement participants can devise more effective tactics if they critically assess the dynamics of previous protest campaigns inside and outside the country. Similarly, the

Example in Modular Political Phenomena: The Diffusion of Bulldozer/Rose/Orange/Tulip Revolutions." *Perspectives on Politics* 5(2): 259–76; Beissinger, Mark. 2009. "An Interrelated Wave." *Journal of Democracy* 20(1): 74–77; Bunce, Valerie, and Sharon Wolchik. 2010. "Defeating Dictators: Electoral Change and Stability in Competitive Authoritarian Regimes." *World Politics* 43(1): 43–86; Bunce, Valerie, and Sharon Wolchik. 2011. *Defeating Authoritarian Leaders in Post-Communist Countries*. New York: Cambridge University Press; Fenger, Menno. 2007. "The Diffusion of Revolutions: Comparing Recent Regime Turnovers in Five Post-communist States." *Demokratizatsiya: Journal of Post-Soviet Democratization* 15(1): 5–27.

[3] On belonging to the post-Soviet generation as a basis for the attribution of similarity, see Nikolayenko, Olena. 2007. "The Revolt of the Post-Soviet Generation: Youth Movements in Serbia, Georgia, and Ukraine." *Comparative Politics* 39(2): 169–88.

[4] McAdam, Doug. 1983. "Tactical Innovation and the Pace of Insurgency." *American Sociological Review* 48(6): 735–54, p. 736.

incumbent government can deploy more effective countermobilization tactics if it takes cues from prior upheavals in politically affinitive contexts. The pace of learning by civic activists and autocratic incumbents accounts, to some extent, for cross-country differences in state-movement interactions.

This research seeks to contribute to three bodies of literature. First, this study adds to comparative democratization literature by examining the development of youth movements in the post-communist region. In recent years, copious research has analyzed origins of the so-called color or electoral revolutions in Eastern Europe.[5] Likewise, the Arab Spring – a wave of protest events in the Middle East – has reinvigorated a debate over the causes of the autocrat's downfall.[6] One of the crucial factors that determined the incumbent's loss of power was a remarkably high level of citizen participation in antigovernment protests. Young people played a prominent

[5] See, for example, Aslund, Anders, and Michael McFaul, eds. 2006. *Revolution in Orange: The Origins of Ukraine's Democratic Breakthrough*. Washington, DC: Carnegie Endowment for International Peace; Beacháin, Donnacha Ó., and Abel Polese, eds. 2010. *The Colour Revolutions in the Former Soviet Republics: Successes and Failures*. London: Routledge; Beissinger, Mark. 2007. "Structure and Example in Modular Political Phenomena: The Diffusion of Bulldozer/Rose/Orange/Tulip Revolutions"; Bunce, Valerie, and Sharon Wolchik. 2011. *Defeating Authoritarian Leaders in Post-Communist Countries*; Cummings, Sally, ed. 2010. *Domestic and International Perspectives on Kyrgyzstan's 'Tulip Revolution': Motives, Mobilization, and Meanings*. New York: Routledge; Forbig, Joerg, and Pavol Demes, eds. 2007. *Reclaiming Democracy: Civil Society and Electoral Change in Central and Eastern Europe*. Washington, DC: German Marshall Fund; Hale, Henry. 2006. "Democracy or Autocracy on the March?: The Colored Revolutions as Normal Dynamics of Patronal Presidentialism." *Communist and Post-Communist Studies* 39: 305–29; Lane, David, and Stephen White, eds. 2013. *Rethinking the "Coloured Revolution"*. London: Routledge; McFaul, Michael. 2005. "Transitions from Postcommunism." *Journal of Democracy* 16(3): 5–19; Mitchell, Lincoln. 2011. *Uncertain Democracy: U.S. Foreign Policy and Georgia's Rose Revolution*. Philadelphia: University of Pennsylvania Press; Spoerri, Marlene. 2014. *Engineering Revolution: The Paradox of Democracy Promotion in Serbia*. Philadelphia: University of Pennsylvania Press; Way, Lucan. 2008. "The Real Causes of the Color Revolutions." *Journal of Democracy* 19(3): 55–69; Wheatley, Jonathan. 2005. *Georgia from National Awakening to Rose Revolution: Delayed Transition in the Former Soviet Union*. Aldershot, UK: Ashgate.

[6] On the Arab Spring, see Anderson, Lisa. 2011. "Demystifying the Arab Spring: Parsing the Differences between Tunisia, Egypt, and Libya." *Foreign Affairs* 90(3): 2–7; Bayat, Asef. 2013. *Life as Politics: How Ordinary People Change the Middle East*, 2nd ed. Stanford, CA: Stanford University Press; Bellin, Eva. 2012. "Reconsidering the Robustness of Authoritarianism in the Middle East: Lessons from the Arab Spring." *Comparative Politics* 44(2): 127–49; Gelvin, James. 2012. *The Arab Uprisings: What Everyone Needs to Know*. New York: Oxford University Press; Haas, Mark, and David Lesch, eds. 2012. *The Arab Spring: Change and Resistance in the Middle East*. Boulder, CO: Westview Press; Howard, Philip, and Muzammil Hussain. 2013. *Democracy's Fourth Wave?: Digital Media and the Arab Spring*. New York: Oxford University Press; Korany, Bahgat, and Rabab El-Mahdi. 2014. *Arab Spring in Egypt: Revolution and Beyond*. Cairo: American University in Cairo Press; Masoud, Tarek. 2011. "The Road to (and from) Liberation Square." *Journal of Democracy* 22(3): 20–34.

role in these political processes, coordinating the organization of protest events, permanently occupying city squares, and spreading information via leaflets or, more recently, social media. Insufficient attention, however, has been devoted to youth movements as an agent of social change.[7] Addressing this oversight, this book traces how youth movements in five post-communist states sought to mobilize citizens against the regime on the eve of national elections.

Second, this research contributes to social-movement scholarship by analyzing state-movement interactions in political regimes falling somewhere between democracy and dictatorship. The bulk of empirical work on the topic has been done in advanced industrial democracies and hardcore autocracies.[8] The proliferation of hybrid regimes in the post–Cold War period provides an understudied context for the analysis of contentious politics.[9] This study argues

[7] To date, there are few academic books on the topic, and most research has been published in the form of journal articles or book chapters. See Bunce, Valerie, and Sharon Wolchik. 2006. "Youth and Electoral Revolutions in Slovakia, Serbia, and Georgia." *SAIS Review* 26(2): 55–65; Bunce, Valerie, and Sharon Wolchik. 2007. "Youth and Postcommunist Electoral Revolutions: Never Trust Anyone over 30?" In *Reclaiming Democracy: Civil Society and Electoral Change in Central and Eastern Europe*, eds. Pavol Demes and Joerg Forbig. Washington, DC: German Marshall Fund, pp. 191–204; Demes, Pavol, and Joerg Forbig. 2006. "Pora – 'It's Time' for Democracy in Ukraine." In *Revolution in Orange: The Origins of Ukraine's Democratic Breakthrough*, eds. Anders Aslund and Michael McFaul. Washington, DC: Carnegie Endowment for International Peace, pp. 85–102; Kuzio, Taras. 2006. "Civil Society, Youth, and Societal Mobilization in Democratic Revolutions." *Communist and Post-Communist Studies* 39(3): 365–86; Lim, Merlyna. 2012. "Clicks, Cabs, and Coffee Houses: Social Media and Oppositional Movements in Egypt, 2004–2011." *Journal of Communication* 62(2): 231–48; Nikolayenko, Olena. 2012. "Tactical Interactions between Youth Movements and Incumbent Governments in Post-Communist States." *Research in Social Movements, Conflicts, and Change* 34: 27–61; Rosenberg, Tina. 2011. *Join the Club: How Peer Pressure Can Transform the World*. New York: Norton and Williams; Sanders, Christoph. 2013. "Building Resistance: Dynamics of Egyptian Youth Activism in Non-Violent Movements between 2000 and 2011." In *Democracy in Crisis: The Dynamics of Civil Protest and Civil Resistance*, eds. Bert Preiss and Claudia Brunner. Munster, Germany: LIT Verlag, pp. 155–84.

[8] See, for example, Banaszak, Lee Ann, Karen Beckwith, and Dieter Rucht, eds. 2003. *Women's Movements Facing the Reconfigured State*. New York: Cambridge University Press; Boudreau, Vincent. 2004. *Resisting Dictatorship: Repression and Protest in Southeast Asia*. New York: Cambridge University Press; Goodwin, Jeff. 2001. *No Other Way Out: States and Revolutionary Movements, 1945–1991*. New York: Cambridge University Press; Johnston, Hank. 2011. *States and Social Movements*. Malden, MA: Polity Press; Yashar, Deborah. 1997. *Demanding Democracy: Reform and Reaction in Costa Rica and Guatemala, 1870s–1950s*. Stanford, CA: Stanford University Press; Zwerman, Gilda, and Patricia Steinhoff. 2005. "When Activists Ask for Trouble: State-Dissident Interactions and the New Left Cycle of Resistance in the United States and Japan." In *Repression and Mobilization*, eds. Christian Davenport, Hank Johnston, and Carol Mueller. Minneapolis, MN: University of Minnesota Press, pp. 85–107.

[9] On the conceptualization of the hybrid regime, see Diamond, Larry. 2002. "Thinking about the Hybrid Regimes." *Journal of Democracy* 13(2): 21–35; Levitsky, Steven, and Lucan Way. 2010. *Competitive Authoritarianism: Hybrid Regimes after the Cold War*. New York: Cambridge University Press.

that the regime type affects the timing of mass mobilization, the scope of movement demands, the repertoire of contention, and the toolkit of state repression.

Third, this study contributes to the bourgeoning body of research on nonviolent action.[10] Within this literature, analysis of defeated unarmed insurrections is greatly outnumbered by examination of the triumphant use of nonviolent action. Unlike most previous work, this study includes cases of both successful and failed mobilization. Specifically, this book examines the development of such understudied challenger organizations as Maqam, Yeni Fikir, Yokh, and Zubr. Though the Azerbaijani and Belarusian youth movements were unable to mobilize a sufficiently large number of young people against the regime, the analysis of their tactical missteps and the governments' countermoves can advance scholarly understanding of nonviolent resistance and inform youth's ongoing struggle for political change.

The remainder of this chapter lays out a theoretical framework for explaining the level of youth mobilization against the regime, explains the case selection, and describes data sources.

THE SIGNIFICANCE OF TACTICS

This study argues that tactics adopted by youth movements and incumbent governments influence the level of youth mobilization against the regime. While strategy is a long-term plan of action, tactics denote specific means to execute a

[10] Ackerman, Peter, and Jack DuVall. 2000. *A Force More Powerful: A Century of Nonviolent Conflict*. New York: St. Martin's Press; Bartkowski, Maciej, ed. 2013. *Recovering Nonviolent History: Civil Resistance in Liberation Struggles*. Boulder, CO: Lynne Rienner; Chenoweth, Erica, and Maria Stephan. 2011. *Why Civil Resistance Works: The Strategic Logic of Nonviolent Conflict*. New York: Columbia University Press; Engler, Mark, and Paul Engler. 2016. *This Is an Uprising: How Nonviolent Revolt Is Shaping the Twenty-First Century*. New York: Nation Books; Martin, Brian, and Wendy Varney. 2003. *Nonviolence Speaks: Communicating against Repression*. Cresskill, NJ: Hampton Press; Nepstad, Sharon Erickson. 2011. *Nonviolent Revolutions: Civil Resistance in the Late 20th Century*. New York: Oxford University Press; Nepstad, Sharon Erikson. 2015. *Nonviolent Struggle: Theories, Strategies, and Dynamics*. New York: Oxford University Press; Popovic, Srdja, Andrej Milivojevic, and Slobodan Djinovic. 2006. *Nonviolent Struggle: 50 Crucial Points*. Belgrade, Serbia: Centre for Applied Non-Violent Action and Strategies; Popovic, Srdja. 2015. *Blueprint for Revolution*. New York: Spiegel & Grau; Roberts, Adam, and Timothy Garton Ash, eds. 2009. *Civil Resistance and Power Politics: The Experience of Nonviolent Action from Gandhi to the Present*. Oxford: Oxford University Press; Schock, Kurt. 2005. *Unarmed Insurrections: People Power Movements in Nondemocracies*. Minneapolis: University of Minnesota Press; Schock, Kurt, ed. 2015. *Comparative Perspectives on Civil Resistance*. Minneapolis: University of Minnesota Press; Sharp, Gene. 2005. *Waging Nonviolent Struggle: Twentieth Century Practice and Twenty-First Century Potential*. Boston: Porter Sargent; Stephan, Maria, ed. 2009. *Civilian Jihad: Nonviolent Struggle, Democratization, and Governance in the Middle East*. New York: Palgrave Macmillan; Zunes, Stephen, Lester Kurtz, and Sarah Beth Asher, eds. 1999. *Nonviolent Social Movements: A Geographical Perspective*. Malden, MA: Blackwell.

strategy. This analysis focuses on three types of movement tactics based on the target of their action: (1) recruitment tactics targeted at the youth population, (2) tactics vis-à-vis allies, and (3) tactics vis-à-vis opponents. Recruitment tactics are critical to the political activation of youth because they determine the scope and the methods of the movement's growth. Tactics vis-à-vis allies also affect the level of youth mobilization because the challenger organization needs to forge alliances with other civil society actors to tip the balance of power in its favor. Furthermore, tactics vis-à-vis opponents influence the level of youth mobilization because novel forms of civil resistance might draw a larger pool of youngsters into a movement.

By the same token, this study singles out different types of countermovement tactics. State repression is often defined as "behavior that is applied by governments in an effort to bring about political quiescence and facilitate the continuity of the regime through some form of restrictions or violation of political and civil liberties."[11] Broadly speaking, this study distinguishes between coercion, or the use of force, and channeling, a subtler form of repressive action "meant to affect the forms of protest available, the timing of protests, and/or flows of resources to movements."[12] In addition, this study considers the government's support for regime-friendly youth organizations as state action directed against challenger organizations.

In analyzing movement tactics and state countermoves, this book applies the concept of tactical interaction. As defined by McAdam, tactical interaction consists of two components: tactical innovation by the challenger organization and tactical adaptation by its adversary.[13] A related concept describing the dynamic relationship between the social movement and its opponents is Sharp's idea of "political jiu-jitsu," which refers to the process in which nonviolent action can turn the opponent's repression into a liability by generating shifts in public opinion and tilting power relationships in favor of nonviolent activists.[14] More recently, Hess and Martin develop the concept of backfire to define "a public reaction of outrage to an event that is publicized and perceived as unjust."[15]

The concept of tactical interaction brings closer to each other two strands of research. One line of inquiry has focused on movement strategies and protest tactics.[16] A major finding in this literature is that social movements tend to

[11] Davenport, Christian, ed. 2000. *Paths to State Repression: Human Rights Violations and Contentious Politics*. Lanham, MD: Rowman & Littlefield, p. 6.

[12] Earl, Jennifer. 2003. "Tanks, Tear Gas, and Taxes: Toward a Theory of Movement Repression." *Sociological Theory* 21(1): 44–68, p. 48.

[13] McAdam, Doug. 1983. "Tactical Innovation and the Pace of Insurgency." *American Sociological Review* 48(6): 735–54.

[14] Sharp, Gene. 1973. *The Politics of Nonviolent Action*. Boston: Porter Sargent.

[15] Hess, David, and Brian Martin. 2006. "Repression, Backfire, and the Theory of Transformative Events." *Mobilization* 11(1): 249–67, p. 249.

[16] Beckwith, Karen. 2000. "Strategic Innovation in the Pittson Coal Strike." *Mobilization* 5(2): 179–99; Chabot, Sean. 2000. "Transnational Diffusion and the African American Reinvention of

deploy a recurrent set of tactics to pursue their goals. Tilly develops the concept of the repertoire of contention to describe "a limited set of routines that are learned, shared, and acted out through a relatively deliberate process of choice."[17] Strike, for example, is a common form of protest used by labor unions. Scholars also recognize that the repertoire of contention may undergo transformation, and a period of heightened protest activity can engender the development of innovative tactics. Tarrow, for example, finds that Italian workers devised new forms of strike during the protest cycle of the 1960s and 1970s.[18] Empirical evidence further indicates that a significant political defeat may trigger the transformation of movement tactics.[19] This body of literature suggests that movement participants can exercise a great deal of creativity in campaigning for their cause.

Another strand of research has analyzed patterns of state repression.[20] A consistent finding in this literature is that dissent provokes a repressive action.

Gandhian Repertoire." *Mobilization* 5(2): 201–16; Gamson, William. 1990. *The Strategy of Social Protest*, 2nd edn. Belmont, CA: Wadsworth Publishing; Ganz, Marshall. 2000. "Resources and Resourcefulness: Strategic Capacity in the Unionization of California Agriculture: 1959–1966." *American Journal of Sociology* 105: 1003–62; Ganz, Marshall. 2009. *Why David Sometimes Wins: Strategy, Leadership, and the California Agricultural Movement*. New York: Oxford University Press; Jasper, James. 1997. *The Art of Moral Protest: Culture, Biography, and Creativity in Social Movements*. Chicago: University of Chicago Press; Jasper, James. 2004. "A Strategic Approach to Collective Action: Looking for Agency in Social Movement Choices." *Mobilization* 9(1): 1–16; McCammon, Holly. 2012. *The US Women's Jury Movements and Strategic Adaptation: A More Just Verdict*. New York: Cambridge University Press; Meyer, David, and Suzanne Staggenborg. 2008. "Opposing Movement Strategies in U.S. Abortion Politics." *Research in Social Movements, Conflicts and Change* 28: 207–38; Minkoff, Debra. 1999. "Bending with the Wind: Strategic Change and Adoption by Women's and Racial Minority Organizations." *American Journal of Sociology* 104: 1666–703; Taylor, Verta, Katrina Kimport, Nella van Dyke, and Ellen Ann Andersen. 2009. "Culture and Mobilization: Tactical Repertoires, Same-Sex Weddings, and the Impact on Gay Activism." *American Sociological Review* 74: 865–90.

17 Tilly, Charles. 1995. "Contentious Repertoires in Great Britain, 1758–1834." In *Repertoires and Cycles of Collective Action*, ed. Mark Traugott. Durham, NC: Duke University Press, pp. 15–42, p. 26. See also Tilly, Charles. 1986. *The Contentious French*. Cambridge, MA: Harvard University Press; Tilly, Charles, and Sidney Tarrow. 2015. *Contentious Politics*, 2nd edn. New York: Oxford University Press.

18 Tarrow, Sidney. 1993. "Cycles of Collective Action: Between Moments of Madness and the Repertoire of Contention." *Social Science History* 17: 281–307.

19 McCammon, Holly. 2003. "Out of the Parlors and into the Streets: The Changing Tactical Repertoire of US Women's Suffrage Social Movements." *Social Forces* 81(3): 787–818.

20 See, for example, Boycoff, Jules. 2007. "Limiting Dissent: The Mechanisms of State Repression in the USA." *Social Movement Studies* 6(3): 281–310; Carley, Michael. 1997. "Defining Forms of Successful State Repression of Social Movement Organizations: A Case Study of the FBI's COINTELPRO and the American Indian Movement." *Research in Social Movements, Conflicts and Change* 20: 151–76; Davenport, Christian. 2005. "Understanding Covert Repressive Action." *Journal of Conflict Resolution* 49(1): 120–40; Della Porta, Donatella, and Herbert Reiter, eds. 1998. *Policing Protest: The Control of Mass Demonstrations in Western Democracies*. Minneapolis: University of Minnesota Press; Earl, Jennifer, Sarah Soule, and John McCarthy. 2003. "Protest under Fire? Explaining the Policing of Protest." *American Sociological Review* 68(4): 581–606; Earl,

Davenport refers to this empirical regularity as the law of coercive responsiveness.[21] The movement's opponents, however, are not "actors devoid of strategic ability" who are "either blind to protests or able to crudely repress activists using the levers of the state."[22] Like protesters, the ruling elite can deploy a wide arsenal of tactics to safeguard its privileged position. Specifically, the coercive apparatus may modify its tactics to respond more effectively to a political threat. Della Porta, for example, demonstrates the evolution of policing styles in Italy and Germany from the 1950s to the 1980s.[23] In sum, both the repertoire of contention and the toolkit of state repression may change over time as a result of tactical interactions between the social movement and the incumbent government.

This book extends the existing literature by examining state-movement interactions in hybrid regimes. Most empirical research on tactical interactions has been done in advanced industrial democracies.[24] There is also rich empirical literature on protests and repression in full-blown autocracies.[25]

Jennifer. 2004. "Controlling Protest: New Directions for Research on the Social Control of Protest." *Research in Social Movements, Conflicts, and Change* 25: 55–83; Soule, Sarah, and Christian Davenport. 2009. "Velvet Glove, Iron Fist or Even Hand? Protest Policing in the United States, 1960–1990. " *Mobilization* 14(1): 1–22; Starr, Amory, Luis A. Fernandez, and Christian Scholl. 2011. *Shutting Down the Streets: Political Violence and Social Control in the Global Era.* New York: New York University Press.

21 Davenport, Christian. 2007. "State Repression and Political Order." *Annual Review of Political Science* 10: 1–23, p. 8.

22 Ingram, Paul, Lori Qingyuan Yue, and Hayagreeva Rao. 2010. "Trouble in Store: Probes, Protests, and Store Openings by Wal-Mart, 1998–2007." *American Journal of Sociology* 116(1): 53–92, p. 54.

23 Della Porta, Donatella. 1995. *Social Movements, Political Violence, and the State.* New York: Cambridge University Press.

24 See, for example, Banaszak, Lee Ann, Karen Beckwith, and Dieter Rucht, eds. 2003. *Women's Movements Facing the Reconfigured State.* New York: Cambridge University Press; Karapin, Roger. 2007. *Protest Politics in Germany: Movements on the Left and Right since the 1960s.* University Park: Pennsylvania State University Press; Zwerman, Gilda and Patricia Steinhoff. 2005. "When Activists Ask for Trouble: State-Dissident Interactions and the New Left Cycle of Resistance in the United States and Japan." In *Repression and Mobilization*, eds. Christian Davenport, Hank Johnston, and Carol Mueller. Minneapolis: University of Minnesota Press, pp. 85–107.

25 Boudreau, Vincent. 2004. *Resisting Dictatorship: Repression and Protest in Southeast Asia.* New York: Cambridge University Press; Francisco, Ronald. 1995. "The Relationship between Coercion and Protest: An Empirical Evaluation in Three Coercive States." *Journal of Conflict Resolution* 39(2): 263–82; Johnston, Hank, 2012. "State Violence and Oppositional Protest in High-Capacity Authoritarian Regimes." *International Journal of Conflict and Violence* 6(1): 55–74; Johnston, Hank, and Carol Mueller. 2001. "Unobtrusive Practices of Contention in Leninist Regimes." *Sociological Perspectives* 44: 351–76; Kubik, Jan. 1994. *The Power of Symbols against the Symbols of Power.* University Park: Pennsylvania State University Press; Shriver, Thomas, and Alison Adams. 2010. "Cycles of Repression and Tactical Innovation: The Evolution of Environmental Dissent in Communist Czechoslovakia." *Sociological Quarterly* 51: 329–54; Trejo, Guillermo. 2012. *Popular Movements in Autocracies: Religion, Repression, and Indigenous Collective Action in Mexico.* New York: Cambridge University Press; Viola, Lynne.

Hornsby, for example, uses the recently declassified archival material to examine protests and repression in the Soviet Union under Nikita Khrushchev.[26] Since the collapse of communism, the rise of hybrid regimes provides an understudied political context for analyzing the interplay between social movements and their opponents.

The state-movement interactions in hybrid regimes are distinct in several ways.[27] First, the regime type affects the timing of mass mobilization. In theory, protest events in democracies may fall on any date due to the systematic provision of political rights and civil liberties. For example, the Occupy Wall Street Movement organized its first march in New York City on September 17, US Constitution Day, during an off-election year.[28] Compared with social movements in democracies, challenger organizations in autocracies face more cumbersome hurdles to organizing a protest campaign because autocrats routinely suppress citizens' expression of political grievances in the public domain. Situated between these two extremes, social movements in hybrid regimes might observe a political opening during an election year due to the government's half-hearted attempt to put up a facade of democracy. From this perspective, the elections might be seen as a prime opportunity for contentious collective action.[29]

Second, the regime type has an impact on the scope of movement demands. Social movements in democracies can tackle a wider variety of political issues than their counterparts in nondemocracies given the nature of the political regime. Moreover, the regime type affects the urgency of certain political issues, which, in turn, influences the movement's choice of political demands. The most pressing issue for challenger organizations in

2003. *Contending with Stalinism: Soviet Power and Popular Resistance in the 1930s*. Ithaca, NY: Cornell University Press; Yashar, Deborah. 1997. *Demanding Democracy: Reform and Reaction in Costa Rica and Guatemala, 1870s-1950s*. Stanford, CA: Stanford University Press; Zhao, Dingxin. 2000. "State-Society Relations and the Discourses and Activities of the 1989 Beijing Student Movement." *American Journal of Sociology* 105: 1592–632.

[26] Hornsby, Robert. 2013. *Protest, Reform and Repression in Khrushchev's Soviet Union*. New York: Cambridge University Press.

[27] For an in-depth treatment of this topic, see Robertson, Graeme. 2011. *The Politics of Protest in Hybrid Regimes: Managing Dissent in Post-Communist Russia*. New York: Cambridge University Press.

[28] On the movement's history, see Milkman, Ruth, Stephanie Luce, and Penny Lewis. 2012. *Changing the Subject: A Bottom-Up Account of Occupy Wall Street in New York City*. New York: Murphy Institute, CUNY.

[29] On the linkage between fraudulent elections and antigovernment protests, see Forbig, Joerg, and Pavol Demes, eds. 2007. *Reclaiming Democracy: Civil Society and Electoral Change in Central and Eastern Europe*. Washington, DC: German Marshall Fund; Kuntz, Philipp, and Mark Thompson. 2009. "More than Just the Final Straw: Stolen Elections as Revolutionary Triggers." *Comparative Politics* 41(3): 253–72; Lindberg, Staffan, ed. 2009. *Democratization by Elections: A New Mode of Transition*. Baltimore, MD: John Hopkins University Press; Tucker, Joshua. 2007. "Enough! Electoral Fraud, Collective Action Problems, and Post-Communist Colored Revolutions." *Perspectives on Politics* 5(3): 537–53.

hybrid regimes is free and fair elections because it is widely regarded as a critical step toward democratization. A related popular demand in hybrid regimes is state provision of the freedom of expression and the freedom of assembly.

Third, the regime type affects movement choices regarding the repertoire of contentious collective action.[30] Social movements in democracies can choose a wider range of protest tactics without fear of state repression. In contrast, the imminent threat of political violence imposes significant constraints on the repertoire of contention in autocracies. The political context in hybrid regimes, falling somewhere between democracy and dictatorship, compels social movements to display a great deal of resourcefulness in developing their repertoires of contention. Specifically, civic activists in hybrid regimes try to combine protest tactics allowed in liberal democracies with those deployed in full-blown autocracies to maneuver in repressive regimes with a semblance of democratic institutions.

Furthermore, the regime type influences the toolkit of state repression. In dealing with social movements, governments in democracies are under public pressure to uphold the rule of law. In contrast, autocrats have a freer rein to unleash violence against civic activists and safeguard their monopoly on power. In hybrid regimes, however, the incumbent tries to secure a modicum of political legitimacy, which precludes the deployment of an overt violent campaign against challenger organizations. Instead, state authorities in hybrid regimes need to exercise ingenuity in manipulating laws and devising extralegal means to strip social movements of power.

LEARNING THROUGH EXPERIENCE AND EXAMPLE

An additional argument presented in this book is that learning is critical to the development of effective tactics. This study singles out two learning mechanisms: (1) engagement in previous protest campaigns and (2) the cross-national diffusion of ideas. It is plausible to assume that the domestic history of civic activism affects the dynamics of state-movement interactions. Participation in previous protest campaigns may enable civic activists to strengthen their organizational skills and advance their grasp of various protest tactics. Furthermore, previous episodes of contention may create "organizational holdovers" that can be activated at a later point in time.[31] Similarly, the incumbent may respond to an outburst of contentious collective action more effectively if he takes a long-term view of state-society relations in

[30] For an in-depth treatment of this topic, see Tilly, Charles. 2006. *Regimes and Repertoires*. Chicago: University of Chicago Press.

[31] Almeida, Paul D. 2003. "Opportunity Organizations and Threat-Induced Contention: Protest Waves in Authoritarian Settings." *American Journal of Sociology* 109(2): 345–400.

the country. In addition, a systematic policing of protest events may bolster coercive capacities of the state. In the absence of recent episodes of mass mobilization, it becomes more challenging for youth activists to effectively stage civil resistance from scratch and for state authorities to suppress a sudden spike in civic activism.

The importance of "dress rehearsals" – prior episodes of contention – has been widely acknowledged in the literature.[32] As Boudreau put it, "interactions between states and societies create an institutional, political and cultural terrain that shapes subsequent contention."[33] Earlier episodes of contention affect not only the likelihood of a political opening but also the development of social movements. Prior research demonstrates the negative consequences of a defeat on the movement's capacity to mobilize activists and enlist third-party support. Yet the positive impact of a loss on subsequent mobilization efforts is understudied in the literature. As shown by Bunce and Wolchik, the electoral model adopted by civil society actors in the post-communist region was shaped by a series of prior civic campaigns.[34] For example, post-election protests in 1996–97 informed the opposition's strategizing on the eve of the 2000 election in Serbia. More specifically, Otpor activists built on the use of humor during the 1996–97 student protests to develop a wider range of humorous nonviolent acts against the regime.[35] Likewise, the defeat of the Ukraine without Kuchma Movement of 2000–01 influenced civil resistance during the 2004 election in Ukraine.[36] Similarly, mass protests against the detention of a parliamentarian in Aksy in March 2002 affected the behavior of the political opposition during the

[32] Many episodes of contention end in a defeat of the civic campaign or the demise of a social movement. On the effects of defeats, see, for example, Beckwith, Karen. 2016. "All Is Not Lost: The 1984–85 British Miners' Strike and Mobilization after Defeat." In *The Consequences of Social Movements: People, Policies and Institutions*, eds. Lorenzo Bosi, Marco Giugni, and Katrin Uba. Cambridge: Cambridge University Press, pp. 41–65; Beckwith, Karen. 2015. "Narratives of Defeat: Explaining the Effects of Loss in Social Movements." *Journal of Politics* 77(1): 2–13; Gupta, Devashree. 2009. "The Power of Incremental Outcomes: How Small Victories and Defeats Affect Social Movement Organizations." *Mobilization* 14(4): 417–32; McCammon, Holly. 2003. "Out of the Parlors and into the Streets: The Changing Tactical Repertoire of US Women's Suffrage Social Movements." *Social Forces* 81(3): 787–818.

[33] Boudreau, Vincent. 2004. *Resisting Dictatorship: Repression and Protest in Southeast Asia*. New York: Cambridge University Press, p. 152.

[34] Bunce, Valerie, and Sharon Wolchik. 2011. *Defeating Authoritarian Leaders in Post-Communist Countries*. New York: Cambridge University Press, p. 260.

[35] For an extensive treatment of this topic, see Sombatpoonsiri, Janjira. 2015. *Humor and Nonviolent Struggle in Serbia*. Syracuse, NY: Syracuse University Press.

[36] See, for example, D'Anieri, Paul. 2006. "Explaining the Success and Failure of Post-communist Revolutions." *Communist and Post-Communist Studies* 39(3): 331–50; Kuzio, Taras. 2007. "Oligarchs, Tapes, and Oranges: 'Kuchmagate' to the Orange Revolution." *Journal of Communist Studies and Transition Politics* 23(1): 30–56; Nikolayenko, Olena. 2015. "Youth Mobilization before and during the Orange Revolution: Learning from Losses." In *Comparative Perspectives on Civil Resistance*, ed. Kurt Schock. Minneapolis: University of Minnesota Press, pp. 93–120.

Tulip Revolution in Kyrgyzstan in spring 2005.[37] Recent studies also show that the Egyptian Movement for Change (Kifaya) formed in 2004 had an impact on the organization of antigovernment protests in 2011.[38] In sum, a movement's loss can present a valuable opportunity for political learning.

The cross-national diffusion of ideas, broadly defined as "the flow of social practices among actors within some larger system,"[39] supplies another opportunity for learning. Both youth movements and incumbent governments can exchange ideas with structurally equivalent actors to achieve their objectives.[40] Della Porta and Tarrow coin the term "interactive diffusion" to describe the cross-national spread of protest and police tactics in interaction with each other.[41] The model of nonviolent resistance – a set of innovative tactics against the regime – is here considered as the main diffusing item. Another diffusing item is the repertoire of countermovement tactics. The transmission of these conflicting ideas may occur through relational and nonrelational channels. Relational channels of diffusion involve direct contact between the transmitter and the adopter of the diffusing item, whereas the use of nonrelational channels implies reliance on such impersonal mechanisms as the mass media.[42] It should also be noted that the attribution of similarity provides a basis for the diffusion of ideas.[43] The fact that members of the selected youth movements belonged

[37] On this point, see Lewis, David. 2010. "The Dynamics of Regime Change: Domestic and International Factors in the 'Tulip Revolution'." In *Domestic and International Perspectives on Kyrgyzstan's 'Tulip Revolution': Motives, Mobilization, and Meanings*, ed. Sally Cummings. New York: Routledge, pp. 43–55; Radnitz, Scott. 2010. *Weapons of the Wealthy: Predatory Regimes and Elite-Led Protests in Central Asia.* Ithaca, NY: Cornell University Press, pp. 103–30; Tursunkulova, Bermet. 2008. "The Power of Precedent?" *Central Asian Survey* 27(3–4): 349–62.

[38] Onodera, Henri. 2009. "The Kifaya Generation: Politics of Change among Youth in Egypt." *Suomen Antropologi: Journal of the Finnish Anthropological Society* 34(4): 44–64; Sanders, Christoph. 2013. "Building Resistance: Dynamics of Egyptian Youth Activism in Non-Violent Movements between 2000 and 2011." In *Democracy in Crisis: The Dynamics of Civil Protest and Civil Resistance*, eds. Bert Preiss and Claudia Brunner. Munster, Germany: LIT Verlag, pp. 155–84; Shahin, Emad el-Din. 2012. "The Egyptian Revolution: The Power of Mass Mobilization and the Spirit of Tahrir Square." *Journal of the Middle East and Africa* 3: 46–69.

[39] Quoted from Soule, Sarah. 2004. "Diffusion Processes within and across Movements." In *The Blackwell Companion to Social Movements*, eds. by David A. Snow, Sarah A. Soule, and Hanspeter Kriesi. Malden, MA: Blackwell, pp. 294–310, p. 275.

[40] On the concept of structural equivalence, see Burt, Ronald. 1987. "Social Contagion and Innovation: Cohesion versus Structural Equivalence." *American Journal of Sociology* 92: 1287–335.

[41] Della Porta, Donatella, and Sidney Tarrow. 2012. "Interactive Diffusion: The Coevolution of Police and Protest Behavior with an Application to Transnational Contention." *Comparative Political Studies* 45(1): 119–52, p. 122.

[42] For an overview of diffusion literature, see Strang, David, and Sarah Soule. 1998. "Diffusion in Organizations and Social Movements: From Hybrid Corn to Poisonous Pills." *Annual Review of Sociology* 24: 265–90.

[43] On this concept, see McAdam, Doug, and Dieter Rucht. 1993. "The Cross-National Diffusion of Movement Ideas." *Annals of the American Academy of Political and Social Science* 528: 56–74.

to the post-Soviet generation and lived in repressive political regimes laid the foundation for a cross-national exchange of ideas. In turn, common socialization experiences under communism and strong opposition to democratization processes united autocrats in the region.

Beissinger advances the study of modular political phenomena, "action based in significant part on emulation of the prior successful example of others,"[44] by meticulously documenting cross-case influences and modeling elite behavior in response to modular political processes. He develops two models of elite behavior. The elite defection model predicts that the ruling elite might withdraw support for the current regime and defect to the political opposition in reaction to the perceived vulnerability of the political system. Alternatively, the elite learning model posits that the incumbent government might learn from previous cases of success and failure and impose additional institutional constraints on the political opposition to secure the status quo. The former model explains well the spread of nationalist mobilization during the late Gorbachev period in the Soviet Union and the spread of electoral revolutions among early risers in the protest cycle in the post-communist region, whereas the latter model is more relevant to the modular phenomena among late risers. An implication of these findings is that the impact of prior example is contingent on the temporal location of a case in the modular process and elite behavior (defection versus learning).[45]

Another major contribution to the field was made by Bunce and Wolchik. Based on an in-depth analysis of eleven elections held between 1998 and 2008 in post-communist Europe and Eurasia, Bunce and Wolchik conclude that the adoption of innovative and sophisticated strategies explains the defeat of autocrats.[46] In particular, their work shows that the presence of "collaborative networks" composed of local nongovernmental organizations (NGOs), members of the international democracy assistance community, and participants in earlier electoral revolutions facilitated the diffusion of innovative tactics in Eastern Europe.[47] Bunce and Wolchik, for example, illustrate how Slovak civic

[44] Beissinger, Mark. 2007. "Structure and Example in Modular Political Phenomena: The Diffusion of Bulldozer/Rose/Orange/Tulip Revolutions," p. 259.

[45] *Ibid.*, p. 273.

[46] Bunce, Valerie, and Sharon Wolchik. 2010. "Defeating Dictators: Electoral Change and Stability in Competitive Authoritarian Regimes." *World Politics* 43(1): 43–86; Bunce, Valerie, and Sharon Wolchik. 2011. *Defeating Authoritarian Leaders in Post-Communist Countries*. New York: Cambridge University Press; Bunce, Valerie, and Sharon Wolchik. 2011. "International Diffusion and Democratic Change." In *The Dynamics of Democratization: Dictatorship, Development, and Diffusion*, ed. Nathan Brown. Baltimore, MD: John Hopkins University Press, pp. 283–310.

[47] On the importance of transnational social networks, see Bunce, Valerie, and Sharon Wolchik. 2006. "International Diffusion and Postcommunist Electoral Revolutions." *Communist and Post-Communist Studies* 39: 283–304.

activists shared their expertise on the organization of a get-out-the-vote (GOTV) campaign with their counterparts in Serbia. Likewise, Petrova traces how Polish and Slovak civic activists provided assistance for civil society in Belarus and Ukraine.[48]

Moreover, bourgeoning research examines how autocrats respond to the cross-national diffusion of regime-threatening ideas.[49] In particular, the behavior of the Russian government has attracted a great deal of scholarly attention. Using the cases of China and Russia, Koesel and Bunce demonstrate that incumbents take preemptive action to "diffusion-proof" their political regimes from social turmoil.[50] Ambrosio further distinguishes three elite strategies: (1) insulate the country from cross-border influences, (2) bolster politically affinitive regimes, and (3) subvert politically dissimilar ones.[51]

As mentioned earlier, this book seeks to contribute to the literature by highlighting the impact of learning on tactical interactions between social movements and their opponents. Despite the importance of accumulated protest experience, scholars tend to focus on proximate causes of mass mobilization. In addition, the Western media frequently depict protest events as spontaneous action of the disgruntled population, losing sight of the long-term struggle for social change in a country. Yet the confrontation between challenger organizations and the ruling elite often lasts for an extended period of time. An examination of previous protest campaigns can deepen our understanding of state-movement interactions at a particular moment in the country's history.

[48] Petrova, Tsveta. 2014. *From Solidarity to Geopolitics: Support for Democracy among Postcommunist States* New York: Cambridge University Press.

[49] See, for example, Ambrosio, Thomas. 2009. *Authoritarian Backlash*. Burlington, VT: Ashgate; Finkel, Evgeny, and Yitzhak Brudny. 2012. "No More Colour! Authoritarian Regimes and Colour Revolutions in Eurasia." *Democratization* 19(1): 1–14; Horvath, Robert. 2013. *Putin's Preventive Counter-Revolution: Post-Soviet Authoritarianism and the Spectre of Velvet Revolution*. New York: Routledge; Oates, Sarah. 2013. *Revolution Stalled: The Political Limits of the Internet in the Post-Soviet Sphere*. New York: Oxford University Press; Silitski, Vitali. 2010. "Contagion Deterred: Preemptive Authoritarianism in the former Soviet Union (the Case of Belarus)." In *Democracy and Authoritarianism in the Postcommunist World*, eds. Valerie Bunce, Michael McFaul, and Kathryn Stoner-Weiss New York: Cambridge University Press; Silitski, Vitali. 2010. "Survival of the Fittest:" Domestic and International Dimensions of the Authoritarian Reaction in the Former Soviet Union Following the Colored Revolutions." *Communist and Post-Communist Studies* 43(4): 339–50; von Soest, Christian. 2015. "Democracy Prevention: The International Collaboration of Authoritarian Regimes." *European Journal of Political Research* 54(4): 623–38; Whitehead, Laurence. 2014. "Anti-Democracy Promotion: Four Strategies in Search of a Framework." *Taiwan Journal of Democracy* 10(2): 1–24.

[50] Koesel, Karrie, and Valerie Bunce. 2013. "Diffusion-Proofing: Russian and Chinese Responses to Waves of Popular Mobilizations against Authoritarian Rulers." *Perspectives on Politics* 11(3): 753–68.

[51] Ambrosio, Thomas. 2007. "Insulating Russia from a Colour Revolution: How the Kremlin Resists Regional Democratic Trends." *Democratization* 14(2): 232–52, pp. 236–37.

THE SALIENCE OF NONVIOLENT ACTION

The use of nonviolent methods is a salient attribute of the selected youth movements. The term "nonviolent action" implies that action "does not involve physical violence or the threat of physical violence against human beings – and it is active – it involves activity in the collective pursuit of social or political objectives."[52] As illustrated in subsequent chapters, most youth activists shared the view that a nonviolent campaign, rather than a violent one, would be more effective in bringing about political change. This assumption was based on the belief that nonviolence would enable movement participants to gain a greater amount of legitimacy in the international community and enlist a higher level of domestic support for their cause.[53]

The emergence of nonviolent youth movements in the post-communist region can be considered as a part of "a global wave of unarmed insurrections."[54] As Schock points out, there has been an explosion in the number of "organized popular challenges to government authority that depend primarily on the methods of nonviolent action" in nondemocracies from the late 1970s to the early 1990s.[55] The triumph of such nonviolent social movements as the people's power movement in the Philippines and the Solidarity movement in Poland captured media attention and inspired civic activists around the globe in the 1980s. More recently, there has been a wave of electoral revolutions in Eastern Europe and popular uprisings in the Middle East. These episodes of contention illustrate how civic activists in nondemocracies effectively used nonviolent methods of resistance to press for political change. In particular, young people displayed a great deal of creativity to undermine the strength of the regime.

This study adds to the growing body of research on civil resistance by comparing the use of nonviolent methods in several post-communist states. Spectacular images of electoral revolutions and victories of the political opposition in Georgia, Serbia, and Ukraine sparked a lot of academic interest. In contrast, the sight of relatively small post-election protests and the opposition's losses in Azerbaijan and Belarus attracted much less academic attention. This book assumes that the analysis of failed cases can advance our understanding of factors associated with the success of nonviolent action.

ADDITIONAL FACTORS

The choice of tactics alone cannot fully explain the level of youth mobilization against the regime because there is a limit to the power of strategic thinking. The

[52] Schock, Kurt. 2005. *Unarmed Insurrections: People Power Movements in Nondemocracies*. Minneapolis: University of Minnesota Press, p. 6.

[53] On the effectiveness of nonviolent campaigns, see Stephan, Maria, and Erica Chenoweth. 2008. "Why Civil Resistance Works: The Strategic Logic of Nonviolent Conflict." *International Security* 33(1): 7–44.

[54] Schock, Kurt. 2005. *Unarmed Insurrections*, p. 5.

[55] *Ibid.*, p. xvi.

degree of political openness, the existence of social networks, and access to resources also affect the level of civil resistance.[56] Nonetheless, it requires resourcefulness to take full advantage of openings in the political system and effectively use preexisting social networks and available resources. As Ganz put it, "strategy is how we turn what we have into what we need to get what we want."[57]

In describing the political context in which the selected youth movements emerged, this study focuses on five dimensions of the political opportunity structure: elite divisions, security defections, alignments within the opposition, media access, and influential allies. The political opportunity structure refers to "consistent – but not necessarily formal or permanent – dimensions of the political struggle that encourage people to engage in contentious politics."[58] The emergence of divisions within the ruling elite may undermine the government's response to nonviolent resistance against the regime and thus increase the level of youth's engagement in high-risk activism. In particular, security defections might embolden a larger number of citizens to get involved in antigovernment protests.[59] Furthermore, the unification of chronically fragmented political opposition and the emergence of a viable alternative to the incumbent are likely to propel citizens into action. In addition, the development of independent media resulting in the growing supply of alternative information may augment citizens' opposition to the regime.[60] Finally, shifts in world politics might affect the level of protest activity because external support tends to strengthen the position of challenger organizations

[56] On the importance of these factors, see Diani, Mario, and Doug McAdam, eds. 2003. *Social Movements and Networks: Relational Approaches to Collective Action.* New York: Oxford University Press; McAdam, Doug. 1982. *Political Process and the Development of Black Insurgency, 1930–1970.* Chicago: University of Chicago Press; Jenkins, Craig. 1983. "Resource Mobilization Theory and the Study of Social Movements." *Annual Review of Sociology* 9: 527–83; Krinsky, John, and Nick Crossley. 2014. "Social Movements and Social Networks: Introduction." *Social Movement Studies* 13(1): 1–21; McAdam, Doug, and Ronnelle Paulsen. 1993. "Specifying the Relationship between Social Ties and Activism." *American Journal of Sociology* 99(3): 640–67; McCarthy, John, and Mayer Zald. 2002. "The Enduring Vitality of the Resource Mobilization Theory of Social Movements." In *Handbook of Sociological Theory*, ed. Jonathan Turner. New York: Plenum Press, pp. 533–65; Meyer, David. 2004. "Protest and Political Opportunity." *Annual Review of Sociology* 30: 125–45.

[57] Ganz, Marshall. 2009. *Why David Sometimes Wins*, p. 8.

[58] Tarrow, Sidney. 1998. *Power in Movement: Social Movements, Collective Action, and Politics*, 2nd edn. New York: Cambridge University Press, pp. 19–20.

[59] On the significance of security defections, see Nepstad, Sharon Erickson. 2011. *Nonviolent Revolutions.*

[60] On the importance of media access in nondemocracies, see Osa, Maryjane, and Cristina Corduneanu-Huci. 2003. "Running Uphill: Political Opportunity in Non-democracies." *Comparative Sociology* 2(4): 605–29; Schock, Kurt. 1999. "People Power and Political Opportunities: Social Movement Mobilization and Outcomes in the Philippines and Burma." *Social Problems* 46 (3): 355–75.

vis-à-vis the incumbent.[61] Among the movement's influential allies might be international NGOs and Western governments.

The existence of mobilizing structures is another critical condition for civil resistance. The concept of mobilizing structures refers to "collective vehicles, informal as well as formal, through which people mobilize and engage in collective action."[62] The activation of preexisting social networks may enable youth activists to seize an opportunity for political change. Moreover, preexisting social networks can serve as a vehicle for the diffusion of ideas. This study views youth organizations and student unions as formal organizations that have the potential to rally young people around a particular cause. In addition, informal social networks bound by common values might develop in the aftermath of a protest event, providing a launching pad for further contentious collective action. This study seeks to determine the presence of preexisting social networks through the examination of protest campaigns preceding the emergence of the selected youth movements.

Furthermore, the movement's access to resources increases the level of mass mobilization. According to the resource mobilization theory, resource-poor movements are less likely to achieve their goals.[63] This study distinguishes between tangible and nontangible resources.[64] Monetary resources fall into the category of tangible assets, whereas human resources belong to nontangible assets of the social movement. Based on the publicly available data, this analysis discusses the extent to which the selected youth movements enlisted support of influential allies and secured the assistance of the international donor community. This study, however, places a higher value on the quality of human resources rather than the amount of monetary funds in explaining the level of youth mobilization because the development of savvy, innovative tactics hinges on the presence of competent movement leaders.

The added value of studying tactics lies in illuminating how civic activists can alter the political climate, take advantage of preexisting social networks, and

[61] Voluminous research has examined the international dimensions of democratization. See, for example, Carothers, Thomas. 1999. *Aiding Democracy Abroad: The Learning Curve*. Washington, DC: Carnegie Endowment for International Peace; Whitehead, Laurence, ed. 1996. *The International Dimensions of Democratization: Europe and the Americas*. New York: Oxford University Press; Youngs, Richard. 2005. *International Democracy and the West: The Role of Governments, Civil Society, and Multinational Business*. New York: Oxford University Press.

[62] McAdam, Doug, John McCarthy, and Mayer Zald. 1996. "Introduction: Opportunities, Mobilizing Structures, and Framing Processes – Toward a Synthetic Comparative Perspective on Social Movements." In *Comparative Perspectives on Social Movements: Political Opportunities, Mobilizing Structures, and Cultural Framings*, eds. Doug McAdam, John McCarthy, and Mayer Zald. New York: Cambridge University Press, p. 3.

[63] McCarthy, John, and Mayer Zald. 1977. "Resource Mobilization and Social Movements: A Partial Theory." *American Journal of Sociology* 82(6): 1212–41.

[64] Freeman, Jo. 1979. "Resource Mobilization and Strategy." In *The Dynamics of Social Movements*, eds. Mayer Zald and John McCarthy. Cambridge, MA: Winthrop Press, pp. 167–89.

use available resources to mobilize a large number of citizens. First, it is reasonable to assume that the social movement can introduce favorable changes in the political environment through the deployment of effective tactics. The challenger organization, for example, can engender an opening in the political opportunity structure by skillfully pushing for the unity of opposition political parties around a presidential candidate on the eve of elections. Second, the social movement can increase the value of preexisting social networks by building a horizontal organizational structure and cultivating a sense of solidarity among movement participants. Furthermore, the resource-poor movement can overcome its disadvantaged position by displaying creativity in the disbursement of scarce resources. For these reasons, the analysis of tactics contributes to a fuller understanding of factors associated with a high level of civil resistance.

It should also be born in mind that there exists a dynamic relationship between movement tactics and structural conditions. As mentioned earlier, the use of innovative tactics can help social movements overcome a structural disadvantage. Civic activists, for example, might devise a savvy plan for the dissemination of movement ideas in spite of the government's crackdown on the broadcasting media. *Samizdat* – "self-published literature" – was a common means of overcoming state censorship in the Soviet Union.[65] Nowadays, social media is widely used as a venue for spreading uncensored news in a repressive political regime.[66] The cultivation of a working relationship with the international donor community, especially in the absence of a large middle class, provides another example of how civic activists might alter the political opportunity structure by virtue of savvy tactics. As Otpor leader Srdja Popovic put it, "Political space is never granted. It is always conquered."[67]

Concurrently, unfavorable structural conditions may thwart the effectiveness of innovative tactics. Most importantly, the strength of civil society influences social movement outcomes. In particular, the success of youth movements depends on the strength of opposition political parties. It is

[65] On the use of samizdat, see Kind-Kovacs, Friederike, and Jessie Labov, eds. 2013. *Samizdat, Tamizdat, and Beyond: Transnational Media during and after Socialism*. New York: Berghahn Books; Komaromi, Ann. 2015. *Uncensored: Samizdat Novels and the Quest for Autonomy in Soviet Dissidence*. Chicago: Northwestern University Press.

[66] It must be noted that such social media as Facebook, Twitter, and YouTube were nonexistent in the early 2000s, so the selected youth movements organized protest events and disseminated information in the absence of such digital technology. For an overview of recent scholarship on the role of social media in repressive political regimes, see Dencik, Lina, and Oliver Leistert, eds. 2015. *Critical Perspectives on Social Media and Protest: Between Control and Emancipation*. London: Rowman & Littlefield International; Trottier, Daniel, and Christian Fuchs, eds. 2014. *Social Media, Politics and the State: Protests, Revolutions, Riots, Crime and Policing in the Age of Facebook, Twitter and YouTube*. New York: Routledge.

[67] Quoted from Rosenberg, Tina. 2011. "Revolution U: What Egypt Learned from Students Who Overthrew Milosevic." *Foreign Policy*, February 16, www.foreignpolicy.com/articles/2011/02/16/revolution_u?page=full.

difficult for youth activists to mobilize the electorate against the incumbent in the absence of a trustworthy opposition politician. A high level of state repression also imposes enormous constraints on citizens' engagement in protest activity. Under such circumstances, the use of humor might be insufficient to break a climate of fear in the country.

In sum, this book emphasizes the importance of tactics in explaining the level of mass mobilization, but it acknowledges the effects of structural conditions on state-movement interactions. An earlier discussion in this chapter pointed out how the regime type influences tactical interactions between challenger organizations and state authorities. Cross-national diffusion of ideas also presupposes that social movements tailor their novel tactics to local circumstances. Clearly, movement tactics affect and are affected by the political environment.

CASE SELECTION

Youth movements are here defined as "organized and conscious attempts on the part of young people to initiate or resist change in the social order."[68] This study focuses on the following youth movements: Kmara (Georgia), Maqam (Azerbaijan), Otpor (Serbia), Pora (Ukraine), Yeni Fikir (Azerbaijan), Yokh (Azerbaijan), and Zubr (Belarus). A common feature of these youth movements is the adoption of similar strategies. Otpor is viewed here as an initiator movement that engendered the emergence of similar youth movements in the region.[69] The paired comparison method guides the selection of the remaining cases.[70] The first pair includes the youth movements from Belarus and Ukraine, whereas the second pair consists of Azerbaijani and Georgian youth movements. This grouping is based on the type of national elections and the extent of cultural affinity. The youth movements in Belarus and Ukraine were formed on the eve of the presidential elections, while the youth movements in Azerbaijan and Georgia emerged in the run-up to the parliamentary elections. Moreover, the paired cases are embedded in a similar cultural context. Belarus and Ukraine are former Soviet republics located between the European Union and Russia and sharing a common Slavic heritage. Likewise, Azerbaijan and Georgia are

[68] Braungart, Richard G., and Margaret M. Braungart. 1990. "Youth Movements in the 1980s: A Global Perspective." *International Sociology* 5(June): 157–81, p. 157.

[69] On the conceptualization of initiator and spin-off movements, see McAdam, Doug. 1995. "'Initiator' and 'Spin-Off' Movements: Diffusion Processes in Protest Cycles." In *Repertoires and Cycles of Collective Action*, ed. Mark Traugott. Durham, NC: Duke University Press, pp. 217–39.

[70] On the advantages of paired comparison as a research strategy, see Tarrow, Sydney. 2010. "The Strategy of Paired Comparison: Toward a Theory of Practice." *Comparative Political Studies* 43(2): 230–59.

neighboring states lying at the crossroads between Europe and Asia. A brief description of each movement is provided in the following paragraphs.

The youth movement Otpor was formed by a group of university students in reaction to the new laws restricting press freedom and academic freedoms in Serbia. Between 1998 and 2000, the movement spread from a few university campuses to over one hundred cities and towns throughout the country. Movement participants organized a large-scale campaign targeting the incumbent president and a GOTV campaign aimed at young voters in the run-up to the 2000 federal elections. Otpor activists distributed stickers with provocative slogans, spray painted graffiti with its symbol of the clenched fist, and staged street performances infused with humor. These courageous acts of nonviolent resistance boosted youth voter turnout and contributed to Milosevic's electoral defeat. More broadly, Otpor was successful in creating a culture of resistance that appealed to Serbian youth and became a source of inspiration for civic activists worldwide.

Belarusian civic activists were the first to adopt Otpor's model of nonviolent resistance in the post-Soviet region. A group of youth activists set up the social movement Zubr on the eve of the 2001 presidential election. Like Otpor, Zubr launched a negative campaign "It's Time to Clean Up" and a positive campaign "It's Time to Choose" to press for political change. In particular, Zubr sought to engage Russian-speaking urban youth in nonviolent struggle against the regime. The Belarusian youth movement, however, was unable to mobilize a significantly large share of youth in favor of political change. The movement's strength further declined after the reelection of the incumbent president, and Zubr formally self-dissolved in 2006.

Compared with Zubr, Ukrainian youth activists mobilized a larger number of young people in advance of the 2004 presidential election. Inspired by Otpor, two youth movements with the same name – Pora – were established during the election year. Based on the color of their insignia, these movements were often labeled as "black Pora" and "yellow Pora." Black Pora became known for its street action directed against the current regime, whereas yellow Pora focused on voter education and voter mobilization campaigns. Movement participants were among the first to set up tents in Kyiv's main square and permanently occupy the public space until the annulment of the fraudulent election results.

Another attempt to emulate Otpor's tactics was undertaken in Georgia. Kmara was founded by leaders of a student government and participants in prior protest campaigns against the ruling elite. Youth activists spray painted graffiti, performed street actions, and organized community events demanding political change during the 2003 parliamentary election. As a result, the youth movement became known as an agent of radical social change. In particular, Kmara struck a chord with rural youth frequently neglected by the national government.

Compared with Kmara, the Azerbaijani youth movements recruited a smaller fraction of the youth population on the eve of the 2005 parliamentary election. As in earlier cases, movement participants distributed leaflets and spray-painted slogans to demand free and fair elections. But Maqam, Yeni Fikir, and Yokh were unable to generate large-scale public outrage over state repression, and they self-dissolved in the wake of the ruling party's electoral victory.

DATA SOURCES

This research is based on a combination of sources, including semistructured interviews with former movement participants, public opinion polls, NGO publications, and media reports. A principal advantage of semistructured interviewing is that it opens up an opportunity to uncover the logic behind the movement's action and identify themes overlooked or misrepresented in the mass media.[71] Using the snowball sampling method, I identified key informants, "a small number of knowledgeable participants who observe and articulate social relationships for the researcher."[72] The main criterion for choosing respondents was a leadership role in the movement. For example, 8 of 11 founding members of Otpor participated in this study.[73] A total of 54 former movement participants were interviewed.[74] I conducted most interviews during my field trips to the region in January–April 2008 and March–April 2010. The interviews consisted of open-ended questions about movement tactics and state countermoves.

To date, it remains problematic to secure interviews with high-ranking officials responsible for the execution of repressive measures in the region. This methodological challenge arises from the fact that most post-Soviet states still struggle with their authoritarian legacies or continue to be ruled by autocrats. The government of Serbia has yet to open police files pertinent to the Milosevic period. Furthermore, there was lack of lustration in the aftermath of Ukraine's Orange Revolution, and the country experienced a resurgence of authoritarianism during Viktor Yanukovych's presidency from 2010 to 2014. At the time of this writing, Azerbaijan and Belarus remain closed political regimes in which the incumbents regularly use repressive methods against

71 On the advantages of this research method, see Blee, Kathleen M., and Verta Taylor. 2002. "Semi-Structured Interviewing in Social Movement Research." In *Methods of Social Movement Research*, eds. Bert Klandermans and Suzanne Staggenborg. Minneapolis: University of Minnesota Press, pp. 92–117.

72 Seidler, John. 1974. "On Using Informants: A Technique for Collecting Quantitative Data and Controlling Measurement Error in Organizational Analysis." *American Sociological Review* 39(6): 816–31, p. 816.

73 Otpor's eleven founding members were Ivan Andric, Slobodan Djindovic, Slobodan Homen, Milja Jovanovic, Nenad Konstantinovic, Ivan Marovic, Vladimir Pavlov, Vukasin Petrovic, Srdja Popovic, Dejan Randic, and Andreja Stamenkovic.

74 A full list of interviewees is provided in the Appendix. The number of interviewees is lower in Azerbaijan and Belarus because they either continue to reside in a repressive political regime or have left the country out of fear of state repression.

regime opponents. Under these circumstances, most government officials are unlikely to divulge information that might threaten their job security or pose a risk to their physical well-being.

To compensate for the absence of semistructured interviews with representatives of the coercive apparatus, I collected data from government documents, NGO publications, and media reports. In particular, I consulted several web-based news sources that supplied regular coverage of protest events in each country: *Charter 97* (Belarus), *Civil Georgia* (Georgia), *Free Serbia* (Serbia), *Ukrainska Pravda* (Ukraine), and *Zerkalo* (Azerbaijan). These online publications are widely regarded as authoritative sources on domestic politics. I gathered additional data about state repression from reports prepared by international NGOs (e.g., Amnesty International, Article 19, and Human Rights Watch) and local human rights organizations (e.g., Belarus's Human Rights Center Viasna, Serbia's Humanitarian Law Center, and Ukraine's Kharkiv Human Rights Group). A combination of these sources enabled me to trace the government's response to the emergence of regime-threatening youth movements.

STRUCTURE OF THE BOOK

This book focuses on nonviolent youth movements in Azerbaijan, Belarus, Georgia, Serbia, and Ukraine. Chapter 2 describes the political context in the aforementioned states on the eve of national elections. Chapter 3 estimates the level of youth mobilization against the regime. The subsequent chapters analyze state-movement interactions in each country in a chronological order, starting with the 2000 election in Serbia and ending with the 2005 election in Azerbaijan. Chapter 4 scrutinizes tactical interactions between the incumbent government and Otpor in Serbia. Chapter 5 analyzes the adoption of Otpor's ideas and the deployment of countermovement tactics during the 2001 presidential election in Belarus. Chapter 6 examines the interplay between the youth movement Kmara and the incumbent government during the 2003 parliamentary election in Georgia. Chapter 7 is concerned with state-movement interactions in the course of the 2004 presidential election in Ukraine. Chapter 8 investigates civil resistance and state countermoves during the 2005 parliamentary election in Azerbaijan. The book concludes by summarizing cross-country differences in state-movement interactions and laying out the implications of these findings.

2

Elections as an Opportunity for Political Change

The regular conduct of national elections has become a near-universal phenomenon. Between 2000 and 2006, for example, direct elections for national office were held in almost 94 percent of independent states around the globe.[1] Strikingly, most autocrats adopted this seemingly democratic procedure despite their resistance to political change. The ubiquitous use of elections provoked a scholarly debate about the role of elections in a nondemocratic setting.[2] A major argument in recent political science literature is that elections in nondemocracies fulfill a variety of functions aimed at extending the incumbent's longevity and bolstering the regime's survival. First, elections might provide a mechanism for the maintenance of patronage networks and the distribution of spoils among members of the ruling elite.[3] Magaloni, for example, conceptualizes elections as an instrument for power sharing between an autocrat and a ruling coalition.[4] Second, elections might serve as a device for gathering information about the incumbent's allies and

[1] These estimates are based on data from Hyde, Susan. 2011. "International Dimensions of Elections." In *The Dynamics of Democratization: Dictatorship, Development, and Diffusion*, ed. Nathan Brown. Baltimore: John Hopkins University Press, pp. 266–82, p. 266. Hyde reports that national elections were held in 161 of 172 states, with a population of over 250,000 people, at the beginning of the twenty-first century.

[2] For a recent review of literature on the functions of elections in nondemocracies, see Gandhi, Jennifer, and Ellen Lust-Okar. 2009. "Elections under Authoritarianism." *Annual Review of Political Science* 12: 403–22.

[3] See, for example, Blaydes, Lisa. 2011. *Elections and Distributive Politics in Mubarak's Egypt*. New York: Cambridge University Press; Koehler, Kevin. 2008. "Authoritarian Elections in Egypt: Formal Institutions and Informal Mechanisms of Rule." *Democratization* 15(5): 974–90; Magaloni, Beatriz. 2006. *Voting for Autocracy: Hegemonic Party Survival and Its Demise in Mexico*. New York: Cambridge University Press; Lust-Okar, Ellen. 2006. "Elections under Authoritarianism: Preliminary Lessons from Jordan." *Democratization* 13(6): 456–71; Sjöberg, Fredrik. 2011. "Competitive Elections in Authoritarian States: Weak States, Strong Elites, and Fractional Societies in Central Asia and Beyond." Ph.D. dissertation, Uppsala University, Sweden.

[4] Magaloni, Beatriz. 2008. "Credible Power-Sharing and the Longevity of Authoritarian Rule." *Comparative Political Studies* 41(4–5): 715–41.

detecting pockets of resistance to the current regime.[5] Furthermore, autocrats might use elections as a tool to enhance their international reputation and mitigate external pressures for democracy.[6]

Another perspective on electoral politics in a nondemocratic setting considers elections as a propitious moment for ushering in political change.[7] Despite an uneven playing field,[8] elections inject an element of uncertainty in the political system. Electoral outcomes are not fully predetermined in hybrid regimes. There remains a possibility that the political opposition garners a sizable share of popular vote, undermining the incumbent's grip on power. The ruler also faces a threat of elite defections. In addition, international actors impose constraints on the autocrat's capacity to tamper with the electoral process. Under some circumstances, international election monitoring might limit the scope of electoral irregularities in nondemocracies.[9] Moreover, the country's long-term economic, political, and social ties with the West increase democratizing pressures on the authoritarian incumbent.[10]

5 See, for example, Boix, Carles, and Milan Svolik. 2013. "The Foundations of Limited Authoritarian Government: Institutions, Commitment, and Power-Sharing in Dictatorships." *Journal of Politics* 75(2): 300–16; Herron, Erik. 2011. "Measuring Dissent in Electoral Authoritarian Societies." *Comparative Political Studies* 44(11): 1557–83; Miller, Michael. 2015. "Elections, Information, and Policy Responsiveness in Autocratic Regimes." *Comparative Political Studies* 48(6): 691–727.

6 See, for example, Beaulieu, Emily, and Susan Hyde. 2009. "In the Shadow of Democracy Promotion: Strategic Manipulation, International Observers, and Election Boycotts." *Comparative Political Studies* 43(3): 392–415; Hyde, Susan. 2011. *The Pseudo-Democrat's Dilemma: Why Election Observation Became an International Norm.* Ithaca, NY: Cornell University Press.

7 On democratizing effects of elections, see Hadenius, Axel, and Jan Teorell. 2007. "Pathways from Authoritarianism." *Journal of Democracy* 18(1): 143–57; Howard, Marc Morjé, and Philip G. Roessler. 2006. "Liberalizing Electoral Outcomes in Competitive Authoritarian Regimes." *American Journal of Political Science* 50(2): 365–81; Lindberg, Staffan, ed. 2009. *Democratization by Elections: A New Mode of Transition.* Baltimore: John Hopkins University Press; Schedler, Andreas. 2013. *The Politics of Uncertainty: Sustaining and Subverting Electoral Authoritarianism.* New York: Oxford University Press.

8 On the importance of a level playing field, see Levitsky, Steven and Lucan Way. 2010. "Why Democracy Needs a Level Playing Field." *Journal of Democracy* 21(1): 57–68.

9 On the role of international election monitoring in non democracies, see Donno, Daniela. 2013. *Defending Democratic Norms: International Actors and the Politics of Electoral Misconduct.* New York: Oxford University Press; Hyde, Susan. 2008. "How International Election Observers Detect and Deter Fraud." In *Election Fraud: Detecting and Deterring Electoral Manipulation*, eds. Michael Alvarez, Thad Hall and Susan Hyde. Washington, DC: Brookings Institution Press; Hyde, Susan and Nikolay Marinov. 2014. "Information and Self-Enforcing Democracy: The Role of International Election Observation." *International Organization* 68(2): 329–59; Kelley, Judith. 2012. *Monitoring Democracy: When International Election Observation Works, and Why It Often Fails.* Princeton, NJ: Princeton University Press.

10 On the significance of cross-national linkages and Western leverage, see Levitsky, Steven and Lucan Way. 2006. "Linkage versus Leverage. Rethinking the International Dimension of Regime Change." *Comparative Politics* 38(4): 379–400; Way, Lucan and Steven Levitsky.

Recent scholarship on electoral revolutions in Eurasia demonstrates how fraudulent elections might provide an impetus for antigovernment protests.[11] One contention in the literature is that vote rigging was "the final straw" that fueled political action against the regime. Beissinger, for example, argues that rejection of the political regime as a whole, rather than a narrowly defined political grievance, provided a motivation for citizens' participation in post-election protests in Ukraine.[12] In contrast, Kuntz and Thomas contend that a stolen election in itself was a trigger for mass mobilization against the regime.[13] Furthermore, Tucker posits that electoral fraud was "a focal point for solving collective action problems" in repressive political regimes.[14]

This study argues that elections in nondemocracies might create favorable conditions for mass mobilization against the regime. Elections are usually associated with an increased level of political engagement despite the government's encroachment on political rights and civil liberties. Opinion polls indicate that voting is the most common type of political participation among all age groups, including youth.[15] As a result, electoral malfeasance affects a large proportion of the country's voting-age population and provides a basis for building a heterogeneous coalition against the incumbent government.[16] The

2007. "Linkage, Leverage, and the Post-Communist Divide." *East European Politics and Societies* 21(1): 48–66.

[11] See, for example, Fournier, Anna. 2010. "Ukraine's Orange Revolution: Beyond Soviet Political Culture?" In *Orange Revolution and Aftermath: Mobilization, Apathy, and the State in Ukraine*, ed. Paul D'Anieri. Baltimore: Johns Hopkins University Press, pp. 110–28; Hash-Gonzalez, Kelli. 2013. *Popular Mobilization and Empowerment in Georgia's Rose Revolution*. Lanham, MD: Lexington Books; Kulov, Emir. 2008. "March 2005: Parliamentary Elections as a Catalyst of Protests." *Central Asian Survey* 27(3–4): 337–47; Kuzio, Taras. 2013. "Democratic Revolutions from a Different Angle: Social Populism and National Identity in Ukraine's 2004 Orange Revolution." *Journal of Contemporary European Studies* 20(1): 41–54; Onuch, Olga. 2014. *Mapping Mass Mobilization: Revolutionary Moments in Argentina and Ukraine*. Basingstoke, UK: Palgrave Macmillan; Wheatley, Jonathan. 2005. *Georgia from National Awakening to Rose Revolution: Delayed Transition in the Former Soviet Union*. Aldershot, UK: Ashgate.

[12] Beissinger, Mark. 2011. "Mechanisms of Maidan: The Structure of Contingency in the Making of the Orange Revolution." *Mobilization* 16(1): 25–43.

[13] Kuntz, Philipp, and Mark Thompson. 2009. "More than Just the Final Straw: Stolen Elections as Revolutionary Triggers." *Comparative Politics* April: 272–53.

[14] Tucker, Joshua. 2007. "Enough! Electoral Fraud, Collective Action Problems, and Postcommunist Colored Revolutions." *Perspectives on Politics* 5(3): 535–51, p. 536.

[15] See, for example, Colton, Timothy. 2000. *Transitional Citizens: Voters and What Influences Them in the New Russia*. Cambridge, MA: Harvard University Press; Dominguez, Jorge, ed. 2013. *Parties, Elections, and Political Participation in Latin America*, 2nd edn. New York: Routledge; Lindberg, Staffan. 2006. *Democracy and Elections in Africa*. Baltimore: John Hopkins University Press; Youniss, James, and Peter Levine, eds. 2009. *Engaging Young People in Civic Life*. Nashville, TN: Vanderbilt University Press.

[16] On the importance of negative coalitions, see Beissinger, Mark. 2013. "The Semblance of Democratic Revolution: Coalitions in Ukraine's Orange Revolution." *American Political Science Review* 107(3): 574–92.

clarity of responsibility further boosts the odds of antigovernment protests during an election year.[17] Since state authorities are charged with the task of upholding the quality of elections, blame for electoral irregularities can be clearly placed at the door of the incumbent government. Another favorable characteristic of the election period is that it is often associated with an increase in the flow of resources to civil society, given increased attention of the international donor community, human rights organizations, and the mass media to violations of democratic procedures in the country.[18]

This chapter examines the political landscape on the eve of specific national elections in five countries (in the chronological order): Serbia (2000), Belarus (2001), Georgia (2003), Ukraine (2004), and Azerbaijan (2005). Multiparty, multicandidate elections were regularly held in these post-communist societies, but democratic procedures were systematically violated to the extent the turnover of power was hardly possible. In the absence of viable democratic institutions, citizens considered the street as an alternative vehicle for expressing their political grievances. To gauge the likelihood of antigovernment protests, this chapter analyzes five dimensions of the political opportunity structure: (1) elite divisions, (2) security defections, (3) alignments within the opposition, (4) media access, and (5) influential allies. In addition, the chapter discusses socioeconomic conditions as a contextual factor. Analysis of the political environment supplies a partial explanation for cross-country differences in the level of youth mobilization against the regime.

SERBIA

Serbia was the largest republic in the Socialist Federal Republic of Yugoslavia (SFRY), with a population of over 7 million people.[19] Four of six constituent republics – Bosnia-Herzegovina, Croatia, Macedonia, and Slovenia – declared national independence in 1991–92, but the Serbian government opposed the disintegration of the multiethnic communist state, plunging the Balkan region into one of the bloodiest twentieth-century conflicts since the end of

[17] On the link between mass protests and blame attribution, see Javeline, Debra. 2003. "The Role of Blame in Collective Action: Evidence from Russia." *American Political Science Review* 97 (1): 107–21.

[18] In his seminal article, Carothers calls into question the predominant use of election-focused democracy assistance programs and emphasizes the need for a broader conceptualization of democracy assistance. Nonetheless, elections continue to attract considerable attention in the democracy promotion community. See Carothers, Thomas. 2002. "The End of the Transition Paradigm." *Journal of Democracy* 13(1): 5–21.

[19] This chapter reports the size of a country's population during the selected election year. On population statistics, see US Census Bureau's *International Database*, www.census.gov/population/international/data/idb/informationGateway.php.

World War II.[20] The exact number of war casualties has yet to be determined,[21] but the death toll is estimated to be as high as 300,000 people.[22] The United Nations High Commissioner for Refugees (UNHCR) estimated that there were 212,000 internally displaced persons (IDPs) in Serbia and Montenegro in 2000.[23] Overall, human rights activists documented "serious violations of international humanitarian law" in the territory of the former Yugoslavia, and, to date, the International Criminal Tribunal for the Former Yugoslavia (ICTY) indicted 161 persons – mostly Serbs or Bosnian Serbs – for war crimes.[24]

Slobodan Milosevic rose to power on a wave of Serbian nationalism.[25] In particular, his speech marking the six-hundredth anniversary of the Battle of Kosovo (ending in Serbian defeat by the Ottoman Empire) unleashed bottled-up nationalist sentiments in the republic.[26] As a communist apparatchik, Milosevic was not a principled nationalist, but he skillfully appropriated the nationalist rhetoric to amass power. According to the last prime minister of SFRU Ante Markovic, Milosevic "was quite simply somebody who was ready to use everything at his disposal to secure power for himself ... And if that was nationalism, well, then he used nationalism."[27] Milosevic transformed the League of Communists of Yugoslavia into the Socialist Party of Serbia (*Socijalisticka Partija Srbije* [SPS]) and won 65 percent of popular vote in the first Serbian multiparty presidential election held on December 9, 1990.[28] In 1992, Milosevic presided over the formation of the Federal Republic of Yugoslavia (FRY), made up of Serbia and its junior partner Montenegro. Given presidential term limits, the Serbian strongman shifted executive

[20] On the causes of the Yugoslav wars, see Ramet, Sabrina, ed. 2005. *Thinking about Yugoslavia: Scholarly Debates about the Yugoslav Breakup and the Wars in Bosnia and Kosovo*. New York: Cambridge University Press.

[21] On methodological challenges pertinent to the estimation of casualties, see Tabeau, Ewa, ed. 2009. *Conflict in Numbers: Casualties of the 1990s Wars in the Former Yugoslavia (1991–1999)*. Belgrade, Serbia: Helsinki Committee for Human Rights in Serbia.

[22] Leitenberg, Milton. 2006. "Deaths in Wars and Conflicts in 20th Century." Peace Studies Program Occasional Paper No. 29. Cornell University, Ithaca, NY, p. 79.

[23] United Nations High Commissioner for Refugees. 2001. *The Global Report 2000*. Geneva, Switzerland: UNHCR, p. 400.

[24] For details of these crimes, see the web site of ICTY. www.icty.org/sid/24.

[25] On Milosevic's rule, see Cohen, Leonard. 2000. *Serpent in the Bosom: The Rise and Fall of Slobodan Milosevic*. Boulder, CO: Westview Press; Ramet, Sabrina, and Vjeran Pavlakovic, eds. 2005. *Serbia since 1989*. Seattle: University of Washington Press; Thomas, Robert. 1999. *The Politics of Serbia in the 1990s*. New York: Columbia University Press.

[26] The full text of Milosevic's speech delivered on June 28, 1989 is available at http://cmes.arizona.edu/sites/cmes.arizona.edu/files/SLOBODAN%20MILOSEVIC_speech_6_28_89.pdf.

[27] International Criminal Tribunal for the Former Yugoslavia. 2003. *The Case of Milosevic, Slobodan (IT-02–54) "Kosovo, Croatia, and Bosnia": Transcripts for 23 October 2003*. The Hague, Netherlands: ICTY, p. 28,042. Retrieved from www.icty.org/x/cases/slobodan_milosevic/trans/en/031023ED.htm.

[28] For a summary of election results, see *Balkan Insight*. 2012. "Serbian Elections since 1990." April 1. www.balkaninsight.com/en/article/serbian-presidential-elections-since-1990.

powers to the FRY presidency and won the 1997 federal presidential election. In anticipation of another electoral victory, Milosevic initiated constitutional amendments introducing the direct election of the president of FRY, rather than a vote in the Federal Assembly, so that he could serve two additional terms as president of FRY under new rules. To leave little time for the consolidation of fragmented political opposition, the incumbent president announced on July 27, 2000 that the federal presidential and parliamentary elections would be held on September 24, 2000, almost a year prior to the expiration of his term in office.

In addition to Milosevic, four presidential candidates were placed on the ballot: (1) Vojislav Kostunica, a single candidate from the democratic opposition, (2) Vojislav Mihailovic, leader of the Serbian Renewal Party, (3) Tomislav Nikolic, leader of the Serbian Radical Party, and (4) Miodrag Vidojkovic, a little-known member of the Affirmative Party. This section examines various dimensions of the political environment on the eve of the 2000 election.

Elite Divisions

Assassination of several individuals associated with Milosevic's inner circle provided a backdrop for the emergence of elite divisions in Serbia.[29] A black market ring leader, Vlada Kovacevic (d. February 1997), a former deputy minister of interior, Radovan Stojicic (d. April 1997), and a director of an oil company, Zoran Todorovic (d. October 1997), were reportedly gunned down by professional hit men. Similarly, paramilitary leader Zeljko Raznatovic and Minister of Defense Pavle Bulatovic were assassinated in the winter of 2000. Rumor had it that Milosevic was behind this string of assassinations to eliminate key witnesses of his war crimes in anticipation of an ICTY case against him.[30]

A breakdown of Milosevic's political alliances occurred in 1999–2000. Two political parties – SPS, founded by Milosevic himself, and the Yugoslav United Left (*Jugoslovenska Ujedinjena Levica* [JUL]), led by his wife, Mirjana

[29] BBC. 2000. "Serbian Warlord Shot Dead." January 15. http://news.bbc.co.uk/2/hi/europe/605172.stm; BBC. 2000. "Yugoslav Defence Minister Killed." February 8. http://news.bbc.co.uk/2/hi/europe/634714.stm; Hedges, Chris. 1997. "Fatal Fight over Spoils by Insiders in Belgrade." *New York Times*. November 9. www.nytimes.com/1997/11/09/world/fatal-fight-over-spoils-by-insiders-in-belgrade.html; Wilkinson, Tracy. 1997. "Yugoslavia: Leader of Milosevic's Feared Security Forces Is Slain in Attack inside Belgrade Restaurant." *Los Angeles Times*. April 12. http://articles.latimes.com/1997-04-12/news/mn-48018_1_serbian-president; Wilkinson, Tracy. 1997. "Ally of Milosevic's Wife Shot to Death." *Los Angeles Times*. October 25. http://articles.latimes.com/1997/oct/25/news/mn-46570.

[30] Erlanger, Steven. 2000. "Milosevic Government Denies Role in Killing of Serbia Warlord." *New York Times*. January 19. www.nytimes.com/2000/01/19/world/milosevic-government-denies-role-in-killing-of-serbian-warlord.html.

Milosevic – provided a bedrock of his rule. In addition, several political parties allied with the incumbent president in exchange for political favors. In collusion with SPS, for example, the Serbian Radical Party (*Srpska Radikalna Stranka* [SRS]) and the Serbian Renewal Movement (*Srpski Pokret Obnove* [SPO]) voted out of office the mayor of Belgrade Zoran Djindjic in September 1997. A crack in the Yugoslav government appeared when SPO leader Vuk Draskovic was sacked from the post of deputy prime minister in April 1999, and three cabinet ministers resigned in defiance of his dismissal.[31] The right-wing political party SRS broke off its alliance with SPS in September 2000,[32] undermining Milosevic's position a few weeks prior to the federal elections.

Security Defections

A few army generals defected to the political opposition in 2000. General Momcilo Perisic, former chief of the general staff of the FRY military, came out in support of Kostunica by calling for the army's nonintervention in electoral politics.[33] Media reports also indicate that his successor, Nebojsa Pavkovic, objected to the use of force against civilians during antigovernment protests in Belgrade on October 5, 2000.[34] Furthermore, there was a great deal of disillusionment with Milosevic's foreign policy among rank-and-file soldiers. Thousands of young men dodged the draft during the Yugoslav wars; some army reservists and their families participated in antigovernment protests demanding an end to war.[35] Similarly, some police officers displayed a lack of loyalty to the incumbent president by refusing to shoot at Kolubara coal miners who went on strike in October 2000.[36] These security defections reduced the likelihood of violence against participants in post-election protests.

[31] BBC. 1999. "Draskovic Fired over Kosovo Remarks." April 28. http://news.bbc.co.uk/2/hi/europe/330609.stm; Partos, Gabriel. 1999. "Dissent and Disunity in Belgrade." BBC. April 29. http://news.bbc.co.uk/2/hi/europe/331159.stm.

[32] Strauss, Julius. 2000. "Milosevic Abandoned by Old Ally." *Telegraph*. September 14. www.telegraph.co.uk/news/worldnews/1355442/Milosevic-abandoned-by-old-ally.html.

[33] McGeary, Johanna. 2000. "The End of Milosevic." CNN. October 9. http://edition.cnn.com/ALLPOLITICS/time/2000/10/16/cover.html.

[34] Sunter, Daniel. 2002. "Serbia: Pavkovic Changes Sides." *Balkans: Regional Reporting and Sustainable Training*. BCR Issue 328. http://iwpr.net/report-news/serbia-pavkovic-changes-sides.

[35] For example, thousands of army reservists participated in antigovernment protests in May 1999. See Bideleux, Robert, and Ian Jeffries. 2007. *The Balkans: A Post-Communist History*. London: Routledge Press, p. 262.

[36] Erlanger, Steven. 2000a. "Serbian Strikers, Joined by 20,000, Face down Police." *New York Times*. October 5. www.nytimes.com/2000/10/05/world/serbian-strikers-joined-by-20000-face-down-police.html; Erlanger, Steven. 2000b. "Showdown in Yugoslavia: The Overview; Yugoslavs Claim Belgrade for New Leader." *New York Times*. October 6. www.nytimes.com/2000/10/06/world/showdown-in-yugoslavia-the-overview-yugoslavs-claim-belgrade-for-new-leader.html?pagewanted=all&src=pm.

Unity of the Opposition Political Parties

The fragmentation of the political opposition was a chronic problem in Serbian politics.[37] In particular, political coalitions formed during an election campaign did not last long. The Democratic Movement of Serbia (*Demokratski Pokret Srbije* [DEPOS]) founded by five political parties (Democratic Party of Serbia, New Democracy, the People's Peasant Party, the Serbian Liberal Party, and the Serbian Renewal Movement) received 20 percent of the vote in the 1992 parliamentary election and broke down in the wake of the 1993 parliamentary election.[38] Likewise, the coalition Together (*Zajedno*) formed on the eve of the 1996 local elections fell apart in the run-up to the 1997 presidential election.[39] Compared with previous political alliances, the Democratic Opposition of Serbia (DOS) established in advance of the 2000 federal election was the largest. Eighteen political parties joined DOS and nominated 56-year-old Kostunica as a single candidate from the democratic opposition.

Public opinion polls indicated that Kostunica could beat Milosevic at the ballot box.[40] Trained as a lawyer, Kostunica was a founding member of the Democratic Party (*Demokratska Stranka* [DS]) in 1989 and the first chairperson of the Democratic Party of Serbia (*Demokratska Stranka Srbije* [DSS]), formed as a result of its split from DS in 1992. Since Kostunica espoused nationalist views and was an outspoken critic of the NATO bombing of Serbia, he could appeal to the electorate previously captured by Milosevic. As a *New York Times* reporter put it, Kostunica "was a bridge over which many Milosevic supporters could walk into opposition."[41] The nomination of a viable presidential contender increased the likelihood of mass mobilization against the incumbent.

Media Access

The media environment under Milosevic was marred with "murdered, jailed and harassed journalists, closed radio and television stations, fines imposed

[37] For an overview, see Bieber, Florian. 2003. "The Serbian Opposition and Civil Society: Roots of the Delayed Transition in Serbia." *International Journal of Politics, Culture, and Society* 17(1): 73–90, pp. 74–82.

[38] Miller, Nicholas. 1997. "A Failed Transition: The Case of Serbia." In *Politics, Power, and the Struggle for Democracy in South-East Europe*, eds. Karen Dawisha and Bruce Parrott. New York: Cambridge University Press, pp. 146–88.

[39] Dinomore, Guy. 1997. "New Elections Don't Offer Cynical Serbs Hope." *Chicago Tribune*. November 20. http://articles.chicagotribune.com/1997-11-20/news/9711200294_1_serbian-presidency-opposition-coalition-zajedno-president-of-federal-yugoslavia.

[40] Slavujevic, Zoran. 2007. *Izborne kampanje: Pohod na birace, slucaj Srbije od 1990 do 2007 godine* [Election Campaigns: Struggle for Voters, the Case of Serbia from 1990 to 2007]. Belgrade: Friedrich Ebert Stiftung, Faculty of Political Sciences, and Institute of Social Sciences, p. 343.

[41] Erlanger, Steven. 2000. "Man in the News; Reluctant Revolutionary: Vojislav Kostunica." *New York Times*. October 9. www.nytimes.com/2000/10/09/world/man-in-the-news-reluctant-revolutionary-vojislav-kostunica.html?src=pm.

according to the Public Information Act, hijacked or stolen equipment, restrictions on newsprint supply and expelled foreign journalists."[42] A startling example of the alleged government's attack on the press was the murder of Slavko Curuvija, owner of the daily *Dnevni Telegraf*, in April 1999.[43] The media bias on state-controlled television was another indicator of the state crackdown on the mass media. Almost 70 percent of newscasts on the state-run TV channel RTS was devoted to positive coverage of Milosevic, his government, and the ruling coalition in 2000.[44]

Nonetheless, a significant change in the media landscape occurred in the aftermath of the 1996 local elections. The opposition-controlled city councils initiated the creation of small-scale TV channels and radio stations. By 2000, there were as many as 100 privately owned TV stations and 300 privately owned radio stations in Serbia, operating primarily at the local level.[45] These media outlets provided a valuable platform for the political opposition on the eve of the 2000 elections, increasing citizen access to uncensored news.

In addition, Serbia experienced a tenfold increase in the number of Internet users between the two presidential elections, ranging from 40,000 people in 1997 to 400,000 people in 2000.[46] Furthermore, the number of Internet hosts with the domain name "yu" increased nearly five times from 2,885 in 1997 to 14,199 in 2000.[47] With the assistance of the Fund for an Open Society, the Internet service provider OpenNet was set up to facilitate the free flow of information in the repressive political regime.[48] The emerging Internet infrastructure enabled the radio station Radio B2-92, although banned by the government on several occasions, to reach approximately 60 percent of the population by rebroadcasting the news via the Internet and satellite in

[42] Association of Independent Electronic Media. 2001. "Serbia and Montenegro." In *2000 World Press Freedom Review*. Vienna, Austria: International Press Institute Retrieved from. www.free-media.at/cms/ipi/freedom_detail.html?country=/KW0001/KW0003/KW0079/&year=2000.

[43] Committee to Protect Journalists. 1999. "Journalists Killed/Yugoslavia: Slavko Curuvija." CPJ. April 11. www.cpj.org/killed/1999/slavko-curuvija.php.

[44] OSCE. 2000. *Elections in the Federal Republic of Yugoslavia, 24 September 2000: Preliminary Findings and Conclusions*. Warsaw, Poland: ODIHR.

[45] Bardos, Gordon. 2001. "Yugoslavia." In *Nations in Transit 2001: Civil Society, Democracy, and Markets in East Central Europe and the Newly Independent States*, eds. Adrian Karatnycky, Alexander Motyl, and Amanda Schnetzer. New York: Freedom House, pp. 418–34, p. 424.

[46] Agence France-Presse. 2000. "Internet the Rising Star of Yugoslav Elections." September 21. www.nettime.org/Lists-Archives/nettime-l-0009/msg00200.html.

[47] Internet Systems Consortium's Internet Domain Survey is conducted semiannually worldwide. The host is defined as "a domain name that has an IP record associated with it, i.e., any computer system connected to the Internet." Retrieved from www.isc.org/services/survey.

[48] United States Institute of Peace. 1996. "Preserving the Free Flow of Information on the Internet: Serbs Thwart Milosevic Censorship, Round Two" [summary of a public event]. Retrieved from www.usip.org/events/preserving-free-flow-information-internet-serbs-thwart-milosevic-censorship-round-two.

cooperation with its regional partners.[49] Still, the Internet has not been used in Milosevic's Serbia to the same extent as in more recent cases of electoral revolutions.

Influential Allies

Serbian civil society developed against the backdrop of violent conflicts in the territory of the former Yugoslavia. Of 2,000 nongovernmental organizations registered in 2000,[50] several were originally founded in the early 1990s to campaign for a peaceful resolution of ethnic conflicts. Among the most prominent ones were the Center for Anti-War Action and Women in Black. Since its inception in 1991, the antimilitarist peace organization Women in Black organized street action in which female activists dressed in black stood in silence in the street.[51] The black color symbolized their grief for war victims, whereas their bodies expressed disobedience to the politics of war mongering. Another NGO named the Humanitarian Law Center was established in 1992 to document human rights violations during the armed conflicts in the former Yugoslavia.[52] A group of antiwar movement activists founded the NGO Civic Initiatives in 1996 with the intent to strengthen civil society through civic education, promotion of democratic values, and support of active citizenship.[53] Notably, Civic Initiatives focused its attention on the development of the NGO sector outside Belgrade and established ties with NGOs in small towns and rural areas. These NGOs played an instrumental role in building a nationwide network of civic activists and implementing a GOTV campaign in 2000. The Center for Anti-War Action, for example, organized a conference titled "The Role of Non-Governmental Sector and Local Civil Movement in the Changes of the System" in December 1999, whereas Civic Initiatives held another conference titled "Preparation for the Future" in June 2000 in an attempt to coordinate NGO action against the current regime.[54] More than 150 NGOs participated in a pre-election campaign titled "Exit 2000 – Non-Governmental Organizations for Free and Democratic Elections" (*Izlaz 2000*), which took almost a year to

[49] On the role of the radio station in Serbian politics, see Collin, Mathew. 2001. *This Is Serbia Calling: Rock 'n' Roll Radio and Belgrade's Underground Resistance*. London: Serpent's Tail.

[50] United States Agency for International Development. 2001. *The 2000 NGO Sustainability Index for Central and Eastern Europe and Eurasia*. Washington, DC: USAID Bureau for Europe and Eurasia, Office of Democracy and Governance, p. 144.

[51] On the history of Women in Black, see Zajovic, Stasa, Slavica Stojanovic, and Milos Urosevic, eds. 2013. *Women for Peace*. Belgrade: Women in Black.

[52] On the Center's mission, see www.hlc-rdc.org.

[53] A brief English-language history of Civic Initiatives is available at www.gradjanske.org/page/about/en.html.

[54] For details, see the English-language news archive of the Belgrade-based Center for Development of Non-Profit Sector. www.crnps.org.rs/arhivavesti/news_arhive.htm.

prepare.[55] Serbian NGOs implemented 50 projects aimed at boosting voter turnout among various segments of the electorate, including women and youth.

Independent election monitoring was another critical function performed by civil society. Founded in 1997, the Center for Free Elections and Democracy (*Centar za Slobodne Izbore i Demokratiju* [CeSID]) monitored electoral processes in Serbia despite repeated official rejections of the NGO's requests to register its representatives as election observers. As a result of its work, CeSID developed a network of 16 regional offices and recruited thousands of volunteers so that they could be placed outside polling stations to monitor election processes.

Serbian civil society experienced a significant increase in Western financial and technical assistance when "Milosevic's image changed from a peacemaker from Dayton to a butcher from the Balkans."[56] An increased level of funding for Serbian NGOs reflected, in no small degree, a shift in US foreign policy. The US government stopped treating Milosevic as a credible negotiating partner and threw its weight behind a military intervention in the Balkans. The NATO military campaign, lasting from March through June 1999, was a hallmark of Milosevic's confrontation with the West. At the end of the NATO air strike, the amount of US government assistance to Serbia more than doubled, increasing from $10.7 million in 1999 to $25 million in 2000.[57] In addition, Serbian civil society received financial and technical assistance from Western foundations. In particular, the Fund for an Open Society Yugoslavia established by the American financier and philanthropist George Soros in 1991 supported a wide range of civic initiatives in the region.[58] The fund's expenditures for the year 2000 stood at $6,475,000, with $1,215,000 earmarked for independent media and another $1 million for local NGOs, think tanks, and independent trade unions.[59] Another US-based NGO – the International Republican Institute (IRI) – sponsored a training program for more than 15,000 opposition party polling station workers and advised DOS on the design and

[55] For an overview of Exit 2000, see Paunovic, Zarko, Natasa Vuckovic, Miljenko Dereta, and Maja Djordevic. 2000. *Exit 2000: Non-governmental Organizations for Democratic and Fair Elections*. Belgrade: Verzal Printing House.

[56] Author's interview with Tanja Azanjac, program coordinator, NGO Civic Initiatives, Belgrade, Serbia, February 7, 2008.

[57] Lancaster, John. 2000. "US Funds Help Milosevic's Foes in Election Fight." *Washington Post*. September 19. www.washingtonpost.com/ac2/wp-dyn?pagename=article&contentId=A13155-2000Sep15.

[58] On the Fund's work, see Fund for an Open Society/Soros Yugoslavia Foundation. 2001. *Fund for an Open Society, Ten Years On*. Belgrade: Fund for an Open Society; Korpivaara, Ari, William Kramer, Laura Silber, and Beka Vuco, eds. 2011. *Building Open Society in the Western Balkans, 1991–2011*. New York: Open Society Foundations.

[59] Open Society Institute. 2001. *Building Open Societies: Soros Foundations Network 2000 Report*. New York: OSI, p. 84.

implementation of parallel vote count.[60] The increasing flow of Western assistance enhanced the opposition's capacity to contest the fraudulent elections.[61]

Socioeconomic Conditions

The Serbian economy was heavily hit by the Yugoslav wars and international isolation. In response to Milosevic's belligerent foreign policy, the UN Security Council introduced economic sanctions against FRY in May 1992, mandating the cessation of any international trade with FRY and the freezing of its foreign assets.[62] UN Security Council Resolution 820 of April 1993 further toughened an economic embargo against FRY.[63] The national economy collapsed, and the country experienced one of the world's largest hyperinflations in the early 1990s.[64] Between October 1993 and January 1995, prices increased by five quadrillion percent.[65] More recently, growth in real gross domestic product (GDP) plummeted from 1.9 percent in 1998 to −18.0 percent in 1999.[66] According to official statistics, the private sector contributed almost 40 percent to FRY's GDP and employed 27 percent of Yugoslavia's workforce.[67] But most economic power was concentrated in the hands of Milosevic and his inner circle.[68]

This economic meltdown led to steep impoverishment of the population. The unemployment rate surged from 23.1 percent in 1994 to 40.5 percent in 2000.[69]

[60] International Republican Institute. 2001. *International Republican Institute 2000 Annual Report*. Washington, DC: IRI, p. 8.

[61] On the role of foreign aid, see Carothers, Thomas. 2001. "Ousting Foreign Strongmen: Lessons from Serbia." Policy Brief. Carnegie Endowment for International Peace, Washington, DC.

[62] Lewis, Paul. 1992. "UN Votes 13–0 for Embargo on Trade with Yugoslavia: Air Travel and Oil Curbed." *New York Times*. May 31. www.nytimes.com/1992/05/31/world/un-votes-13-0-for-embargo-on-trade-with-yugoslavia-air-travel-and-oil-curbed.html?pagewanted=all&src=pm.

[63] UN Security Council Resolution 820, April 17, 1993. Retrieved from www.nato.int/ifor/un/u930417a.htm.

[64] Bartlett, William. 2008. *Europe's Troubled Region: Economic Development, Institutional Reform and Social Welfare in the Western Balkans*. New York: Routledge Press, pp. 42–48.

[65] Lyon, James. 1996. "Yugoslavia's Hyperinflation, 1993–1994: A Social History." *East European Politics and Societies* 10(2): 293–327.

[66] European Bank for Reconstruction and Development. 2007. *Transition Report 2007: People in Transition*. London, UK: EBRD, p. 35.

[67] Bardos, Gordon. 2001. "Yugoslavia." In *Nations in Transit 2001: Civil Society, Democracy, and Markets in East Central Europe and the Newly Independent States*, eds. Adrian Karatnycky, Alexander Motyl, and Amanda Schnetzer. New York: Freedom House, pp. 418–34, p. 429.

[68] Miljkovic, Maja, and Marko Attila Hoare. 2005. "Crime and the Economy under Milosevic and his Successors." In *Serbia since 1989: Politics and Society under Milosevic and After*, eds. Sabrina P. Ramet and Vjeran Pavlakovic. Seattle, WA: University of Washington Press, pp. 192–226.

[69] Bardos, Gordon. 2001. "Yugoslavia." In *Nations in Transit 2001: Civil Society, Democracy, and Markets in East Central Europe and the Newly Independent States*, p. 418.

In addition, the monthly minimum wage of $40 was an insufficient amount of money to cover basic living expenses.[70] Serbia's GDP per capita PPP was nearly half of Croatia's GDP per capita PPP in 2000 ($5,816 versus $10,907).[71] Moreover, according to World Bank estimates, the level of absolute poverty in FRY was twice as high in 2000 as in 1990.[72] The deteriorating quality of living standards eventually eroded mass support for Milosevic.

In sum, significant changes occurred in Serbia's political environment in the run-up to the 2000 elections. The unification of the opposition political parties around a viable presidential contender, security defections, the growth of local media, and the increasing flow of Western assistance to the NGO sector increased the likelihood of antigovernment protests. Furthermore, Milosevic miscalculated his odds of being reelected when he unveiled his plan for snap elections. An opinion poll conducted in August 2000 indicated that less than one-third of the electorate was going to vote for Milosevic in the upcoming elections.[73]

BELARUS

Belarus is an East European state with a population of almost 10 million people. The chair of the national parliament, Stanislau Shushkevich, hosted a historic meeting of party leaders in Belovezhskaia Pushcha in December 1991, resulting in a formal agreement between three Slavic republics about the dissolution of the Soviet Union.[74] Yet Belarus and Russia signed a treaty on the creation of a union state in December 1999, reviving the Kremlin's ambition to install a new Moscow-led political entity in the post-Soviet region.[75] From the political perspective, Belarus is important to Russia because it helps the Kremlin sustain the myth of Slavic unity. From the economic standpoint, Belarus is a major transit country for Russian energy resources. Located between the European Union and Russia, this small state transports 20 percent of Russian gas and 50 percent of Russian oil exports to Europe.[76] To date, however, the

[70] *Ibid.*, pp. 418–34, p. 434.

[71] GDP per capita PPP is gross domestic product converted to international dollars using purchasing power parity rates. See World Bank. 2013. *World Development Indicators Database: GDP per Capita, PPP.* Retrieved from http://data.worldbank.org/indicator/NY.GDP.PCAP.PP.CD.

[72] European Bank for Reconstruction and Development. 2001. *Transition Report 2001: Energy in Transition.* London, UK: EBRD, p. 143.

[73] Bideleux, Robert, and Ian Jeffries. 2007. *The Balkans: A Post-Communist History.* London: Routledge Press, p. 266.

[74] For a detailed account of this meeting, see Sivy, Ales. 2005. "Stanislau Shushkevich: We Worked in Belovezhskaia Pushcha, We Did Not Drink." *Narodnaya volia.* November 26. http://bp21.org.by/en/art/a051126a.html.

[75] Wines, Michael. 1999. "Russia and Belarus Agree to Join in a Confederation." *New York Times.* December 9. www.nytimes.com/1999/12/09/world/russia-and-belarus-agree-to-join-in-a-confederation.html.

[76] Balmaceda, Margarita. 2005. *Belarus: Oil, Gas, Transit Pipelines and Russian Foreign Energy Policy.* London, UK: GMB Publishing.

government of Belarus resists full political and economic integration with its eastern neighbor on Russian terms.[77]

Following a short period of political liberalization in the early 1990s, Belarus experienced democratic regression.[78] Once elected as the president of Belarus in 1994, Alyaksandar Lukashenka, a former head of a collective farm and chair of a parliamentary anticorruption committee, began to consolidate all the power in his hands. Defying democratic procedures, Lukashenka staged a referendum on the expansion of presidential powers and disbanded the national parliament in opposition to the incumbent president in 1996. He also used the adoption of constitutional amendments as a pretext for extending his first five-year presidential term until 2001. The opposition's attempt to organize shadow presidential elections in May 1999 and challenge the legitimacy of Lukashenka's continuous rule was met with repression.[79] Belarus on the eve of the 2001 presidential election remained one of the most Soviet republics in the post-Soviet region due to the government's use of Soviet-style social control mechanisms.[80]

Nonetheless, Lukashenka sought to maintain a facade of competitive elections. The Central Election Commission registered four presidential candidates in 2001: (1) the incumbent president, (2) Siarhei Haidukevich, leader of the Liberal Democratic Party, (3) Uladzimir Hancharyk, head of the Federation of Belarusian Trade Unions since its foundation in 1990, and (4) Siamion Domash, chair of the Coordinating Council of the civic coalition Hrodna Initiative formed by leaders of NGOs and opposition political parties in 1999. Since Domash withdrew his candidacy after Hancharyk's nomination as a single candidate from the opposition, the names of only three presidential contenders were placed on the ballot.

Elite Divisions

The incumbent president commanded fear to suppress elite defections. There were widespread rumors that the security apparatus was responsible for disappearances of former Minister of Interior Yury Zakharanka, former head

[77] For an in-depth analysis of Belarus-Russia relations, see Danilovich, Alex. 2006. *Russian-Belarusian Integration: Playing Games behind the Kremlin Walls*. Burlington, VT: Ashgate.

[78] For an overview of Belarusian politics, see Marples, David. 1999. *Belarus: A Denationalized Nation*. Amsterdam: Harwood Academic Publishers; White, Stephen, Elena Korosteleva, and John Lowenhardt, eds. 2005. *Postcommunist Belarus*. Oxford, UK: Rowman & Littlefield; Wilson, Andrew. 2011. *Belarus: The Last Dictatorship in Europe*. New Haven, CT: Yale University Press.

[79] Padhol, Uladzimir, and David Marples. 1999. "Belarus: The Opposition and the Presidency." *Harriman Review* 12(1): 11–18.

[80] For an overview of the political situation, see the transcript of the Hearing before the Commission on Security and Cooperation in Europe. 2000. "Belarus: Stalled at the Crossroads." 106th US Congress, Second Session, March 9. Retrieved from www.csce.gov.

of the Central Election Commission Viktar Hanchar, local businessman Anatol Krasouski, and Lukashenka's former official cameraman Dzmitry Zavadsky in 1999–2000.[81] Zakharanka went missing on May 7, 1999, shortly before the unofficial presidential election scheduled by the political opposition for May 16 in defiance of Lukashenka's arbitrary extension of his first presidential term from five to seven years. Zakharanka worked on a campaign for one of the presidential candidates, former Prime Minister Mykhail Chyhir, arrested for alleged embezzlement of state funds in March 1999. Despite police harassment, Hanchar played a leading role in organizing the 1999 presidential election and "disappeared" with his friend, Anatol Krasouski, on September 16, 1999, three days before a meeting of the disbanded parliament. Zavadsky worked as a reporter in Chechnya before his "disappearance" in Minsk on July 7, 2000. The government of Belarus obstructed police investigations into these cases, and the bodies of the four missing men were never recovered.[82] These cases of political violence served as a deterrent for further elite defections, creating a climate of fear on eve of the 2001 election.

Security Defections

Lukashenka inhibited high-profile defections in the security apparatus through cabinet reshuffling.[83] Between 1994 and 2001, the KGB of Belarus was chaired by Uladzimir Yagorow (1994–95), Uladzimir Matsekvich (1995–2000), and Leanid Tsikhanavich (2000–04). Likewise, there was a turnover of power in the Ministry of Interior: the minister's post was held by Zakharanka (1994–95), Yury Siwakow (1995–2000), and Uladzimir Navumaw (2000–09). Lukashenka also pitted the Ministry of Interior against the KGB of Belarus to secure his political longevity.

In addition, priority funding for the security apparatus increased the likelihood of its loyalty to the current regime. Policemen earned more than twice that of an average Belarusian and received plum welfare benefits, including subsidized housing and reduced fare.[84] Moreover, the size of the Belarusian police doubled during Lukashenka's first presidential term, climbing from 45,000 people in the late Soviet period to 89,000 people in

81 Amnesty International. 2001. "Belarus: Briefing for the UN Commission against Torture." April 17, www.amnesty.org/en/library/info/EUR49/002/2001/en.

82 Amnesty International. 2002. "Belarus: Without Trace: Uncovering the Fate of Belarus 'Disappeared.'" August 31. www.amnesty.org/en/library/info/EUR49/013/2002/en.

83 On cabinet appointments in Belarus, see *Belorusskaia Delovaia Gazeta*. 2013. "Who Is Who in Belarus." http://who.bdg.by/obj.php?&kod=2.

84 Maltsev, Valentin. 2009. "Boiazlivyi, nedoverchivyi, no neplokho zarabatyvauishchii: Usrednennyi portret belorusskogo militsionera." *Chastnyi Kurjer*. December 14. www.chaskor.ru/article/boyazlivyj_nedoverchivyj_no_neploho_zarabatyvayushchij__13365.

the early 2000s.[85] Many police recruits were young men who moved from rural areas to the city in pursuit of better job opportunities and acquired a personal stake in safeguarding the current regime.

Unity of the Opposition Political Parties

As in Serbia, disunity of the political opposition presented an obstacle to political change.[86] Such leading opposition political parties as the Belarusian Popular Front (*Belaruski Narodny Front* [BNF]), the Communist Party of Belarus (*Partia Komunistau Belarusi* [PKB]), and the United Civic Party of Belarus (*Abjednanaia Hramadzianskaia Partia Belarusi* [*AGPB*]) disagreed over ideological and strategic issues. In particular, émigré leader of BNF Zianon Pazniak opposed the party's alliance with "the communist nomenclature," including politicians who held government positions in the early 1990s and went into opposition to the incumbent president in the late 1990s.[87] The 2000 parliamentary election further revealed intraopposition divisions over the use of protest tactics: the Communist Party of Belarus and the Liberal Democratic Party participated in the elections, while the remainder of the opposition political parties boycotted due to anticipated electoral malpractices.[88]

Lack of unity had a debilitating effect on negotiation processes regarding the nomination of a single candidate from the opposition in 2001. Political bargaining dragged on until July 21, nearly seven weeks prior to election day. The politicians eventually agreed on Hancharyk's candidacy, disregarding a widely held belief that Domash was a more viable presidential candidate.[89] This decision was, to a large extent, driven by Western diplomats who observed Kostunica's electoral victory over Milosevic in October 2000 and erroneously assumed that the same scenario could play out in Belarus.[90] Western analysts suggested that a moderate candidate, rather than an outspoken regime

[85] Fedorovich, Viktor. 2013. "Skolko v Belarusi militsionerov?" *TutBy*. March 4. http://news.tut.by/society/337374.html.

[86] For an overview of political parties in Belarus, see Feduta, Aleksandr, Oleg Bogutskii, and Viktor Martinovich, eds. 2003. *Politicheskie partii Belarusi – neobkhodimaia chast grazhdanskogo obshchestva: Materialy seminara*. Minsk, Belarus: Friedrich Ebert Stiftung.

[87] *Monitor*. 1999. "Split in the Popular Front." September 30. www.jamestown.org/single/?no_cache=1&tx_ttnews[tt_news]=11849&tx_ttnews[backPid]=213.

[88] OSCE. 2001. *Belarus Parliamentary Elections 15 and 29 October 2000: Technical Assessment Mission Final Report*. Warsaw, Poland: ODIHR, p. 7.

[89] The five presidential candidates who participated in negotiations were former Prime Minister Chyhir, former Mayor of Hrodna Domash, trade union leader Hancharyk, leader of the Communist Party of Belarus Siarhej Kaliakin, and former Minister of Defense Paval Kazlouski.

[90] Silitski, Vital. 2010. "Chas Nazad N1: Iak belarusy adzinaga kandydata abirali." *Nasha Niva*. June 8. http://nn.by/?c=arprint&i=39499; Wilson, Andrew. 2011. *Belarus: The Last Dictatorship in Europe*. New Haven, CT: Yale University Press, pp. 194–95.

opponent, would be in a better position to compete against the incumbent president. Most Belarusian civic activists, on the contrary, felt that Hancharyk's candidacy undermined the ability of challenger organizations to mobilize citizens against the regime.[91]

Media Access

According to official statistics, there were hundreds of newspapers, 165 TV channels, and more than 40 radio stations in Belarus,[92] but state-run media occupied a dominant position in the media market.[93] The government exercised near-total control over the broadcasting media, whereas 10 leading independent newspapers, including *Belarusskaia Delovaia Gazeta* (*Belarusian Business Daily*), *Narodnaia Volia* (*People's Will*), and *Nasha Niva* (*Our Field*), jointly accounted for only one-tenth of prnt media circulation.[94] Independent newspapers were placed at a disadvantage by the government's policy of higher production and distribution costs for private media. Moreover, state authorities drove independent media out of business by slapping hefty fines on any publication critical of the current regime. In this media environment, Belarusian challenger organizations could reach a relatively small percentage of the population.

At the turn of the twenty-first century, the Internet as an alternative news source was in its embryonic stage in Belarus. There were nearly as many Internet hosts with the country's domain name in Belarus in 2001 as in Serbia in 1996 (1,545 versus 1,631).[95] Only 4 of 100 Belarusians were Internet users in 2001.[96] Still, several Belarusian NGOs were active on the net during the election campaign. The website of the NGO Charter 97 (http://charter97.org), for example, supplied regular coverage of protest events in the country. Likewise, the human rights center Viasna (http://spring96.org), founded in the wake of 1996 protests against the incumbent president, regularly compiled analytical reports on human rights violations and distributed them via the web. But the low level of public access to the Internet constrained the effectiveness of this medium of mass communication on the eve of the 2001 election.

[91] For a scathing criticism of Hancharyk's candidacy, see Kobets, Vladimir. 2003. "Odnazhdy v sentiabre." Charter 97. September 9. http://charter97.org/rus/news/2003/09/09/zubr.

[92] Kuzio, Taras. 2001. "Belarus." In *Nations in Transit 2001: Civil Society, Democracy, and Markets in East Central Europe and the Newly Independent States*, pp. 100–11, p. 106.

[93] For an overview, see Urbanovich-Sauka, Ilona, ed. 2002. *Srodki masavai informatsyi u Belarusi u 2002 godze*. Minsk, Belarus: Belarusian Association of Journalists.

[94] Kuzio, Taras. 2001. "Belarus." In *Nations in Transit 2001: Civil Society, Democracy, and Markets in East Central Europe and the Newly Independent States*, pp. 100–11, p. 106.

[95] Internet Systems Consortium's Internet Domain Survey. www.isc.org/services/survey.

[96] European Bank for Reconstruction and Development. 2007. *Transition Report 2007: People in Transition*. London, UK: EBRD, p. 108.

Influential Allies

Lukashenka's presidency delivered a serious blow to the development of civil society in Belarus.[97] The presidential decree of January 1999 initiated the reregistration of all NGOs, reducing the number of registered NGOs from 2,500 to 1,300.[98] Instead, the government supported the establishment of government-controlled NGOs to create an illusion of civil society. According to some estimates, there were approximately 2,500 registered NGOs and "nearly as many unregistered ones" in 2001.[99] A number of democracy-oriented NGOs attempted to coordinate their activities by setting up the Assembly of Democratic Nongovernmental Organizations. Moreover, the civic initiative Independent Observation (*Nezalezhnae Naziranne*), launched in June 2001, brought together approximately 200 Belarusian NGOs.[100] The NGO coalition built a nationwide network of independent election observers and trained more than 16,000 people for the purpose of election monitoring.[101]

One of the largest Western foundations in support of Belarusian civil society was the Soros-funded Open Society Institute (OSI). Between 1994 and 1997, OSI spent more than $13 million on the development of education, science, and civil society in Belarus.[102] For its prominent role in Belarusian society, OSI faced state harassment, and its Minsk office was closed down in 1997. Nonetheless, OSI continued to support Belarusian NGOs and allocated $1,958,000 for the OSI-Paris Belarus Project in 2001.[103]

Western governments also supported election-related projects in the country. The NGO sector was a main recipient of US government assistance to Belarus, totaling $37.78 million dollars in 2001.[104] The National Endowment for Democracy (NED), for example, received $500,000 from US State Department's

97 For an overview, see Lenzi, Mark. 2002. "Lost Civilization: The Thorough Repression of Civil Society in Belarus." *Demokratizatsiya: Journal of Post-Soviet Democratization* 10(3): 401–24.

98 Zagorskaia, Marina. 2007. "1991–2006. Itogi ot Vladimira Rovdo." *Salidarnats*. May 11. http://gazetaby.com/cont/art.php?sn_nid=6486.

99 USAID. 2002. *The 2001 NGO Sustainability Index for Central and Eastern Europe and Eurasia*. Washington, DC: United States Agency for International Development, p. 40.

100 Kesner, Genadz. 2001. "Zvysh za 200 gramadzkih arganizatsyia Belarusi buduts sumesna dzeinichats u chase nazirannia za prezydentskimi vybarami." Radio Ratsyia. June 12. http://news.tut.by/society/6742.html.

101 Shalayka, Alaksandar, and Syarhey Mackevich. 2002. "Nongovernmental Organizations and the Presidential Election in Belarus in 2001: The First Step Made, We Are Moving On." In *Belarus – The Third Sector: People, Culture, Language*, eds. Pawel Kazanecki and Marta Pejda. Warsaw, Poland: East European Democratic Center – IDEE, pp. 82–86, p. 85.

102 Miller, Judith. 1997. "Soros Closes Foundation in Belarus." *New York Times*. September 4. www.nytimes.com/1997/09/04/world/soros-closes-foundation-in-belarus.html.

103 Open Society Institute. 2002. *Building Open Societies: Soros Foundations Network 2001 Report*. New York: OSI, p. 149.

104 US State Department. 2002. *US Government Assistance to and Cooperative Activities with Eurasia: FY 2001 Annual Report*. Washington, DC: Office of the Coordinator of US Assistance to Europe and Eurasia, p. 42.

Human Rights and Democracy Fund to award subgrants on election-related projects by Belarusian civic organizations.[105] Funded by the US government, the Belarusian Service of Radio Free Europe/Radio Liberty increased its number of broadcasting hours to provide more extensive coverage of the election campaign.[106] Among European states, Lithuania and Poland provided strong backing for the Belarusian NGO sector. Vilnius and Warsaw hosted numerous workshops for Belarusian civic activists to facilitate the transfer of knowledge between NGOs in the post-communist region. For example, the Warsaw-based Eastern European Democratic Center received grants from NED, OSI, and the Charles Stewart Mott Foundation to administer projects in support of Belarusian NGOs and independent media in 2001.[107]

This volume of Western assistance to Belarusian civil society was counterbalanced by Russia's political and economic assistance to Lukashenka. The government of Belarus received from Russia a stabilization loan of approximately $200 million (4.5 billion Russian rubles), enabling the incumbent president to increase government spending and thus appease his core electorate.[108] The first tranche, worth $51 million, was released in July 2001, with the next tranche available during the election month. Moreover, Lukashenka met with Russian President Vladimir Putin during his visit to Moscow on June 20, 2001, and secured a promise that the Commonwealth of Independent States would send its own delegation of election observers to Belarus to legitimize the incumbent's "elegant victory."[109] Putin also signaled his support for Lukashenka by attending the annual art festival Slavic Bazaar held in Belarus on July 25–26 2001.[110]

Socioeconomic Conditions

The country's economic performance fared well for the incumbent president. The living standard improved during Lukashenka's first presidential term, compared with the early 1990s. GDP growth increased from −11.7 percent in 1994 to 4.7 percent in 2001,[111] and GDP per capita PPP climbed from $3,766 in

105 *Ibid.*, p. 45.

106 NewsRu. 2001. "Radio Svoboda rasshiriaet veshchanie na Belorussiu." August 7. http://txt.newsru.com/world/07Aug2001/liberty.html.

107 Eastern European Democratic Center. 2002. *Annual Report 2001*. Warsaw, Poland: EEDC. Retrieved from http://eedc.org.pl/eng/www/raporty/raport2001.htm.

108 Charter 97. 2001. "Belarusian Authorities Swindle with Russian Stabilization Loan." February 28. http://charter97.org/eng/news/2001/02/28/01.

109 *TutBy*. 2001. "A. Lukashenko sumel ugovorit Putina." June 25. http://news.tut.by/society/32810.html.

110 *Monitor*. 2001. "Slavic Bazaar in Belarus." July 30. www.jamestown.org/single/?no_cache=1&tx_ttnews[tt_news]=23360&tx_ttnews[backPid]=215#.Uboo_9geS_I.

111 World Bank. 2013. *World Development Indicators Database*. Retrieved from http://data.worldbank.org/data-catalog/world-development-indicators.

1994 to $5,618 in 2001.[112] Moreover, the average monthly income rose from $76 in 2000 to $97 in 2001.[113] Notably, the survival of an enormous state sector and a Soviet-style welfare system strengthened the government's position vis-à-vis regime opponents.[114] In particular, most village inhabitants endorsed the preservation of collective farms (*kolkhozes*) and backed the incumbent.

The government's control over the economy limited the opposition's access to financial resources in the country. Given the lack of economic liberalization reforms, the private sector contributed only 20 percent to the country's GDP in 1999–2001.[115] Furthermore, wealthy businessmen sympathizing with the political opposition were driven out of the country. According to Anatoly Lashkevich, a local businessman in favor of Hancharyk, one could do business in Belarus only on Lukashenka's consent.[116] Meanwhile, given the large size of the unionized public sector, state authorities systematically undermined the mobilizing potential of labor unions by eliminating their independence and handpicking political conformists as their leaders.

In sum, the chances of a public uprising appeared to be quite slim in Belarus. From the political standpoint, the nomination of an uncharismatic trade union leader as a single candidate from the opposition diminished the likelihood of revolt against the popular incumbent. Furthermore, the country's economic outlook on the eve of the presidential election undermined the opposition's call for political change. An opinion poll conducted in August 2001 showed that Lukashenka's approval rating stood at 52 percent, and only 29 percent of the electorate reported the intent to vote for Hancharyk.[117] Based on pre-election opinion polls, it appears that Lukashenka would have won even in the absence of gross manipulations of electoral results.

GEORGIA

Georgia is a former Soviet republic with a population of 4.7 million people. It is one of the oldest states that adopted Christianity as the state religion in the

[112] World Bank. 2013. *World Development Indicators Database: GDP per Capita, PPP*. Retrieved from http://data.worldbank.org/indicator/NY.GDP.PCAP.PP.CD.

[113] International Monetary Fund. 2002. *IMF Country Report: Republic of Belarus*. Washington, DC: IMF, p. 8. Retrieved from www.imf.org/external/pubs/ft/scr/2002/cr0223.pdf.

[114] For an overview, see Lawson, Colin. 2003. "Path-Dependence and the Economy of Belarus: The Consequences of Late Reforms." In *Contemporary Belarus: Between Democracy and Dictatorship*, eds. Elena Korosteleva, Colin Lawson, and Rosalind Marsh. London: Routledge, pp. 125–36.

[115] European Bank for Reconstruction and Development. 2005. *Transition Report 2005: Business in Transition*. London, UK: EBRD, p. 108.

[116] Sekhovich, Vadim. 2007. "1991–2006. Itogi. Chastnyi biznes." *Salidarnats*. April 3. www.gazetaby.com/cont/art.php?sn_nid=5886.

[117] Independent Institute of Socio-Economic and Political Studies. 2001. *IISEPS Newsletter* (in Russian). September Issue. www.iiseps.org/arhiv.html.

fourth century.[118] According to the 2002 Census, ethnic Georgians make up 83.7 percent of the population, most of whom self-identify with Christianity.[119] Situated at the crossroads of Europe and Asia, Georgia is currently a major transit point for Caspian oil. With the support of Western oil companies, Azerbaijan, Georgia, and Turkey agreed on the construction of the Baku-Tbilisi-Ceyhan (BTC) oil pipeline stretching more than 1,000 miles from Azerbaijan's oil fields to a Mediterranean seaport via Georgian territory. The multibillion-dollar project was expected to boost economic development in the region and loosen the Russian stranglehold on energy exports to Europe.[120] Moreover, this cross-border initiative challenged the idea of South Caucasus as land within Russia's sphere of influence. In view of its geostrategic importance, the BTC project, although incomplete in 2003, raised the stakes of political stability in the country.

Since the dissolution of the Soviet Union, Georgia was ravaged by a civil war and secessionist movements in Abkhazia and South Ossetia.[121] Approximately 20 percent of the country's territory, including the two breakaway regions and adjacent areas, fell under control of the Russian military.[122] As a result of these conflicts, there remained 261,600 IDPs in Georgia in 2002.[123] The political situation further destabilized when the first president of Georgia, Zviad Gamsakhurdia (1991–92), was removed from office via a coup d'état, triggering a civil war between Gamsakhurdia's supporters and his opponents.[124]

Eduard Shevardnadze, former leader of the Communist Party of Soviet Georgia and Soviet Foreign Minister, made a political comeback in 1992. As the acting head of state in 1992–95, he pulled the country out of a political

[118] On the spread of Christianity in Georgia, see Suny, Grigor Ronald. 1994. *The Making of the Georgian Nation*, 2nd edn. Bloomington: Indiana University Press, pp. 20–41.

[119] National Statistics Office of Georgia. 2003. *General Population Census of 2002: Major Findings*. Retrieved from www.geostat.ge/index.php?action=page&p_id=677&lang=eng.

[120] On the significance of the BTC project for Georgia, see Papava, Vladimer. 2005. "The Baku-Tbilisi-Ceyhan Pipeline: Implications for Georgia." In *The Baku-Tbilisi-Ceyhan Pipeline: Oil Window to the West*, eds. Frederick Starr and Svante Cornell. Washington, DC: Central Asia-Caucasus Institute and Silk Road Studies Program, Johns Hopkins University-SAIS, pp. 85–102.

[121] For an overview of Georgian politics, see Ekedahl, Carolyn McGiffert, and Melvin Allan Goodman. 1997. *The Wars of Eduard Shevardnadze*. College Park: Penn State University Press; Jones, Stephen.1997. "Georgia: The Trauma of Statehood." In *New States, New Politics: Building the Post-Soviet Nations*, eds. Ian Bremmer and Ray Taras. New York: Cambridge University Press; Wheatley, Jonathan. 2005 *Georgia from National Awakening to Rose Revolution: Delayed Transition in the Former Soviet Union*. Aldershot, UK: Ashgate.

[122] On security challenges, see Center for Strategic and International Studies. 2012. *Georgia's Security Challenges and Policy Recommendations* [policy brief]. Washington, DC: CSIS.

[123] United Nations High Commissioner for Refugees. 2003. *The Global Report 2002*. Geneva, Switzerland: UNHCR, p. 399.

[124] On Gamsakhurdia's presidency, see Nodia, Ghia. 1996. "Political Turmoil in Georgia and the Ethnic Policies of Zviad Gamsakhurdia." In *Contested Borders in the Caucasus*, ed. Bruno Coppieters. Brussels: VUB Press.

crisis. Given his statesmanship, Shevardnadze received 74.3 percent of the vote in the 1995 presidential election and 79.8 percent of the vote in the 2000 presidential election.[125] But his popularity began to dwindle amid the spread of corruption and the enrichment of his entourage in the poverty-stricken society. An opinion poll conducted in May 2003 found that 68 percent of Georgians held a negative opinion of the incumbent president, and 83 percent of citizens felt that the country was heading in the wrong direction.[126] In light of his dwindling popularity, 73-year-old Shevardnadze resigned as the chair of the Citizens' Union of Georgia and declared his intent to step down at the end of his second presidential term.[127] Shevardnadze's anticipated resignation elevated the importance of the upcoming parliamentary elections.

The 2003 parliamentary election was widely seen as a dress rehearsal for the 2005 presidential election. The Central Election Commission registered 39 political parties for participation in the parliamentary elections.[128] Among major political parties in terms of anticipated share of the vote were the Citizens' Union of Georgia (CUG), the Labor Party, the National Movement, and the United Democrats. It was widely upheld that a political party with a plurality of votes would be in a better position to jockey for the presidency.

Elite Divisions

Founded by Shevardnadze in 1993, CUG was closely associated with the current regime. The ruling party received 41.8 percent of votes in the 1999 election, compared with 23.7 percent of votes in the 1995 election (in electoral districts based on the proportional representation system).[129] But the CUG began to disintegrate in the early 2000s.[130] A few wealthy businessmen led by

[125] Nodia, Ghia, and David Usupashvili. 2002. *Electoral Processes in Georgia*. Discussion Paper No. 4. Sweden, Stockholm: International Institute for Democracy and International Assistance, p. 9.

[126] The Georgian National Voter Study was conducted by the International Republican Institute, Baltic Surveys, Ltd./The Gallup Organization, and Institute of Polling and Marketing with funding from the United States Agency for International Development.

[127] *Civil Georgia*. 2001. "President Resigns from CUG Chairmanship." September 17. www.civil.ge/eng/article.php?id=202; *Civil Georgia*. 2002. "Shevardnadze Rules Out Prolongation of Presidential Term." March 25. www.civil.ge/eng/article.php?id=1633.

[128] International Election Observation Mission. 2003. *Parliamentary Elections, Georgia – 2 November 2003*. Statement of Preliminary Findings and Conclusions, p. 5.

[129] Nodia, Ghia, and Alvaro Pinto Scholbach, eds. 2006. *The Political Landscape of Georgia: Political Parties: Achievements, Challenges, and Prospects*. Amsterdam: Eburon Academic Publishers, p. 14.

[130] *Civil Georgia*. 2001. "Various Factions Bid for Control over CUG." December 10. www.civil.ge/eng/article.php?id=845; Kalandadze, Giorgi. 2001. "Battle for Citizens Union Party: Will the CUG Be for or against the President?" *Civil Georgia*. December 12. www.civil.ge/eng/article.php?id=865.

David Gamkrelidze broke off from the CUG and set up the New Rights Party in September 2001.[131] In that year, Mikheil Saakashvili resigned from the post of the Minister of Justice and founded the National Movement in opposition to the current regime.[132] Having attempted to reform the CUG from within, Zurab Zhvania, the first secretary general of CUG and former speaker of the national parliament, left the ruling party with a team of young reformers and placed his faction on the party list of the tiny Christian Conservative Party just in time to run in the 2002 local elections.[133] Nino Burjanadze, another high-profile CUG member, abandoned her party membership in 2000 and later allied with Zhvania's newly formed party.

The CUG's disintegration affected the outcome of the 2002 municipal elections. Seven political parties, including the Labor Party (25.5 percent), the National Movement (23.7 percent), the New Rights Party (11.3 percent), and the Christian Conservative Party (7.3 percent), crossed the 4 percent threshold and secured seats in the Tbilisi City Council (*sacrebulo*). In contrast, the CUG experienced a crushing defeat, with only 2.5 percent of the vote in the capital city.[134] Within two weeks of the local elections, Zhvania announced the establishment of a new political party – the United Democrats – based on the CUG's reformist faction.[135] In alliance with smaller political parties, a conservative faction of the CUG formed the political coalition For a New Georgia. Still, electoral losses of the pro-Shevardnadze party in the local elections exposed the vulnerability of the current regime.

Security Defections

The so-called Tbilisi syndrome reduced the likelihood of military intervention in a confrontation between the incumbent government and the political opposition. The phrase "Tbilisi syndrome" was coined in the aftermath of the Soviet deployment of force against peaceful protesters in Tbilisi and referred to

[131] On the party's history, see www.nrp.ge/new-rights/history.html?lang=en-GB.

[132] *Civil Georgia*. 2001. "Saakashvili Dissociates from Shevardnadze's Corrupted Government." September 20. www.civil.ge/eng/article.php?id=225; *Civil Georgia*. 2001. "Saakashvili: Preliminary Elections Needed." November 8. www.civil.ge/eng/article.php?id=619; *Civil Georgia*. 2002. "Reformers Form Democratic Coalition." March 25. www.civil.ge/eng/article.php?id=1641.

[133] *Civil Georgia*. 2001. "Reformers Plan to Take over CUG." December 7. www.civil.ge/eng/article.php?id=825; *Civil Georgia*. 2002. "Zhvania's Team in Christian Conservative Party." May 8. www.civil.ge/eng/article.php?id=1808.

[134] On the 2002 local election, see Council of Europe. 2002. *Report on Local Elections in Georgia (2 June 2002)*. Strasbourg, France: Council of Europe. Retrieved from https://wcd.coe.int/ViewDoc.jsp?id=853173&Site=DC.

[135] Civil Georgia. 2002. "Zurab Zhvania Forms Party." June 17. www.civil.ge/eng/article.php?id=2098.

"military resentment toward civilian politicians" for their misuse of the army in political games.[136] Acting on the party's order, the Soviet army violently dispersed an antiregime protest on April 9, 1989, resulting in the death of 19 civilians aged between 16 and 70.[137] The communist leadership, however, refused to take responsibility for their action and shifted blame for the killing of civilians on the military. Colonel General Igor Rodionov, commander of the Caucasian Military District, was framed as the main culprit, while Mikhail Gorbachev and Shevardnadze claimed ignorance of the military operation.[138] This incident underpinned the military's reluctance to intervene in state-society relations.

Moreover, inadequate state funding for the army and the police brewed disloyalty to the incumbent government. Like most public-sector employees, the military suffered from wage arrears.[139] In May 2001, for example, a National Guard battalion stationed 25 miles northeast of Tbilisi revolted against the government, demanding the timely payment of wages and an improvement in living conditions.[140] Likewise, the police received meager state funding, engendering rampant corruption. Given state failure, the coercive apparatus was unlikely to obey the president's orders to suppress antigovernment protests.

Unity of the Opposition Political Parties

Taking into account the existence of more than 50 political parties,[141] leaders of the political opposition attempted to unite on the eve of the 2003 parliamentary election. As early as January 2003, Saakashvili and Zhvania proposed the establishment of a broad-based coalition in opposition to the current regime.[142] By May 2003, the Labor Party, the National Movement, the New Rights Party, and the United Democrats agreed on the creation of an anticrisis

[136] Barylski, Robert. 1998. *The Soldier in Russian Politics: Duty, Dictatorship, and Democracy under Gorbachev and Yeltsin*. New Brunswick, NJ: Transaction Publishers, pp. 63–67.

[137] *Ibid.*, p. 63.

[138] Balmasov, Sergei. 2011. "Igor Rodionov: Sovetskih soldat v Tbilisi sdelali palachami." *PravdaRu*. April 8. www.pravda.ru/world/formerussr/georgia/08–04-2011/1073043-rodionovv-0/; Remnick, David. 1989. "Tbilisi Role Disavowed by Kremlin; Georgian Officials Blamed in Crackdown." *Washington Post*. April 26. P. A21.

[139] On the state of the military during Shevardnadze's presidency, see Darchiashvili, David. 2005. "Georgian Defense Policy and Military Reform." In *Statehood and Security: Georgia after the Rose Revolution*, eds. Bruno Coppieters and Robert Legvold. Cambridge, MA: MIT Press, pp. 117–51.

[140] *Washington Post*. 2001. "Battalion Revolts at Base in Georgia." May 26. P. A22.

[141] On party politics, see Nodia, Ghia, and Alvaro Pinto Scholbach, eds. 2006. *The Political Landscape of Georgia: Political Parties: Achievements, Challenges, and Prospects*. Amsterdam: Eburon Academic Publishers.

[142] *Civil Georgia*. 2003. "Broad Opposition Alliance Proposed." January 21. www.civil.ge/eng/article.php?id=3041.

center aimed at preventing electoral fraud.[143] Zhvania and Burjanadze formed the electoral bloc Burjanadze–United Democrats in August 2003, but the National Movement did not join this alliance.[144] At the very least, Saakashvili and Zhvania reportedly agreed to target the incumbent government rather than attack each other in their election campaigns.

Another factor in favor of the political opposition was Saakashvili's charismatic personality.[145] As a recent graduate of the Columbia Law School, the young Georgian politician passionately campaigned for social change. The National Movement promised to double pensions, abolish the land tax for small land owners, and provide tax breaks for small business.[146] These campaign pledges resonated with ordinary citizens.

Media Access

The Georgian media market was filled with more than 200 newspapers, 47 TV channels, and a dozen of radio stations.[147] All the print media was de jure private. Newspapers with the largest circulation included *Kviris Palitra* (circulation 35,000), *Asaval Dasavali* (23,000), *Alia* (12,000), and *Akhali Taoba* (9,000). Among pro-government newspapers were former press organs of the Communist Party *Sakartvelos Respublika* (in Georgian) and *Svobodnaia Gruziia* (in Russian). Compared with print media, the broadcasting sector had a stronger presence of state-owned outlets. Two state TV channels had near-universal reach, whereas Rustavi-2, a leading private TV channel, could broadcast only in large cities and relied on local media partners to rebroadcast its programming in the provinces. According to an opinion poll, the state-owned TV channels Channel 1 and Channel 2 had approximately 32 percent of the market share in 2002, whereas Rustavi-2 captured 18.4 percent of market share.[148] Founded in 1994 and nearly closed down by state authorities in 2001, Rustavi-2 became known for investigative journalism. It

[143] *Civil Georgia*. 2003. "Leading Opposition Parties Agree on Cooperation." May 13. www.civil.ge/eng/article.php?id=4202.

[144] *Civil Georgia*. 2003. "Burjanadze, Zhvania Officially Presented New Election Bloc." August 21. www.civil.ge/eng/article.php?id=4800.

[145] On Saakashvili's charismatic personality, see Greenberg, Ilan. 2004. "The Not-So-Velvet-Revolution." *New York Times*. May 30. www.nytimes.com/2004/05/30/magazine/the-not-so-velvet-revolution.html?src=pm&pagewanted=1; Nanava, Nino. 2003. "Mikhail Saakashvili: New Romantic or Modern Realist?" *Open Democracy*. December 11. www.opendemocracy.net/democracy-protest/article_1637.jsp.

[146] Alkhazashvili, K. 2003. "Saakashvili's Economic Pledges Prove Effective." *The Messenger*. November 6. P. 3.

[147] Duve, Freimut. 2001. *Current Media Situation in Georgia: Fifth Report*. Vienna, Austria: The Office of the OSCE Representative on Freedom of the Media.

[148] These estimates are based on results from a survey conducted on February 22–March 2, 2002 (*N* = 1,000). For details, see Georgian Opinion Research Business International. 2002. *Georgian Media Facts: Eleventh Edition* [PowerPoint slides]. Tbilisi, Georgia: GORBI.

was widely believed that Giorgi Sanaia, a popular 26-year-old news anchor on Rustavi-2, was murdered for his investigative work in July 2001.[149] Imedi ("Hope"), a new private TV channel funded by the Georgian billionaire Badri Patarkatsishvili, started broadcasting in March 2003.[150] These private TV channels provided an opportunity for spreading news critical of the incumbent government.

Unlike traditional media, web-based publications could reach a tiny fraction of the electorate in 2003. There were 2,565 Internet hosts with the domain name "ge" at the beginning of the election year,[151] with 2.6 Internet users per 100 people.[152] One of the most popular news websites (available in Georgian, English, and Russian) was the news portal Civil Georgia, established by the NGO United Nations Association of Georgia. Yet, given the underdevelopment of the Internet infrastructure and the impoverishment of local population, the Internet was much less influential than the broadcasting media during the 2003 parliamentary elections.

It must also be noted that the level of press freedom varied across Georgian regions.[153] The Autonomous Republic of Ajara, located on the border with Turkey and populated with Muslim Georgians, was notorious for systematic violations of political freedoms. Since 1991, Aslan Abashidze ruled the region with an iron fist and suppressed dissent. Ajara was "the only part of Georgia where people whisper criticisms of the government in a fear of being overheard by the special services."[154] In addition, local authorities in the Samtskhe-Javakheti region, predominantly populated with ethnic Armenians, and the Kvemo Kartli region, mostly populated with ethnic Azerbaijanis, bluntly propagated mass support for the incumbent government via ethnic media.

Influential Allies

Shevardnadze's presidency was associated with the development of a vibrant civil society.[155] In 2002, there were 3,848 registered civic associations and 500

[149] *Civil Georgia*. 2001. "A Famous Georgian Journalist Giorgi Sanaia Has Been Murdered." July 27. www.civil.ge/eng/article.php?id=91.

[150] Civil Georgia. 2003. "TV Channel Run by Influential Tycoon Starts Broadcasting." March 13. www.civil.ge/eng/article.php?id=3339.

[151] Internet Systems Consortium's Internet Domain Survey. Retrieved from www.isc.org/services /survey.

[152] European Bank for Reconstruction and Development. 2007. *Transition Report 2007: People in Transition*. London, UK: EBRD, p. 136.

[153] Nodia, Ghia. 2002. "Country Report: Georgia." In *Nations in Transit 2002*. New York: Freedom House, pp. 182–95, p. 183.

[154] Bakhtadze, Revaz. 2002. "Aslan Abashidze, a Man of Feudal Loyalty and Pride." *Civil Georgia*. December 21. www.civil.ge/eng/article.php?id=2917.

[155] For an in-depth analysis, see Angley, Robyn. 2010. "NGOs in Competitive Authoritarian States: The Role of Civic Groups in Georgia's Rose Revolution." Ph.D. dissertation, Boston University.

foundations dealing with a wide range of issues, including civic education, conflict resolution, and human rights.[156] Notably, 60 Georgian NGOs involving up to 700 active members focused on women's issues, indicating the prominent role of women in Georgian civil society.[157] Several leading NGOs were established in the late 1990s and lobbied the national parliament for legal reforms in support of democratic development. Founded in 1994, the Georgian Young Lawyers' Association (GYLA), with a membership of nearly 600 people, promoted the rule of law and transparency in the public sector. GYLA organized an independent election observation mission and dispatched its representatives to polling stations in Tbilisi, Adjara, and Kvemo Kartli during the 2003 parliamentary elections.[158] A larger election monitoring project was undertaken by the Georgian NGO International Society for Fair Elections and Democracy (ISFED). The NGO planned to deploy 3,000 observers to 2,500 of 3,000 precincts to monitor the elections and conduct parallel vote count.[159] The Caucasus Institute for Peace, Democracy and Development (CIPDD), founded in 1992, and the Liberty Institute, established by several former Rustavi-2 reporters in 1996, also played an active role during the 2003 parliamentary election. These leading NGOs set up a coordination council to facilitate NGO cooperation on election-related issues and drafted a list of 10 steps necessary for Georgia's democratic development.[160]

The Open Society Georgia Foundation (OSGF), established by Soros in 1994, systematically supported the growth of civil society and the protection of human rights in Georgia. Given the significance of the 2003 parliamentary elections, OSGF launched the Election Support Program to assist local civic activists with the implementation of projects promoting free, fair, and democratic elections. Specifically, the OSGF provided funding for the conduct of pre-election opinion polls and an exit poll in 2003.[161] Overall, OSGF expenditures increased from $3,299,000 in 2002 to 4,600,000 in 2003.[162]

[156] Stuart, Jennifer, ed. 2003. *The 2002 NGO Sustainability Index for Central and Eastern Europe and Eurasia*. Washington, DC: United States Agency for International Development, p. 74.

[157] Nodia, Ghia. 2002. "Country Report: Georgia." In *Nations in Transit 2002*. New York: Freedom House, pp. 182–95, p. 186.

[158] *Civil Georgia*. 2003. "GYLA Protects the Rights of Electorate." November 6. www.civil.ge/eng/article.php?id=7337.

[159] Sepashvili, Giorgi. 2003. "ISFED to Conduct Parallel Vote Tabulation." *Civil Georgia*. October 30. www.civil.ge/eng/article.php?id=5329.

[160] *Civil Georgia*. 2003. "Civil Society Organizations for Fair and Democratic Elections." May 12. www.civil.ge/eng/article.php?id=7314; Giorgadze, Julie. 2003. "Ten Steps towards Liberty: Civil Society Leaders Unveil Program to Promote Democracy." *Civil Georgia*. October 17. www.civil.ge/eng/article.php?id=5132.

[161] *Civil Georgia*. 2003. "US Company to Conduct Exit Polls." October 29. www.civil.ge/eng/article.php?id=5312.

[162] Open Society Institute. 2003. *Building Open Societies: Soros Foundations Network 2002 Report*. New York: OSI, p. 25; Open Society Institute. 2004. *Building Open Societies: Soros Foundations Network 2003 Report*. New York: OSI, p. 103.

In contrast, the amount of US government assistance to Georgia dropped from $187 million in 2002 to $141.16 million in 2003.[163] A total of $21.06 million was allocated for democratic reform programs, including election-related projects. The US government, for example, funded the compilation of computerized voter lists and training of domestic election observers. Moreover, former US Secretary of State James Baker was designated as a presidential envoy to Georgia to impress on Shevardnadze the importance of free and fair parliamentary elections.[164]

Socioeconomic Conditions

Georgia was dubbed a failed state in the 1990s.[165] The national government lost control over Abkhazia, South Ossetia, and, to a large extent, Ajara. The Pankisi Gorge, a mountainous area on the border with Chechnya, became a haven for drug trafficking, kidnapping, and terrorism.[166] In addition to national security failures, the state lacked the capacity to collect revenues. According to some estimates, the shadow economy contributed 70 percent to the country's GDP.[167] Moreover, the cash-strapped state was unable to provide adequate public-sector services and pay wages to state employees, including the coercive apparatus. A Georgian civic activist recalled how police officers extracted money from ordinary citizens to cover their living expenses:

> Once a police officer stopped my friend inside the subway station. He was searched and the police didn't find anything on him. In fact, the policeman openly admitted that he just needed some money to buy lunch. He asked for a few coins to buy a sandwich and a bottle of lemonade. That's how poor the policemen were during Shevardnadze's presidency.[168]

[163] US State Department. 2003. *US Government Assistance to and Cooperative Activities with Eurasia: FY 2002 US Assistance to Eurasia.* Washington, DC: Bureau of European and Eurasian Affairs. Retrieved from www.state.gov/p/eur/rls/rpt/23621.htm; US State Department. 2004. *US Government Assistance to and Cooperative Activities with Eurasia: FY 2003 US Assistance to Eurasia.* Washington, DC: Bureau of European and Eurasian Affairs. Retrieved from www.state.gov/p/eur/rls/rpt/37655.htm.

[164] Baker, James, and Steve Fiffer. 2008. "*Work Hard, Study and ... Keep out of Politics!": Adventures and Lessons from an Unexpected Public Life.* London: Penguin Books, pp. 397–98; White House. 2003. "Presidential Envoy James Baker to Visit Tbilisi, Georgia." Statement by the Press Secretary. July 3. Retrieved from http://georgewbush-whitehouse.archives.gov/news/releases/2003/07/20030703-15.html.

[165] Malek, Martin. 2006. "State Failure in the South Caucasus: Proposals for an Analytical Framework." *Transition Studies Review* 13(2): 441–60.

[166] Silverman, Jeffrey. 2002. "Pankisi Gorge Kidnappings Hint at Chaos in Georgian Government." *Eurasianet.* January 28. www.eurasianet.org/departments/insight/articles/eav012902.shtml.

[167] US State Department. 2004. *US Government Assistance to and Cooperative Activities with Eurasia: FY 2003 US Assistance to Eurasia.* Washington, DC: Bureau of European and Eurasian Affairs. Retrieved from www.state.gov/p/eur/rls/rpt/37655.htm.

[168] Author's interview with David Darchiashvili, Tbilisi, Georgia, February 16, 2008.

A high incidence of poverty was a defining attribute of the weak state. GDP per capita PPP was $2,950 in 2003,[169] and the monthly family income for 54 percent of Georgian households was $47.6 (GEL100) or less.[170] Though the share of agriculture in GDP declined from 66 percent in 1993 to 23 percent of GDP in 2003,[171] more than half of the economically active population was officially employed in agriculture. Almost all rural households practiced subsistence farming. The low level of living standards dampened mass support for the incumbent president.

A protracted parliamentary debate over the law on minimum wages further damaged the pro-presidential electoral bloc. The opposition's accomplishment lay in pushing through the parliament a law raising the minimum wage from $9.1 (GEL20) to $54.7 (GEL115) starting in July 2003.[172] Implementation of this law required an additional $55.2 million for the 2003 state budget, which presented an insurmountable challenge for the incumbent government. Shevardnadze vetoed the law and suggested a gradual increase in the minimum wage to lighten the economic burden on the state. In line with the president's proposal, the national parliament passed an amendment to the Labor Code increasing the size of the minimum wage to $16.6 (GEL35).[173] While the United Democrats lost this parliamentary battle, the opposition scored political points with the impoverished electorate.

Overall, the political conditions were ripe for political change in Georgia. The breakdown of the ruling party, the ascendancy of new reform-oriented political parties, and investigative reporting by Rustavi-2 increased the odds of a popular revolt against the incumbent. Moreover, a high incidence of poverty and corruption alienated the majority of voters from the government. A public opinion poll conducted on October 19–22, 2003 found that the National Movement was a frontrunner in the upcoming parliamentary elections, with 22.8 percent of popular support; the Burjanadze–United Democrats bloc came in second with 19.8 percent; while the electoral bloc For New Georgia trailed behind with 8.7 percent.[174]

169 World Bank. 2013. *World Development Indicators Database: GDP per Capita, PPP*. Retrieved from http://data.worldbank.org/indicator/NY.GDP.PCAP.PP.CD.

170 Georgian Opinion Research Business International. 2002. *Georgian Media Facts: Eleventh Edition* [PowerPoint slides]. Tbilisi, Georgia: GORBI. The official exchange rate for the Georgian national currency lari (GEL) against US$1 was 2.1 in 2003. See the National Bank of Georgia, www.nbg.ge/index.php?m=582&lng=eng.

171 Kegel, Hannah. 2003. "The Significance of Subsistence Farming in Georgia as an Economic and Social Buffer." In *Subsistence Agriculture in Central and Eastern Europe: How to Break the Vicious Circle?*, eds. Steffen Abele and Klaus Frohberg. Leibniz, Germany: Institute of Agricultural Development in Central and Eastern Europe, pp. 147–60, p. 154.

172 Sepashvili, Giorgi, and Jaba Devdariani. 2003. "United Democrats Corner President Shevardnadze." *Civil Georgia*. March 5. www.civil.ge/eng/article.php?id=3289.

173 *Civil Georgia*. 2003. "Parliament Approves Increase of Minimal Salary." May 7. www.civil.ge/eng/article.php?id=4161.

174 Sepashvili, Giorgi. 2003. "Exit Poll to Be Held, Despite Government Opposition." *Civil Georgia*. October 29. www.civil.ge/eng/article.php?id=5316.

UKRAINE

Like Belarus, Ukraine is a former Soviet republic located between the European Union and Russia. With 34 million hectares of arable land and fertile black soil, Ukraine was once nicknamed "the breadbasket of the Soviet Union."[175] More recently, it became a vital transit country for energy resources from Russia to the European Union. Eighty percent of Russian gas bound for European states passed through Ukraine in 2004, making the country's pipelines a coveted asset for the Russian gas company Gazprom.[176] More broadly, this second largest former Soviet republic, with a population of 47.3 million people, posed a threat to Russia's hegemonic rule in the post-Soviet region. As Zbigniew Brzezinski put it, Russia would not be an empire without Ukraine.[177]

Ukraine had three competitive presidential elections between 1991 and 2004.[178] The former leader of the Communist Party, Leonid Kravchuk, was the first president of Ukraine from 1991 to 1994. Leonid Kuchma, former manager of the Soviet Union's largest missile factory in the city of Dnipropetrovsk, beat the incumbent in the 1994 election and won reelection in 1999. Kuchma toyed with the idea of running for a third term through the manipulation of legal procedures,[179] but he eventually endorsed Viktor Yanukovych as his successor.

Twenty-four candidates registered for participation in the 2004 presidential election,[180] but it was primarily a political battle between two former prime ministers named Viktor. Viktor Yanukovych, incumbent prime minister and leader of the Party of Regions of Ukraine, was a governor of Donetsk *oblast* (province) before his entry into national politics. His convictions for robbery and assault,[181] as well as his alleged connections with a Donetsk business clan,

[175] Rachkevych, Mark. 2012. "Agriculture: Room for Profitable Growth in the Fields of Black Earth." *Financial Times*. September 17. www.ft.com/intl/cms/s/0/268d74fc-f8e0-11e1-8d92-00144feabdc0.html#axzz2Xaj5iofc.

[176] Elder, Miriam. 2009. "Behind the Russia-Ukraine Gas Conflict." *Business Week*. January 3. www.businessweek.com/globalbiz/content/jan2009/gb2009013_045451.htm.

[177] Brzezinski, Zbigniew. 1994. "The Premature Partnership." *Foreign Affairs* 73(2): 67–82.

[178] On Ukrainian politics, see D'Anieri, Paul. 2007. *Understanding Ukrainian Politics: Power, Politics, and Institutional Design*. Armonk, NY: M.E. Sharpe; Harasymiw, Bohdan. 2002. *Post-communist Ukraine*. Toronto, ON: Canadian Institute of Ukrainian Studies; Kuzio, Taras. 2005. "Regime Type and Politics in Ukraine under Kuchma." *Communist and Post-Communist Studies* 38: 167–90.

[179] On Kuchma's proposal of constitutional amendments, see Haran, Olexiy, and Rostyslav Pavlenko. 2003. "Political Reform or a Game of Survival for President Kuchma?" PONARS Policy Memo 294.

[180] For a full list of presidential candidates, see OSCE. 2005. *Ukraine Presidential Election 31 October, 21 November and 26 December 2004: OSCE/ODIHR Election Observation Mission Final Report*. Warsaw, Poland: ODIHR, p. 45.

[181] *Ukrainska Pravda*. 2004. "Imidzh Yanukovycha – khlorkoi!" May 13. www.pravda.com.ua/rus/news/2004/05/13/4378553/; *Ukrainska Pravda*. 2004. "Yanukovych shapok ne voroval. Ego osudili za krazhu chasov." May 27. www.pravda.com.ua/rus/news/2004/05/27/4378868/.

stirred a debate over the moral qualities of the national leader. Yanukovych's candidacy was endorsed by Russia's increasingly authoritarian government.[182] Compared with Yanukovych, Viktor Yushchenko had a cleaner reputation. Yushchenko was former head of the National Bank of Ukraine and Kuchma's prime minister before his dismissal in spring 2001. Trained as an economist and married to a Chicago-born Ukrainian American, Yushchenko was seen as a stronger champion of democratic and market reforms.

Elite Divisions

The emergence of oligarchic groups was a source of elite divisions during Kuchma's presidency. In the Ukrainian context, the term "oligarch" refers to "a very wealthy and politically well-connected businessman ... who was the main owner of a conglomerate of enterprises and had close ties to the president."[183] Based on the main industry in a region, three major clans emerged in the 1990s: (1) the Donetsk clan, with specialization in metallurgy; (2) the Dnipropetrovsk clan, with a focus on metallurgy and the financial sector; and (3) the Kyiv clan, with a heavy presence in the energy sector, banking, and media.[184] These clans sought to protect their business interests by wielding power in domestic politics.

One of the earliest challengers to the incumbent president was Dnipropetrovsk-born Pavlo Lazarenko. As prime minister in 1996–97, Lazarenko began to amass a lot of political power and fell out of favor with Kuchma. On his resignation, Lazarenko, along with 22 members of his political party Community (*Hromada*), was elected to the national parliament,[185] sparking rumors about his run for presidency. Yet Lazarenko had to abandon his political ambitions and flee the country in February 1999 due to the threat of imprisonment for embezzlement of state property and attempted assassination of high-ranking officials.[186]

[182] On Russian foreign policy in 2004, see Petrov, Nikolai, and Andrei Ryabov. 2006. "Russia's Role in the Orange Revolution." In *Revolution in Orange: The Origins of Ukraine's Democratic Breakthrough*, eds. Anders Aslund and Michael McFaul. Washington, DC: Carnegie Endowment for International Peace, pp. 145–64.

[183] Aslund, Anders. 2009. *How Ukraine Became a Market Economy and Democracy*. Washington, DC: Peterson Institute for International Economics, p. 107.

[184] For an overview of the oligarchic clans, see Matuszak, Slawomir. 2012. *The Oligarchic Democracy: The Influence of Business Groups on Ukrainian Politics*. Warsaw, Poland: Centre for European Studies, pp. 14–15.

[185] Central Election Committee. 1998. *Vybory narodnykh deputativ Ukrainy 29.03.1998: Zvedeni vidomosti pro nalezhnist narodnykh deputativ do partii (blokiv)*. Retrieved from www.cvk.gov.ua/pls/vd2002/webprocov?kodvib=1&rejim=0.

[186] BBC. 2006. "The Case against Pavlo Lazarenko." August 25. http://news.bbc.co.uk/go/pr/fr/-/2/hi/europe/4780743.stm. For an in-depth analysis of Lazarenko's crimes, see Leshchenko, Serhiy. 2013. *Amerykanska saga Pavla Lazarenka*. Kyiv, Ukraine: Nezalezhnyi kulturologichnyi zhurnal "I".

In addition, two main defections from the incumbent president occurred on the eve of the 2002 parliamentary elections. Yulia Tymoshenko, Lazarenko's business partner and Minister of Energy in 2000–01, joined the opposition camp in the early 2000s. She founded the political party Fatherland (*Batkivshchyna*) that received 22 seats in the 450-member national parliament. A bigger political winner in the 2002 parliamentary elections was Yushchenko's electoral bloc Our Ukraine (*Nasha Ukraina*), securing 112 seats in parliament.[187] In light of their electoral victories, Tymoshenko and Yushchenko became the main opposition figures during the 2004 presidential election.

Given competing business interests, the 2004 presidential election was dubbed a revolution of "millionaires against billionaires."[188] Yanukovych was backed by the Donetsk clan and in particular the billionaire Rinat Akhmetov. In contrast, less wealthy representatives of big business sided with Yushchenko. Petro Poroshenko, a chocolate magnate and former member of a pro-presidential party, and David Zhvania, another wealthy businessman, were among Yushchenko's strongest supporters in 2004.

Security Defections

From the start of Kuchma's presidency, the police increasingly intervened in electoral processes.[189] Minister of Interior Mykola Bilokon was allegedly ready to deploy special police units from Donetsk *oblast* and the Crimea to disperse post-election protests in Kyiv in case of such an order from Kuchma.[190] But the outgoing president proclaimed his commitment to a peaceful resolution of the political standoff.[191]

Splits within the security apparatus reduced the incidence of violence against protesters. A faction of Ukraine's top intelligence officers cooperated with the political opposition during the election campaign. Specifically, Ihor Smeshko, chief of the State Security Service (*Sluzhba bezpeky Ukrainy* [SBU]), and Oleksandr Galaka, chief of the military intelligence board in the Ministry of

[187] Central Election Committee. 2002. *Vybory narodnykh deputativ Ukrainy 31.03.2002: Iakisnyi sklad Verkhovnoi Rady. Nalezhnist do partii (blokiv)*. Retrieved from www.cvk.gov.ua/pls/vd2002/WEBPROCoV.

[188] Grin, Grigoriy. 2012. "Konets sroka ekspluatatsii Ukrainskoi SSR." *Maidan*. October 19. http://maidanua.org/2012/10/konets-sroka-ekspluatatsyy-ukraynskoj-ssr/; Hoagland, Jim. 2005. "Ukraine's Lesson for Putin." *Washington Post*. January 23. www.washingtonpost.com/wp-dyn/articles/A40072-2005Jan26.html; Levchenko, Aleksandr. 2005. "Pokhvala oligarkhii." *Zerkalo Nedeli*. November 4. http://gazeta.zn.ua/POLITICS/pohvala_oligarhii.html.

[189] Khavroniuk, Mykola, and Mykola Melnyk. 2004. "Pravookhorontsi pered vyborom: Moment istyny." *Dzerkalo tyzhnia*. October 29. http://gazeta.dt.ua/LAW/pravoohorontsi_pered_viborom_moment_istini.html.

[190] Koshkina, Sonia. 2007. "Bilokon: Prikazhi Kuchma razognat Maidan – my by vypolnili." *Obozrevatel*. February 16. http://obozrevatel.com/news/2007/2/14/156487.htm.

[191] Kuchma, Leonid. 2008. *Posle maidana: Zapiski prezidenta2005–2006*. Kyiv, Ukraine: Dovira, Vremia, p. 8.

Defense, reportedly maintained contacts with representatives of Yushchenko's camp.[192] The SBU chief allegedly warned the Minister of Interior against the use of violence when armored police units advanced to the capital city on November 28.[193] In addition, some rank-and-file police officers publicly sided with the political opposition in November 2004. For example, a police officer from Donetsk published an open letter in support of Yushchenko,[194] while a group of cadets from the national police academy backed his candidacy by attending a protest event in Kyiv.[195] These security defections increased the chances of large post-election protests.

Unity of the Opposition Political Parties

Dozens of political parties representing a broad political spectrum were formed in post-Soviet Ukraine.[196] A major right-wing political party in favor of democratic development was the People's Movement of Ukraine (*Narodnyi Rukh Ukrainy* [NRU]), founded as an independence movement in 1989 and registered as a political party in 1993. But the sudden death of party leader Taras Chornovil on the eve of the 1999 presidential election and a subsequent split within the party undermined NRU's strength in the early 2000s.[197] Among main left-wing political parties were the Communist Party of Ukraine and the Socialist Party of Ukraine, whose leaders – Petro Symonenko and Oleksandr Moroz – received 22.2 and 11.3 percent of the vote, respectively, in the 1999 presidential election.[198] But disagreements between right- and left-wing political parties undercut their effectiveness in challenging the current regime. In contrast, the political opposition appeared to be united during the 2004 election. Tymoshenko struck a deal with Yushchenko, putting on hold her presidential ambitions in exchange for the

192 Chivers, C. J. 2005. "How Top Spies in Ukraine Changed the Nation's Path." *New York Times*. January 17. www.nytimes.com/2005/01/17/international/europe/17ukraine.html?_r=0.

193 Smeshko did not officially confirm his role during the Orange Revolution. For a critical assessment of Smeshko's role, see Kuzio, Taras. 2005. "Did Ukraine's Security Service Really Prevent Bloodshed during the Orange Revolution?" *Eurasia Daily Monitor*. January 23.

194 *Ukraina Moloda*. 2004. "Moment istyny: Dlia vysokogo militseiskogo chyna poliagaje u tomu, shcho vin obyraje Yushchenka." November 17. www.umoloda.kiev.ua/number/309/176/11184/.

195 Kyivska miska rada. 2004. "Kursanty MVS z narodom." November 26. http://kmr.gov.ua/news.asp?IdType=1&Id=31923.

196 For an overview, see Kononchuk, Svitlana, and Oleg Yarosh. 2013. *Ideologichne pozytsionuvannia politychnykh partii v Ukraini*. Kyiv, Ukraine: Agentsvo Ukraina.

197 A faction of NRU party members led by Yuri Kostenko broke off and set up the Ukrainian People's Party (*Ukrainska narodna partiia* [UNR]) in 1999. On NRU's weakness, see Tychina, Andrei. 2001. "Bolshoi perepolokh iz-za malogo rukha." *Zerkalo nedeli*. November 16. http://gazeta.zn.ua/POLITICS/bolshoy_perepoloh_iz-za_malogo_ruha.html.

198 OSCE. 2000. *Ukraine Presidential Elections 31 October and 14 November 1999*. Warsaw, Poland: ODIHR, p. 30.

post of prime minister, and Moroz backed Yushchenko during post-election protests against vote rigging.

Media Access

More than 800 TV and radio stations and 2,551 newspapers existed in Ukraine on the eve of the 2004 election.[199] According to official statistics, 95 percent of broadcasting media and 70 percent of print media were privately owned.[200] Yet the incumbent president exercised political control over a large segment of the media market through his ties with wealthy businessmen. Viktor Pinchuk, Kuchma's son-in-law, reportedly owned such TV channels as ICTV, STB, and Novyi Kanal, whereas Viktor Medvedchuk, Kuchma's chief of staff, controlled Inter and Channel 1+1.[201] Moreover, most local newspapers, founded on the basis of Soviet-era press organs, fell under the influence of business cliques or city councils. Local newspapers, on average, had a larger circulation than national ones. But the Russian-language tabloid *Fakty i Kommentarii* (*Facts and Comments*), owned by Pinchuk, was the largest, with a daily circulation of more than 1 million copies. Since September 2001, major media outlets received from the presidential administration the so-called *temnyky*, detailed instructions on how to cover current events.[202] Recalcitrant media faced the threat of defamation suits, unscheduled tax audits, or intimidation of journalists.

Founded by Poroshenko in 2003, Channel 5 positioned itself as a "channel of trustworthy news." Unlike most private TV channels, Channel 5 provided ample airtime for the political opposition in the run-up to the 2004 presidential election. Moreover, Channel 5 broadcast around-the-clock news from the Maidan, the main site of post-election protests, to inform the general public of happenings in Kyiv and to minimize the use of violence against peaceful protesters. With intermittent interruptions, approximately half of Ukraine's population could watch Channel 5 via cable TV. State authorities put pressure on local cable providers to limit the channel's reach and temporarily froze the channel's bank account in an attempt to disrupt its work.[203] In reaction to the government's

199 Freedom House. 2005. "Country Report: Ukraine." In *Nations in Transit Report*. New York: Freedom House. Retrieved from www.freedomhouse.org/report/nations-transit/2005/ukraine.

200 Freedom House. 2004. "Country Report: Ukraine." In *Nations in Transit Report*. New York: Freedom House. Retrieved from www.freedomhouse.org/report/nations-transit/2004/ukraine.

201 On the ownership structure, see Dyczok, Marta. 2005. "Breaking through the Information Blockade: Election and Revolution in Ukraine 2004." *Canadian Slavonic Papers* 47(3–4): 241–64.

202 Human Rights Watch. 2003. *Negotiating the News: Informal State Censorship of Ukrainian Television.*

203 Krushelnycky, Askold. 2004. "Ukraine: TV Channel Finds Itself under Hostile Fire in Fight for Country's Presidency." Radio Free Europe/Radio Liberty. October 22. www.rferl.org/features article/2004/10/790dcfb1-4279-4c90-9145–357970930849.html.

crackdown on the mass media, more than 300 journalists from various media outlets signed an open letter demanding the protection of press freedom during the 2004 election campaign.[204] A number of journalists on leading private TV channels refused to deliver state-censored news in October–November 2004, which increased the opposition's access to the mass media.

Compared with Belarus of 2001, Ukraine had a higher Internet penetration, with 8 Internet users per 100 people in 2004.[205] The number of Internet hosts with the domain name "ua" was 130,144 in 2004, up from 22,766 in 1999.[206] One of the most popular online publications was *Ukrainska Pravda* (*Ukrainian Truth*, http://www.pravda.com.ua), founded by investigative journalist Georgiy Gongadze. Gongadze's murder in September 2000 engendered the Ukraine without Kuchma Movement. The website *Maidan* (http://maidanua.org) was initially set up by civic activists to provide extensive coverage of the movement's activities. By 2004, *Maidan* became a popular news site and online forum, fostering a community of like-minded individuals in opposition to the regime. These online publications were able to exercise a greater degree of press freedom than broadcast media, providing an impetus for youth political action.[207]

Influential Allies

The number of registered Ukrainian NGOs grew from 4,000 in 1995 to 35,000 in 2003.[208] The largest share of NGOs focused on such issues as charity, gender, culture, ethnic minorities, and youth.[209] In addition, a few NGOs were concerned primarily with democratic development and transparent elections. Since its inception in 1994, the Committee of Voters of Ukraine (CVU) systematically monitored electoral processes and implemented voter education programs in the

[204] Ligachova, Natalia, and Lesia Ganzha, eds. 2005. *Zhurnalistska revolutsiia 2004: Podii, liudy, duskusii*. Kyiv, Ukraine: Vistka, pp. 17–20.

[205] European Bank for Reconstruction and Development. 2007. *Transition Report 2007: People in Transition*. London, UK: EBRD, p. 204.

[206] Internet Systems Consortium's Internet Domain Survey is conducted semiannually in January and July. The reported data come from July surveys. Retrieved from www.isc.org/services/survey.

[207] On the role of digital technology, see Goldstein, Joshua. 2007. *The Role of Digital Networked Technologies in the Ukrainian Orange Revolution*. Cambridge, MA: Berkman Center for Internet and Society, Harvard Law School; Lysenko, Volodymyr, and Kevin Desouza. 2010. "Role of Internet-based Information Flows and Technologies in Electoral Revolutions: The Case of Ukraine's Orange Revolution." *First Monday: Peer-Reviewed Journal on the Internet*. http://firstmonday.org/htbin/cgiwrap/bin/ojs/index.php/fm/article/viewArticle/2992/2599.

[208] Freedom House. 2004. "Country Report: Ukraine." In *Nations in Transit Report*. New York: Freedom House. Retrieved from www.freedomhouse.org/report/nations-transit/2004/ukraine.

[209] Kolodii, Antonina. 2001. "Stanovlennia gromadianskogo suspilstva v Ukraini." *Nezalezhnyi kultorologichnyi chasopys 'I'* 22. www.ji.lviv.ua/n22texts/kolodij.htm.

country.[210] In October 2003, the CVU, in cooperation with such leading NGOs as the Ukrainian Independent Center of Political Research, the Foundation "Democratic Initiatives," and the Europe XXI Fund, unveiled the formation of a civic coalition, New Choice 2004.[211] Approximately 100 NGOs joined this coalition to campaign for free and fair presidential elections. Another NGO coalition named the Wave of Freedom was formed on the eve of the 1999 presidential election and continued its election monitoring and voter education work in 2004.[212] According to the coalition's coordinator, Vladyslav Kaskiv, the number of member organizations grew from 250 NGOs in 1999 to 370 NGOs in 2004.[213] Several NGOs monitored parliamentary by-elections or mayoral elections held in Ukraine immediately prior to the 2004 presidential election. CVU representatives also served as international election observers for the 2003 parliamentary elections in Georgia and the 2003 presidential election in Azerbaijan, providing Ukrainian civic activists with another perspective on electoral malpractices in the post-Soviet region.[214]

Both NGO coalitions received grants from the international donor community. The International Renaissance Fund (IRF), established by the Soros Foundations, provided funding for the organization of roundtables, workshops, and press conferences by the NGO coalition New Choice 2004, whereas the NGO coalition Wave of Freedom received a grant to monitor mayoral elections in the city of Mukachevo in April 2004.[215] With a total budget of $8,242,000 in 2004, the IRF spent $1,550,000 on media development projects, an additional $1,125,000 on the information society, and $913,000 on civil society initiatives.[216] The total amount of US government

210 For an overview of CVU activities, visit the website www.cvu.org.ua.

211 Ukrainian Independent Center of Political Research. 2003. "Prezentatsiia gromadskoi koalitsii Novyi vybir-2004." October 31. www.ucipr.kiev.ua/publications/prezentatciia-gromadskoii-koalitciii-novii-vibir-2004/lang/tab02.

212 Committee of Voters of Ukraine. 1999. "Stvorennia koalitsii organizatsii" [press release]. March 22. www.cvu.org.ua/doc.php?lang=ukr&mid=docs&id=350; Gulenko, Liudmila. 1999. "Svoboda vyboru – vybir svobody." *Den*. July 27. www.day.kiev.ua/uk/article/den-ukrayini/svoboda-viboru-vibir-svobodi.

213 Dokukin, Yuriy. 2004. "Vzhe na nastupnyi den pislia opryliudnennia nashoi zaiavy na pidtrymku GK 'Pora' stalysia obshuky ofisu koalitsii 'Svoboda vyboru' i osobysto v mene vdoma." *Gromadskyi zakhysnyk* 20(24), p. 3. Retrieved from www.zahysnyk.org.ua/pdf/gz0024.pdf.

214 Committee of Voters of Ukraine. 2004. *Zvit pro dialnist VGO "Komitet vybortsiv Ukrainy" u 2003 rotsi*. Retrieved from www.cvu.org.ua/doc.php?lang=ukr&mid=yreport&doc_type=&id=631&lim_beg=0.

215 International Renaissance Fund. 2005. *Spryiannia spravedlyvym i chesnym vyboram 2004 roku*. Retrieved from www.irf.ua/index.php?option=com_content&view=article&id=4586:irf-news-uk-298&catid=27:news-irf&Itemid=59.

216 Open Society Institute. 2005. *Building Open Societies: Soros Foundations Network 2004 Report*. New York: OSI, p. 93. There is a mismatch between the total budget for Ukraine reported by the OSI and the total budget reported by the IRF in part due to the fact that the OSI figure includes $989,068 provided by non-Soros entities for public health projects in Ukraine.

assistance to Ukraine was $161.06 million in 2004.[217] Of $42.34 million allocated for democratic reform programs, $18.3 million was earmarked for projects promoting free and fair presidential elections. A central component of the US election program was "support for nonpartisan domestic and international election monitoring, parallel vote tabulations, and exit polling."[218] The NDI and IRI received grants to train independent election observers and party activists to improve their capacities to campaign and monitor elections. Moreover, the US government provided funding for the Poland-America-Ukraine Cooperation Initiative facilitating the transfer of Western expertise through the prism of Polish experience to Ukrainian civil society.[219]

Socioeconomic Conditions

The national economy was booming on the eve of the 2004 election, with high international demand for metal (the country's main export commodity), rapid growth in the construction sector, and recovery in agricultural output.[220] The rate of growth in real GDP improved from −12.2 percent in 1995 to 12.1 percent in 2004.[221] Another positive trend was an increase in GDP per capita PPP from $2,998 in 1999 to $5,222 in 2004.[222] Two-thirds of the country's GDP was generated by the private sector.[223] This economic boom gave rise to a sizable middle class in Ukraine. According to some estimates, the proportion of the middle class in the total population increased from 14.9 percent in 2000 to 19.5 percent in 2002.[224] Unlike Belarus, however, positive economic growth did not lead to a high level of satisfaction with the incumbent government.

217 US State Department. 2005. *US Government Assistance to and Cooperative Activities with Eurasia: FY 2004 US Assistance to Eurasia*. Washington, DC: Bureau of European and Eurasian Affairs. Retrieved from www.state.gov/p/eur/rls/rpt/55799.htm.

218 *Ibid.*

219 Marung, Steffi. 2012. "Moving Borders and Competing Civilizing Missions: Germany, Poland, and Ukraine in the Context of the EU's Eastern Enlargement." In *Walls, Borders, Boundaries: Spatial and Cultural Practices in Europe*, eds. Marc Silberman, Karen Till, and Janet Ward. Oxford, UK: Berghahn Books, pp. 131–52, p. 135.

220 On this point, see European Bank for Reconstruction and Development. 2005. *Annual Report 2004*. London, UK: EBRD, p. 46.

221 European Bank for Reconstruction and Development. 2007. *Transition Report 2007: People in Transition*. London, UK: EBRD, p. 35.

222 World Bank. 2013. *World Development Indicators Database: GDP per Capita, PPP*. Retrieved from http://data.worldbank.org/indicator/NY.GDP.PCAP.PP.CD.

223 European Bank for Reconstruction and Development. 2005. *Transition Report 2005: Business in Transition*. London, UK: EBRD, p. 196.

224 These estimates are based on survey research conducted by the marketing company GfK Ukraine in 2000–2. Such criteria as education, employment status, income level, and household asset ownership were used as markers of the middle class. International Center for Policy Studies. 2002. *The Report of Preliminary Research "Ukraine Middle Class."* Kyiv, Ukraine: ICPS. Retrieved from http://icps.com.ua/eng/arh/pub/ep/3411.html.

Opinion polls indicate that only 15 percent of Ukrainians placed trust in the incumbent president in February 2004.[225] Specifically, owners of small and medium-sized enterprises were discontent with the strangulation of small business by oligarchic groups and backed the Orange Revolution.[226]

Overall, several positive changes in the political environment occurred on the eve of the 2004 presidential election. The unification of the political opposition around a viable presidential candidate and splits within the ruling elite increased the odds of mass mobilization against the regime. Dioxin poisoning disfigured Yushchenko's face and got him off the election trail for a few weeks,[227] but it backfired against the regime. Moreover, Kuchma's endorsement of the most antagonistic politician – a former convict – as his successor caused public outrage. In particular, the emerging middle class turned to the street in support of a reform-oriented candidate.

Nonetheless, Yanukovych's electoral defeat should not be taken for granted because Ukrainian voters were divided along regional lines.[228] Pre-election opinion polls consistently showed that Yushchenko was a frontrunner in western and central parts of Ukraine, while Yanukovych was more popular in eastern and southern parts of the country.[229] According to an opinion poll conducted in early October 2004, 77.7 percent of respondents from western Ukraine reported their intention to vote for Yushchenko, whereas 81.7 percent

[225] Panina, Natalia, ed. 2005. *Ukrainske suspilstvo 1994–2004: Sotsiologichnyi monitoring*. Kyiv, Ukraine: Zapovit, p. 20. The survey was conducted by the Institute of Sociology of the National Academy of Science in cooperation with the Foundation "Democratic Initiatives" and the public opinion company Socis in January–February 2004 ($N = 1{,}800$).

[226] Denysenko, Marina. 2004. "Middle Class Backs Orange Revolution." *BBC World Service*. December 1. http://news.bbc.co.uk/2/hi/europe/4057839.stm; Zhdanov, Igor, and Yuriy Yakimenko. 2005. "Formula pomaranchevoi peremogu: Notatky nestoronnikh sposteriga-chiv." *Dzerkalo tyzhnia*. January 22.

[227] Holley, David, and Sonya Yee. 2004. "Ukrainian Poisoning Confirmed." *Los Angeles Times*. December 12. http://articles.latimes.com/2004/dec/12/world/fg-ukraine12.

[228] The region has been the strongest predictor of voting in post-Soviet Ukraine. On this point, see Barrington, Lowell, and Erik Herron. 2004. "One Ukraine or Many? Regionalism in Ukraine and Its Political Consequences." *Nationalities Papers* 32(1): 53–86; Wolczuk, Kataryna. 2007. "Whose Ukraine? Language and Regional Factors in the 2004 and 2006 Elections in Ukraine." *European Yearbook of Minority Issues* 5: 521–47.

[229] These regional differences can be attributed in part to the impact of historical legacies. Ukrainian land was divided up between various empires in the pre-Soviet period. Western parts of the country fell in the domain of the Polish-Lithuanian Commonwealth and the Austro-Hungarian Empire, whereas eastern and southern parts of the country were colonized by the Russian Empire. Moreover, Halychyna (Ivano-Frankivsk, Lviv, and Ternopil *oblasts*), Volyn (Khmelnytsky, Rivne, Volyn, and Zhytomir *oblasts*), and parts of Bessarabia (part of Odesa *oblast*) and Bukovina (Chernivtsi *oblast*) were forcefully integrated into the Soviet Union in the post–World War II period, whereas east Ukrainian *oblasts* formed the core of Soviet Ukraine since its establishment in the 1920s. As a result of divergent colonization experiences, the Ukrainian nation remains culturally and politically divided along geographic lines. Furthermore, the ruling elite systematically reinforce the salience of regional differences to undermine the strength of civil society and maintain its grip on power.

of respondents from eastern Ukraine favored Yanukovych.[230] As a result of these regional differences, Yushchenko's margin of victory was anticipated to be quite narrow. When prompted to choose between Yushchenko and Yanukovych, 42.4 percent of respondents preferred the former and 40.7 percent the latter. A high level of mass mobilization against the current regime was critical to Yushchenko's electoral victory.

AZERBAIJAN

Like Georgia, Azerbaijan is a former Soviet republic located in the South Caucasus. According to official statistics, 96 percent of the country's 8.8 million population is Muslim, with a significant share of Shia Muslims.[231] But opinion polls indicate that the majority of people do not observe religious rituals, which is, to a large extent, a product of the Soviet-era policy of atheism. For example, an opinion poll conducted in 1999–2000 found that 82 percent of self-identified Muslims did not perform the daily prayer (*namaz*), and 71.4 percent did not fast during the month of Ramadan.[232] Another distinguishing characteristic of Azerbaijan is its endowment with natural resources. According to 2002 estimates by British Petroleum, Azerbaijan's proven oil reserves were 7 billion barrels.[233] Consistent with the "resource-curse argument," the economy's dependence on the oil sector hindered economic development and decreased the chances of democratization.[234]

The Nagorno-Karabakh conflict was another significant factor in Azerbaijan's political development.[235] The mountainous region predominantly populated with ethnic Armenians became a site of ethnic violence in the late Soviet period, and a full-scale military conflict between the two former Soviet republics ensued in the early 1990s. Like Georgia, Azerbaijan lost nearly 20 percent of its territory

230 The survey was conducted on October 6–12, 2004 (N = 2,000). For details, see Democratic Initiatives and Kyiv International Institute of Sociology. 2004. "Prezydentski vybory-2004: Reityngy ta prognozy" [press release]. Retrieved from http://dif.org.ua/ua/polls/2004_polls/prezii-ta-prognozi.htm.

231 On religious demography, see US State Department. 2005. *International Religious Freedom Report 2005*. Washington, DC: Bureau of Democracy, Human Rights, and Labor. Retrieved from www.state.gov/j/drl/rls/irf/2005/51540.htm.

232 Faradov, Tair. 2001. "Religiosity in Post-Soviet Azerbaijan: A Sociological Survey." *ISIM Newsletter* 8: 28. Retrieved from https://openaccess.leidenuniv.nl/handle/1887/17523.

233 For comparison, the United States has proven oil reserves of 30.7 billion barrels and Russia has 76 billion barrels of oil. See British Petroleum. 2013. *BP Statistical Review of World Energy 2013*. London, UK: BP, p. 6. Retrieved from www.bp.com/en/global/corporate/about-bp/statistical-review-of-world-energy-2013/downloads.html.

234 On this point, see Hoffman, David. 1999. "Oil and Development in Post-Soviet Azerbaijan." *NBR Analysis* 10(3): 5–28.

235 On the origins of the conflict, see Cornell, Svante. 1999. *The Nagorno-Karabakh Conflict*. Report No. 46. Department of East European Studies, Uppsala University.

to a Russia-backed secessionist movement.[236] By the time of ceasefire in 1994, over 25,000 people on both sides had been killed, and a population exchange between Armenia and Azerbaijan involved the movement of more than 500,000 people.[237] According to UNHRC estimates, there were 572,000 IDPs in Azerbaijan in 2000.[238]

The government's failure to resolve the conflict was a cause of coup d'états in the 1990s.[239] The first president of Azerbaijan, Ayaz Mutalibov, elected in a single-candidate election on September 8, 1991, held the post for less than a year. In the aftermath of numerous military losses and the massacre of ethnic Azerbaijanis in the city of Khojaly, Mutalibov was deposed in 1992. Another coup d'état, staged in June 1993, removed from office the popularly elected president of Azerbaijan Abulfaz Elchibey.

The restoration of political stability was associated with the return to power by Heidar Aliyev, former Communist Party leader and former chief of Azerbaijan's branch of the KGB. Under Aliyev's leadership, Azerbaijan signed a ceasefire with Armenia and launched the development of the oil industry. Aliyev was reelected for a second term in office with 76.1 percent of the vote in 1998.[240] At the age of 80, however, the ailing president withdrew his candidacy from the 2003 presidential race and endorsed his 42-year-old son as his successor. The election campaign was marred with a higher than ever level of electoral malpractices.[241] According to official results, the incumbent's son won a landslide victory, while the leader of the Musavat Party, Isa Gambar, called for a run-off.[242] Notwithstanding post-election protests against electoral fraud,[243] Ilham Aliyev took over the presidency from his father and began to consolidate political power in his hands.

A total of 2,063 candidates representing 48 political parties and blocs registered for participation in the parliamentary elections scheduled for November 6, 2005. In accordance with new electoral rules abolishing the

[236] Yalcin-Heckmann, Lale. 2010. *The Return of Private Property: Rural Life after Agrarian Reform in the Republic of Azerbaijan*. Münster, Germany: LIT Verlag, p. 167.

[237] MacFarlane, Neil and Larry Minear. 1997. *Humanitarian Action and Politics: The Case of Nagorno-Karabakh*. Occasional Paper No. 25. Thomas J. Watson Jr. Institute for International Studies, Brown University, p. 1.

[238] United Nations High Commissioner for Refugees. 2001. *The Global Report 2000*. Geneva, Switzerland: UNHCR, p. 351.

[239] On post-Soviet politics in Azerbaijan, see Cornell, Svante. 2011. *Azerbaijan since Independence*. Armonk, NY: M.E. Sharpe; Goltz, Thomas. 1998. *Azerbaijan Diary: A Rogue Reporter's Adventures in an Oil-Rich, War-Torn Post-Soviet Republic*. Armonk, NY: M.E. Sharpe.

[240] OSCE. 1998. *Presidential Election in the Republic of Azerbaijan 11 October 1998*. Warsaw, Poland: ODIHR, p. 7.

[241] On state repression during the pre-election period, see Human Rights Watch. 2003. "Azerbaijan: Presidential Elections 2003." Human Rights Watch Briefing Paper.

[242] OSCE. 2003. *The Republic of Azerbaijan Presidential Election 15 October 2003*. Warsaw, Poland: ODIHR, p. 25

[243] On state repression in the post-election period, see Human Rights Watch. 2004. *Crushing Dissent: Repression, Violence, and Azerbaijan's Elections*.

proportional representation system, all the delegates to the 125-member national parliament were to be elected in single-member districts. Since 1995, the majority of seats in the national parliament had been controlled by the New Azerbaijan Party (*Yeni Azerbaijan Party* [YAP]).[244] Among main opposition political parties were the Azerbaijan Popular Front Party (APFP) and the Musavat Party. As a result of the 2000 parliamentary elections, YAP received 72 seats in the national parliament, the APFP five seats, and the Musavat Party two seats.[245] Prospects for a stronger representation of the political opposition in the next session of the national parliament were rather bleak.

Elite Divisions

The ruling elite in Azerbaijan consisted of the communist-era apparatchiks, oligarchs, and kinship networks associated with the Aliyevs.[246] Many senior government positions handed out in the 1990s went to bureaucrats who began their careers under Heidar Aliyev in the 1970s or 1980s.[247] From the start of his presidency, Aliyev Jr. continued to rely on a cadre of the old guard. In addition, the incumbent presided over competing regional clans.[248] The Nakhchivanis had a dominant position in domestic politics because the Aliyevs elevated the status of their family members and associates from the region. A rival faction – the Yerazis – was composed of ethnic Azerbaijanis from Armenia.[249]

A native of Nakhchivan and a former speaker of the national parliament, Rasul Guliyev was driven out of the country for challenging the power of the Aliyevs.[250] State authorities prevented the exiled politician from coming back in the run-up to the 2003 presidential election and, once again, prior to the 2005 parliamentary elections by seeking his arrest on embezzlement charges.[251]

244 On the party's official history, see www.yap.org.az/view.php?lang=en&menu=4.

245 OSCE. 2001. *The Republic of Azerbaijan Parliamentary Elections 5 November 2000 and 7 January 2001: Final Report*. Warsaw, Poland: ODIHR, p. 27.

246 International Crisis Group. 2010. *Azerbaijan: Vulnerable Stability*. Europe Report No. 207, pp. 10–12.

247 Rohozinski, Rafal. 2005. *E-Governance in Azerbaijan: UNDP Contribution to Promoting Transparency and Accountability in Public Administration*. Baku: UNDP Azerbaijan, p. 12.

248 For an overview, see Guliyev, Farid. 2012. "Political Elites in Azerbaijan." In *Challenges of the Caspian Resource Boom: Domestic Elites and Policy-Making*, eds. Andreas Heinrich and Heiko Pleines. Houndmills, UK: Palgrave Macmillan, pp. 117–30.

249 The derogatory term "Yerazis" is an abbreviation for Yerevani Azerbaijanis (Yerevan is the capital city of Armenia).

250 Radio Free Europe/Radio Liberty. 2011. "Does Rasul Quliyev Fancy Himself as Azerbaijan's Bidzina Ivanishvili?" December 8. www.rferl.org/content/is_rasul_quliyev_azerbaijans_bidzina_ivanishvili/24416012.html.

251 *EurasiaNet*. 2003. "Azerbaijani Opposition Figure Rasual Guliyev Detained Overnight in the Netherlands." May 1. www.eurasianet.org/departments/insight/articles/eav050203.shtml; Ismailova, Gulnara. 2005. "Rasul Guliyev Failed to Return to Azerbaijan." *Central Asia-Caucasus Analyst*. November 2. http://new.cacianalyst.org/publications/field-reports/item/10420-field-reports-caci-analyst-2005-11-2-art-10420.html.

Another blow to Guliyev's political aspirations was the arrest of his political allies for their alleged involvement in plotting a coup d'état in advance of his anticipated visit to Baku in October 2005. Among the detainees were Minister of Health and leader of the Yerazis clan Ali Insanov, Minister of Economic Development Farhad Aliyev, Minister of Finance Fikret Yusifov, and deputy chair of the Azerbaijan Democratic Party Natiq Efendiyev.[252] While Insanov allegedly admitted his financial support for an attempted coup and awaited a trial on these charges,[253] he was sentenced to 11 years in prison for bribery, embezzlement, and forgery, with the confiscation of his private property.[254] These repressive actions signaled the strength of the incumbent president in dealing with high-profile political opponents.

Security Defections

The coercive apparatus appeared to be united against regime opponents. Given the arrests of several ministers, high-ranking military and police personnel seemed to be fearful of siding with the opposition. Unlike Lukashenka, Aliyev favored the stability of cadres in the coercive apparatus. Rasul Usubov held the post of the Minister of Interior since 1994.[255] Similarly, Javanshir Mammadov occupied a leadership position in the Ministry's Public Security Department since 1994.[256] Furthermore, the incumbent government provided positive incentives for their loyalty to the regime. Compared with Shevardnadze, Aliyev allocated significantly more resources for the coercive apparatus. From the start of his presidency, Ilham Aliyev annually increased the state budget for internal troops by 40 percent. According to the commander of internal troops Zakir Hasanov, the military was ready to "stop the action of any destructive elements" in the country.[257]

Unity of the Opposition Political Parties

Domestic politics was marked by divisions within the opposition camp. Like Ukraine's NRU, the APFP was established on the basis of an independence movement and split into two factions on the death of its founding member, Abulfaz Elchibey. Since 2000, Ali Kerimli stood at the helm of the APFP, while

[252] Ismayilov, Rovshan. 2005. "Recent Arrests Fuel Controversy, but Bets Are Off on Outcome." *EurasiaNet.* November 1. www.eurasianet.org/azerbaijan/news/coup_20051101.html.

[253] *TodayAz.* 2005. "Ali Insanov Turns to Be Donor of the Coup Attempt." October 21. www.today.az/news/politics/20905.html.

[254] Radio Free Europe/Radio Liberty. 2007. "Former Azerbaijani Minister Sentenced to 11 Years." April 20. www.rferl.org/content/article/1075997.html.

[255] For details, see the website of the Ministry of Internal Affairs of Azerbaijan, www.mia.gov.az/index.php?/en/content/298/.

[256] Mammadov was deputy head of the Ministry's Public Security Department from 1994 to 2001. He has headed the department since 2001. See www.mia.gov.az/index.php?/en/content/306/.

[257] Rashidoglu, A. 2005. "Elektorat oppozitsii rastet s kazhdym dnem." *Zerkalo*, July 12.

Gurat Hasanguliyev broke off and founded the Whole Azerbaijan Popular Front Party (WAPFP). The Musavat Party also vied for a leading position in the opposition camp, tracing its origins to a ruling party in the Democratic Republic of Azerbaijan in 1918–20.[258] In addition, there existed over 40 political parties in Azerbaijan.[259] Though the Musavat Party and APFP disagreed over the boycott of the 2000 parliamentary elections, they formed a strategic alliance in the run-up to the 2003 presidential election. The electoral bloc Our Azerbaijan (*Bizim Azerbaycan*), composed of more than 20 political parties, nominated Gambar as a candidate from the opposition,[260] but this electoral bloc again collapsed in the post-election period. As Lala Shevket put it, "[T]he weakest link was always found to inhibit the possibility of presenting a united front" against the regime.[261]

Two new electoral blocs were formed on the eve of the 2005 parliamentary elections.[262] The electoral bloc Freedom (*Azadlyq*) was set up by the APFP, the Azerbaijan Democratic Party (ADP), and the Musavat Party in July 2005. Another electoral bloc, New Policy (*Yeni Siyaset* [YeS]) brought together the Azerbaijan Social Democratic Party, the National Independence Party of Azerbaijan, representatives of smaller political parties, and independent candidates in opposition to the incumbent government. These electoral blocs competed against the ruling party.

Media Access

There was little quantitative change in the media sector in the early 2000s. Since adoption of a new law on mass media in 2002, the National Council on TV and Radio, staffed with presidential appointees, did not approve any new broadcasting license. There were 12 regional and 5 national broadcasting companies in the country, with the dominant position held by the state-run TV channel AzTV.[263] With the exception of ANS, such private TV channels as ATV, Lider, and Space were associated with Aliyev's family members or his allies. Unlike Georgia, Azerbaijan lacked a private TV channel critical of the incumbent government. There was more political pluralism in print media, with

258 On the party's timeline, see www.isagambar.az/musavat-tarixi-en.htm.

259 For an overview, see Ishiyama, John. 2008. "Political Party Development and Party 'Gravity' in Semi-Authoritarian States: The Cases of Azerbaijan, Kyrgyzstan, and Tajikistan." *Taiwan Journal of Democracy* 4(1): 33–53.

260 Kusov, Oleg. 2003. "Kampania po vyboram prezidenta Azerbaijana." Radio Svoboda. July 9. http://archive.svoboda.org/programs/cauc/2003/cauc.070903.asp.

261 Suanly, Makhmud. 2007. "Lala Shevket: V Azerbaidzhane net politicheskoiborby." *Realnyi Azerbaidzhan*. April 5. http://lalashevket.az/new3/pub/ru/523/.

262 Fuller, Liz. 2005. "Azerbaijan: The Parliamentary Elections by the Numbers." Radio Free Europe/Radio Liberty. September 23. www.rferl.org/content/article/1061640.html.

263 Haraszti, Miklos. 2005. *Assessment Visit to Azerbaijan: Observations and Recommendations*. Vienna, Austria: OSCE Representative on Freedom of the Media, p. 8.

only 30 state-owned of 200 registered newspapers, but print media had a much smaller audience than television. When prompted to identify main media sources, no more than 5 percent of the population mentioned such publications as *Azadlyq, Azerbaycan, Ekho, Yeni Musavat*, or *Zerkalo*.[264] *Azadlyq* and *Yeni Musavat* were Azerbaijan-language newspapers associated with major opposition political parties, whereas *Azerbaycan* was a mouthpiece of the ruling party. In contrast, *Ekho* and *Zerkalo* were Russian-language publications supplying a more neutral coverage of domestic politics. State authorities induced self-censorship, threatening journalists with imprisonment or physical attacks. The criminal code provided for imprisonment for up to six years for defaming or insulting the incumbent president. The murder of investigative reporter and editor of the weekly magazine *Monitor*, Elmar Huseynov, in March 2005 also had "a chilling effect" on independent media in Azerbaijan, further limiting the opposition's access to mass media.[265]

Compared with Georgia, Azerbaijan had a higher rate of Internet penetration on the eve of the parliamentary elections. According to European Bank for Reconstruction and Development (EBRD) estimates, the number of Internet users was 8.1 per 100 people in 2005.[266] But the volume of online content was lower in Azerbaijan. There were 5.5 times fewer Internet hosts with the country's domain name in Azerbaijan in 2005 compared with Georgia in 2003 (460 versus 2,656).[267] Overall, the mobilizing potential of this medium was not fully exploited during the 2005 election.

Influential Allies

Azerbaijan had a less vibrant civil society than Georgia on the eve of the parliamentary elections. According to the NGO Sustainability Index, Azerbaijan's score for 2005 was 5, compared with Georgia's score of 4.1 for 2003, with a higher number indicating a lower level of sustainability and development.[268] Only one-fifth of 3,000 existing NGOs were "active and

[264] International Foundation for Election Systems. 2006. *Public Opinion in Azerbaijan 2006: Findings from a Public Opinion Survey*. Washington, DC: IFES, p. 37.

[265] Gojayev, Vugar. 2010. "Remembering a Brave Journalist in Azerbaijan." *Human Rights House Foundation News*. March 2. http://humanrightshouse.org/noop/page.php?p=Articles/13614.html&d=1.

[266] European Bank for Reconstruction and Development. 2007. *Transition Report 2007: People in Transition*. London, UK: EBRD, p. 104.

[267] *Internet Systems Consortium's Internet Domain Survey*, www.isc.org/services/survey.

[268] The NGO Sustainability Index is estimated based on seven dimensions: legal environment, organizational capacity, financial viability, advocacy, service provision, infrastructure, and public image. The index ranges on a scale from 1 to 7, with a higher number corresponding to a lower level of NGO sustainability. For details, see United States Agency for International Development. 2006. *The 2005 NGO Sustainability Index for Central and Eastern Europe and Eurasia*. Washington, DC: USAID Bureau for Europe and Eurasia, Office of Democracy and Governance.

visible" in 2005,[269] with more than two-thirds of them based in the capital city of Baku.[270] A large share of local NGOs dealt with Nagorno-Karabakh refugees, women's rights, and environmental issues. Among leading national NGOs was the Azerbaijan Foundation for the Development of Democracy (AFDD), established by a former political prisoner, Murad Sadaddinov, in 2001, and the Institute for Peace and Democracy, founded by Leyla Yunus in 1995. Over the years, the Institute expanded its scope of activities from conflict resolution and IDPs to women's rights and political prisoners.[271] At the local level, the Social Union of Sumgait Youth played an active role in educating young voters and training election observers in the city of Sumgait, located 20 miles northwest of Baku. Yet civic organizations deemed as threatening to the regime were subject to state repression. For example, the eviction of a Muslim congregation from the Juma Mosque and the arrest of its religious leader, Ilgar Allahverdiyev, were widely believed to be a politically motivated case given the imam's open support for Gambar during the 2003 presidential election.[272]

State authorities systematically obstructed NGO engagement in electoral processes. The law on NGOs passed in 2000 prohibited election monitoring by local NGOs that received more than one-third of their funding from foreign sources.[273] In accordance with the law, a coalition of 150 NGOs, Free Elections, Free Will, was not allowed to monitor the conduct of a national referendum in 2002.[274] Similarly, the NGO coalition For Free and Fair Elections faced obstacles in its attempt to organize an election observation mission during the 2003 presidential election.[275] Local NGOs had to go through the cumbersome process of registering individually every volunteer as an election observer until the adoption of a presidential decree nearly two weeks prior to the 2005 parliamentary election. Despite legal hurdles, the Election Monitoring Center (ECM), founded in July 2001, monitored the 2002 national referendum, the 2003 presidential election, and the 2004 municipal elections. In

269 United States Agency for International Development. 2006. *The 2005 NGO Sustainability Index for Central and Eastern Europe and Eurasia*, p. 49.

270 Cornell, Svante. 2003. "Country Report: Azerbaijan." In *Nations in Transit 2003*. New York: Freedom House, pp. 100–22, p. 109.

271 Atayeva, Nadejda, Yodgor Grudges, and Dmitry Belomestnov. 2011. "Azerbaijan: Bulldozer Demolished the Institute for Peace and Democracy." *Civil Society Leadership Network News*. August 11. http://csln.info/en/news/urn:news:12990E4.

272 On the details of the case, see European Court of Human Rights. 2013. *Decision. Application No. 15405/04: Juma Mosque Congregation and Others against Azerbaijan*. Strasbourg, France: ECHR. Retrieved from http://hudoc.echr.coe.int/sites/eng/pages/search.aspx?i=001-116090.

273 The full text of the law on NGOs is available at www.sulesy.org/eng/index.php?option=com_content&task=view&id=18&Itemid=31.

274 Cornell, Svante. 2003. "Country Report: Azerbaijan." In *Nations in Transit 2003*. New York: Freedom House, pp. 100–22, p. 110.

275 OSCE. 2003. *The Republic of Azerbaijan Presidential Election 15 October 2003*. Warsaw, Poland: ODIHR, pp. 16–17.

2005, ECM trained and deployed 2,115 observers in 2,315 of 5,139 precincts in the country.[276]

Western foundations and foreign governments provided some assistance for the NGO sector in Azerbaijan. With a total budget of $3,198,000 for the election year, OSI Assistance Foundation Azerbaijan allocated the largest amount of money – $905,000 – for the development of civil society.[277] In addition, NED awarded grants to such local NGOs as AFDD ($39,140) and EMC ($43,450) for election-related projects.[278] Overall, the US government spent $17.1 million on democratic reform programs in Azerbaijan in 2005,[279] slightly down from $16.1 million in 2003.[280] The bilateral relations between the United States and Azerbaijan were constrained by US sanctions against Azerbaijan in compliance with Section 907 of the Freedom Support Act of 1992.[281] In light of the Nagorno-Karabakh conflict and Armenia's lobbying in Washington, DC, Azerbaijan was singled out as the only former Soviet republic ineligible to receive any US government assistance, with the exception of aid for democratization, counterproliferation, and humanitarian relief. The US Congress revisited this policy in the wake of 9/11 and granted the US president the right to annually waver these sanctions to facilitate cooperation on defense issues. US Defense Secretary Donald Rumsfeld made the first visit to South Caucasus in December 2001 to boost cross-border cooperation against terrorism in return for US military assistance.[282] Another Rumsfeld's visit on the eve of the 2005 parliamentary election stirred rumors about the opening of a US military base on the border with Iran in exchange for US backing of Aliyev.[283]

[276] Election Monitoring Center. 2006. *Final Report on the Results of the Monitoring of the Elections to the Milli Majilis of the Republic of Azerbaijan Held on November 6, 2005*. Baku, Azerbaijan: EMC, p. 5. Retrieved from www.smdt.az/files/file/Parlament%20seckileri/Final_Report_Parlament_2005.pdf.

[277] Open Society Institute. 2006. *Building Open Societies: Soros Foundations Network 2005 Report*. New York: OSI, p. 179.

[278] National Endowment for Democracy. 2006. *NED Annual Report 2005*. Retrieved from www.ned.org/publications/annual-reports/2005-annual-report/eurasia/description-of-2005-grants/azerbaijan.

[279] US State Department. 2006. *US Government Assistance to and Cooperative Activities with Eurasia: FY 2005 US Assistance to Eurasia*. Washington, DC: Bureau of European and Eurasian Affairs. Retrieved from www.state.gov/p/eur/rls/rpt/63172.htm.

[280] US State Department. 2004. *US Government Assistance to and Cooperative Activities with Eurasia: FY 2003 US Assistance to Eurasia*. Washington, DC: Bureau of European and Eurasian Affairs. Retrieved from www.state.gov/p/eur/rls/rpt/37650.htm.

[281] This bill was passed to support political and economic reform in the former Soviet republics (102nd US Congress, 1991–92). The full bill text is available through the online legislative database of the US Library of Congress, http://thomas.loc.gov/home/LegislativeData.php?&n=BillText&c=102.

[282] Garamone, Jim. 2001. "Rumsfeld Meets with Leaders of Caucasus Nations." American Services Press Service. December 16. www.defense.gov/News/NewsArticle.aspx?ID=44351.

[283] Talyshli, Alman. 2005. "Rumsfeld's Baku Trip Stirs Controversy." *EurasiaNet*. April 12. www.eurasianet.org/departments/insight/articles/eav041305.shtml; *PravdaRu*. 2005. "*USA*

Socioeconomic Conditions

Compared with Georgia, resource-rich Azerbaijan achieved a higher level of economic development. The rate of economic growth was, on average, 10 percent between 1998 and 2004, and it accelerated to 26.4 percent in 2005 due to an increase in oil-generated revenues.[284] Oil production jumped from 309,000 barrels per day in 2004 to 445,000 barrels in 2005.[285] As a result of oil-driven development, Azerbaijan's GDP per capita PPP for 2005 ($8,540) was nearly three times higher than Georgia's GDP per capita PPP for 2003.[286] The private sector contributed 60 percent to Azerbaijan's GDP.[287]

The economic recovery generated a gradual decline in the level of poverty. According to the official figures, 29.3 percent of people lived in extreme poverty, on less than $32 per month, in 2005, down from 39.7 percent in 2003.[288] The incidence of poverty was higher in urban areas, where nearly half the population resided, due to a scarcity of nonagriculture employment opportunities and a lack of resources for engagement in subsistence farming.[289] Furthermore, nearly 70 percent of IDPs did not have a permanent job and depended on state transfers and humanitarian aid.[290] Still, 54 percent of the population reported satisfaction with the current economic situation in 2004 compared with only 17 percent in 2002.[291]

Overall, there were unfavorable political conditions for mass mobilization against the regime on the eve of the 2005 parliamentary elections. The security apparatus remained loyal to the incumbent government and harshly penalized elite defections by framing Aliyev's opponents as participants in a coup d'état. Most citizens had limited access to uncensored news in the absence of an accessible Internet infrastructure and a private TV channel in opposition to the current regime. Moreover, the country's endowment with natural resources enabled the incumbent president to flex his political muscle in domestic politics and silence his international critics.

Plans to Expand Military Presence in Azerbaijan to Strike Iran." April 13. http://english.pravda.ru/world/americas/13-04-2005/8056-azerbaijan-0/.

284 European Bank for Reconstruction and Development. 2007. *Transition Report 2007: People in Transition*. London, UK: EBRD, p. 105.

285 British Petroleum. 2013. *BP Statistical Review of World Energy 2013*. London, UK: BP, p. 8.

286 World Bank. 2013. *World Development Indicators Database: GDP per Capita, PPP*. Retrieved from http://data.worldbank.org/indicator/NY.GDP.PCAP.PP.CD.

287 European Bank for Reconstruction and Development. 2007. *Transition Report 2007: People in Transition*. London, UK: EBRD, p. 104.

288 *Ibid.*

289 International Monetary Fund. 2003. *Azerbaijan Republic: Poverty Reduction Strategy Paper*. IMF Country Report No. 03/105. Washington, DC: IMF, p. 7.

290 *Ibid.*, p. 8.

291 Sharma, Rakesh. 2005. *Azerbaijan Looks to Its Future: Social Attitudes and Trends 2004*. Washington, DC: International Foundation for Election Systems, p. 11.

Another trend in favor of the ruling elite was a low level of mass support for opposition political parties. When prompted to name political parties that most effectively represented interests and aspirations of people like them, only 5.9 percent of survey respondents mentioned the Musavat Party and 1.7 percent the APFP in June 2005, five months prior to the elections.[292] Similarly, few respondents named the Musavat Party (6 percent) or the APFP (5 percent) as a party that represented their best interests in October 1998, shortly after Aliyev's victory in the presidential election.[293] A persistently low level of popular support for opposition political parties did not bode well for the political opposition in the run-up to the parliamentary elections.

CONCLUSION

This chapter has found multiple cross-country similarities in political conditions on the eve of national elections. First, the fragmentation of the political opposition was a gargantuan impediment to democratic change in these societies. Most political alliances formed by opposition political parties lasted a short period of time, and fierce competition for a leadership position in the opposition camp deadened the politicians' call for political change. Nonetheless, the opposition forces in each country attempted to nominate a single candidate from the opposition or form a multiparty electoral bloc on the eve of national elections to increase the odds of mass mobilization against the regime. Second, there was an increase in press freedom violations in advance of the elections. For example, cross-national analysis shows that each country experienced a spike in physical attacks on investigative reporters. Among journalists killed for their professional activities were Curuvija (Serbia 1999), Gongadze (Ukraine 2000), Huseynov (Azerbaijan 2005), Sanaia (Georgia 2001), and Zavadsky (Belarus 2000). Another common trend was an escalation in state repression against local NGOs. Specifically, state authorities interfered with the implementation of election monitoring projects by tampering with the registration of NGO-led election observation missions and harassing independent election observers. This comparative analysis demonstrates that the political environment in all five states was hostile to the rise of youth movements in opposition to the current regime.

A closer look at the political climate in each country uncovers discernible differences. First, the degree of the opposition's access to mass media varied across the countries. Unlike Georgia and Ukraine, Azerbaijan and Belarus lacked a private TV channel with an ostensibly antiregime stance, limiting citizens' exposure to uncensored news. Second, the incumbents differed in the severity of their responses to elite defections. Specifically, the governments of

[292] *Ibid.*, p. 16.

[293] Wagner, Steve. 1998. *Public Opinion in Azerbaijan 1998*. Washington, DC: International Foundation for Election Systems, p. A21.

Azerbaijan and Belarus reacted more harshly to elite defections, masterminding the physical disappearance of high-profile government critics or imprisoning them for long terms. In contrast, Saakashvili and Zhvania appeared to be physically safe after their defections from Shevardnadze. Moreover, following a 42-day imprisonment in 2001, Tymoshenko ran an election campaign and received a seat in the national parliament the next year.[294] Apparently there remained room for political maneuvering in these repressive political regimes.

Notably, opposition political parties affected the odds of mass mobilization against the regime through their choice of a single candidate from the opposition. Some incumbents faced more charismatic opposition leaders than others, which explains cross-country variations in the competitiveness of national elections. There was a stark contrast between 50-year-old Yushchenko, whose "ruggedly handsome looks"[295] were considered a strong asset of the 2004 election campaign in Ukraine, and 61-year-old Hancharyk, whose "not even marginally charismatic"[296] candidacy damaged the opposition's call for ousting a popular incumbent in Belarus. Likewise, 35-year-old Saakashvili, a charismatic leader of the National Movement,[297] stood a better chance of winning the hearts and minds of young voters than 48-year old Gambar, who chaired the Musavat Party for a decade longer than Aliyev Jr. held the presidency at the time of the parliamentary elections. The popularity of a political leader was found to be a significant factor in shaping citizens' vote choice due to the presence of an underdeveloped party system in the post-Soviet region. In Georgia, for example, two-thirds of the electorate reported on the eve of the 2003 parliamentary election that the identity of a political leader was more important than the party label in determining their vote choice.[298] Since the list of names on the ballot was decided by political parties, the old opposition affected the capacity of the youth movements to bring young people to polling stations and protest events in support of a certain political figure.

[294] Leshchenko, Sergei. 2011. "Istoriia areshtiv Yulii Tymoshenko." *Ukrainska Pravda.* August 10. www.pravda.com.ua/articles/2011/08/10/6475266/.

[295] CBC. 2004. "Yushchenko Tested for Signs of Poison." *CBC News.* December 10. www.cbc.ca/news/world/story/2004/12/10/ukraine-yushchenko-041210.html; *Time.* 2009. "Top Ten Contested Elections: Revolution in Orange." June 19. www.time.com/time/specials/packages/article/0,28804,1905660_1905666_1905673,00.html.

[296] Wines, Michael. 2001. "Street Theater and Graffiti: Belarus Dissidents Make News by Making Noise." *New York Times.* August 11. www.nytimes.com/2001/08/19/world/street-theater-and-graffiti-belarus-dissidents-make-news-by-making-noise.html?pagewanted=all&src=pm.

[297] *The Messenger.* 2012. "Charisma in Modern Georgian Politics." July 6. www.messenger.com.ge/issues/2644_july_6_2012/2644_edit.html.

[298] International Republican Institute. 2004. *Georgian National Voter Study* [PowerPoint presentation]. Retrieved from www.iri.org/explore-our-resources/public-opinion-research/public-opinion-polls#three. The survey was administered in May 2003 (N = 1,400). The question wording was, "When considering which party to vote for, what is more important: party is more important or the leader is more important?"

With hindsight, one might conclude that the concept of political opportunity structure is sufficient to explain cross-country variations in the level of youth mobilization against the regime. But a structure-focused account of mass protests is incomplete. As Bunce and Wolchik have argued, the vulnerability of a political regime "did not necessarily translate in automatic fashion into" a victory of the opposition forces.[299] It was incumbent on civic activists to seize an opportunity for political change and craft savvy tactics. The choice of tactics is critical to our understanding of cross-country variations in the level of youth political participation. Before taking a closer look at protest tactics and state countermoves in each country, Chapter 3 estimates the level of youth mobilization against the regime.

299 Bunce, Valerie, and Sharon Wolchik. 2011. *Defeating Authoritarian Leaders in Post-Communist Countries*, p. 159.

3

Youth's Revolt against the Regime

Youth is widely seen as an agent of social change. Life-cycle theory, as well as generational theory, provides an explanation for youth's vanguard role in challenging the political order. According to life-cycle theory, political behavior of individuals is affected by their life stage.[1] Young people display the propensity to protest due to their position on a variety of biological and psychosocial dimensions. Compared with adults, youngsters are less saddled with job and family responsibilities, increasing the chances of their availability for civic engagement.[2] Furthermore, youth's quest for social identity might increase the likelihood of their revolt against state authorities. Another contention in the literature is that individuals' political behavior is influenced by membership in a political generation.[3] Each generation is defined by "the common location in the social and historical process" during formative years.[4] From this perspective, conflict might erupt as a result of intergenerational differences in political values. In addition, intragenerational cleavages might exacerbate social tensions because members of the same generation might react to a political phenomenon in a different manner. One generation unit, for example, might come out in favor of revolutionary change, while another segment of the same generation might advocate gradual reforms. It is usually

[1] For an overview, see O'Rand, Angela, and Margaret Krecker. 1990. "Concepts of the Life-Cycle: Their History, Meanings, and Uses in the Social Sciences." *Annual Review of Sociology* 16: 241–62.

[2] On the significance of biographical availability, see Petrie, Michelle. 2004. "A Research Note on the Determinants of Protest Participation: Examining Socialization and Biographical Availability." *Sociological Spectrum* 24(5): 553–74; Wiltfang, Gregory, and Doug McAdam. 1991. "The Costs and Risks of Social Activism: A Study of Sanctuary Movement Activism." *Social Forces* 69(4): 987–1010.

[3] On the concept of political generations, see Rintala, Marvin. 1968. "Generations: Political Generations." In *International Encyclopedia of the Social Sciences*, ed. David Sills. New York: Macmillan and Free Press, p. 93.

[4] Mannheim, Karl. 1952 [1928]. "The Problem of Generations" In *Essays on the Sociology of Knowledge by Karl Mannheim*, ed. Paul Kleckemeti. London: Routledge and Kegan, p. 291.

assumed that generational membership has an enduring impact on the individual's political outlook.[5]

This study argues that the rise of the post-Soviet generation explains the emergence of youth movements at a particular moment in post-Soviet history. This generation was born in the late Soviet period and grew up under conditions of dramatic social change.[6] As adolescents, they witnessed at least three transitions: (1) from a one-party rule to a multiparty political system, (2) from a planned economy to a market economy, and (3) from a constituent part of a multiethnic communist state to an independent country with a distinct national culture.[7] The demise of the communist regime signified a relaxation of institutional constraints on youth political participation. Young people were no longer required to profess Marxist-Leninist ideology and join the Youth League of the Communist Party. Instead, multiple political parties vied for youth electoral support. Moreover, the breakdown of the planned economy drastically affected youth's participation in the labor market, expanding opportunities for entrepreneurship and diminishing state provision of welfare services. In addition, the young generation saw the installment of new state institutions and the revival of national culture, combating the deleterious effects of Russification. Concurrently, post-communist youth gained greater exposure to Western cultural products and practices and experimented with their adoption to the local context.[8] Notwithstanding these dramatic changes, transition from communism did not lead to the consolidation of democracy. As discussed in Chapter 2, another type of a nondemocratic regime emerged on the debris of the communist state.

[5] On this point, see Jennings, Kent. 1987. "Residues of a Movement: The Aging of the American Protest Generation." *American Political Science Review* 81(June): 367–82; Sears, David, and Nicholas Valentino. 1997. "Politics Matters: Political Events as Catalysts for Preadult Socialization" *American Political Science Review* 91(1): 45–65.

[6] For a detailed discussion of youth development in the post-Soviet region, see Roberts, Kenneth, S. C. Clark, Colette Fagan, and Jochen Tholen. 2000. *Surviving Post-Communism: Young People in the Former Soviet Union.* Cheltenham, UK: Edward Elgar; Walker, Charles, and Svetlana Stephenson, eds. 2013. *Youth and Social Change in Eastern Europe and the Former Soviet Union.* London: Routledge.

[7] It must be noted, however, that the depth and breadth of these transitions varied across the postcommunist region. For example, the former Soviet Union and the former Yugoslavia differed in the extent to which the communist regime exercised control over the economy, which influenced the adoption of economic policies since the collapse of communism. For an overview of multiple transitions, see Offe, Claus, and Adler Pierre. 1991. "Capitalism by Democratic Design? Theory Facing the Triple Transition in East Central Europe." *Social Research* 58 (Winter): 865–81; Kuzio, Taras. 2001. "Transition in Post-Communist States: Triple or Quadruple?" *Politics* 21 (September): 168–77.

[8] On youth and globalization in the post-Soviet region, see Blum, Douglas. 2011. *National Identity and Globalization: Youth, State, and Society in Post-Soviet Eurasia.* New York: Cambridge University Press; Kirmse, Stefan. 2013. *Youth and Globalization in Central Asia: Everyday Life between Religion, Media, and International Donors.* Frankfurt-on-Main, Germany: Campus Verlag; Pilkington, Hilary, et al. 2002. *Looking West? Cultural Globalization and Russian Youth Cultures.* University Park: Pennsylvania State University Press.

These political, socioeconomic, and cultural transformations had a profound impact on political attitudes of the young generation. Public opinion polls indicate that young people displayed greater support for democracy than older citizens.[9] However, contrary to their political aspirations, youth observed a resurgence of nondemocratic procedures in the post-communist period. Faced with the threat of the consolidation of authoritarianism, a visible minority of the post-Soviet generation mobilized in favor of genuine political change in the 2000s.

As shown in previous research,[10] people of different ages participated in post-election protests. However, it is important to bear in mind the length and depth of their engagement in civil resistance. Most citizens attended protest events in the aftermath of fraudulent elections. In contrast, youth activists performed acts of civil resistance for months prior to election day. Young people played a vital role in combating apathy and mitigating skepticism about the possibility of political change. Rather than simply joiners, youth were innovators and leaders in a nonviolent struggle against the regime.

A more recent episode of contention in contemporary Ukraine provides additional support for the generational argument. According to numerous accounts,[11] young professionals in their mid-30s comprised a large share of participants in antigovernment protests in 2013–14, commonly known as the *EuroMaidan*. These middle-aged protesters were university students during the Orange Revolution and turned to the street en masse again in 2013–14. Volodymyr Viatrovych, for example, pointed out that "in 2004, 60–70 percent of activists were students who could break away from their ordinary life for an extended period of time, while it is now young professionals who work and can spend the maximum of 2–4 days in Kyiv."[12] Among participants in the 2013–14 protests were such Pora

9 See, for example, Diuk, Nadia. 2012. *The Next Generation in Russia, Ukraine and Azerbaijan: Youth, Politics, Identity, and Change*. Washington, DC: Rowman & Littlefield.

10 Beissinger, Mark. 2011. "Mechanisms of Maidan: The Structure of Contingency in the Making of the Orange Revolution." *Mobilization* 16(1): 25–43; Hash-Gonzalez, Kelli. 2013. *Popular Mobilization and Empowerment in Georgia's Rose Revolution*. Lanham, MD: Lexington Books; Onuch, Olga. 2014. *Mapping Mass Mobilization: Revolutionary Moments in Argentina and Ukraine*. Basingstoke, UK: Palgrave Macmillan; Wheatley, Jonathan. 2005. *Georgia from National Awakening to Rose Revolution: Delayed Transition in the Former Soviet Union*. Aldershot, UK: Ashgate.

11 Berdynskyh, Kristina. 2014. *Ye liudy: Tepli istorii z Maidanu [Maidaners: Warm Stories from Maidan]*. Kyiv: Bright Books; Kovtunovych, Tetiana, and Tetiana Pryvalko, eds. 2015. *Maidan vid pershoi osoby: 45 istorii Revoliutsii gidnosti [Maidan from the First Person: 45 Stories about the Revolution of Dignity]*. Kyiv: KIS; Onuch, Olga. 2014. "Who Were the Protesters?" *Journal of Democracy* 25(3): 44–51; *Ukrainska Pravda*. 2014. "Imena Revoluitsii." November 21. www.pravda.com.ua/rus/photo-video/2014/11/21/7044957/.

12 Petsukh, Mariana. 2013. "Volodymyr Viatrovych: My povynni vyity z Maidanu iak organizovana syla [We need to come out of Maidan as an organized force]." *Ukrainska Pravda*. December 23. www.pravda.com.ua/articles/2013/12/23/7008042/.

activists as Andriy Kohut, Olha Salo, Volodymyr Viatrovych, and Yaryna Yasynevych.[13] Similarly, some Azerbaijani youth activists and Belarusians representative of the Malady Front generation[14] continued their engagement in civil resistance after their transition to adulthood.

The remainder of this chapter discusses the political behavior of the young generation. The chapter investigates the prevalence of pro-democracy attitudes and the degree of political engagement in the 1990s before turning to a discussion of the recent upsurge in youth participation in contentious politics.

YOUTH POLITICAL BEHAVIOR IN THE 1990S

Youth political behavior in the 1990s can be summarized in terms of two major trends. On the one hand, young people professed a great deal of support for democratic ideas and principles. On the other hand, the rate of youth political participation was rather low. This disjuncture between political values and political action can be attributed to a lack of political efficacy, the individual's belief in the capacity to influence political processes.

Opinion polls consistently showed that support for democracy was higher among youth.[15] Based on the analysis of EuroBarometer data, for example, Haerpfer concludes that 18–29-year-old respondents were the strongest supporters of democratic values in 12 of 15 post-communist states included in the study.[16] Similarly, the data from the third wave of the World Values Survey demonstrate that at least two-thirds of 18–29-year-old respondents in the selected states viewed democracy as the best form of government (Table 3.1). With the exception of Azerbaijan, there are statistically significant cross-age differences in the level of democratic support. For example, the level of support for democracy increased from 54.5 percent among those over 55 to 72.4 percent among 18–29-year-old respondents in Belarus. These public opinion data

[13] Tytysh, Halyna. 2013. "Ia divchynka. Ia ne khochu sukniu, ia khochu zminyty tsiu systemu: Molod iaka tvoryt myrnyi protest [I am a girl. I do not want a new dress, I want to change this system: Youth who stages nonviolent resistance]." *Ukrainska Pravda*. December 12. http://life.pravda.com.ua/society/2013/12/19/146507/.

[14] The phrase "Malady Front generation" was coined by a leader of the Belarusian youth movement Youth Front. For details, see Seviarynets, Paval. 2002. *Pakalennia Maladoga Frontu*. Minsk: Malady Front. Retrieved from http://mfront.net/pakalen.html.

[15] See, for example, Gibson, James, Raymond Duch, and Kent Tedin. 1992. "Democratic Values and the Transformation of the Soviet Union." *Journal of Politics* 54(2): 329–71; Reisinger, William, Arthur Miller, Vicki Hesli, and Kristen Hill Maher. 1994. "Political Values in Russia, Ukraine, and Lithuania: Sources and Implications for Democracy." *British Journal of Political Science* 24(2): 183–223; Rose, Richard, William Mishler, and Christian Haerpfer. 1998. *Democracy and Its Alternatives: Understanding Post-Communist Societies*. Baltimore, MD: John Hopkins University Press.

[16] Haerpfer, Christian. 2002. *Democracy and Enlargement in Post-Communist Europe: The Democratisation of the General Public in Fifteen Central and Eastern European Countries, 1991–1998*. London: Routlege, pp. 52–54.

TABLE 3.1 *Cross-Age Support for Democracy*

Country (survey year)	Age (in years)			Number of respondents	Cramer's V
	18–29	30–54	>55		
Azerbaijan (1997)	85.6	82.7	81.4	1,943	.034
Belarus (1996)	72.4	69.6	54.5	2,092	.126***
Georgia (1996)	76.3	81.2	71.5	2,507	.070***
Serbia (1996)	79.2	79.9	71.5	1,275	.118***
Ukraine (1996)	60.3	56.1	41.1	2,811	.109***

Note: The WVS was administered in Belarus, Georgia, Serbia, and Ukraine in September–December 1996 and in Azerbaijan in 1997. The question wording was, "I'm going to read off some things that people sometimes say about a democratic political system. Could you please tell me if you agree strongly, agree, disagree, or disagree strongly, after I read each one of them? *Democracy may have problems, but it's better than any other form of government.*" A combined percentage of those who "strongly agree" and "agree" with the statement is reported in the table. The value of the correlation coefficient Cramer's V, estimating the strength of the correlation between age and support for the democratic political system, is reported in the last column. The correlation coefficient is significant at the .001 level in all countries, except Azerbaijan. $^{***}p < 0.01$; $^{**}p < 0.05$; $^{*}p < 0.1$.
Source: The World Values Survey, Wave 3, 1995–7.

suggest that youth might act as a champion of democratic reforms. Interestingly, the level of youth support for the democratic political system was found to be the highest in Azerbaijan (85.6 percent) and the lowest in Ukraine (60.3 percent) in the mid-1990s, while Ukrainian youth movements mobilized a larger number of citizens than their Azerbaijani counterparts in the early 2000s. In part, the timing of the survey explains these paradoxical findings. Economic decline, along with the proliferation of corruption, peaked in Ukraine in the mid-1990s, causing some disillusionment with the democratic political system.[17] According to the World Values Survey, Ukrainians were significantly less satisfied with their financial situation than Azerbaijanis in the mid-1990s.[18] Within each country, however, youth reported a higher level of satisfaction with their financial situation than older age groups. These findings suggest that most young people saw themselves as winners of market reforms.

17 Using the World Values Survey data, the empirical analysis finds a significant positive correlation between support for democracy as the best form of government and financial satisfaction in Ukraine.

18 The question wording was, "How satisfied are you with the financial situation of your household? If '1' means you are completely dissatisfied on this scale and '10' means you are completely satisfied, where would you put your satisfaction with your household's financial situation?" The mean for Azerbaijan was 4.5, and the mean for Ukraine was 3.0, with a higher number indicating a higher level of financial satisfaction.

TABLE 3.2 *Perceived Link between Democracy and Bad Economy*

Country (survey year)	Age (in years)			Number of respondents	Cramer's V
	18–29	30–54	>55		
Azerbaijan (1997)	12.8	18.0	18.2	1,634	.067*
Belarus (1996)	31.2	36.2	46.7	1,796	.121***
Georgia (1996)	30.6	30.4	37.0	2,235	.058*
Serbia (1996)	27.1	27.7	32.6	1,075	.051
Ukraine (1996)	34.8	40.5	53.0	2,033	.138***

Note: The question wording was, "I'm going to read off some things that people sometimes say about a democratic political system. Could you please tell me if you agree strongly, agree, disagree, or disagree strongly, after I read each one of them? *In democracy, the economic system runs badly.*" A combined percentage of those who "strongly agree" and "agree" with the statement is reported in the table. The value of the correlation coefficient Cramer's V is reported in the last column. The correlation coefficient is significant at the .05 level in all the countries, with the exception of Serbia.
$***p < 0.01$; $**p < 0.05$; $*p < 0.1$.
Source: The World Values Survey, Wave 3, 1995–7.

Furthermore, young people in the former Soviet republics were significantly less likely than older citizens to associate democracy with a bad economy.[19] As seen in Table 3.2, 31.2 percent of 18–29-year-old Belarusians, compared with 46.7 percent of those over 55, and 34.8 percent of 18–29-year-old Ukrainians, compared with 53 percent of those over 55, agree with the statement that "the economic system runs badly in democracy." The magnitude of cross-age differences is smaller, albeit statistically significant, in Azerbaijan and Georgia. For example, 12.8 percent of 18–29-year-old Azerbaijanis, compared with 18.2 percent of older respondents, associate the democratic political system with a bleak performance of the national economy.

The perceived link between democracy and human rights provides another reason for youth's inclination to act in favor of democracy. Various public opinion polls found that young people in the former Soviet Union were more likely than older citizens to associate democracy with political freedoms and civil liberties. When prompted to describe what democracy meant for them, a larger fraction of Ukrainian youth mentioned the freedom of expression (43 versus 31 percent), the freedom of assembly (13.1 versus 7.3 percent), and the protection of human rights (70.6 versus

[19] Age does not have a significant effect on the perceived connection between democracy and economic performance in Serbia.

55.6 percent) than those over 55 in 2004.[20] Likewise, the results from an opinion poll conducted on the eve of the 2005 parliamentary election in Azerbaijan indicate that 52.8 percent of 18–29-year-old respondents, compared with 37.9 percent of those over 55, associated democracy with multiple types of freedom.[21] Given their conceptions of democracy, youth critically assessed the quality of democracy in the region.

The overwhelming majority of youth in the former Soviet republics was dissatisfied with a gradual rollback of democratic reforms. For example, the data from the fourth wave of the World Values Survey show that 84 percent of 18–29-year-old Ukrainians, as well as 79.4 percent of 18–29-year-old Belarusians, were dissatisfied with the way democracy was developing in their country.[22] Specifically, 77 percent of young people in Belarus and Ukraine felt that there was little respect for individual human rights in the country.[23] Yet youth's awareness of the government's wrongdoings and their dissatisfaction with the current regime did not necessarily translate into political action.

Consistent with a global trend, youth turnout is usually lower than general voter turnout in the post-communist states. An opinion poll administered by the International Foundation for Electoral Systems (IFES), for example, finds that only one-fifth of 18–29-year-old Azerbaijanis, compared with half of those over 55, voted in the 2000 parliamentary election.[24] Likewise, according to another IFES opinion poll, 30.8 percent of 18–29-year-old people, compared with 56.6 percent of those over 55, participated in the 1999 local election in Belarus.[25] In particular, first-time voters tend to abstain from exercising their newly acquired right to vote. In Serbia, for example, only 5 percent of first-time voters cast a ballot in the pre-2000 elections.[26] A low rate of youth's electoral participation stems, in part, from low levels of political efficacy.[27]

[20] International Foundation for Electoral Systems. 2004. *Public Opinion in Ukraine 2004* [data file]. Washington, DC: International Foundation for Electoral Systems.

[21] International Foundation for Electoral Systems. 2005. *Public Opinion in Azerbaijan 2005* [data file]. Washington, DC: International Foundation for Electoral Systems.

[22] The survey was administered in Belarus in March–April 2000 and in Ukraine in December 1999. For furthermore information, see www.worldvaluessurvey.org.

[23] World Values Survey, Wave IV. The question wording was, "How much respect is there for individual human rights nowadays in our country? Do you feel there is (1) a lot of respect for individual human rights, (2) some respect, (3) not much respect, (4) no respect at all?" A combined percentage of the last two categories is reported in the text.

[24] International Foundation for Electoral Systems. 2005. *Public Opinion in Azerbaijan 2005* [data file]. For details, see Sharma, Rakesh. 2005. *Azerbaijan Looks to Its Future: Social Attitudes and Trends 2004*. Washington, DC: International Foundation for Electoral Systems.

[25] International Foundation for Electoral Systems. 1999. *Public Opinion in Belarus 1999* [data file]. Washington, DC: International Foundation for Electoral Systems.

[26] Paunovic, Zarko, Natasa Vuckovic, Miljenko Dereta, and Maja Djordevic. 2000. *Exit 2000: Non-governmental Organizations for Democratic and Fair Elections*. Belgrade: Verzal Printing House, p. 31.

[27] On the importance of psychological involvement with politics, see, for example, Finkel, Steven. 1985. "Reciprocal Effects of Participation and Political Efficacy: A Panel Analysis." *American*

TABLE 3.3 *Youth Participation in Protests, Mid-1990s*

Country	Petition sgning	Demonstration	Boycott	Strike	Occupying a building
Azerbaijan (1997)	8.2	16.9	2.3	7.4	0.2
Belarus (1996)	8.6	15.3	4.2	3.5	0.2
Georgia (1996)	7.3	24.7	7.3	14.0	1.5
Serbia (1996)	24.3	10.2	8.8	6.7	1.3
Ukraine (1996)	13.7	16.4	6.3	3.9	0.9

Note: The question wording was, "Now I'd like you to look at this card. I'm going to read out some different forms of political action that people can take, and I'd like you to tell me, for each one, whether you have actually done any of these things, whether you might do it, or would never, under any circumstances, do it." The percentages of respondents who have actually taken political action are reported in the table. *N* = 10,778.
Source: The World Values Survey, Wave 3, 1995–7.

The rate of youth's participation in protest activity, on the contrary, tends to be higher. The conventional view is that young people are more prone to revolt due to their location in the life cycle and their lack of access to positions of power.[28] Nonetheless, only a small fraction of youth in the former Soviet republics turned to the street in the 1990s. Table 3.3 displays the percentage of 18–29-year-old people who reported participation in different types of protest activity in the mid-1990s. Attendance at a public rally is found to be the most common form of protest in all five countries. Approximately 16 percent of 18–29-year-old respondents in Azerbaijan, Belarus, and Ukraine reported joining a demonstration in the mid-1990s. The next most common type of protest activity was signing a petition. For example, 8 percent of youth in Azerbaijan and Belarus reported signing a petition. Remarkably, one-quarter of Serbs signed a petition during that period. The level of youth participation in boycotts and strikes was lower. Less than 4 percent of Belarusian and Ukrainian youth went on strike. Likewise, the percentage of youthful participation in boycotts ranged from 2.3 percent in Azerbaijan to 8.8 percent in Serbia. Occupation of a building was the least popular type of political action, with an average participation rate of nearly 1 percent.

Political Science Review 29(4): 891–913; Soderlund, Peter, Hanna Wass, and Andre Blais. 2011. "The Impact of Motivational and Contextual Factors on Turnout in First- and Second-Order Elections." *Electoral Studies* 30(4): 689–99; Sabucedo, Jose, and Duncan Cramer. 1991. "Sociological and Psychological Predictors of Voting in Great Britain." *Journal of Social Psychology* 131(5): 647–54.

28 On this point, see Karklins, Rasma, and Roger Petersen. 1993. "Decision Calculus of Protesters and Regimes." *Journal of Politics* 55: 588–615.

According to data from the third wave of the World Values Survey, Georgian youth were the most rebellious in the mid-1990s. As seen in Table 3.3, 24.7 percent of 18–29-year-old Georgians attended a public rally, 14 percent of them went on strike, 7.3 percent signed a petition or joined a boycott, and 1.5 percent occupied a building. Azerbaijani youth, on the contrary, were the least active in contentious politics in the 1990s. Twice fewer Azerbaijani youth than their Georgian peers joined a strike or a boycott. As discussed later in this chapter, these cross-country differences in the level of youth political participation persisted into the next decade.

A relatively low level of youth engagement in politics might be attributed to lack of public confidence in citizens' capacity to influence political processes in the country. For example, 71 percent of 18–29-year-old Ukrainians polled on the eve of the 1999 presidential election agreed with the statement, "People like me have little or no influence on the way things are run in Ukraine."[29] Similarly, 76.5 percent of 18–29-year-old Belarusians concurred in spring 1999 that they had little influence on "what's going on in Belarus."[30] In another IFES survey, two-thirds of young people reported a lack of belief in their ability to influence politics in Azerbaijan in the summer of 2004.[31]

The youth movements under study represented an attempt by a small fraction of the post-Soviet generation to overcome a sense of powerlessness in post-communist societies. The significance of these youth movements lies in mobilizing youth against the regime. Before turning to the analysis of youth political participation during the selected time period, the next section estimates the size of the youth population in each country.

THE SIZE OF THE YOUTH POPULATION

The revolutionary role of youth might be contingent on the size of the youth population. The presence of a youth bulge – a disproportionately high percentage of youth in the total population – is often seen as a source of social unrest.[32] It is usually assumed that the country is more susceptible to political

29 International Foundation for Electoral Systems. 1999. *Public Opinion in Ukraine June 1999* [data file]. Washington, DC: International Foundation for Electoral Systems. *N* = 1,200.

30 International Foundation for Electoral Systems. 1999. *Public Opinion in Belarus 1999* [data file]. Washington, DC: International Foundation for Electoral Systems. *N* = 1,012. The survey was conducted from April 28 to May 7, 1999.

31 International Foundation for Electoral Systems. 2004. *Public Opinion in Azerbaijan 2004* [data file]. Washington, DC: International Foundation for Electoral Systems. *N* = 1,620. The survey was conducted between June 21 and July 21, 2004.

32 Fuller, Gary, and Forrest Pitts. 1990. "Youth Cohorts and Political Unrest in South Korea." *Political Geography Quarterly* 9(1): 9–22; Goldstone, Jack. 2002. "Population and Security: How Demographic Change Can Lead to Violent Conflict." *Journal of International Affairs* 56(1): 1–22; Huntington, Samuel. 1996. *The Clash of Civilizations and the Remaking of World Order*. New York: Simon & Schuster, pp. 116–20; Urdal, Henrik. 2006. "A Clash of Generations? Youth Bulges and Political Violence." *International Studies Quarterly* 50(3): 607–29.

instability when the proportion of 15–24-year-old people exceeds 20 percent of the total population. A large size of the youth population increases competition for scarce resources, and the government's inability to meet youth's growing needs provokes youth's revolt against the moribund political system.

Youth is here conceptualized as a distinct life stage between adolescence and adulthood.[33] This life stage is marked by dramatic changes in one's educational attainment, employment status, and personal relationships. At this life stage, individuals tend to complete their education and move into the labor force. It is also a common phase for courtship and marriage. Furthermore, youth is a period of experimentation before settlement into enduring adult roles. Given the peculiarities of this life stage, youth are well poised to act as agents of social change.

For the purpose of statistical analysis, the United Nations defines youth as "those between the ages of 15 and 24."[34] In accordance with the UN definition, the youth population constitutes 1.2 billion people, or approximately one-fifth of the world's population.[35] The size of the youth population in the post-communist region falls below the world's average. Of the five selected states, Azerbaijan has the largest youth population (20.1 percent), and Serbia has the lowest (13.6 percent). These statistics, however, do not take into account the legal definition of youth and the dominant social norms in post-communist societies.

This study defines youth as persons between the ages of 15 and 29. These age boundaries are a better fit with the legal definition of youth in the selected states than the UN definition of youth. As shown in Table 3.4, the government of Azerbaijan defines youth as 14–29-year-old persons,[36] while the governments of Belarus and Serbia further extend the legal definition of youth by one or two years.[37] Since 1993, Ukraine's legal definition of youth covered 14–35-year-old people.[38] In contrast, the age brackets for youth are the shortest in Georgia.[39]

[33] On the conceptualization of youth, see Keniston, Kenneth. 1971. *Youth and Dissent: The Rise of a New Opposition*. Orlando, FL: Harcourt Brace.

[34] United Nations. 2007. *World Youth Report. Young People's Transition to Adulthood: Progress and Challenges*. New York: Department of Economic and Social Affairs, Population Division, p. vi.

[35] *Ibid.*, p. xv.

[36] Hajyev, Farhad. 2011. *Reviews on Youth Policies and Youth Work in the Countries of South East Europe, Eastern Europe and Caucasus: Azerbaijan*. Strasbourg, France: Council of Europe, p. 5.

[37] Nicolic, Tamara. 2011. *Reviews on Youth Policies and Youth Work in the Countries of South East Europe, Eastern Europe and Caucasus: Serbia*. Strasbourg, France: Council of Europe, p. 7; Oleinik, Yaroslav. 2011. *Reviews on Youth Policies and Youth Work in the Countries of South East Europe, Eastern Europe and Caucasus: Belarus*. Strasbourg, France: Council of Europe, p. 5.

[38] Borenko, Yaryna. 2010. *Reviews on Youth Policies and Youth Work in the Countries of South East Europe, Eastern Europe and Caucasus: Ukraine*. Strasbourg, France: Council of Europe, p. 8.

[39] The country's legal definition of youth is extrapolated from a law that defines youth organizations as noncommercial entities in which 18–26-year-old citizens constitute no

TABLE 3.4 *Size of the Youth Population*

Country	Legal definition of youth (in years) (a)	Youth population, 15–24 years old (b)	Youth population, 15–29 years old (c)	Youth population as percent of the total population (d)
Azerbaijan	14–29	1,770,048	2,458,320	27.9% (8,825,439)
Belarus	14–31	1,565,293	2,283,000	22.8% (9,999,789)
Georgia	18–26	719,534	1,033,586	21.9% (4,710,921)
Serbia	15–30	1,031,651	1,544,545	20.3% (7,604,335)
Ukraine	14–35	7,466,977	10,883,529	23.0% (47,305,388)

Note: The legal definition of youth is retrieved from country reports prepared by Council of Europe experts. Population statistics for the election year are retrieved from the US Census Bureau's International Database. Entries in column d report the size of the youth population as a percentage of the country's total population, with the size of the total population in parentheses.
Sources: Country reports for *Reviews on Youth Policies and Youth Work in the Countries of South East Europe, Eastern Europe and Caucasus* by Council of Europe experts; US Census Bureau's International Database. Retrieved from www.census.gov/population/international/data/idb/informationGateway.php.

A pattern of recent demographic changes in the post-communist region provides another reason for a contextualized definition of youth. The mean age at first marriage increased in all the selected states, with the exception of Azerbaijan.[40] In Serbia, for example, the mean age at first marriage climbed from 27.5 years for men and 24.0 years for women in 1995 to 29.6 for men and 26.3 for women in 2007. Similarly, the mean age at first marriage increased from 27.1 for men and 23.6 for women in 1995 to 29.4 for men and 25.6 for women in 2007 in Georgia. In contrast, the timing of first marriage hardly changed in Azerbaijan,[41] with 27.5 as

less than two-thirds of members. See Asanidze, Vakhtang. 2011. *Reviews on Youth Policies and Youth Work in the Countries of South East Europe, Eastern Europe and Caucasus: Georgia*. Strasbourg, France: Council of Europe, p. 7.

40 See United Nations. 2011. "Mean Age at First Marriage, in the United Nations." In *World Fertility Report 2009*. New York: Department of Economic and Social Affairs, Population Division, table A3. Retrieved from www.un.org/esa/population/publications/WFR2009_Web/Data/DataAndSources.html.

41 The mean age at first marriage for men slightly dropped from 27.5 in 1995 to 27.4 in 2007, while the mean age at first marriage for women increased from 23.0 in 1995 to 23.3 in 2007.

the mean age at first marriage for men and 23.0 as the mean age at first marriage for women. The percentage of persons ever married by a certain age is another indicator of youth's delayed transition to adulthood. The percentage of ever-married 20–24-year-old persons stood at 9.7 percent in Serbia (2002), 15.2 percent in Azerbaijan (2006), 25.5 percent in Ukraine (2007), and 29.8 percent in Belarus (1999).[42] By age 29, the share of ever-married people surged to 40 percent in Serbia, 63.9 percent in Azerbaijan, 67.4 percent in Ukraine, and 72.3 percent in Belarus. By the same token, there is a gradual trend toward the delay of first childbirth.[43] In Belarus, for example, the mean age at first childbirth increased from 22.9 years in 1995 to 24.2 years in 2007. The mean age at first childbirth was lowest in Azerbaijan (23.7 years) and highest in Serbia (26.2years) in 2007. Based on these demographic trends, it is reasonable to extend the definition of youth into the late twenties.

As seen in Table 3.4, the youth population comprised of 15–29-year-old people represents approximately 20 percent of the total population in the selected countries. The size of the youth population is above the region's average in Azerbaijan because this former Soviet republic continues to sustain positive population growth in the post-Soviet period.[44] Though demographic patterns in the selected states reflect a global trend of the increasingly aging population, youth plays an important symbolic role in post-communist societies. As a former Otpor activist put it:

> Youth are small in numbers in the former Soviet republics, these are "old nations." But students are perceived as the future of the nation. If they turn to the street, it signals to the rest of people that something is wrong. They don't stand only for themselves, but also for their families.[45]

SIZE OF THE YOUTH MOVEMENTS

As shown in Table 3.5, there are discernible differences in the size of the youth movements. The Serbian youth movement clearly developed the most extensive network of activists. With approximately 70,000 members in 130 branches across

[42] The data are unavailable for Georgia. See United Nations. 2011. "Percentage Ever Married by Age Group, in the United Nations." In *World Fertility Report 2009*. New York: Department of Economic and Social Affairs, Population Division, table A5. Retrieved from www.un.org/esa/population/publications/WFR2009_Web/Data/DataAndSources.html.

[43] See United Nations. 2011. "Mean Age at First Childbirth, in the United Nations." In *World Fertility Report 2009*. New York: Department of Economic and Social Affairs, Population Division, table A9. Retrieved from www.un.org/esa/population/publications/WFR2009_Web/Data/DataAndSources.html.

[44] On population growth rates in the region, see the United Nations. 2008. *Demographic Yearbook 2006*. New York: Department of Economic and Social Affairs, Population Division, pp. 58–69.

[45] Author's interview with Srdja Popovic, Belgrade, Serbia, January 23, 2008.

TABLE 3.5 *Sizes of the Youth Movements*

Country	Estimated size of the movement, absolute numbers	As percentage of the youth population
Azerbaijan	100 each	0.004%
Belarus	5,000	0.22%
Georgia	3,000	0.29%
Serbia	70,000	4.5%
Ukraine	35,000	0.32%

Note: The sizes of the youth movements are estimated as a percentage of the country's youth population, defined as individuals aged between 15 and 29 years. Population statistics come from the US Census Bureau's International Database. Retrieved from www.census.gov/population/international/data/idb/informationGateway.php.

Sources: Interviews with former movement participants; Cohen, Roger. 2000. "Who Really Brought Down Milosevic?," *New York Times*, November 26. Retrieved from www.nytimes.com/2000/11/26/magazine/who-really-brought-down-milosevic.html?src=pm; Kandelaki, Giorgi. 2006. "Georgia's Rose Revolution: A Participant's Perspective." *Special Report 167* (July). Washington, DC: United States Institute of Peace; Kaskiv, Vladyslav, Iryna Chupryna, Anastasiya Bezverkha, and Yevhen Zolotariov. 2005. *A Case Study of the Civic Campaign Pora and the Orange Revolution in Ukraine*. Retrieved from www.pora.org.ua.

the country,[46] Otpor recruited more than 4 percent of Serbian youth by September 2000. A smaller fraction of the youth population reportedly joined the challenger organizations in Georgia and Ukraine. According to the most optimistic estimates, Kmara's membership reached 3,000 people at the peak of the movement's activity.[47] Kaskiv et al. report that Pora had more than 35,000 movement participants,[48] while other Ukrainian activists provide lower estimates of the movement's size.[49] Zubr's membership peaked at 5,000 people in the fall of 2001,[50] which constitutes nearly the same fraction of the youth population as in Ukraine. But in raw numbers the size of the Ukrainian youth movement was nearly seven times bigger. Finally, the Azerbaijani youth movements mobilized the smallest percentage of the youth population, albeit the exact size of these youth

46 Cohen, Roger. 2000. "Who Really Brought Down Milosevic?" *New York Times*. November 26. www.nytimes.com/2000/11/26/magazine/who-really-brought-down-milosevic.html?src=pm.

47 Kandelaki, Giorgi. 2006. "Georgia's Rose Revolution: A Participant's Perspective." *Special Report 167 (July)*. Washington, DC: United States Institute of Peace, p. 8.

48 Kaskiv, Vladyslav, Iryna Chupryna, Anastasiya Bezverkha, and Yevhen Zolotariov. 2005. *A Case Study of the Civic Campaign Pora and the Orange Revolution in Ukraine*. Retrieved from www.pora.org.ua.

49 Author's interviews with several Ukrainian activists, Kyiv, Ukraine, April 2008.

50 Author's interview with Zubr member Uladzimir (via Skype), March 11, 2012.

movements is disputable. According to a few Yeni Fikir spokespeople, the youth movement recruited between 2,000 and 3,000 young people.[51] But Maqam leader Emin Huseynov estimates that the Azerbaijani youth movements retained no more than 100 people each by November 2005.[52] The estimated size of the youth movements shortly before election day is reported in the table because movement activity was geared toward mass mobilization during this critical period in domestic politics.

The reported statistics, however, should be interpreted with great caution. First, the self-definitions of the movements' membership were quite ambiguous. Maqam, for example, designated 50 members as activists, an additional 50 members as individuals responsible for "tasks related to the internal affairs of the group," and another 100 people as "general members."[53] Second, most challenger organizations refrained from the systematic collection and storage of membership information due to security concerns. Furthermore, the use of self-reports is problematic because movement leaders tend to exaggerate their movements' sizes. Notwithstanding data limitations, it is clear that some youth movements were more successful than others in recruiting young people to demand political change.

In addition to the sizes of the youth movements, this study uses several indicators of youth mobilization against the regime. For this purpose, the study distinguishes two modes of political participation: voting and protest activity. Voter turnout is a standard measure of electoral participation. It is plausible to assume that regime opponents in hybrid regimes turn out at a higher rate to reduce the incidence of electoral fraud.[54] But it is also possible that political conformists vote at a higher rate due to their endorsement of the current regime and the government's provision of positive incentives for compliant activism. A more accurate measure of youth's opposition to the current regime is vote choice. A high level of youth vote for an opposition political party or a presidential candidate from the united opposition may signify youth's action against the regime. The two measures of youth's engagement in protest activity are the size and the length of post-election protests, given the focal point of elections in the movement's history.

[51] Author's interview with Said Nuri (via Skype), October 17, 2014; Muradova, Mina, and Rufat Abbasov. 2005. "Youth Groups in Azerbaijan Encounter Difficulties during Run-up to Parliamentary Elections." *EurasiaNet*. November 3. Retrieved from www.eurasianet.org/azerbaijan/news/youth_20051103.html.

[52] Author's interview with Emin Huseynov, Baku, Azerbaijan, February 22, 2008.

[53] Huseynov, Emin. 2006. "Open Letter to US President George Bush." April 26. www.idee.org/Azerbaijan%20Youth%20Appeal%202006.html.

[54] On the significance of voter turnout in fraudulent elections, see Myagkov, Mikhail, Peter Ordershook, and Dimitri Shakin. 2009. *The Forensics of Electoral Fraud*. New York: Cambridge University Press.

YOUTH VOTING

Public opinion polls based on a national representative sample provide an empirical basis for the analysis of youth voting behavior in the region.[55] The use of survey data makes it possible to compare voting behavior across different segments of the population. The survey-based estimates of voter turnout, however, should be interpreted with caution given the tendency of survey respondents to over-report their rate of electoral participation.[56]

One of the findings that emerges from the cross-national analysis is that youth turnout, along with general turnout, varies depending on the type of election. As shown in Table 3.6, voter turnout was higher for the presidential elections in Belarus, Serbia, and Ukraine than for the parliamentary elections in Azerbaijan and Georgia. For example, 87.9 percent of polled Belarusians reported voting in the 2001 presidential election, whereas 63.8 percent of Azerbaijanis reportedly cast a ballot in the 2005 parliamentary election. This is consistent with a general trend in voting behavior research, indicating that voters tend to participate in presidential elections at a higher rate. Nonetheless, the absolute level of self-reported voter participation in the selected presidential elections is

[55] The Belgrade-based Centre for Political Studies and Public Opinion Research of the Institute of Social Sciences and the Independent Institute of Socio-Economic and Political Studies founded by Aleh Manau polled voters almost a month after the elections, in November 2000 and October 2001, respectively (N = 1,504 for Serbia and N = 1,465 for Belarus). The Institute of Sociology of the National Academy of Science of Ukraine conducted a survey of the voting-age population in March 2005 (N = 1,800). The amount of publicly available survey data from the South Caucasus is more limited. While the International Foundation for Electoral Systems released data from a public opinion survey conducted in Azerbaijan on November 17–December 20, 2006 (N = 1,400), the International Republican Institute restricted access to the raw survey data from the Georgian National Voter Study collected on February 11–17, 2004 (N = 1,494). Instead, this study uses data from the Caucasus Barometer administered in Tbilisi, the capital city of Georgia, in June 2004, three months after the rerun of the parliamentary elections in 150 electoral districts (N = 1,472). For details, see Caucasus Research Resource Centers. 2007. *The Data Initiative: A Brief Overview, V.1.0, Phases 1–3*. Tbilisi, Georgia: CRRC; The Centre for Political Studies and Public Opinion Research. 2001. *Public Opinion of Serbia 2000/18* [data file]. Belgrade, Serbia: Institute of Social Sciences; Independent Institute of Socio-Economic and Political Studies. 2001. *Novosti NIESPI*. December issue. www.iiseps.org/arhiv.html; International Foundation for Electoral Systems. 2006. *Public Opinion in Azerbaijan 2006: Findings from a Public Opinion Survey*. Washington, DC: International Foundation for Electoral Systems; International Republican Institute. 2004. *Georgian National Voter Study* [PowerPoint Presentation]. Retrieved from www.iri.org/explore-our-resources/public-opinion-research/public-opinion-polls#three; Panina, Natalia. 2005. *Ukrainske suspilstvo 1994–2005: Sotsiologichnyi monitoring*. Kyiv, Ukraine: Institute of Sociology of the National Academy of Science of Ukraine and the Foundation "Democratic Initiatives."

[56] On over-reporting of voting, see Ansolabehere, Stephen, and Eitan Hersh. 2012. "Validation: What Big Data Reveal about Survey Misreporting and the Real Electorate." *Political Analysis* 20(4): 437–59; Highton, Benjamin. 2005. "Self-Reported Versus Proxy-Reported Voter Turnout in the Current Population Survey." *Public Opinion Quarterly* 69(1): 113–23.

TABLE 3.6 *Youth Vote*

Country	Youth turnout	General turnout	Youth vote for the opposition	General vote for the opposition
Azerbaijan (2005)	47.8	63.8	N/A	12.0
Belarus (2001)	83.3	87.9	27.2	21.0
Georgia (2003)	51.5	70.1	N/A	36.8
Serbia (2000)	86.0	90.0	80.7	70.2
Ukraine (2004)	82.7 85.0 83.7	90.4 90.2 89.2	53.7 60.5 61.6	50.2 60.3 62.4

Note: The turnout rates reported in this table are based on self-reports of voter participation in the selected elections. The table reports voter turnout for Tbilisi only, rather than Georgia as a whole. For Ukraine, the table reports voter turnout for all three rounds of the presidential elections held on October 31, November 21, and December 26. The percentage of vote for the electoral bloc Azadlyq is reported based on the results of an exit poll conducted by Mitofsky International and Edison Media Research.

Sources: The Caucasus Research Resource Centers. 2007. *Caucasus Barometer* [data file]. Tbilisi, Georgia: CRRC; The Centre for Political Studies and Public Opinion Research. 2000. *Public Opinion of Serbia 2000/18* [data file]. Belgrade, Serbia: Institute of Social Sciences; Independent Institute of Socio-Economic and Political Studies. 2001. *Novosti NIESPI*, December Issue. Retrieved from www.iiseps.org/arhiv.html; Institute of Sociology. 2005. *Ukrainian Society 2005: Social Monitoring* [data file]. Kyiv, Ukraine: National Academy of Science of Ukraine; International Foundation for Electoral Systems. 2006. *Public Opinion in Azerbaijan 2006* [data file]. Washington, DC: International Foundation for Electoral Systems; OSCE. 2003. *Georgia Parliamentary Elections: Post-Election Interim Report (November 3–25, 2003)*. Warsaw, Poland: Office for Democratic Institutions and Human Rights; Simsek, Ayhan. 2005. "Aliyev Wins Victory, Opposition Rejects Results." *Journal of Turkish Weekly*, November 9. Retrieved from www.turkishweekly.net/news/21447/aliyev-wins-victory-opposition-rejects-results.html.

quite striking. Nine of 10 survey respondents reported voting in Belarus, Serbia, and Ukraine.

The magnitude of cross-age differences in voter turnout is another indicator of cross-country differences in youth political participation. As displayed in Table 3.6, the percentage difference between youth turnout and general turnout is quite small in Serbia and Ukraine. Remarkably, 86 percent of 18–29-year-old survey respondents, compared with 90 percent of all the voting-age respondents, reported voting in the 2000 election in Serbia. Similarly, the level of youth turnout in Belarus (83.3 percent) and Ukraine (>82 percent in each round of the elections) nearly matched the level of voter turnout for all citizens. In contrast, the age gap in voter turnout is much wider in Azerbaijan and Georgia, where nearly half of young voters abstained from voting in the parliamentary elections.

The severity of over-reporting voting is usually estimated based on the comparison of self-reported voter participation with the official turnout rates. But the central election commissions in the selected states are notorious for the manipulation of electoral results, so the official turnout rates are highly unreliable. If we assume the accuracy of official turnout rates, then the highest level of over-reporting is found to be in Azerbaijan: the turnout estimate based on the IFES opinion poll is 22 percent higher than the official turnout rate.[57] Similarly, the official turnout rate is 18 percent lower in Serbia and at least 10 percent lower in Georgia.[58] The differences between the survey-based turnout estimates (82–85 percent) and the official turnout rates (75–80 percent) are smaller in Ukraine.[59] Strikingly, the survey-based turnout estimate in Belarus closely corresponds to the official turnout rate released by the central election commission (83.6 percent).[60] At least these cross-country differences in estimates of voter turnout should be kept in mind when comparing levels of youth's participation in elections.

Turning to vote choice, the analysis finds cross-country differences in the size of the youth vote for the political opposition, either opposition political parties in the case of the parliamentary elections in Azerbaijan and Georgia or a single candidate from the united opposition in the case of the presidential elections in Belarus, Serbia, and Ukraine. As shown in Table 3.6, the level of mass support for a presidential contender from the united opposition was much higher in Serbia and Ukraine than in Belarus. Specifically, 80.7 percent of young Serbs and 60 percent of young Ukrainians, compared with only 27.2 percent of young Belarusians, reported voting for an opposition candidate. Another major finding is that the share of votes cast for the opposition by young people was only slightly higher than the share of votes cast for the opposition by older voters. This study, for example, finds that approximately the same proportion of Ukrainians across age groups voted for the opposition candidate in 2004.

[57] The official voter turnout rate reported by the central election commission was 42 percent. See OSCE. 2006. *Republic of Azerbaijan Parliamentary Elections (6 November 2005): OSCE/ODIHR Final Report*. Warsaw, Poland: Office for Democratic Institutions and Human Rights, p. 20.

[58] On the official voter turnout rates, see the *IDEA Voter Turnout Database*. Retrieved from www.idea.int/vt/.

[59] On the official results of the 2004 presidential election, visit the web site of the Central Election Commission of Ukraine: www.cvk.gov.ua/pls/vp2004/wp0011.html.

[60] OSCE. 2001. *Republic of Belarus Presidential Elections (9 September 2001): OSCE/ODIHR Limited Election Observation Mission Final Report*. Warsaw, Poland: Office for Democratic Institutions and Human Rights, p. 26.

This is somewhat surprising given the common assumption of a higher level of youth support for democratic values. Apparently, the east-west regional cleavage trumped age differences in determining the vote choice during the 2004 presidential election in Ukraine.[61] At one end of the political spectrum, 100 percent of survey respondents from Lviv oblast reported voting for Yushchenko in the second round of the 2004 presidential election. At another end of the political spectrum, only 9.1 percent of 18–29-year-old respondents from Donetsk oblast, along with 3.4 percent of those over 55, reported casting a ballot for Yushchenko on November 21, 2004. The statistical analysis finds insignificant cross-age differences in vote choice in the 2004 presidential election in Ukraine. These findings suggest that two generation units were formed in post-communist Ukraine due to the persistence of historical legacies. One generation unit based primarily in western and central Ukraine was more inclined than another generation unit based predominantly in eastern and southern Ukraine to act in defense of Ukraine's national independence and democratic development.

The cross-age analysis of vote choice in Azerbaijan and Georgia is limited due to the dearth of publicly available survey data. The 2006 IFES survey omitted the use of a direct question about one's vote choice. Instead, the survey respondents were prompted to name a political party that best represented aspirations of people like them. One-third of young Azerbaijanis mentioned the Yeni Azerbaijan Party closely associated with the incumbent president, Ilham Aliyev, and only 3.7 percent of 18–29-year-old Azerbaijanis named one of the three political parties that formed the electoral bloc Azadlyq (the Musavat Party, the Popular Front Party of Azerbaijan, and the Democratic Party of Azerbaijan). Notably, approximately 60 percent of all Azerbaijanis reported that no political party represented well their interests, signifying the absence of a trustworthy opposition party in the country. Given a low level of identification with opposition political parties, it is not surprising that they were weakly represented in the national parliament. An exit poll by US-based pollsters Mitofsky International and Edison Media Research revealed that Azadlyq received 15 percent of the popular vote, qualifying for 12 seats in the

[61] On the importance of the regional factor in Ukrainian elections, see Barrington, Lowell, and Erik Herron. 2004. "One Ukraine or Many?: Regionalism in Ukraine and Its Political Consequences." *Nationalities Papers* 32(1): 53–86; Clem, Ralph, and Peter Craumer. 2005. "Shades of Orange: The Electoral Geography of Ukraine's 2004 Presidential Election." *Eurasian Geography and Economics* 46(5): 364–85; Craumer, Peter, and James Clem. 1999. "Ukraine's Emerging Electoral Geography: A Regional Analysis of the 1998 Parliamentary Elections." *Post-Soviet Geography and Economics* 39(1):1–26; Holdar, Sven. 1995. "Torn between East and West: The Regional Factor in Ukrainian Elections." *Post-Soviet Geography* 36(2): 112–32; Kubicek, Paul. 2000. "Regional Polarization in Ukraine: Public Opinion, Voting, and Legislative Behavior." *Europe-Asia Studies* 52(2): 273–24.

125-seat national parliament[62] (the Central Election Commission of Azerbaijan allotted Azadlyq only six seats).[63] In contrast, the level of popular support for the political opposition was higher in Georgia. According to the parallel voter tabulation, the two main opposition forces in Georgia – the National Movement and the Burjanadze-Democrats – received a total of 36.8 percent of the votes in November 2003.[64] Moreover, 93 percent of Georgians polled in February 2004 agreed that it was the right thing for President Eduard Shevardnadze to resign.[65] In sum, available empirical evidence indicates that Azerbaijani voters, including youth, were less inclined to vote for the opposition than the electorate in neighboring Georgia.

Youth Participation in Post-Election Protests

This study compares the size of post-election protests to gauge the level of youth participation in protest events. Public opinion polls show that young people protested against vote rigging at a higher rate than older age groups during the selected period. For example, an opinion poll conducted by the Institute of Sociology finds that 8.2 percent of 18–29-year-old Ukrainians, compared with 3.4 percent of 30–54-year-old respondents and 2.1 percent of those over 55, participated in Kyiv protests during the Orange Revolution.[66] Moreover, 17.8 percent of young Ukrainians versus 13.2 percent of 30–54-year-old respondents and 9 percent of those over 55 were involved in protests outside the capital city. Similarly, the data from the fourth wave of the World Values Survey reveal a spike in youth political participation in Serbia.[67] The whopping 41.8 percent of 18–29-year-old Serbs, compared with 12.4 percent of those over 55, reported attending a protest rally in the early 2000s. A possible explanation for this phenomenon is a high level of youth participation in protest events during the 2000 federal election. The level of protest potential on the eve of stolen elections also attests to cross-age differences in the level of citizen participation in protest

[62] Simsek, Ayhan. 2005. "Aliyev Wins Victory, Opposition Rejects Results." *Journal of Turkish Weekly*. November 9. www.turkishweekly.net/news/21447/aliyev-wins-victory-opposition-rejects-results.html.

[63] OSCE. 2006. *Republic of Azerbaijan Parliamentary Elections (6 November 2005): OSCE/ODIHR Final Report*. Warsaw, Poland: Office for Democratic Institutions and Human Rights, p. 20.

[64] OSCE. 2003. *Georgia Parliamentary Elections: Post-Election Interim Report (3–25 November 2003)*. Warsaw, Poland: Office for Democratic Institutions and Human Rights, p. 5.

[65] International Republican Institute. 2004. *Georgian National Voter Study* [PowerPoint presentation]. Retrieved from www.iri.org/explore-our-resources/public-opinion-research/public-opinion-polls#three.

[66] Institute of Sociology. 2005. *Ukrainian Society 2005: Social Monitoring* [data file]. Kyiv, Ukraine: National Academy of Science of Ukraine.

[67] The survey was administered in Serbia on October 29–November 8, 2001 ($N = 1{,}200$).

events. In May 2000, for example, 46.8 percent of 18–29-year-old people, compared with 29.8 percent of 40–49-year-old people, were willing to participate in protest rallies organized by the political opposition in Serbia.[68] By the same token, the media coverage of protest events stresses the role of youthful protesters as catalysts for change.[69] In light of this empirical evidence, the overall size of post-election protests can give us a good proxy for the level of youth participation in these protests.

Based on the media coverage of protest events,[70] this study estimates cross-country differences in the size of post-election protests. By any account, the largest post-election protests were held in Serbia and Ukraine. The number of protesters in Belgrade swelled from 20,000 people on September 26 to as many as 700,000 people on October 5 due to the arrival of citizens from different parts of the country.[71] Similarly, the number of protesters in Kyiv surged to almost 1 million people, while the first post-election rally on November 22 attracted more than 100,000 people.[72] At least 50,000 people, representing more than 4 percent of Tbilisi's population, turned to the street in November 2003.[73] In contrast, the number of participants in post-election protest rallies fluctuated between 15,000 and 20,000 people in

[68] Centre for Political Studies and Public Opinion Research. 2003. *Public Opinion of Serbia 2000/3* [data file]. Belgrade, Serbia: The Institute of Social Sciences. $N = 1{,}152$.

[69] See, for example, Chivers, C. J. 2004. "Youth Movement Underlies the Opposition in Ukraine." *New York Times*. November 28. www.nytimes.com/2004/11/28/international/europe/28ukraine.html; Cohen, Roger. 2000. "Who Really Brought Down Milosevic?" *New York Times*, November 26; Corwin, Julie. 2005. "Fledgling Youth Groups Worry Post-Soviet Authorities." *Radio Free Europe/Radio Liberty*. April 22. www.rferl.org/content/article/1347179.html; Rubin, Joe. 2000. "The Kids Who Could Topple Milosevic." *Mother Jones*. September 26. http://motherjones.com/politics/2000/09/kids-who-confronted-milosevic.

[70] The police records as an alternative source of information about protest events are inaccessible to the public given the nature of the current regimes in these states.

[71] Erlanger, Steven. 2000. "Yugoslavia's Opposition Leader Claims Victory over Milosevic." *New York Times*. September 26. www.nytimes.com/2000/09/26/world/yugoslavia-s-opposition-leader-claims-victory-over-milosevic.html?pagewanted=all&src=pm; Erlanger, Steven. 2000. "Milosevic Foes Stage Protests to Force Him to Concede." *New York Times*. September 30. www.nytimes.com/2000/09/30/world/milosevic-foes-stage-protests-to-force-him-to-concede.html?pagewanted=all&src=pm; Vinci, Alessio. 2000. "Mayor Tells Inside Story of Belgrade Uprising." CNN. October 12. www.cnn.com/2000/WORLD/europe/10/11/yugo.storm/index.html?iref=allsearch

[72] BBC. 2004. "Ukraine Poll Protests Escalate." November 23. http://news.bbc.co.uk/2/hi/europe/4034287.stm; Chivers, C. J. 2004. "Ukraine Protests Grow, as Crisis Deepens." *New York Times*. November 24. www.nytimes.com/2004/11/24/international/europe/24ukraine.html; Finn, Peter. 2004. "Rally against Ukraine Vote Swells." *Washington Post*. November 24, p. A01; Radio Free Europe/Radio Liberty. 2004. "Protests over Presidential Vote Continue in Kyiv." *Newsline*. November 23. www.rferl.org/content/article/1143287.html.

[73] Nodia, Ghia. 2005. "Breaking the Mold of Powerlessness: The Meaning of Georgia's Latest Revolution." In *Enough! The Rose Revolution in the Republic of Georgia 2003*, ed. Zurab Karumidze and James V. Wertsch. New York: Nova Science Publishers, pp. 61–74.

TABLE 3.7 *Level of Protest Activity*

Country	Size of post-election protests (% of the city's population)	Length of post-election protests
Azerbaijan	20,000 (1.05%)	4 days (Nov. 9, 13, 19, 26)
Belarus	5,000 (0.3%)	3 days (Sept. 9–10, 13)
Georgia	50,000 (4.5%)	12 days (Nov. 4–5, 8–14, 21–23)
Serbia	700,000 (63.6%)	12 days (Sept. 24 – Oct. 5)
Ukraine	1 million (35.7%)	17 days (Nov. 22 – Dec. 8)

Note: The approximate size of the largest post-election rally is reported in raw numbers and as a percentage of the population in the capital city in parentheses. The population statistics were retrieved from *The World Factbook*.

Sources: Cole, Victor, ed. 2001. "Lukashenka Triumphant but Doomed, Say Papers." *Belarus Update,* 4(37). New York: International League for Human Rights. Retrieved from www.ilhr.org/ilhr/regional/belarus/updates/2001/37. htm; Nodia, Ghia. 2005. "Breaking the Mold of Powerlessness: The Meaning of Georgia's Latest Revolution." In *Enough! The Rose Revolution in the Republic of Georgia 2003*, ed. Zurab Karumidze and James V. Wertsch. New York: Nova Science Publishers, pp. 61–74; Radio Free Europe/ Radio Liberty. 2005. "Azerbaijani Opposition Convenes Rally in Baku," *RFE/RL Newsline.* November 14. www.rferl.org/content/article/1143519.html; *The World Factbook.* 2005. Washington, DC: Central Intelligence Agency. Retrieved from www.cia.gov/library/ publications/the-world-factbook.

Baku.[74] As the least rebellious population, less than 1 percent of Minsk residents attended a protest rally on election night.[75]

In addition, this study identifies cross-country differences in the length of post-election protests. The longest protest campaign was held in Ukraine, in part, due to the permanent occupation of the main square and the installment

[74] Radio Free Europe/Radio Liberty. 2005. "Azerbaijani Opposition Convenes Protest Rally." *RFE/RL Newsline.* November 10. www.rferl.org/content/article/1143518.html; Radio Free Europe/Radio Liberty. 2005. "Azerbaijani Opposition Convenes Rally in Baku." *RFE/RL Newsline.* November 14. www.rferl.org/content/article/1143519.html.

[75] Cole, Victor, ed. 2001. "Lukashenka Triumphant but Doomed, Say Papers." In *Belarus Update 4(37).* New York: International League for Human Rights. Retrieved from www.ilhr.org/ilhr/regional/belarus/updates/2001/37.htm.

of a tent city.[76] Thousands of Ukrainians stayed in the tent city from November to December 2004. Most people protested until the Supreme Court's ruling invalidated the fraudulent election results on December 3 and the national parliament passed laws to provide a legal framework for cleaner elections on December 8, while a few activists stayed on the Maidan until December 26, election day for the unprecedented rerun of the second round of the presidential election.

Another relatively long protest campaign was held in Georgia.[77] The opposition political parties organized the first post-election protest rally in Tbilisi on November 4, two days after the parliamentary election. Subsequently, a round-the-clock protest rally was held in front of the parliamentary building from November 8 to November 14. After a week-long break, the Georgian opposition forces resumed protest rallies and eventually ousted the incumbent president from office. Likewise, the protest events were held in Serbia for nearly two weeks until the president's resignation. In contrast, the Azerbaijani opposition parties convened only four state-sanctioned rallies in the post-election period, and the opposition leaders rejected youth's call for installment of the tent city on November 13.[78] Similarly, the Belarusian opposition parties did not organize a sit-in action on the closure of polling stations, and post-election rallies lasted only three days, starting on election night and ending shortly after the terrorist attack on US soil.

CONCLUSION

This chapter has analyzed the level of youth mobilization against the regime during the national elections. The empirical analysis distinguished two modes of political participation: voting and protest. The study compared the rate of electoral participation and vote choice of young people. In addition, this chapter estimated the size of the youth movement and the level of citizens' engagement in post-election protests.

The empirical analysis finds cross-country differences in the level of youth political participation. The Serbian youth movement recruited the largest share of the youth population, while the total membership of the Azerbaijani youth movements was the lowest. It is not surprising that youth voter turnout was much higher during the presidential elections in Belarus, Serbia, and Ukraine than during the parliamentary elections in Azerbaijan and Georgia. What is striking is that only 27.2 percent of young Belarusians, compared with 60.5

[76] On postelection protests in Ukraine, see the online archive of *Ukrainska Pravda*, www.pravda.com.ua/archives/year_2004/.

[77] For a timeline of protest events in Georgia, see *Civil Georgia*, www.civil.ge/eng.

[78] Radio Free Europe/Radio Liberty. 2005. "Azerbaijani Opposition Rally Ends Peacefully in Baku." November 9. www.rferl.org/content/article/1062793.html.

percent of young Ukrainians (during the second round of the presidential election), cast a ballot for a single candidate from the opposition in the elections under study. Similarly, the popular vote for opposition political parties was estimated to be three times lower in Azerbaijan than in Georgia. These results suggest that the political opposition in Azerbaijan and Belarus failed to secure the electoral support of most young voters. A related finding that emerges from this cross-national analysis is that post-election protests drew a larger number of people and lasted for a longer period of time in Georgia, Serbia, and Ukraine than in Azerbaijan and Belarus. The chapters that follow investigate why some youth movements were more successful than others in mobilizing youth against the regime.

4

Otpor's Resistance until Victory in Serbia

On January 13, 2000, approximately 3,000 people gathered in downtown Belgrade to celebrate the Orthodox New Year. The sounds of rock music entertained the cheerful crowd. At midnight, however, the festivities abruptly stopped. A large screen on the main stage began to display grim images of war-torn Serbia in the aftermath of the NATO bombing campaign. Boris Tadic, then a member of the parliament, read the names of soldiers and civilians who died during the military operation. The count of casualties ended with the statement, "This year, life finally must win in Serbia."[1] On that winter night people were told to go home and reflect on the political situation in the country so that they would have a real reason for celebration the next year. In this dramatic way, Otpor launched a public campaign titled "This is THE Year" (*Ovo je TA godina*). In response to Otpor's call for action, thousands of young people became engaged in nonviolent resistance to the regime. Otpor branches sprang up in more than 100 towns and cities across Serbia. Youth challenged state authorities by spray painting the movement's symbol of resistance (the clenched fist), distributing stickers with provocative slogans, and wearing Otpor T-shirts.

As a countermove, government officials labeled Otpor as a terrorist organization. Between May and September 2000, more than 2,000 Otpor members were arrested, and 95 percent of them were photographed and fingerprinted in violation of the law on criminal proceedings.[2] Yet the escalation of state repression backfired. The size of the social movement grew in defiance of political violence. Antiregime struggle culminated in massive protests against electoral fraud and the resignation of the incumbent president in October 2000.

[1] See York, Steve. 2001. *Bringing Down a Dictator* [documentary]. Washington, DC: York Zimmerman.

[2] Humanitarian Law Center. 2001. *Police Crackdown on Otpor*. Belgrade: HLC, p. 7.

This chapter demonstrates how state-movement interactions explain a remarkably high level of youth mobilization against the regime in Serbia. The chapter begins with an overview of main student protests during the Milosevic period, demonstrating that protest campaigns of 1991, 1992, and 1996–97 informed the strategic thinking of Otpor activists. In addition, this study traces how the cross-national diffusion of ideas influenced the development of Otpor's tactics. The remainder of the chapter is devoted to an analysis of movement tactics and state countermoves during the 2000 election.

STUDENT PROTESTS IN THE 1990S

Student engagement in protest events was a prominent feature of Serbian politics in the 1990s. In March 1991, Belgrade students protested against the government's crackdown on the mass media and police violence against peaceful protesters. The next year students occupied university buildings and demanded political reforms in favor of democratization. The winter of 1996–97 saw another spectacular outburst of political discontent. For several weeks, young people daily marched through the streets of Belgrade, pressing for the official recognition of the opposition's electoral victories and the reinstatement of university autonomy. These episodes of student activism contributed to the development of informal social networks and advanced the organizational skills of future Otpor leaders. This section provides a synopsis of these protest events.

March 1991

One of the first protests against Milosevic occurred on March 9, 1991, four months after the first multiparty elections in Serbia. The SPO leader Draskovic organized a protest rally to challenge the government's ironclad control over the editorial policy of the state-run Radio Television of Serbia (*Radio-televizija Srbije* [RTS]). In particular, Draskovic campaigned against the negative bias toward the opposition political party in the mass media. To secure more balanced media coverage, the political opposition demanded the resignation of RTS management. In a fiery speech in front of approximately 100,000 protesters, Draskovic called for a march on *TV Bastille*, a derogatory term for the state media company. In response, the police dispersed the crowd with batons, water cannons, rubber bullets, and tear gas.[3] The event claimed the lives of two people, a student and a police officer. At least 200 people were

[3] B92 Online. 2007. "March 1991 Protest Anniversary." March 9. www.b92.net/eng/news/politics-article.php?yyyy=2007&mm=03&dd=09&nav_id=40041; Lukovic, Petar. 2000. "The March 9 Legacy." *Balkan Crisis Report*. March 7. www.iwpr.net/index.php?apc_state=hen&s=o&o=p=bcr&l=EN&s=f&o=247789; Pakula, Andrew. 1991. "Letter from Belgrade." *Peace Magazine* 7(4): 11–14. Retrieved from http://archive.peacemagazine.org/v07n4p11.htm.

injured, and 100 protesters were arrested. Among the detainees was Draskovic himself. For the first time since the end of World War II, the tanks of the Yugoslav National Army rolled into the city to deter further mass protests.

Another protest rally involving a large number of Belgrade students was held on March 10. Thousands of students marched from dormitories in a remote part of the city to downtown Belgrade to demand the removal of the military from the streets, the resignation of Minister of Interior Radmilo Bogdanovic, and the release of SPO leadership from detention. Protesters occupied Terazije Square and blockaded traffic in the main streets to put pressure on the government. On the spur of the moment, students set up the Forum of Terazije Parliament so that they could act as "a restraint, both on the regime and the opposition."[4] As a battle cry, students chanted the phrase, "It is time for justice; it is time for the truth" (*Vreme je za pravdu; vreme je za istinu*). This slogan was borrowed from a song by the Serbian band Spinal Discipline (*Disciplina Kicme*). Subsequently, the title of Otpor's GOTV campaign It's Time (*Vreme Je!*) had a symbolic connection with the 1991 protest campaign.

In turn, the ruling party organized a counter-rally on March 11. The authorities bused supporters from other parts of Serbia to boost the legitimacy of the incumbent president. In addition, state-controlled TV channels showed images of Milosevic sympathizers to marginalize regime opponents. At that time, Milosevic commanded genuine popular support among a plurality of citizens. Nonetheless, anti-incumbent protests continued for a few days, posing a threat to political stability.

The protest campaign had both short- and long-term consequences for domestic politics. In the short term, protesters extracted concessions from the government. The unpopular Minister of Interior, along with the head of RTS, stepped down. Milosevic, however, quickly regained control over the political situation and diverted citizens' attention to conflicts in Bosnia and Herzegovina and Croatia. The country's engagement in military operations in the territory of the former Yugoslavia sparked an exodus of young men trying to dodge the draft. According to some estimates, more than 100,000 young people, including college-age youth, left Serbia in the 1990s.[5] In the long term, the March 1991 protest gained a symbolic meaning in Serbian society. The political opposition would use the protest event as an occasion for commemorating victims of police violence and fueling public outrage over state action. In the spring of 1992 and 1997, for example, the opposition political parties held rallies to reassert the opposition's commitment to the struggle for political change. In addition, students organized their own events to pay tribute to victims of the regime and boost youth's political engagement.

[4] Susak, Bojana. 2000. "An Alternative to War." In *The Road to War in Serbia: Trauma and Catharsis*, ed. Neboisa Popov. Budapest: Central European University Press, pp. 479–508, p. 500.

[5] Schapiro, Mark. 1999. "Serbia's Lost Generation." *Mother Jones* 24(5): 48–53.

June–July 1992

University students launched another protest campaign in June 1992 to demand dramatic political change.[6] Young people called for the resignation of the incumbent president, the disbandment of the national parliament, and the schedule of new parliamentary elections. Students also protested against the government's version of draft laws on universities and student standards, tightening state control over universities. The "Declaration of University of Belgrade Students" summarized students' demands. Likewise, the slogan "Enough! We want to live now!" reflected the prevailing mood among Serbian youth.

Students employed a wide range of nonviolent methods, including strike, the occupation of university buildings, and street performances. On June 15, more than 12,000 students gathered on the Student Square and voted for the start of a general strike. Students occupied university buildings and declared them a "free territory." Young people also organized symbolic off-campus events. One of the most spectacular street events was the "prison walk," symbolizing the suffocating political environment in the country. To reach a large audience, students published the magazine *Dosta* ("Enough") and prepared programs for the radio station B92. The protest campaign lasted 26 days and ended without the attainment of the students' demands.

The protest campaign was met with state propaganda and repression. The state-controlled media framed the takeover of university buildings as a frivolous party of reckless youth in times of war. The government further undermined the legitimacy of the protest campaign by circulating rumors about the involvement of faculty and students of non-Serb ethnic backgrounds in planning antigovernment protests. The rector of the university Rajko Vracar was removed from office for his support of student protesters. Furthermore, the University of Belgrade lost whatever autonomy it previously exercised. In August 1992, the government adopted a new law on universities, asserting greater state control over institutions of higher education.

Nonetheless, the production of antiregime discourse was a tangible outcome of the 1992 protest campaign. Students stimulated a public debate over current events through their actions. In particular, students organized public talks profiling prominent intellectuals and covering a wide range of issues, including "the properties of authoritarian political culture, reform of the armed forces, the role of the (Orthodox) church in contemporary society, and a possible restoration of the monarchy."[7] Furthermore, students contributed to

[6] Dordević, Dragoljub, and Saša Dukić. 1992. *Sile mraka i bezumlja: niški studentski protest '92: pokušsaj sociološke interpretacije*. Niš: Naucni podmladak SKC; Kuzmanović, Bora. 1993. *Studentski protest 1992: Socialno-psihološka studija društvenog dogadaja*. Belgrade: Institute of Psychology; Prosic-Dvornic, Mirjana. 1993. "Enough! Student Protest'92: The Youth of Belgrade in Quest of 'Another Serbia.'" *Anthropology of East Europe Review* 11 (1–2).

[7] Prosic-Dvornic, Mirjana. 1993. "Enough! Student Protest'92."

Belgrade folklore by concocting antigovernment slogans and rhymes. The last symbolic event of this protest campaign was the funeral procession to commemorate the death of the national university at the hands of the new law on universities.

November 1996–March 1997

The government's annulment of the 1996 municipal election results triggered massive civic and student protests in 1996–97.[8] The opposition political parties organized protests to defend their electoral victories. Independent of politicians, university students carried out another protest campaign. Like student protesters in the spring of 1991 and the summer of 1992, a new cohort of university students sought to distance itself from political parties. The student-written "Declaration of Decency" stated that young people were "not taking sides between the party in power and the opposition."[9] In addition to the recognition of stolen votes, students pressed for the resignation of Dragutin Velickovic, SPS-backed rector of the University of Belgrade, and Vojin Djurdjevic, the student vice-chancellor. In general, the main slogan of the protest campaign was "Justice" (*Pravo*).

The mobilization of students occurred through student protest committees formed in almost every faculty of the university. A Main Council of the Student Protest, composed of two representatives from each faculty, was set up to coordinate protest activities. Approximately seventy students sat on the Main Council and made all the major decisions through debate and vote. Dusan Vasiljevic, a 23-year-old political science student, acted as spokesperson for the student protest campaign.

A prominent feature of these student protests was the use of symbolic action to express grievances against state institutions.[10] Students employed a variety of low-cost prompts to send a message to incumbent authorities. Young people tossed toilet paper at the building of the Federal Election Commission and threw condoms at the building of the Supreme Court as a token of their dissatisfaction with political conformism inside these institutions. Protesters also hurled eggs at the RTS headquarters, condemning a media bias in the news coverage. In another street action, students spray painted graffiti on the wall of the parliamentary building with the chalk used in local households as a

[8] Babović, Marija, et al., eds. 1997. *'Ajmo, 'Aide, Svi u Šetnju! Gradanski i Studentski Protest 96/97*. Belgrade: Medija Centar; Lazic, Mladen, ed. 1999. *Winter of Discontent: Protest in Belgrade*. Budapest: Central European University Press; Milić, Anđelka, and Lilijana Cickarić. 1998. *Generacija u Protestu*. Belgrade: University of Belgrade Press.

[9] Walch, Jim, and James Walch. 1999. *In the Net: An Internet Guide for Activists*. London: Zed Books, pp. 124–25.

[10] For a daily account of the 1996–97 student protests, visit the home page of the Student Protest of the School of Mathematics and Natural Sciences, University of Belgrade, www.yurope.com/mirrors/protest96/pmf/index.html.

disinfestation method against cockroaches. Targeting university management, students rolled up paper and looked into the sky, trying to find the university's rector on Mars.

Another salient feature of the protest campaign was the creation of a carnivalesque atmosphere during protest events. Whistle-blowing was a signature element of the protest marches in the winter of 1996–97. Additionally, protesters used ringing alarm bells to symbolize the imminent end of Milosevic's presidency. Later, the image of the alarm clock would appear on Otpor's stickers, suggesting that it was time to vote the incumbent out of office. The opposition forces, including political parties and student protesters, organized one of the largest New Year's street parties on December 31, 1996. To call for a new phase in Serbian politics, students showcased a rubber reptile with the sign "The Last Slobosaurus," referring to Milosevic's first name.

Given the lack of access to the state-controlled national media, the student protesters identified alternative venues for the dissemination of protest-related information. Young people published a newsletter titled *Boom* and aired news reports on the student radio station. Serbian students also established their presence online. Students enrolled in the School of Electrical Engineering, the School of Mechanical Engineering, the School of Mathematics and Natural Sciences, and the School of Philosophy created special websites to provide a daily account of protest events. In addition, e-mail correspondence had become a novel tool of internal and external communication. In an interview with the Serbian newspaper *Nasa Borba*, Vasiljevic commented on the use of the new medium:

> Several days into the protest we realized that it is much easier to communicate with Novi Sad and other cities in Serbia via the Internet than using inadequate telephone links and faxes. We achieved two things: established communications with our colleagues within Serbia and, what seems to be very, very important, informed the whole world about what we are doing and what our demands are. I have to admit that until recently I hadn't realized the potential of electronic mail ... we are in contact with students all over the planet and from their reactions we can tell that our voice is heard and that they are interested in the situation in Serbia.[11]

There was a low-key fund-raising campaign during the protest period. Few observers of local politics and civic activists anticipated that the student protest campaign would last almost four months. In March 1997, Vasiljevic, along with Oliver Dulic, a member of the Main Council of the Student Protest, traveled to Italy to raise funds for the student radio station Index.[12] Yet a combination of external and internal factors, including the presence of the economic embargo, the absence of a well-developed banking sector, and the lack of technical

[11] Quoted from Banjac, Dragan. 1996. "We Know What We Are Doing and We Are Not Trying to Woo Anyone." *Nasa Borba*, December 12. The English-language translation of the article is available at www.ex-yupress.com/nasaborba/nasaborba8.html.

[12] This information was disclosed in *Boom* 42, March 14, 1997.

expertise, hampered the development of an online fund-raising campaign. An outpouring of international support for student protesters was largely moral rather than financial. As Vasiljevic noted, students from across Europe expressed solidarity with their Serbian peers.

> On Saturday we received a message from Bulgarian students. We've heard that signatures for a petition in our support are being collected in the USA and Canada and that demonstrations in front of the UN building in New York were scheduled for this Sunday. We've also heard from the Slovenian students of political science who had started a petition in support of our movement a few days ago ... we didn't expect this sort of reaction, we just wanted to inform them, but we've received a lot of offers of assistance.[13]

In addition, defections within the military facilitated the mobilization of citizens against the incumbent government. There were rumors that the army would disobey the order to shoot at protesters.[14] In December 1996, military officers stationed in several Serbian towns sent an open letter to Milosevic urging him "to exercise some presidential dignity and sensibility, as [the] one most responsible for Serbia and its people and to side with the interests of the Serbian people as they, the officers, have resolved to do."[15] A delegation of student activists secured a promise from Momcilo Perisic, commander-in-chief of the FRY Army, that he would not deploy the armed forces to intervene in the conflict between the incumbent government and the opposition.[16] In addition, student activists attempted to win support of rank-and-file police officers. Students, for example, staged a beauty contest titled "Miss Student Protest 1996–1997" (*Izbor za mis studentskog protesta*) in front of the police cordons.[17]

On a more personal level, the majority of young people secured parental endorsements for their action. Opinion polls indicate that 53 percent of participants in the 1996–97 student protests had parental backing, compared with 38 percent of participants in the 1992 protest campaign.[18] Furthermore, the large-scale participation of the adult population in civic protests boosted the legitimacy of the student protest due to the congruence of their demands.

[13] Quoted from Banjac, Dragan. 1996. "We Know What We Are Doing and We Are Not Trying to Woo Anyone."

[14] Soloway, Colin. 1996. "Top Generals Deny Split with Milosevic." *Chicago Tribune*. December 31.

[15] The information is retrieved from the mirror website of Students of the School of Mathematics and Natural Sciences, Student Protest 96–97, www.yurope.com/mirrors/protest96/pmf/index.html.

[16] Cohen, Leonard. 2002. *Serpent in the Bosom*, p. 299.

[17] Welch, Matt. 1997. "A Street-Level Account of Milosevic's Biggest Challenge Yet." *Pozor Magazine*. January 15. http://mattwelch.com/belgrade.html.

[18] Popadić, Dragan. 1997. "Studentski protesti – uporedna analiza studentskih protesta 1992 i 1996/97." In *'Ajmo, 'Aide, Svi u Šetnju! Gradanski i Studentski Protest 96/97*, eds. Marija Babović et al. Belgrade: Medija Centar, pp. 65–76.

The incumbent government responded to mass protests in a predictable manner. On December 24, 1996, a counter-rally organized by the ruling party was held in Belgrade. To flaunt popular support for the president, the state-controlled TV channels showed the crowd shouting, "Slobo, we love you!" In February 1997, the government increased the presence of the police in the streets and stepped up countermobilization measures. Several dozen students were arrested and sentenced to imprisonment.[19] By the same token, the government drove a wedge between the opposition political parties and student protesters. Initially, Milosevic conceded to the demands of the opposition political parties but ignored student grievances. Though the opposition politicians called off their protests in February, students continued their protest campaign until March. The government threatened to impose on students an additional year of study to meet graduation requirements, but young people refused to go back to classes until their demands were met.

This episode of contention produced mixed results. In the short term, it looked like a political victory for the opposition. The coalition bloc Zajedno received the majority in 14 of Serbia's 19 biggest cities. The students' main demand – replacement of the university management – was also satisfied, albeit with a delay. On the 106th day of student protests, Velikovic and Djurdjevic announced their resignation. These government concessions led to the radicalization of student demands. In March 1997, approximately 15,000 students picketed the presidential office chanting, "Slobo, you are next!"[20] Milosevic, however, skillfully neutralized the short-term gains of the protest campaign. There remained a wide gap between the formal and actual power of elected officials.[21] Furthermore, an acrimonious power struggle between Draskovic and Djindjic caused a breakdown of the coalition shortly before the 1997 presidential election. Having served two terms as president of Serbia, Milosevic was elected as the president of FRY in the summer of 1997. Another political conformist, Momcilo Babic, was appointed as rector of the University of Belgrade. Overall, the repressive political regime remained in place.

Yet the 1996–97 student protest campaign laid the groundwork for the development of antiregime social networks. At the end of the protests, several student organizations were set up to sustain youth civic engagement. Members of the Main Council of the Student Protest spearheaded the establishment of the Student Parliament independent of the university administration. In spring 1997, approximately 11,000 students participated in the election of a newly

[19] Kandic, Natasa, and Lazar Stojanovic, eds. 1997. *Political Use of Political Violence during the 1996–1997 Protests in Serbia*. Belgrade: Humanitarian Law Center.

[20] Rich, Vera. 1997. "Belgrade Rector Replaced." *The Times of Higher Education*. March 14. www.timeshighereducation.co.uk/story.asp?storyCode=101640&sectioncode=26.

[21] On the political situation in the wake of the 1996–97 protests, see McCarthy, Paul. 1997. "Serbia's Opposition Speaks." *Journal of Democracy* 8(3): 3–16.

formed 70-member student governing body.[22] Slobodan Homen became the president of the Student Parliament. Ivan Bender, Nenad Konstantinovic, Predrag Lecic, and Sinisa Sikman assumed other key positions in the Student Parliament. Another group of former student protesters under the leadership of Aleksa Grgurevic set up the Student Initiative, an NGO-like group that advocated student rights at universities. In addition, Cedomir Antic and Cedomir Jovanovic established the Student Political Club to tackle political issues. In mid-June 1997, the Serbian Student Movement (*Pokret studenata Srbije*) headed by Sikman was formed to serve as an umbrella organization for several student organizations, including the Student Parliament and the Student Initiative. Among other things, the Serbian Student Movement organized a public campaign, "Stop the Tyranny," in August 1997.[23] Ivan Marovic, participant in the 1996–97 student protests and member of the Serbian Student Movement, recalled the movement's biggest event on the day of Milosevic's inauguration as the president of FRY:

> We asked people to bring to the parliament building shoes of those young people who left the country. When Milosevic walked outside the building and got in his car, people were throwing shoes at him. We wanted to show people how much damage Milosevic has done to the country.[24]

Notwithstanding short-term gains, the aforementioned protest campaigns failed to put an end to nondemocratic practices in the country. The absence of genuine political change in the wake of 1996–97 protests motivated youth activists to develop novel methods of nonviolent resistance against the regime. The veterans of the 1996–97 student protest campaign played a crucial role in developing Otpor's strategy.

Lessons Learned from the 1996–97 Protest Campaign

The outcome of the 1996–97 protest campaign informed the formulation of Otpor's main goal. Though the government satisfied the main demands of student protesters in 1997, these concessions kept intact the foundations of the political regime. As a skillful politician, Milosevic managed to undermine the opposition's short-term gains and prolong his rule. These political setbacks provided an impetus for a revision of youth claim making. As Dejan Randic, member of Otpor's marketing department, put it, "We realized that we shouldn't fight against the consequences of Milosevic's regime. We had to fight against the source of all problems – Milosevic himself. We decided that we would put all the

[22] Nicolic, Zoran. 1997. "Students Divided: Belgrade – Struggle against Genes." *AIM*. September 8. www.aimpress.ch/dyn/trae/archive/data/199709/70912-029-trae-beo.htm.

[23] Sekularac, I. 1997. "Danas krece predizborna akcija 'Stop tiraniji.'" *Nasa Borba*. August 13. www.yurope.com/nasa-borba/arhiva/Aug97/1308/1308_15.HTM.

[24] Author's interview with Ivan Marovic, Washington, DC, December 13, 2007.

blame on Milosevic."[25] The incumbent president became the movement's primary target.

Another major lesson that youth activists learned was that they needed to develop a more sophisticated repertoire of contention. Nenad Konstantinovic, member of Otpor's network department, pointed out a disadvantage of using the daily march as a protest tactic in 1996–97. "The model of daily protest marches didn't work. The authorities could just redirect the traffic so that it wouldn't affect them. Besides, people were exhausted to march every day."[26] Instead, Otpor embraced the idea of short and humorous street performances.

Moreover, the 1996–97 protest campaign had an impact on the development of the movement's recruitment tactics. Otpor leadership realized that a viable social movement should spread into the provinces and build a nationwide network of activists. Furthermore, Otpor sought to broaden the social base of movement participants by recruiting nonstudents. Vladimir Pavlov, member of Otpor's network department, said:

> I was allergic to the word "student." Universities represent a pretty close circle of people. At the university, one can easily find a receptive audience, since most students share the same views. But society is more complicated than that. I believed that our base should be larger.[27]

In addition, veterans of the 1996–97 protest campaign realized that a horizontal organizational structure was vital to the survival of the social movement in the nondemocratic setting. According to Slobodan Djindovic, member of Otpor's university/NGOs department, one of the main lessons that Otpor learned from 1996 was that "it is important not to have visible leaders."[28] Though a team of Otpor activists based in Belgrade made key strategic decisions, it was hidden from the public eye. Instead of having a single leader, Otpor rotated its spokespeople each fortnight without compromising the consistency of the movement's political message. This tactic baffled the authorities, who got used to co-opting, dividing, or discrediting a handful of opposition political leaders. An additional advantage of rotating Otpor spokespeople was the generation of favorable mass perceptions about the movement's strength. Specifically, the frequent rotation of spokespeople fostered popular belief about the large size of the movement.

Finally, the 1996–97 protest campaign strengthened youth's belief that youth activists should not count on the support of the opposition political parties. "The 1996–1997 student protests were not supported by political parties; they were used by politicians. None of the political parties reacted to the 1998 Law on Universities," said Tanja Azanjac, program coordinator at the Belgrade-based

[25] Author's interview with Dejan Randic, Belgrade, Serbia, January 30, 2008.

[26] Author's interview with Nenad Konstantinovic, New York City, November 6, 2009.

[27] Author's interview with Vladimir Pavlov, New York City, November 4, 2009.

[28] Author's interview with Slobodan Djindovic, Belgrade, Serbia, January 25, 2008.

NGO Civic Initiatives.[29] In light of these political developments, Otpor reasserted youth's independence from the political parties and built a nonpartisan challenger organization.

CROSS-NATIONAL DIFFUSION OF IDEAS

In the late 1990s, Serbian civic activists engaged in an intense debate over the country's future. The cross-national exchange of ideas about civil resistance informed these debates and influenced the development of Otpor's strategy. The Slovak experience provided a positive example of how to inform voters about their rights, boost voter turnout, train election observers, and expose electoral fraud. Another set of ideas developed by advocates of nonviolent action influenced the opposition's choice of protest tactics.

The Slovak parliamentary election held in September 1998 was widely seen as "a delayed velvet revolution."[30] Under the premiership of Vladimir Meciar, Slovakia missed an opportunity to join NATO and apply for membership in the European Union. Furthermore, the prime minister systematically violated democratic procedures to wield power in the post-communist society. To put the country on the path to democracy, a group of NGOs developed a nonpartisan civic campaign, OK'98 (*Obcianska Kampan '98*), pressing for free and fair elections. The NGO community sought to inform the electorate about voting rights, boost voter turnout, and monitor vote count. Within the framework of the GOTV campaign, Slovak activists carried out the campaign "Rock the Vote" (*Rock volieb '98*). One of the main target audiences for this campaign was first-time voters, constituting approximately 10 percent of the electorate.[31] For example, the Foundation for Civil Society implemented a project titled "The Year of Elections," including a media campaign and rock concerts in 13 major Slovak cities. Slick TV spots featuring popular musicians and athletes spread the message "I Vote, Therefore I Am." As a testament to the campaign's success, the turnout for the 1998 parliamentary elections was 84 percent, almost 10 percent higher than during the previous parliamentary elections. Remarkably, 8 of 10 first-time voters cast a ballot in the 1998 elections. Given effective voter mobilization and election monitoring, a coalition of opposition political parties gained more than half the seats in the national parliament and removed the incumbent prime minister from power.

The Slovak GOTV campaign was, to a large extent, a product of the cross-national diffusion of ideas. Slovak civic activists developed the campaign in

[29] Author's interview with Tanja Azanjac, Belgrade, Serbia, February 7, 2008.

[30] Butora, Martin, Zora Butorova, Sharon Fisher, and Grigorij Meseznikov, eds. 1999. *The 1998 Parliamentary Elections and Democratic Rebirth in Slovakia*. Bratislava, Slovakia: Institute for Public Affairs, p. 10.

[31] Nadacia pre obciansku spolocnos [Foundation for Civil Society]. 1998. *Rock volieb '98 Campaign: Report on Activities and Results, 1998 Slovak Parliamentary Elections*. Retrieved from www.wmd.org/documents/RockVoliebGOTV.pdf.

consultation with their Bulgarian, Romanian, and American counterparts. For example, the US-based nonprofit organization Rock the Vote supplied information on how to use rock concerts as a venue for voter mobilization. Marek Kapusta, national coordinator of Rock the Vote campaign, recalled the impact of face-to-face interactions with Bulgarian and Romanian civic activists:

> It showed us the way, the light appeared at the end of the tunnel and I think that vision was fundamental for OK'98 efforts. Because I think that at the beginning only [a] very handful of people believed it's possible, and that something could really be changed by our activities and exactly that positive example of Romania and Bulgaria ... The bare fact that it is possible, that it has been done in three countries already, is a fascinating thing, I think.[32]

On Meciar's removal from power, Slovak activists began to share their expertise about the organization of a GOTV campaign with civic activists in the region.[33] With funding from the Charles Stewart Mott Foundation, Partners for Democratic Change Slovakia prepared an English-language report providing a detailed analysis of the campaign from the perspective of campaign organizers. The report writers envisioned it "as encouragement mostly to participants and leaders from the third sector in those countries, which still expect their campaign of OK'98 kind."[34] In addition to the preparation of a technical report, Pavol Demes, chairman of OK'98, presented an overview of the GOTV campaign at the Belgrade-based conference titled, "Looking at the Future," organized by Civic Initiatives in September 1999. This conference brought together 206 representatives of 144 local NGOs and 20 foreign participants.[35] According to Demes, "it was an excellent opportunity to meet numerous civic leaders, listen to their evaluation of the difficult Yugoslav situation and observe firsthand how they perceive their role in addressing pressing humanitarian needs, economic hardship, political oppression, international isolation and other issues."[36] Kapusta also observes

[32] Quoted from Berecka, Olga, Natalia Kusnierikova, and Dusan Ondrusek. 1999. *NGO Campaign for Free and Fair Elections OK'98: Lessons Learned*. Bratislava, Slovakia: Partners for Democratic Change Slovakia, p. 48.

[33] In addition to the cross-national transfer of knowledge, Slovak civic activists attempted to dispatch an election observation mission to Serbia. The Slovak Democratic Initiative, a coalition of three Slovak NGOs (Civic Eye, Memo '98, and the Slovak Foundation for Civil Society), tried to conduct a pre-election assessment and train election observers, but members of the election observation mission were denied entry to FRY to monitor the electoral process. See Owen, Trefor, Alexandra Levaditis, Katherine Vittum, and Donika Kacinari. 2000. *Federal Republic of Yugoslavia Parliamentary Election Technical Assistance December 2000*. Washington, DC: International Foundation for Election Systems, p. 3.

[34] Quoted from Berecka, Olga, Natalia Kusnierikova, and Dusan Ondrusek. 1999. *NGO Campaign for Free and Fair Elections OK'98*, p. 5.

[35] Demes, Pavol. 1999. *Civil Society Development in Post-War Serbia: Key Findings and Observations*. A Preliminary Field Report. Washington, DC: Woodrow Wilson Center for International Scholars, p. 21.

[36] Demes, Pavol. 1999. *Civil Society Development in Post-War Serbia: Key Findings and Observations.: A Preliminary Field Report*, p.21.

that the Slovak example "was an important inspiration, and it was a factor in getting things started, but they [Serbs] had their own campaign, which was quite different from what we [Slovaks] had done."[37]

The interviewed Otpor activists were quick to point out the need for the adaptation of foreign ideas to the local context. The political regime under Meciar was less repressive than Serbia under Milosevic. The Slovak political opposition, for instance, had greater access to the mass media. The private TV channel Markiza provided nationwide coverage of the GOTV campaign in Slovakia, whereas national TV channels denied access to the opposition forces in Serbia. In planning a GOTV campaign, Serbian activists had to negotiate airtime with a myriad of local TV channels. Despite these political differences, rock concerts in both countries proved to be an effective tool for voter mobilization. The campaign slogans used during the 1998 Slovak elections also seemed to influence Otpor's campaigning. Consider a TV spot shown in Slovakia in 1998. The spot began with the image of a drop of water transforming into a powerful waterfall and ended with the slogan, "This year you can have a choice." A similar message was propagated by Otpor's campaign, "This is THE year!" launched in January 2000. Both campaigns emphasized the urgency of joint political action against the regime.

Another diffusing item was Gene Sharp's ideas about nonviolent action. Otpor leadership became familiar with Sharp's work almost a year after the movement's inception. In June 1999, the Serbian NGO Civic Initiatives translated into Serbian and printed 5,500 copies of Sharp's book, *From Dictatorship to Democracy: A Conceptual Framework for Liberation.*[38] A workshop organized by IRI provided another venue for learning about nonviolent methods. A few Otpor activists traveled to Budapest to participate in this training. One of the items on the workshop's agenda was a seminar with Robert Helvey, a retired US colonel and a longtime proponent of Sharp's ideas. In an interview with the American filmmaker Steve York, Helvey described his meeting with Otpor activists:

> I think they were looking for something to keep the momentum going. You know, they had done very, very effective work in mobilizing individual groups. But there was something missing to take them beyond protest into actually mobilizing to overthrow the regime ... So we started with the basics of strategic nonviolent struggle theory. And I focused on the pluralistic basis of power. That the sources of power are the skills and knowledge and the numbers of people, the legitimacy, the fear of sanctions, things like that. Why people obey the regime, even though they dislike it ... They had analyzed a lot of it, but one thing they had not analyzed was this idea of pillars of support. I think I was able to show them a different way of looking at society. So that they could use their

[37] Arias-King, Fredo. 2007. "Revolution Is Contagious: Interview with Marek Kapusta." *Demokratizatsiya: Journal of Post-Soviet Democratization* 15(1): 133–37, p. 135.

[38] Albert Einstein Institution. 2004. *Report on Activities 2000–2004*. Boston: AEI, p. 15.

resources much more effectively, and be able to measure the effects of their efforts by looking at each of these institutions.[39]

The exposure to Sharp's ideas, however, produced mixed reactions among Otpor activists. Some of them heeded Helvey's advice regarding the development of movement strategies. Srdja Popovic, member of Otpor's human resources and marketing departments, used the notion of the pillars of support to develop the movement's tactics vis-à-vis the incumbent president.[40] Others held a more critical opinion of Helvey's suggestions. Among them was Stanko Lazendic, member of Otpor's network department (Novi Sad).

The truth is that Helvey didn't make Otpor. Prior to the seminar, Otpor has already developed a full-blown network of activists, but Helvey attributes a lot of Otpor's success to himself. Up to that point, I have been arrested eighteen times. I was even put on the wanted list because the government alleged that I killed a top Vojvodina politician.[41]

Serbia's international isolation had an impact on the cross-national diffusion of ideas. The UN economic sanctions adopted in 1992 included a ban on air travel to and from Belgrade.[42] Given travel restrictions and security concerns, Otpor members held meetings with members of the international donor and human rights community outside the country. Often Serbian activists would travel by car to Budapest, the capital city of Hungary, located approximately 200 miles from Belgrade. Despite these hurdles, Otpor activists were able to maintain contacts with Western donors and obtain financial resources for the movement. The next section discusses Otpor's tactics in greater detail.

RESISTANCE UNTIL VICTORY

Otpor was formed by a dozen of university students in reaction to new laws on universities and the mass media. The Law on Universities eliminated university autonomy and curtailed academic freedoms by putting political conformists in places of power. The law granted the government the right to appoint rectors, deans, and supervisory boards who, in turn, could unilaterally fire dissenting professors and fundamentally alter the curriculum. As a result, approximately forty members of pro-government political parties assumed decision-making positions at the University of Belgrade.[43] These personnel changes entailed

[39] An excerpt from Steve York's interview with Robert Helvey is available at http://web.archive.org/web/20050207072559/http://www.pbs.org/weta/dictator/otpor/ownwords/helvey.html.

[40] Author's interview with Srdja Popovic, Belgrade, Serbia, January 23, 2008.

[41] Author's interview with Stanko Lazendic, Novi Sad, Serbia, January 24, 2008.

[42] Lewis, Paul. 1992. "UN Votes 13-0 for Embargo on Trade with Yugoslavia: Air Travel and Oil Curbed." *New York Times*. May 31. www.nytimes.com/1992/05/31/world/un-votes-13-0-for-embargo-on-trade-with-yugoslavia-air-travel-and-oil-curbed.html?pagewanted=all&src=pm.

[43] Human Rights Watch. 1999. "Deepening Authoritarianism in Serbia: The Purge of the Universities." *Human Rights Watch Report* 11(D).

increasing administrative pressures on students to withdraw from politics. In addition, the Law on Public Information granted the government broad powers to curtail press freedom. This law was applied to impose hefty fines on media outlets critical of the incumbent president. In response to the escalation of state repression, Otpor activists demanded the depoliticization of universities and the provision of press freedom.

Furthermore, radicalization of the movement's goals occurred over time. In the fall of 1999, Otpor members participated in a student protest against the appointment of Radmilo Marojevic as the dean of University of Belgrade's Faculty of Philology. Remarkably, students succeeded in ousting Marojevic from office. In part, this positive outcome served as inspiration for targeting the incumbent president. Otpor spokesperson Branco Ilic commented on the evolution of movement goals:

> We are now trying to say to the Serbian public that there is another dean of this country and his name is Slobodan Milosevic ... and the Serbian people can be successful in dismissing [him].[44]

Once Milosevic announced snap elections in the fall of 2000, the youth movement began to focus on the issue of free and fair elections. Otpor activists assumed that elections would mobilize the largest possible number of people because electoral fraud was a high-salience issue to all voting-age citizens. "If somebody is messing up with your vote, it is personal," Popovic said.[45] To propel Milosevic's electoral defeat, Otpor launched two major campaigns. The first campaign, titled "He's Finished" (*Gotov Je!*), targeted Milosevic as the culprit of all societal problems and involved the use of innovative protest tactics, and the second campaign, titled "It's Time" (*Vreme Je!*), was designed to boost voter turnout and reach, in particular, first-time voters. A detailed discussion of Otpor's tactics is provided in the remainder of the section.

Recruitment Tactics

Otpor's key recruitment strategy was to build a broad-based social movement that cut across political, socioeconomic, and regional divides. Individuals with different ideological leanings were welcomed into the movement, provided that they were in opposition to the incumbent president. As Popovic noted, "Otpor tried to bring together all the opposition forces, from Democratic Christians opposing abortion to those who would vote for legalizing gay marriages."[46] The core of the movement's membership was youth. Illic estimates that 71

[44] Quoted from Brunner, Kira. 2000. "Belgrade: Youth and Resistance." *Dissent*. Fall. www.dissentmagazine.org/article/?article=1434.

[45] Author's interview with Srdja Popovic, Belgrade, Serbia, January 23, 2008.

[46] Author's interview with Srdja Popovic, Belgrade, Serbia, January 23, 2008.

percent of Otpor members were under 25 years of age.[47] Predrag Madzarevic, member of Otpor's network department (Kragujevac), recalled how an Otpor cell was formed in the city of Kragujevac:

In December 1998 I was a freshman in the Faculty of Law at the University of Kragujevac. My friends and I were sitting in a café, and a small group of people walked in. The girl put an Otpor flyer next to me. By that time, I'd heard about Otpor from the mass media. In a few days, we met again at a student club. That's how Otpor was formed in Kragujevac.[48]

The recruitment of youngsters drew their families into nonviolent struggle against Milosevic. This strategy grew, in part, from the assumption that "even if you disagree politically with your children, you are, above all, a parent."[49] In addition, the concentration of universities in four Serbian cities – Belgrade, Kragujevac, Nis, and Novi Sad – contributed to the diffusion of movement ideas from large cities into small towns and villages. Slobodan Djindovic, member of Otpor's university department, recalled the importance of students in propagating movement ideas:

Students were our best messengers. Students came from all parts of Serbia. When they went home to small towns and rural areas, they would spread the word.[50]

The emergence of Otpor Mothers, a group of female sympathizers with the movement's cause, is a telling example of the growing web of regime opponents. A spike in arrests of Otpor members led to the mobilization of women in Novi Sad.[51] In turn, whenever Otpor Mothers were held in detention, the Vojvodina Chamber of Lawyers provided legal assistance to women activists. According to Slobodan Homen, member of Otpor's network department, the movement built a nationwide network of lawyers doing pro bona work.[52] "It was [a] time of genuine friendship and camaraderie," said Vesna Tomic, member of Otpor Mothers in Novi Sad. "It didn't exist in any political organization. People were interested in only one thing – how to topple Milosevic."[53]

Furthermore, Otpor sought to broaden its base of supporters by offering multiple venues for political engagement. Involvement in the campaign "He's Finished" was regarded as high-risk activism due to the explicit targeting of the incumbent president. In contrast, the GOTV campaign "It's Time" entailed engagement in more conventional forms of political participation. As Ivan

[47] Illic, Vladimir. 2001. *Otpor: In or Beyond Politics*. Belgrade: Helsinki Committee for Human Rights in Serbia.
[48] Author's interview with Predrag Madzarevic, Kragujevac, Serbia, February 4, 2008.
[49] Author's interview with Srdja Popovic, Belgrade, Serbia, January 23, 2008.
[50] Author's interview with Slobodan Djindovic, Belgrade, Serbia, January 25, 2008.
[51] Markov, Slobodanka, and Marija Kleut. 2005. "Women in the Popular Movement Resistance (Otpor) in Novi Sad 2000." *Gender Studies* 1(4): 162–70.
[52] Author's interview with Slobodan Homen, Belgrade, Serbia, February 7, 2008.
[53] Author's interview with Vesna Tomic, Novi Sad, Serbia, January 27, 2008.

Andric, a member of Otpor's marketing department, put it, "[T]he GOTV campaign gave the less brave an opportunity to become involved."[54] In addition, the GOTV campaign allowed Otpor to build ties with other civil society actors within the framework of the pre-election campaign *Izlaz 2000* ("Exit 2000").[55]

In February 2000, Otpor formally redefined itself as a broad-based civic movement rather than a youth movement. Mockery of the SPS Annual Congress served as a stimulus for organizing a national meeting of Otpor activists. Otpor's assembly showcased the movement's popularity across Serbia. As Popovic pointed out, "[Y]ou cannot defeat the government by imposing sanctions on it or outspending it. But you can accomplish it by gaining numbers."[56] Given the growing size of the movement, Otpor activists devised numerous ways to maintain a sense of solidarity and foster participant commitment to the movement's cause.

Organizational Structure

Otpor built a horizontal organizational structure without any visible leaders. In part, the rotation of Otpor spokespeople fostered the belief that everybody could be a leader. The movement consisted of autonomous cells in more than 130 Serbian towns, with the main office in Belgrade. The main office was divided into several departments, including action, human resources, marketing, network, press, and university. The action department was responsible for logistically supporting Otpor's activities across the country and coordinating rapid reaction to arrests of Otpor members. The human resources department dealt with recruitment and training of new members, and the network department coordinated within-movement cooperation and cultivated ties with diverse international actors. The university department focused on the movement's contacts with university students. The press department dealt with public relations. Additionally, the marketing department was responsible for the design and production of Otpor's material. Within these departments, activists developed the movement's tactics. And the size of these departments grew with the increasing size of the movement.

> At the very beginning, there were five-six people dealing with marketing. Three of us were designers. I was previously a campaign manager for student anti-war campaigns, and I was actively involved in 1996–1997 student protests. We started by making stencils. After the [NATO] bombing, we began to work in a different way. Our top

[54] Author's interview with Ivan Andric, Belgrade, Serbia, January 28, 2008.

[55] Paunovic, Zarko, Natasa Vuckovic, Miljenko Dereta, and Maja Djordevic. 2000. *Exit 2000: Non-governmental Organizations for Democratic and Fair Elections*. Belgrade: Verzal Printing House.

[56] Author's interview with Srdja Popovic, Belgrade, Serbia, January 23, 2008.

priority was campaigning all the time. Approximately 20–25 people became involved in marketing. It was like a medium-size ad agency.[57]

Another organizational feature of Otpor was a campaign-based division into two wings. For security reasons, Otpor set up one office for execution of the negative campaign and another office for organization of the positive campaign. The two teams were discouraged from communicating with each other. In the public eye, Otpor sought to distance itself from the GOTV campaign so that it could get off the ground without provoking immediate backlash from the authorities. In particular, the rock concerts aimed at boosting voter turnout were held without the use of Otpor's symbols. In addition, the positive campaign involved a greater level of cooperation with other civil society actors.[58]

Notwithstanding these organizational divisions, the organizational structure encouraged the free exercise of creativity and personal initiative in staging nonviolent resistance. While key strategic decisions were made at the leadership level, each cell had a lot of autonomy. Otpor activists in the provinces, for example, could develop original scripts for street action as long as they followed the movement's principles of nonviolent resistance.

We didn't have a system of hierarchy in Otpor. We told Otpor activists that in each city they had their own Milosevic, head of the Socialist Party or the mayor, or somebody else. That person should be a target too. But each cell had a total autonomy. If you create something good, put it on the market. For example, the eclipse-related street action was first staged in Belgrade and then it spread to several cities. In other organizations, everything needs to be controlled. In Otpor, it didn't happen that way. We in Belgrade didn't try to control activities in other cities.[59]

Furthermore, the systematic cultivation of the movement's organizational culture strengthened internal discipline. Otpor members underwent training that introduced them to key principles of nonviolent action and prepared them for detention. As the movement grew, it built a cadre of activists versed in human resources management. Srdja Popovic, sometimes called Otpor's "ideological commissar," played a central role in the organization of Otpor trainings.

I assumed a leadership role in the human resources department when the movement was very small and later recruited and trained a group of eight people. Like in multilevel marketing, these eight people trained approximately 200 people from 30 different towns. These town representatives went back to their communities and trained more people.[60]

[57] Author's interview with Ivan Andric, Belgrade, Serbia, January 28, 2008.
[58] See Paunovic, Zarko, Natasa Vuckovic, Miljenko Dereta, and Maja Djordevic. 2000. *Exit 2000.*
[59] Author's interview with Dejan Randic, Belgrade, Serbia, January 30, 2008.
[60] Author's interview with Srdja Popovic, Belgrade, Serbia, January 23, 2008.

Tactics vis-à-vis Opponents

A pivotal movement's decision was the rejection of violence. To enforce nonviolent discipline, Otpor leadership organized trainings for new members and designated activists in charge of public order at protest events. In addition, the recruitment of female members boosted Otpor's image as a nonviolent movement.

> There was big fear among movement leaders that some people would retaliate against police violence. And they thought how they could control it. At protest events there were several Otpor members responsible for crowd control. They made sure that people wouldn't resort to violence. Young women were often placed in the first row so that the police knew that protesters would not attack them. Young women also carried flowers to show affection for police officers.[61]

The use of nonviolent methods was advantageous to the movement in several ways. First, nonviolent action could mitigate the relevance of the state's military capabilities. As Popovic pointed out, "We couldn't defeat Milosevic by force. NATO couldn't do it, so how could we?"[62] Second, commitment to nonviolence had a positive impact on the movement's recruitment because it appealed to a larger number of citizens in the war-torn country. Finally, the use of nonviolence boosted Otpor's legitimacy in the international community.

Otpor's repertoire of contention included graffiti, stickers, and street performances. A beneficial feature of using graffiti was instant visibility in the public space at a low cost. One of Otpor's slogans spray painted across the country was "Resistance until Victory." As the movement gained access to more resources in the post-NATO bombing period, the distribution of stickers became another commonly used form of protest. According to some reports, Otpor members plastered more than a million stickers in 2000. The use of stickers minimized the incidence of arrests because such small-size print material could be easily carried in a backpack and quickly distributed in a public space. Furthermore, the organization of street performances was a popular form of nonviolent resistance. A number of these street performances were related to current events in the country. Otpor activists, for example, celebrated Milosevic's birthday by placing in city squares posters with the following congratulatory remarks:

> Thank you for the childhood you have taken from us, for the unforgettable war scenes you have given us, for all the crimes you have committed in the name of Serbs, for all the lost battles . . . Happy birthday, Mr. President, may you celebrate the next one with your nearest and dearest on a deserved holiday in the Hague [site of the International Criminal Tribunal for the Former Yugoslavia].[63]

[61] Author's interview with Mladen Joksic, New York City, USA, December 10, 2011.
[62] Author's interview with Srdja Popovic, Belgrade, Serbia, January 23, 2008.
[63] Rubin, Joe. 2000. "The Kids Who Could Topple Milosevic." *Mother Jones*. September 26. http://motherjones.com/politics/2000/09/kids-who-confronted-milosevic.

Street performances were filled with humor to lampoon the regime and break fear within the population. "When you are fighting against [a] brutal force, it is best to put up passive resistance and make funny jokes to show how stupid the regime is. And the Milosevic regime didn't know how to react to it," said Nenad Belcevic, member of Otpor's press department.[64] When the eclipse occurred in Belgrade in August 1999, Otpor activists used this natural phenomenon to make a political statement. Otpor members set up a huge cardboard telescope in the street and invited passers-by to see the falling star dubbed "Slobotea." The makeshift telescope showed a picture of Milosevic, implying his imminent downfall. This street action was similar to what student protesters did during the 1996–97 protest campaign. Back then, students made a so-called rectorscope to send the University of Belgrade's rector to Mars.

Furthermore, a number of street performances were designed to make a parody of public policies under Milosevic. When the government launched a fund-raising campaign, "Dinar for Sowing," and placed donation boxes in public spaces to collect funds for farmers, Otpor responded with its own campaign, "Dinar for Retirement." Otpor members put in the street a barrel decorated with the president's picture and offered passers-by an opportunity to hit the barrel with a bat in exchange for coins. Dejan Randic, member of Otpor's marketing department, recalled it as one of the most resonating street actions:

> [T]he sound [of hitting the barrel] was astounding. After a couple of Otpor activists did it, 15–20 people lined up. It was working by itself. We were just sitting in the nearby café and watching it. The secret police didn't know what to do. They couldn't arrest us because we looked like spectators of the street action. Then they just arrested the barrel. And journalists were there to report it. Then we reproduced this action in several cities. So the following headlines appeared in the media, "The second barrel was arrested," "The third barrel was arrested." We've got a lot of publicity without spending a lot of resources.[65]

Another Otpor method of nonviolent resistance was the rock concert. Rock music is universally associated with revolt against the status quo. In Serbia, rock music was an alternative to turbofolk, the fusion of folk music with pop and dance. State-controlled TV channels kept rock songs off the air and played simple tunes about romance and self-sacrifice.[66] One of the most popular turbofolk performers was Svetlana Raznatovic, better known as Ceca. Her songs dwelled on unhappy romantic relationships and induced acquiescence to the status quo. In contrast, such rock bands as Darkwood Dub, Eyesburn,

[64] Author's interview with Nenad Belcevic, Belgrade, Serbia, February 8, 2008.

[65] Author's interview with Dejan Randic, Belgrade, Serbia, January 30, 2008.

[66] On rock music in Serbia, see Collin, Matthew. 2001. *This is Serbia Calling: Rock 'n' Roll Radio and Belgrade's Underground Resistance*. London: Serpent's Tail; Gordy, Eric D. 1999. *The Culture of Power in Serbia: Nationalism and the Destruction of Alternatives*. University Park: Penn State University Press.

and Kanda, Kodza i Nebojsa provided an impetus for action by portraying the dire political situation in the country.[67] For example, the recurring line in one of Eyesburn's songs was "get out and fight." Within the framework of the GOTV campaign, rock musicians performed in small towns and cities to boost voter turnout. As music critic Dragan Ambrozic stated, these rock concerts "tried to build a context within which change was possible."[68]

Otpor set itself apart from earlier protest campaigns by applying marketing ideas to civil resistance. Taking cues from multinational corporations, the Serbian social movement created a culture of resistance. Otpor's logo, designed by Nenad Petrovic, became a centerpiece of Otpor's branding. Otpor distributed badges, T-shirts, umbrellas, and even matchboxes with the image of the clenched fist. Ivan Marovic, a member of Otpor's press department, stated that branding was an important dimension of the movement's strategy:

> When I ... recently read an article about grassroots marketing, a new trend in the corporate world, I realized that that's exactly what we did. Our product was dissent. Our message was *Jive Otpor* ["Live resistance"]. In other words, you don't support resistance, you live it. We wanted people to join us and live resistance, so we promoted revolution like a fashion line. We had Otpor T-shirts, mugs, and umbrellas. It was a lifestyle promotion.[69]

Using marketing principles, Otpor promoted its brand through a Western-style ad aired on local TV channels. In the TV ad, an aproned woman put a T-shirt with the image of Milosevic inside a washing machine and pushed a button with the symbol of the clenched fist on it. On completion of the washing, the T-shirt was shown to be impeccably clean, without any sign of Milosevic on it. The resounding political message was that Otpor was capable of removing the incumbent president from power.

Another insight the social movement drew from marketing research was the use of survey data to develop the GOTV campaign. Opinion polls showed that young people were more critical of the political regime than older citizens. By the time of the 2000 presidential election, almost half a million youngsters would become eligible to vote. Yet only 5 percent of first-time voters exercised their right to vote in the previous election. The survey data showed that "first-time voters didn't care much about politics" and "the most common fear was that my vote wouldn't count."[70] In light of these survey findings, Otpor sought to bring young voters to the polling stations and thus vote the incumbent president out of office. To stimulate a shift in youth political behavior, youth

[67] Mijatovic, Brana. 2008. "'Throwing Stones at the System': Rock Music in Serbia during the 1990s." *Music and Politics* 2(2): 1–20.

[68] Author's interview with Dragan Ambrozic, Belgrade, Serbia, February 2, 2008.

[69] Author's interview with Ivan Marovic, Washington, DC, December 13, 2007.

[70] Author's interview with Dejan Randic, Belgrade, Serbia, January 30, 2008.

activists stressed the idea that high voter turnout would reduce the number of stolen votes.

The notion of a constant campaign was another idea Otpor borrowed from marketing. "The movement never stopped being present," said Ana Djordjevic, designer and member of Otpor's marketing department. "We live in a consumer society, whereby people tend to forget fast a campaign, and Otpor constantly organized some action. It is also important to keep activists busy and informed. People felt that they were doing something."[71] This approach boosted the movement's visibility and gave members a feeling of accomplishment.

Tactics vis-à-vis Allies

Otpor cultivated ties with both domestic and international actors to accomplish its goals. To undermine the repressive capacities of the state, Otpor sought to enlist the support of the mass media, the police, and the army. In addition, the social movement exerted pressure on opposition political parties to get them united in advance of the elections. Furthermore, Otpor gained technical and financial assistance from the international donor community.

Otpor built its media relations in a hostile political environment. While the government denied the opposition access to national TV channels, local TV channels, radio stations, and newspapers exercised a modicum of freedom in their editorial policies. As Nenad Konstantinovic, a member of Otpor's network department, pointed out, the social movement sought to grab the media's attention through eye-catching street action. "We wanted to be on the front page every day. So we needed a picture every day, and we daily organized events in the street."[72]

Moreover, Otpor attempted to establish informal contacts with the security services and develop a "fraternizing approach" to the police.[73] In the early 1990s, protesters used to employ confrontational tactics in dealing with the police. Instead, Otpor decided to treat police officers as victims of the political regime and show affection for them. One of the PR tactics aimed at the police officers was inspired by the color of their uniforms. The color of both police uniforms and those of the national soccer team was blue (*plavi* in Serbian). At soccer games, Serbs would chant "*Plavi!*" ("Blue men") in support of the national team. Similarly, Otpor members chanted "*Plavi!*" to police officers to get them on the challenger's side or, at least, reduce the magnitude of police violence. In addition, young female activists brought flowers and baked goods to police stations to soften the attitudes of local police officers.

71 Author's interview with Ana Djordjevic, Belgrade, Serbia, January 26, 2008.

72 Author's interview with Nenad Konstantinovic, New York City, November 6, 2009.

73 See Binnendijk, Anika Locke, and Ivan Marovic. 2006. "Power and Persuasion: Nonviolent Strategies to Influence State Security Services in Serbia (2000) and Ukraine (2004)."

Otpor also sought to erode military support for the incumbent president. Though the majority of officers supported the incumbent government, rank-and-file soldiers were less ideologically committed to the regime. Most soldiers were young conscripts with strong ties to local communities. Through these conscripts, Otpor tried to undermine the capacity of the incumbent president to use the military against regime opponents. Mladen Joksic, for example, joined Otpor during his year-long service on the border with Kosovo and disseminated movement ideas inside his unit:

> When I was off duty for a day or two, I would come back with a pack of Otpor stickers. I would hide them among my clothes, and they never searched my belongings. Then I would plaster these stickers at night, and I was never caught. My captain was very angry when he saw Otpor stickers in our barracks. But they didn't find out who did it.[74]

Furthermore, Otpor expanded the political opportunity structure by pushing for unity of the opposition political parties. Acting as an independent force, Otpor members contrived and frequently chanted a provocative slogan ("Traitors are scum") to shame the opposition for internal factionalism. In the long run, the opposition political parties succumbed to popular demands, agreeing on a presidential candidate from the united opposition:

> Initially, 40 percent of our campaign efforts were spent on making the opposition unite. Until the opposition parties were blackmailed, until they realized that they were losing their supporters, they wouldn't unite.[75]

In addition to domestic allies, Otpor found support in the international donor community. As Azanjac noted, Serbia's civil society caught the attention of foreign donors when "Milosevic's image … changed from a peacemaker from Dayton to a butcher from the Balkans."[76] In 1998–99, Otpor built a network of activists without extravagant foreign funding. In the wake of the NATO bombing, however, the United States significantly increased its financial and technical assistance to Serbian civil society actors.[77] Otpor benefited from this shift in US foreign policy. Foreign funding, for example, enabled Otpor to produce a large volume of campaign material. Furthermore, public opinion polls commissioned by IRI supplied Otpor activists with survey data pertinent to the development of antiregime campaigns. Yet, given the preponderance of anti-American sentiments in Serbian society, Otpor made a strategic decision to publicly deny any US connection. Back in the Milosevic period, when asked to comment on sources of their financial support, Otpor activists preferred to

[74] Author's interview with Mladen Joksic, New York City, December 10, 2011.

[75] Author's interview with Srdja Popovic, Belgrade, Serbia, January 23, 2008.

[76] Author's interview with Tanja Azanjac, Belgrade, Serbia, February 7, 2008.

[77] Carothers, Thomas. 2001. "Ousting Foreign Strongmen: Lessons from Serbia." *Policy Brief*. Washington, DC: Carnegie Endowment for International Peace.

exaggerate the role of the Serbian diaspora.[78] The war-ravaged Serbia lacked a middle class that could have provided adequate financial support for the movement:

The main thing that they [critics] are catching Otpor for is cooperation with [the] West... Yes, we are ... yes, we do accept support, financial support from the West, definitely, but that's [critic's condemnation for accepting the West's financial assistance] even worse, because no one in Serbia can invest in Otpor, so that's the worse.[79]

The interviewed Otpor activists emphatically stated that US funding did not dictate their tactical choices. Youth activists, for example, argued that Western funding enabled Otpor to print a million stickers, but Serbian youth was responsible for the design of the print materials and the development of messages that would resonate with the local population. As Aleksandar Maric, a member of Otpor's network department (Novi Sad), put it, "We didn't need Gene Sharp's book to generate ideas. We just needed money to print our material."[80] Given their immersion in local culture, Otpor members felt that they were better positioned than foreigners to develop effective tactics. Youth activists, for instance, rejected the idea of Western-style canvassing on the eve of the 2000 federal election.

Americans advised us to do a door-to-door GOTV campaign. But they didn't take into account the extent of political intolerance in Serbia at that time. For example, an Otpor activist with his wife and a baby [were] thrown out of the house by his in-laws. They [the in-laws] were strong supporters of Milosevic. After his arrest, they found out about his antigovernment activities and told the young couple to leave. It was impossible to campaign from door to door. Some Milosevic supporters could have attacked us.[81]

In sum, Otpor made a number of important strategic decisions. First, the social movement identified elections as an opportunity for large-scale mass mobilization. Second, Otpor focused on the incumbent president as its primary target. Third, the movement built a broad base of support. Fourth, Otpor employed nonviolent methods to challenge the government and applied marketing techniques to create a culture of resistance. Finally, the social movement deftly pushed for unity of the opposition political parties and fostered ties with influential allies. The next section examines how the incumbent government attempted to strangle the movement's growth.

78 Hockenos, Paul. 2003. *Homeland Calling: Exile Patriotism and the Balkan Wars*. Ithaca, NY: Cornell University Press, p. 173.

79 Zakalin Nezic's interview with Otpor member Vladimir Radunovic. Quoted from *Balkan Academic News*. September 20, 2000. http://groups.yahoo.com/group/balkans/message/796.

80 Author's interview with Aleksandar Maric, Novi Sad, Serbia, January 24, 2008.

81 Author's interview with Stanko Lazendic, Novi Sad, Serbia, January 24, 2008.

MILOSEVIC'S REBUTTAL TO "MADLEN JUGEND"

This study finds that state authorities displayed a lack of sophistication in crafting countermovement tactics. A staple set of repressive methods, including state propaganda and mass arrests, was deployed against the challenger organization. Furthermore, the coercive apparatus miscalculated the timing of state repression. A spike in police arrests of movement participants, along with the government's branding of Otpor as a terrorist organization and a foreign mercenary, occurred in spring 2000. By that time, Otpor has already established itself as a nonviolent social movement and secured significant popular support. An escalation in state repression, along with brazen state propaganda, backfired against the regime.

The murder of a Milosevic ally was used as a pretext for a smear campaign in state-controlled media and mass arrests of Otpor activists in May 2000.[82] At a press conference on May 14, 2000, Minister of Information Ivan Markovic accused Otpor of dealing in terrorism:

> Anyone who tries to present Otpor as a student organization or a political party is mistaken. Otpor is a neo-fascist organization in the tradition of the Red Brigades. And the state will use the same means used by the other states when faced with terrorism of such proportions.[83]

In addition, the government attempted to frame Otpor as a foreign mercenary. For example, Gorica Gajevic, SPS secretary general, publicly criticized the challenger organization, claiming that "the aggressor is placing his weapons in the hands of domestic servants in order for them to do their dirty work, to spread fear and chaos."[84] A more covert way of smearing the movement's reputation was allegedly government funding for the production and distribution of posters with the tagline, "*Madlen Jugend.*" This phrase was supposed to invoke the movement's connections to both US Secretary of State Madeleine Albright and the Nazi youth organization Hitler Jugend. The poster portrayed a Nazi soldier holding a flag with Otpor's symbol of the clenched fist. This countermovement framing tapped into anti-US and anti-Nazi sentiments in Serbian society.

In response, Otpor enacted a myriad of savvy countermoves. Movement participants brushed away state allegations about the use of violence by gathering in front of local police stations and humorously introducing to the general public local kids as Otpor members. Youth activists also fended off allegations about foreign funding by claiming support from the diaspora and underscoring their patriotic fervor. In reaction to state propaganda, Otpor

[82] Humanitarian Law Center. 2001. *Police Crackdown on Otpor.*

[83] Quoted from York, Steve. 2001. *Bringing Down a Dictator* [documentary]. Washington, DC: York Zimmerman.

[84] Quoted from Rozen, Lauren. 2000. "Milosevic's Media Blackout." *Salon Magazine.* May 18. www.salon.com/news/feature/2000/05/18/milosevic.

launched a public campaign, titled "Resistance Because I Love Serbia." As Homen put it, "the campaign sought to promote a healthy way of patriotism."[85]

Another discursive strategy used by the state-controlled media was to frame the incumbent president as the guarantor of peace and stability. In particular, state-controlled TV channels tried to convince Serbian youth that they lived in a land of opportunities. Yet the TV spots produced by the youth wing of JUL clashed with political reality and provoked a backlash.

> JUL produced expensive TV spots. They showed green meadows and played upbeat music, but it was completely detached from reality. In a serious way the TV spots tried to show people that life in Serbia was good. In contrast, Otpor delivered serious messages in a humorous way. That's why Otpor messages were much more effective than JUL ads.[86]

In addition to state propaganda, the government tried to obstruct Otpor's access to resources. The confiscation of Otpor's print material was quite common. To mock police behavior, Otpor concocted a street action infused with humor. Movement participants delivered empty boxes to Otpor's main office and slowly carried them as if they were packed with paper. When the police intervened and confiscated the boxes, it became obvious that the youth activists played a prank on the police. The street action exposed the ineptitude of the coercive apparatus.

According to the Belgrade-based Humanitarian Law Center, police action against Otpor members took the following forms: (1) "informational conversation" – summoning an individual to the police station for extensive questioning and subsequent fingerprinting, (2) detention, (3) entry into apartments, search, and confiscation of property, (4) inhumane treatment of detainees, (5) assaults by unidentified individuals, (6) filing misdemeanor complaints, and (7) criminal proceedings.[87] The police routinely arrested movement participants for acts of nonviolent resistance or summoned them to the police station for the so-called informative interviews. Some youth activists were detained several times per week.[88] Another police tactic was fingerprinting of detained movement participants, a procedure formally reserved for suspects in criminal proceedings.

The police recruitment strategy, in part, accounts for the zeal of police officers in dealing with youth activists. The overwhelming majority of law enforcement agents assigned to interrogate Otpor members had a military background. The interviewed Otpor activists stated that most security agents they encountered during their detentions fought in Kosovo. This military

[85] Author's interview with Slobodan Homen, Belgrade, Serbia, February 7, 2008.

[86] Author's interview with Mladen Joksic, New York City, December 10, 2011.

[87] Humanitarian Law Center. 2001. *Police Crackdown on Otpor*.

[88] Helsinki Commission for Human Rights in Serbia. 2000. *Repression – The Regime's Defense Instrument*. Available at www.glypx.com/BalkanWitness/helsinki1.htm.

experience, coupled with state propaganda, solidified the agents' antipathy toward the social movement. In turn, Otpor exposed the magnitude of police violence against movement participants by distributing a poster of a heavily beaten youth activist, fueling public outrage over state repression.

To overcome the fear of arrests, the social movement instituted a set of procedures. Otpor members underwent training on how to behave in case of an arrest and how to answer the most common questions during a police interrogation. Furthermore, Otpor developed the so-called Plan B, a detailed plan of action in response to the detention of Otpor members.[89] The police station would fall under siege. A lawyer would inquire about the detained activist. Journalists would call to inquire about the details of the case. Otpor members would picket the police station. The detainee's relatives would come to the police station as well. Finally, the released activist would be greeted as a national hero.

> The kids who would step out of the police station would be hailed as heroes. Those who were frequently arrested became real heroes. Young people were willing to take risks to earn respect among their peers.[90]

Compared with Otpor, youth wings of SPS and JUL had much less appeal among youth. The regime-friendly youth organizations attempted to lure youth by offering some monetary benefits and promising career advancement. However, most youth were reluctant to become affiliated with the ruling parties.

> It was not cool to join youth wings of SPS or JUL. It was embarrassing. Since young people were ashamed to join, SPS and JUL were buying supporters. Everybody knew that it would be easier to get a job in the public sector if one joined SPS or JUL.[91]

In sum, the incumbent government deployed a mix of framing, channeling, and repression to depress youth mobilization against the regime. The state-controlled media framed Otpor as a terrorist organization and a foreign mercenary. Moreover, the government restricted the opposition's access to resources through political pressures on the mass media and universities. In addition, the police frequently detained movement participants. Yet, despite state repression, thousands of youngsters became Otpor activists. Furthermore, almost 86 percent of 18–29-year-old voters cast their vote in the 2000 election, contributing to the electoral defeat of the incumbent president.[92]

[89] Smiljanovic, Zorana. 2003. *Plan B: Using Secondary Protests to Undermine Repression.* Minneapolis, MN: Center for Victims of Torture/New Tactics in Human Rights Project. Retrieved from www.newtactics.org/en/PlanB.

[90] Author's interview with Srdja Popovic, Belgrade, Serbia, January 23, 2008.

[91] Author's interview with Mladen Joksic, New York City, December 10, 2011.

[92] See Paunovic, Zarko, Natasa Vuckovic, Miljenko Dereta, and Maja Djordevic. 2000. *Exit 2000*, p. 39.

THE BULLDOZER REVOLUTION

The presidential election held in September 2000 was marred by electoral fraud. According to the official results, Milosevic received 38.62 percent of the votes, and Kostunica was ahead of him with 48.96 percent.[93] The Federal Election Commission claimed that a second round was necessary because neither candidate won the majority of votes. CeSID, however, refuted the official results. Based on parallel vote tabulation (PVT) at more than 5,000 polling stations, CeSID estimated that Kostunica won 57.87 percent of votes, and Milosevic received 32.02 percent.[94] Citing PVT results, the opposition political parties demanded the official recognition of Kostunica's victory and called for civil disobedience to put pressure on the incumbent president.

Support for the opposition's demands came from diverse social forces. Thousands of workers at the Kolubara coal mine went on strike, threatening to paralyze Serbia's economy through the disruption of electricity supplies.[95] The mobilization of coal miners against the leader of the Socialist Party dealt a serious blow to the legitimacy of the regime. On October 5, 2000, citizens from small towns and cities arrived in Belgrade to participate in a protest rally. More than half a million people turned to the streets to demand Milosevic's resignation. A bulldozer driver steered his vehicle into the RTS building, later giving a name to these protest events. Under public pressure, the Constitutional Court confirmed Kostunica as the winner of the presidential election, and Milosevic ceded defeat.

CONCLUSION

This chapter demonstrated how the use of innovative tactics by the challenger organization and the deployment of conventional repressive methods by state authorities contributed to a high level of mass mobilization against the regime in Serbia. Otpor's success can be attributed to the savvy adoption of a two-track approach to civil resistance: the development of a negative campaign directed against the incumbent president and a positive campaign aimed at boosting political participation. In particular, the youth movement succeeded in creating a culture of resistance infused with political humor and promoted with the help of marketing techniques. Moreover, Otpor's commitment to nonviolent action

93 Thompson, Mark T. and Philipp Kuntz. 2004. "Stolen Elections: The Case of Serbian October." *Journal of Democracy* 15(4): 159–72, p. 167.

94 Center for Free Elections and Democracy. 2000. *CeSID Parallel Vote Count Report, 2000*. P. 12. Retrieved from http://gndem.net/dommonreport_cesid_pvtreport_eng.

95 Crawshaw, Steve. 2000. "Miners Take Milosevic to the Edge of Meltdown." *The Independent*. October 4. www.independent.co.uk/news/world/europe/miners-take-milosevic-to-the-edge-of-meltdown-635106.html; Erlanger, Steven. 2000. "Striking Serbian Coal Miners Maintain Solidarity." *New York Times*. October 4. www.nytimes.com/2000/10/04/world/striking-serbian-coal-miners-maintain-solidarity.html?src=pm.

was a critical ingredient of the movement's success in a war-torn region. Otpor's ability to assert independence from opposition political parties was also crucial to the movement's appeal in a populace disillusioned with the bleak performance of the divided political opposition. In spite of functioning in a politically suffocating environment, Otpor effectively exposed the government's flaws so that state repression backfired, fueling the movement's growth.

In turn, the recurrent use of repressive methods sapped the regime's strength. A smear campaign against the political opposition, along with the upbeat coverage of the government's performance in state-controlled media, was Milosevic's staple response against his critics. But an avalanche of state propaganda turned out to be an ineffective tool against the rising tide of citizen dissatisfaction with the government because movement participants creatively rebuffed the government's attempts to taint the movement's image. The deployment of political violence against Otpor members further alienated ordinary citizens from the regime because youth activists clearly demonstrated their rootedness in local communities.

Additionally, a set of political and socioeconomic factors discussed in Chapter 3 influenced the odds of popular revolt against the incumbent government. The moribund state of the national economy deprived the incumbent of the capacity to deliver generous welfare benefits to his electorate. Moreover, the NATO bombing campaign dented Milosevic's posture as a legitimate and invincible player in world politics. Eventual defections within the security apparatus signaled cracks in the regime. Still, the regime's declining strength could not explain by itself why thousands of people became engaged in civil resistance. Consider the opposition's access to local media. Otpor's ability to secure airtime on local TV channels was by itself insufficient to guarantee the movement's popularity. Youth activists succeeded in crafting messages and producing TV spots that struck a chord with ordinary citizens.

Otpor's success provided an electrifying example for regime opponents in autocracies worldwide. The movement's struggle was masterfully depicted in the award-winning documentary *Bringing Down a Dictator* produced by Steve York.[96] Furthermore, Slobodan Djindovic and Srdja Popovic set up the Center for Applied Nonviolent Action and Strategies (CANVAS) to foster the cross-national diffusion of ideas about nonviolent resistance.[97] In the following chapters this study examines how youth activists in Belarus (2001), Georgia (2003), Ukraine (2004), and Azerbaijan (2005) sought to emulate Otpor's example and mobilize youth in favor of political change.

[96] For details, see York, Steve. 2001. *Bringing Down a Dictator* [documentary]. Washington, DC: York Zimmerman.

[97] On CANVAS, see www.canvasopedia.org/.

5

Zubr's Struggle against Authoritarianism in Belarus

An extraordinary spectacle awaited visitors to a central park in Minsk on April 21, 2001. An impersonator of the incumbent president wearing a papier-mâché mask with a Lukashenka-like moustache was skiing on the asphalt. He was chased by a few young people in white robes and eventually captured to be taken to a mental asylum. This street action titled "The Final Diagnosis" was organized by the youth movement Zubr. Founded nine months prior to the presidential election, the challenger organization sought to emulate Otpor's example and push for political change through nonviolent action.

The government of Belarus was quick to respond to a threat posed by the youth movement. The police arrested not only participants in the street performance but also local journalists covering the event.[1] Young men wearing masks were put on trial for insulting the president of Belarus and faced the threat of a three-year imprisonment under Article 368 of the Criminal Code. Furthermore, presidential Decree No 11 of May 7, 2001 explicitly authorized the police to disperse any mass action that involved the use of masks or other methods deemed threatening to "public security, life and health of citizens."[2] Like Serbian state officials, the Belarusian authorities framed the opposition as a pawn of the West and an instigator of political chaos.

Compared with Otpor, however, Zubr generated less public outrage over state repression. One of the largest post-election protests in the capital city attracted no more than 5,000 people. Furthermore, the youth vote was split between regime opponents and political conformists.

This chapter demonstrates how Zubr tactics and state countermoves explain, in part, the low level of youth mobilization against the regime during the 2001 election. The chapter begins with an overview of major protest campaigns held

[1] Charter 97. 2001. "Leitenant Novikov opozoril militsiu." April 23. http://charter97.org/bel/news/2001/04/23/02.

[2] Charter 97. 2001. "Lukashenko Bans Rallying in Masks." May 8. http://charter97.org/eng/news/2001/05/08/06.

during Lukashenka's first term in office. In addition, this chapter discusses the development of *Malady Front* ("Youth Front"), an antiregime youth movement formed in the 1990s. Next, the chapter traces the cross-national diffusion of ideas within the post-communist region. Finally, the chapter analyzes Zubr tactics and state countermoves. In particular, the chapter examines state sponsorship of regime-friendly youth organizations to secure political stability in the country.

PROTESTS AND REPRESSION UNDER LUKASHENKA

Spring is a period of heightened protest activity in Belarus. The protest period would begin with the celebration of *Dzen voli* ("Freedom Day") on March 25 and proceed with the organization of the march *Charnobylski shliakh* ("Chernobyl Path") on April 26. In addition, *Marsh svabody* ("Freedom March") was held semiannually in 1999–2000. But the size of these regularly scheduled protest events declined at the end of Lukashenka's first presidential term. The number of participants in the Freedom Day march dropped from approximately 20,000 people in 1996[3] to 5,000 people in 2001.[4] Similarly, the number of participants in the Chernobyl Path march markedly declined from 50,000 people in 1996[5] to 5,000 people in 2001.[6] A closer inspection of these protest campaigns sheds some light on state-society relations in Belarus.

Freedom Day

The organization of antigovernment protests on March 25 became a well-known tradition in Belarus.[7] On this date in March 1918, Belarusian leaders signed a declaration unveiling the creation of the Belarusian National Republic and signaling their opposition to the Russian Bolsheviks. Given the ensuing violence and the installment of the communist regime, the celebration of this event was banned in Soviet Belarus. On the demise of the Soviet Union, the government of Belarus officially marked this date for the first time in 1993, but the date quickly regained its antigovernment overtones and became known as Freedom Day. The main demands of protesters were the resignation of the incumbent president, the introduction of democratic reforms, and the revival

[3] Dubavets, Siargei, ed. 1996. *Menskaia viasna–1996: Kronika, dakumenty, svedchanni*. Minsk, Belarus: Nasha Niva, p. 5.

[4] Radina, Natalia. 2001. "V Den Voli protiv liudei byli brosheny vse silovye podrazdelenia Minska." Charter 97. March 25. www.charter97.org/rus/news/2001/03/25/01.

[5] Dubavets, Siarhei, ed. 1996. *Menskaia viasna–1996: Kronika, dakumenty, svedchanni*. Minsk, Belarus: Nasha Niva.

[6] *Belorusskaia Gazeta*. 2001. "Chernobylskyi Shliakh 26 aprelia: Kak eto bylo." April 30. http://news.tut.by/society/5463.html.

[7] Martynovych, Artem. 2011. "Nastoiashchii Den voli – kogda Pushkin na osle, a glava gosudarstva na mitinge." Euroradio. March 24. http://euroradio.fm/ru/node/15557.

of national culture. At the protest, people would chant "Long Live Belarus!" and "Down with Luka!" to demand political change. The protest consisted of a march through downtown Minsk followed by a public rally and a music concert.

The incumbent government deployed a wide range of repressive methods against protesters, including preemptive arrests of event organizers, heavy policing of the event, and the detention of protesters. In March 2000, for example, at least forty members of the BNF party and the United Civic Party were arrested a few hours prior to the protest, and more than 400 people were detained on conclusion of the rally. In particular, the police targeted journalists to deter further media coverage of protest events.[8] Another frequent target of state repression was youth. Parents of high school students, for example, were coerced into signing documents pledging supervision over their children on March 25. The heavy police presence in downtown Minsk was another deterrent for mass participation in the protest event. According to some estimates, there were two to three police officers per protester in March 2001.[9] By the same token, the government of Belarus began to deny visas to representatives of international organizations and Western political parties, hampering the documentation of human rights violations in the country.

Another common state countermove was the organization of pro-government rallies. Approximately 40,000 people, for example, attended a pro-government rally on March 31, 1996, exceeding the number of participants in an antigovernment protest the previous week.[10] Thousands of people were bused from the provinces to boost the legitimacy of the incumbent president and frame the political opposition as a marginal element in Belarusian society.

Chernobyl Path

The main goal of the annual march, titled Chernobyl Path, was to raise public awareness of environmental issues and commemorate victims of the Chernobyl disaster.[11] Explosions in the Soviet nuclear power plant on April 26, 1986 were approximately 400 times more potent than the atomic bomb dropped on Hiroshima in 1945, with large amounts of radioactive elements released into the air. Though the nuclear plant itself was located in Soviet Ukraine, more than

[8] Dzuba, Vladimir. 2000. "Belarus: A Legal 'Chernobyl' in the Centre of Europe." In *Polls Apart: Media Coverage of the Parliamentary Elections, Belarus, October 2000*, eds. Alan Davis and Mark Grigorian. London: Institute for War and Peace Reporting, p. 34.

[9] Radina, Natalia. 2001. "V Den Voli protiv liudei byli brosheny vse silovye podrazdelenia Minska." Charter 97. March 25. www.charter97.org/rus/news/2001/03/25/01.

[10] Bugrova, Irina. 1996. "Respublika Belarus." In *Political Monitoring – April 1996*. Moscow: International Institute of Political Research. Retrieved from www.igpi.ru/monitoring/1047645476/apr_96/belarus.html.

[11] For an overview of this protest campaign, see Nikolayenko, Olena. 2015. "Marching against the Dictator: Chernobyl Path in Belarus." *Social Movement Studies* 14(2): 230–36.

two-thirds of the radiation fell on the territory of Belarus, which negatively affected the local population and in particular youth.[12] Health specialists found a "sudden and unprecedented rise in thyroid cancer among children in Belarus."[13] Given the devastating effects of the Chernobyl accident, this march took the form of a funeral-like procession, with candles and a bell of grief.

Furthermore, opposition political parties used the event as a platform for articulating a broad spectrum of political grievances. The march usually concluded with a series of politically charged speeches by opposition leaders. In 1996, for example, Pazniak expressed solidarity with antigovernment forces in Russia by commemorating the death of Johar Dudaev, a Chechen leader who fought for the republic's succession from the Russian Federation.[14] The participation of relatives of political prisoners and the "disappeared" regime opponents added political import to the march in 2000. In general, event organizers viewed the provision of political freedoms and civil liberties as a precondition for the exercise of citizens' environmental rights.[15]

The government took multiple measures to undercut this civic initiative. State officials deliberately inhibited the organization of the protest event. The municipal government, for example, sanctioned the relocation of the protest rally to the outskirts of the city in 2001. Delegitimation of the protest campaign was another state countermove. State-controlled media framed Chernobyl Path as a PR stunt by a handful of opposition politicians who coveted public attention to realize their political ambitions. A related state counteraction was preemptive detention of environmental activists who could present an authoritative assessment of the environmental situation in the country. Moreover, participants in the march faced the prospect of police beating, arbitrary detention, and inhumane treatment at police stations.

In turn, the political opposition tried to minimize the magnitude of police violence. The political opposition invited foreign diplomats and Western politicians to participate in the event, increasing the reputational costs of state repression. Another tactic was to arrange the rapid arrival and swift departure of protesters from the site of the gathering. In 2001, protesters were asked to show up on the square approximately five minutes before the scheduled start of the march to reduce the chances of their preemptive detention.

12 On the Chernobyl effects, see Bennett, Burton, Michael Repacholi, and Zhanat Carr, eds. 2006. *Health Effects of the Chernobyl Accident and Special Care Programmes*. Geneva: World Health Organization.

13 Astakhova, L. N., Beebe Anspaugh, Drozdovitch Bouville, and Waclawiw Garber. 1998. "Chernobyl-Related Thyroid Cancer in Children of Belarus: A Case-Control Study." *Radiation Research* 150: 349–56, p. 353.

14 Dudaev was allegedly killed by the Russian military on April 21, 1996.

15 *Belarusian Partisan*. 2013. "Chernobyl Path Will Be Held under the Slogan 'No to the Nuclear Power Plant.'" April 9. www.belaruspartisan.org/politic/231081/.

The organization of this protest event, however, exposed divisions within the opposition camp. Given disagreements over the route of the march, two separate protest events were held in April 2000. Members of the Conservative-Christian Party of BNF organized a rally followed by a minute of silence in Yakub Kolas Square, whereas the BNF *Adrozhdenie* ("Revival") brought protesters to Bangalor Square. As a result, participants in the protest march were split based on their party preferences.

Freedom March

The Freedom March was semiannually organized by a group of civic activists in 1999–2000.[16] Protesters demanded the termination of Lukashenka's presidency, the introduction of democratic reforms, the release of political prisoners, the reinstatement of pre-Soviet state symbols, and the country's integration in the European Union. Like the celebration of Freedom Day, this protest event consisted of a march in downtown Minsk followed by a rally and a concert. The event organizers, however, tried to display creativity in mobilizing citizens against the regime. For the first time in 1999, Belarusian activists used stickers as a tool of mass mobilization.[17] One of the stickers had an image of an orangutan and the tagline, "Come! Don't Be a Freak!" (*Prikhodi! Ne bud' urodom!*), insinuating backwardness of Lukashenka's supporters. Approximately 20,000 people participated in the first march, held on October 17, 1999.[18] The number of protesters peaked at 50,000 on March 15, 2000 and dropped to 15,000 on October 1, 2000.[19]

In turn, the incumbent government sought to discredit protesters as marginal and violent elements in Belarusian society. The state-controlled media dwelled on the idea of cash payments for participants in protest events, questioning the credentials of the political opposition. The incumbent president himself made profuse public statements about his opponents. In the fall of 2000, for example, Lukashenka commented on the outbreak of antigovernment protests:

> We have to stop the activities of certain destructive elements which have come up with a formula for themselves: the worse it is for the people and the state, the better it is for them ... And you must all understand perfectly well that these people are earning money. They got

[16] Charter 97. 2000. "Koordinatsionnaia rada demokraticheskih sil Belarsi zaiavila o nachale 'Vesny-2000' i provedenii Marsha Svobody-2." http://charter97.org/index.phtml?sid=2&did=5&lang=2.

[17] Seviarynets, Paval. 2002. *Pakalennia Maladoga Frontu*. Minsk, Belarus: Malady Front, p. 34. Retrieved from http://mfront.net/pakalen.html.

[18] Charter 97. 1999. "Belorusskie vlasti protiv Marsha Svobody i protiv svobody." www.charter97.org/index.phtml?sid=4&did=MS&lang=2.

[19] Institute of Human Rights. 2000. *Bulletin* 22. March 15. www.hrights.ru/text/belorus/b22/Chapter31.htm; Davis, Alana, and Mark Grigorian, eds. 2000. *Polls Apart: Media Coverage of the Parliamentary Elections, Belarus, October 2000*. London: Institute for War and Peace Reporting, p. 56.

everyone from every corner that they could pay, just over 4,000 people who wanted the money. Some spectators joined in.[20]

Civic activists attempted to counteract state propaganda with humor. Each participant in Freedom March 2 received a fake $100 bill with the logo of Freedom March 2 and the imprinted phrase, "To the Participant in Freedom March." In addition, regime opponents published the newspaper *Navinki*, whose title literally meant news (in Belarusian) and subtly referred to a nickname for a mental asylum in Minsk. The newspaper's staff lampooned the regime by staging a satire-filled street performance in which an impersonator of the incumbent president was portrayed as a patient from the mental asylum.

Another common state countermove was the deployment of violence against protesters. On the eve of the protest, Lukashenka warned would-be protesters that they "would be torn to pieces if they made one step to the left or to the right."[21] The university administration admonished students to stay at home or attend state-sanctioned events. At least 200 participants in Freedom March 1 were arrested and held in custody.[22] Moreover, the security services provoked violent clashes with the police. In February 2000, the independent newspaper *Narodnaia Volia* published an open letter in which an alleged police agent provocateur described his role during the protest event:

> My task was a simple one – to watch and remember the faces of the main activists and, afterwards, detain those whom they told me to detain. However, my major mission was to provoke clashes, insult the police officers and direct the crowd towards the police ambush. Unfortunately, among those throwing stones were some desperate youths, but all of their actions were provoked and planned beforehand. The crowd was purposefully guided toward the place, where the stones were piled. Riot police squads were hiding there in an ambush.[23]

A major lesson that Belarusian youth activists drew from these protest campaigns was that the recurrent use of conventional protest tactics would attract a relatively small number of people. The opposition's plan of action was quite predictable. The opposition political parties would organize a march through downtown Minsk followed by a rally in a city square. In an interview with *BelGazeta*, Andrei Dzmitryeu, 30-year-old campaign manager for the 2010 presidential candidate Uladzimir Niakliayeu, commented on this phenomenon:

[20] Quoted from Davis and Grigorian. 2000. *Polls Apart*, p. 55.

[21] Quoted from *Birzha Informatsii*. 2000. "Marsh Svabody." March 16. www.gazeta.grodno.by/108/.

[22] Neverovsky, Algerd. 1999. "Marsh svobody v SIZO." *Kommersant*. October 20. http://kommersant.ru/doc/228166.

[23] Quoted from Amnesty International. 2000. *Belarus: Dissent and Impunity*. June 20, p. 7. Retrieved from www.amnesty.org/en/library/info/EUR49/014/2000/en.

Maybe, we could have gathered more people if we had television that aired ads of Chernobyl Path for the whole month. But since we don't have such television, we need to deliver people a unique offer, something of interest to them, something that would make them pause when they pass by. In contemporary Belarus it is obviously neither a speech by a politician at the rally nor a simple march.[24]

In particular, the use of novel protest tactics was critical to increase youth participation in protest events. According to an opinion poll conducted in March 1999, 22 percent of 16–30-year-old survey respondents felt that contemporary youth lacked above all freedom in Belarusian society, but only 7 percent of young Belarusians reported participation in protest rallies.[25] A substantial proportion of young Belarusians dissatisfied with the current regime refrained from engagement in protest events. The next section examines how the youth movement Malady Front sought to spur Belarusian youth to action.

THE RISE OF MALADY FRONT

Malady Front, formed initially as a youth wing of the opposition political party BNF, transformed itself into the youth movement in the late 1990s. The founding assembly (*Soim*) held on September 6, 1997 declared struggle for democratic Belarus as the movement's main goal.[26] In addition, the assembly delegates – 236 youth activists from 39 cities – elected three movement leaders: Ales Asiptsov (founder of the Mahilau-based youth organization Patriots of the Motherland – Forward to Europe), Siarhei Paulenka (chair of the Christian-Democratic Youth Union from Hrodna), and Paval Seviarynets (head of the BNF youth wing in Minsk). The establishment of the youth movement was motivated, to some degree, by an attempt to break away from the conflict-stricken party increasingly divided into supporters and opponents of Zianon Pazniak. Many youth activists were also dissatisfied with the party's approach to civil resistance. As a Malady Front activist put it, "BNF works by generating ideas through the press, through the intelligentsia, while we [MF] turn to youth no matter where they are – in secondary school, vocational school, or dormitory, and present our ideas to whoever might be interested in them."[27]

As its name suggests, the core of movement participants were young people. The movement spread throughout the country, with more than 2,500 activists

[24] Ivashchenko, Maksim. 2011. "Shliakh v nikuda. Sbor na Balangor." *BelGazeta.* April 25. http://belgazeta.by/20110425.16/320217021/.

[25] Manaev, Oleg, ed. 1999. *Molodezh i grazhdanskoe obshchestvo: Belorusskii variant.* Minsk, Belarus: Skakun Izdatelstvo, p. 11. The survey was conducted by the Independent Institute of Socio-Economic and Political Studies in March 1999. *N* = 1,700, including 680 respondents aged between 16 and 30.

[26] Seviarynets, Paval. 2002. *Pakalennia Maladoga Frontu*, p. 21.

[27] Quoted from Efimova, Nadezhda. 1999. "Molodezhnye NGOs glazami ikh liderov i uchastnikov." In *Molodezh i grazhdanskoe obshchestvo: Belorusskii variant*, ed. Oleg Manaev. Minsk, Belarus: Izdatelstvo V.M. Skakun, pp. 40–58, p. 55.

in 2001.[28] As an indicator of the movement's growth, youth participation in the protest campaign "Belarus to Europe!" increased from 12 cities in 2000 to 32 cities in 2001.[29] Youth activists were expected to abide by a certain code of behavior. According to Seviarynets, the so-called DJs of Revival were individuals who believed in God, loved Belarus, and displayed commitment to nonviolent struggle.[30]

Malady Front deployed various methods of nonviolent resistance to attract young people. A major protest campaign titled *Gorad nash!* ("The City Is Ours!") involved hanging the banned white-red-and-white flags around the city. Another annual protest campaign held on St. Valentine's Day invited young people to display love of Europe by delivering petitions to Western embassies and distributing little valentines. The use of humor was a prominent feature of the movement's street actions targeting the incumbent president. In particular, the president's moustache was a butt of many jokes. Mocking Lukashenka's looks, Malady Front held a winter competition for the best moustached snowman during the 1998 Winter Olympic Games. On World Meteorological Day in spring 2001, youth activists organized a street action titled *Sasha u proletse* ("Sasha Is Out") and released in the air a large balloon decorated with a Lukashenka-like moustache, signifying the president's anticipated defeat in the upcoming presidential election.[31]

The use of Belarusian-language music constituted another salient element of Malady Front's repertoire of contention. Within the framework of the educational campaign "Belarus Show," movement participants organized high school contests on the knowledge of Belarusian culture and played soundtracks of Belarusian-language music. Civic activists also organized concerts profiling Belarusian bands and produced CDs titled *Volnyia tantsy* ("Free Dances"). The movement leadership saw the promotion of Belarusian culture as a key step toward the development of youth national consciousness, which, in turn, might lead to youth opposition to the current regime.

Malady Front activists, however, disagreed over the importance of Christianity in defining the movement's identity and goals. Some youth activists argued that Christianity was a cornerstone of Belarusian identity, and thus Malady Front should champion the idea of democracy based on Christian values. In his monograph, *Natsionalnaia ideia*, Seviarynets defined the national idea as "Belarusian form – Christian content."[32] Others favored a secular definition of the political system. The 2000 bid for the movement's

[28] "My – Malady Front." 2001. *Vesnyk*. August Issue, p. 1, box 2, Belarusian Subject Collection 1938–2011, Hoover Institution Archives, Stanford University.

[29] For an overview of movement history, see http://mfront.net/history.html.

[30] Radio Svaboda. 2007. "Dy-dzei Adradzhennia-2007 atrymali uznagarody." December 27. http://origin.svaboda.org/content/article/869055.html.

[31] Sasha is a shorter, less formal version of Aleksandr. The Belarusian opposition frequently used the word "Sasha" to refer to the incumbent president.

[32] See Seviarynets, Paval. 1998. *Natsionalnaia ideia.* www.sieviarynets.net.

leadership was a reflection of this internal debate. As an advocate of Christian values, Seviarynets defeated his main opponent, Aleksei Shedlovsky, by 61 votes in July 2000.[33] As a result, the movement officially adopted Seviarynets's vision of democratic Belarus, while several youth activists, including Shedlovsky, left Malady Front and assumed leadership roles in setting up Zubr.

Furthermore, a small group of radical youth split from Malady Front and formed the so-called sports-military organization Krai in 1998. The organization, whose name denotes both the homeland and the edge in the Belarusian language, advocated the use of radical tactics and organized physical drills for its members. Young men dressed in military-style outfit would exercise in the woods to gain physical and moral strength. A typical day of training would begin with physical exercises early in the morning and end with the discussion of Belarusian culture in the evening.[34] At protest events, Krai activists would march in the front row and bear the brunt of police violence against peaceful protesters. In addition, Krai became known for its attempt to conduct an independent investigation into the disappearances of regime opponents.[35]

As a major youth movement in opposition to the regime, Malady Front sought to unite various reform-oriented youth organizations on the eve of the 2001 election so that young people could articulate their political demands in a louder voice.[36] In July 2001, representatives of 87 youth organizations and NGOs participated in the Congress of Belarusian Youth to discuss joint action for free and fair elections. Moreover, the Association of Belarusian Students, the Association of Young Entrepreneurs, the Belarusian Association of Young Politicians, Maladaia Hramada (Youth Community), Malady Front, and the Union of Christian-Social Youth participated in the GOTV campaign titled *Vybirai!* ("Choose!")[37] to boost youth voter turnout.[38] An orange-colored rising sun was selected as the campaign symbol to stand for a new period in Belarusian politics. To drum up support for political change, civic activists

33 A total of 189 delegates attended the 2000 assembly. Forty-five delegates voted for Shedlovsky as the movement's leader, while 106 delegates backed the candidacy of Seviarynets. See Seviarynets, Paval. 2002. *Pakalennia Maladoga Frontu*, p. 49.

34 For a description of Krai training, see Pashkevich. 2000. "Moi pershy vyshkal." *Golas Kraiu*. July–August, Belarusian Subject Collection, 1938–2011, Hoover Institution Archives, Stanford University, p. 3.

35 Charter 97. 2001. "Krai Claims Uglyanitsa Worked for Them." August 31. www.charter97.org/eng/news/2001/08/31/06.

36 On this point, see Neviaroiski, Algerd. 2001. "Kaalitsyia 'Peramenau' pastanavila pravesytsi kangres belaruskai moladzi." Radio Svaboda. May 4. www.svaboda.org/content/article/24868148.html.

37 The Russian-language verb *vybirai* is related to the noun *vybor*, denoting "choice," and the noun *vybory*, denoting "elections." For the sake of convenience, the campaign's slogan is translated as "choose" throughout the text.

38 In addition to youth, the GOTV campaign "Choose!" targeted entrepreneurs, intelligentsia, and women. See "Kantseptsyia kampanii Vybirai." P. 3.

organized rock concerts in 22 Belarusian towns. Kasia Kamotskay, for example, performed in several small towns, urging her audience to turn out on election day. In part, the prior success of civil resistance in Slovakia and Serbia inspired Belarusian youth to apply similar nonviolent tactics during the 2001 presidential election.

THE CROSS-NATIONAL DIFFUSION OF IDEAS

Milosevic's resignation in the aftermath of post-election protests rekindled the opposition's hopes for a peaceful turnover of power in Belarus. In particular, Otpor's success was a source of inspiration for local youth. Capturing this mood, Belarusian activists coined the slogan, "Slobodan Is Finished, Sasha – Be Ready" ("*Slobodan gotov, Sasha bud gotov*"). Within three months of Milosevic's downfall, Belarusian activists formed the youth movement Zubr.

> There was a lot of euphoria in 2001. We [Zubr] were the first in the former Soviet Union to apply Gene Sharp's ideas about nonviolent action.[39]
>
> The most recent inspiration examples for us are Georgia and Serbia. Young people played a very important role there in defeating dictatorship. In the most difficult periods we remember it and it gives us confidence in our victory.[40]

Otpor's model of nonviolent resistance had a strong impact on the development of Zubr's tactics. Like Otpor, Zubr launched two main campaigns. The negative campaign titled *Vremia ubirat* ("It's Time to Clean Up") targeted the incumbent president, and the positive campaign titled *Vremia vybirat* ("It's Time to Choose") was designed to boost voter turnout. To attain its goals, Zubr used such nonviolent methods as stickers, graffiti, and street performances. By the same token, Belarusian activists applied voter mobilization techniques previously used in Slovakia and Serbia.

Zubr's newsletter served as a vehicle for the diffusion of ideas about nonviolent tactics. One of the first newsletter's issues, for example, printed the article "Otpor Earned Public Trust: How Milosevic Was Toppled in Yugoslavia." The article began with a discussion of cross-country similarities (the small size of each state, the persistence of communist legacies, and the rise of nondemocratic rulers) and proceeded with a description of Otpor's tactics. The underlying message was that Belarusian youth could succeed in bringing down the incumbent. The newsletter supplied Zubr's contact information, inviting youth to join the social movement.

In turn, the state-controlled media sought to discredit nonviolent struggle against Milosevic and thus dampen youth aspirations for political change. In particular, the national TV channels framed the Bulldozer Revolution as a Western coup. For example, a host of the TV program "Secret Springs in

39 Author's interview with Iryna, Minsk, Belarus, March 12, 2008.

40 Charter 97. 2004. "French Media about Zubr." July 14. http://charter97.org/eng/news/2004/07/14/zubr.

Politics" claimed that "President of Yugoslavia Kostunica was not elected by anybody; the British Prime Minister Tony Blair just declared him as the president."[41] In lambasting Western governments, the program's producer, Yuri Azarenok, repeatedly drew parallels between Milosevic's Serbia and Lukashenka's Belarus:

Serbs dared to say then: We don't want to live according to your laws ... And they weren't forgiven for it. It [the international community] tried to strangle them with the economic blockade, break them with political sanctions, shoot them with rockets, demoralize them with the deployment of the most dangerous modern weapons – information. The international forces wanted to do something similar to us. Just because of our wish to live according to our own rules.[42]

There was also direct contact between Serbian and Belarusian youth activists prior to the 2001 presidential election. A small group of Belarusian activists, including members of Malady Front and Zubr, visited Serbia.

Several young Belarusians, including me, went to Serbia before the 2001 election. We became familiar with Otpor's methods. In particular, we learned about the distinction between a positive campaign and a negative campaign ... But we heard about protests in Serbia before 2000. We knew about protests in 1997. Afterwards Malady Front began to organize flash mobs, and they became more colorful.[43]

International NGOs frequently used Vilnius as a venue for training and meetings with Belarusian civic activists. For example, IRI opened an office in Vilnius to conduct programs in polling, research, candidate preparation, and youth outreach in the run-up to the 2001 presidential election. Among other things, IRI provided assistance in "building networks between young Belarusian activists and their counterparts in neighboring democracies."[44] In particular, Belarusian civic activists developed contacts with Polish NGOs.[45] In light of the Polish struggle for democracy, *The Little Conspirator*, written in 1983, was translated into Belarusian and Russian and distributed among civic activists. This publication provided practical tips on how to wage an underground struggle against the regime, discussing, for example, how to lose a police tail or organize a clandestine meeting.

41 Charter 97. 2001. "Opiat reforma edintsvennogo telekanala." June 6. http://charter97.org/rus/news/2001/06/14/06.

42 *ZavtraRu.* 1996. "Belarus – ne trus." December 3. www.zavtra.ru/cgi//veil//data/zavtra/96/157/5_NOBEL.html.

43 Author's interview with Ales (via Skype), January 29, 2012.

44 International Republican Institute. 2001. *2001 Annual Report: Guiding Light for Democracy.* Washington, DC: IRI, p. 13.

45 For an extensive treatment of this topic, see Petrova, Tsveta. 2014. *From Solidarity to Geopolitics: Support for Democracy among Postcommunist States.* New York: Cambridge University Press.

Another inspiring example for the Belarusian opposition came from Slovakia. Belarusian civic activists participated in a series of workshops titled "Sharing the OK'98 Experience." One of the first seminars held in Bratislava in March 1999 brought together leaders of the OK'98 campaign and 35 participants from Belarus, Croatia, Kyrgyzstan, Lithuania, Russia, Serbia, Ukraine, and the Caucasus.[46] In addition, the Foundation for Civil Society, later renamed the Pontis Foundation, has been "in active contact" with Belarusian NGOs since 2000.[47] The Slovak NGO provided assistance with the organization of a voter mobilization campaign and coalition building in the NGO community. Despite these cross-national exchanges of ideas, lack of cooperation within civil society crippled the effectiveness of Belarusian NGOs on the eve of the 2001 election. Contrary to the Slovak experience, Kapusta observed the following phenomenon in Belarus:

> These people [NGO staff] are sort of competing with each other, not cooperating, similar to what is happening at the level of political parties. This infighting has devastating effects. That is why people did not trust them so much, why they have been unable to secure a critical mass of people or to fight against the regime's media blockade and communicate effectively with the common people. They spend more time and energy infighting than was necessary.[48]

In addition to palpable internal weaknesses, the Belarusian opposition faced a more potent coercive apparatus than the opposition in Slovakia. To inhibit the cross-national diffusion of ideas, the security services closely monitored international travel of its citizens and restricted the entry of foreigners into the country. Like Serbia, Belarus provided a hostile environment for the organization of Western-funded workshops. In January 2001, 40 representatives of Belarusian opposition political parties went to Lithuania to attend a workshop on nonviolent action organized by the Boston-based Albert Einstein Institution and the Lithuanian NGO Citizens' Defense Support Fund. In response, the embassy of Belarus in Lithuania declared that "such 'training' is directed at the destabilization of the current social and political situation and will create obstacles on the eve of the presidential election campaign in Belarus."[49] Belarusian border patrol officers detained the returning workshop participants and confiscated their training materials. Moreover, the KGB of Belarus hunted down foreigners deemed as threatening to the regime. In March 2001, security

[46] Institute of Development Studies. n.d. Case Study "Civil Campaign OK'98." University of Sussex, UK. www.ids.ac.uk/ids/civsoc/final/slovakia/slo2.doc.

[47] Pontis Foundation. 2015. "Pontis Foundation Celebrates 18 Years." www.nadaciapontis.sk/history-en.

[48] Arias-King, Fredo. 2007. "Revolution Is Contagious: Interview with Marek Kapusta." *Demokratizatsiya: Journal of Post-Soviet Democratization* 15(1): 133–37, p. 136.

[49] Cole, Victor, ed. 2001. "Regime Denounces Seminar, Detains Participant." *Belarus Update.* New York: International League for Human Rights. Retrieved from www.ilhr.org/ilhr/regional/belarus/updates/2001/05.html.

officers deported representatives of Liberal Youth of Denmark to preclude their participation in a seminar on youth-related issues, while the local government reprimanded Belarusian youth for its failure to obtain official permission for such an event.[50] Nonetheless, the government of Belarus could not completely insulate youth activists from exposure to regime-threatening ideas.

THE EMERGENCE OF ZUBR

On January 14, 2001, a group of 40 youth activists gathered in Belovezhskaia Pushcha and declared the establishment of the youth movement Zubr. Both the movement's name and the site of the first meeting held symbolic meaning. The movement was named after the country's national animal, invoking a popular myth that the bison does not live in captivity. The choice of this symbol also challenged the Soviet-era practice of imposing such cultural symbols as the stork and the cornflower onto the Belarusian nation. "The stork has long thin legs; it does not have an image of the strong animal. In contrast, the bison has been glorified through Belarusian literature and folklore for centuries. And this animal cannot be found anywhere else in Europe," explained a Zubr activist.[51] Likewise, Belovezhskaia Pushcha, a forest range placed on the UNESCO World Heritage List as the last remaining mixed forest of the European lowlands, was a source of national pride. Furthermore, the forest occupied a special place in Belarusian modern history because it provided refuge for the partisan movement that waged guerilla warfare against the Nazis during World War II. More recently, Belovezhskaia Pushcha became known worldwide as the meeting place of three former Communist Party leaders – Boris Yeltsin, Leonid Kravchuk, and Stanislau Shushkevich – who signed a treaty putting an end to the Soviet Union.

Initially, Zubr presented itself to the public as an environmental movement advocating protection of the country's natural resources. "We thought that it would not catch the immediate attention of state authorities. But we interpreted the notion of ecology very broadly, as cleansing from all the dirt, including the current regime," said a former Zubr member.[52] In its first English-language press release, Zubr described its goals as follows:

> We call ourselves the ecological resistance Zubr. Lukashenko wants to destroy the natural "lungs" of Europe – Belarusian virgin forests. He wants to turn the country into a radioactive desert. He puts under imminent threat the existence of the giant of Belarusian nature – Zubr. They are not cows. They do not live in bondage. Forest is the natural environment of this animal. And freedom is our natural environment.

[50] Viasna Human Rights Center. 2002. *Obzor-Khronika narushenii prav cheloveka v Belarusi v 2001 godu*. Minsk: Viasna Human Rights Center, p. 160.

[51] Author's interview with Uladzimir (via Skype), March 11, 2012.

[52] Author's interview with Andrei (via Skype), December 19, 2012.

Lukashenko is destroying forests and strangling our freedom. The forest helped partisans to save Belarus from enslavement. We will save our forests and our freedom.[53]

Like Otpor, Zubr sought to mobilize citizens against the incumbent president on the eve of national elections. In exposing the nature of the current regime, the Belarusian youth movement tackled the "disappearance" of regime opponents under Lukashenka. Movement participants held portraits of the "disappeared" in downtown Minsk and picketed the presidential administration. Young people also distributed leaflets with portraits of the "disappeared" and the tagline "They don't go to theaters" at main theaters in Minsk and Mahilau.[54] Zubr's action, however, failed to trigger a large-scale backlash against the incumbent. Lukashenka managed to deflect the threat of an electoral revolution and remain popular with a sizable portion of the electorate.

Recruitment Tactics

To some extent, Zubr positioned itself as an alternative to Malady Front. While Malady Front and in particular Seviarynets advocated the exclusive use of the Belarusian language and championed adherence to Christian principles, Zubr lacked such ideological purity. Like Otpor, Zubr was open to anybody who opposed the incumbent president. Specifically, Zubr sought to appeal to Russian-speaking urban youth. According to a Zubr activist, the minimum age requirement for joining Zubr was 16.[55]

Among sites for the movement's recruitment were preexisting social networks, public spaces, universities, and the workplace. Some Zubr activists, for example, tried to win over working-class youth and propagated movement ideas at local factories. Others closely worked with the student population, so the university was seen as a critical venue for the recruitment of new members. To mobilize students, Zubr activists meticulously mapped an infrastructure of each university by collecting data on student organizations, pressing student problems, potential student leaders, the faculty sympathetic to movement ideas, and the schedule of classes.[56] Zubr organized the so-called leaflet rains on the university grounds in an attempt to win students' support. In March 2001, for example, Zubr activists distributed approximately 1,000 Zubr leaflets in each of the following Minsk-based universities: Belarusian State University, Belarusian State Economic University, Belarusian University of Information Science and Radio-electronics, Belarusian Pedagogical University, and Minsk State Linguistic

[53] Zubr. 2001. "Zubr Showed Up in Belarus." February 13. www.zubr-belarus.com/english/index.php?show=oldnews/march_oldnews001.

[54] Zubr. 2001. "Zubr Visited Theaters." March. www.zubr-belarus.com/english/index.php?show=oldnews/march_oldnews008.

[55] Author's interview with Dzmitry (via Skype), January 21, 2013.

[56] The internal Zubr document, titled "Tsikl raboty s aktivistami" [Work Cycle with Activists], discusses Zubr recruitment strategy and training of new members.

TABLE 5.1 *Zubr's Leaflet, "Think! Decide! Act!"*

THINK! In which Belarus would you like to live?
In Belarus where all the power is in the hands of one man who is simply unaware of what he is doing?
In Belarus where you cannot use the knowledge you acquired?
In Belarus where teenagers after graduation are being assigned to the Chernobyl area?
In the Belarus where the reckless authorities decide for you which music you should listen to and which films you should watch?
DECIDE!
You should decide how to live further.
Either to cringe before our negligent authorities or to dictate your own will.
Despise yourself for faintheartedness or be proud of yourself.
Hope in vain that lethargic and weak-willed politicians could do something or take the responsibility of making the right future for the country.
Wait for somebody to decide everything for you or take decisions on your own.
To exist or to live.
ACT!
If you want to live – not exist – then act.
Be free – our enemy is the slave of his weakness.
Be courageous – our enemy is timorous and weak-willed.
Be honest – our enemy is mendacious and immoral.
Be strong – our enemy is confused.
BE A ZUBR!

Source: Zubr. 2001. "Think! Decide! Act!" March 23. www.zubr-belarus.com/english/index.php?show=oldnews/march_oldnews011.

University.[57] A Zubr activist recalled that "students were not afraid to pick up leaflets from the ground; both students and professors read them."

The leaflet titled "Think! Decide! Act!" is a prime example of how Zubr urged young people to become engaged in civil resistance.[58] As shown in Table 5.1, this leaflet summarized a broad spectrum of political, socioeconomic, and cultural issues that beset Belarusian youth. The social movement denounced the consolidation of power in the hands of the incumbent president and the disappearance of regime opponents. In addition, Zubr drew student attention to the low quality of education and the persistence of the Soviet-era system of mandatory job assignments on graduation from the university. Finally, Zubr

[57] Zubr. 2001. "Think! Decide! Act!" March 23. www.zubr-belarus.com/english/index.php?show=oldnews/march_oldnews011.

[58] *Ibid.*

condemned Lukashenka's cultural policies. The enumeration of these social problems was supposed to provide an impetus for joining the challenger organization.

Once individuals responded to this call for action, the recruitment process proceeded in four stages. In the first stage, a Zubr activist designated as instructor organized a meeting with several volunteers and introduced them to movement goals. In the second stage, volunteers discussed movement activities and filled out application forms to match individuals' qualifications and interests with the movement's needs. The assignment of movement participants to certain departments took place during the third stage. The instructor also reserved the right to reject an application if the individual showed lack of interest in movement ideas. The final stage included training of new members. The interviewed activists defined Zubr as "a fraternity" or "a knight's order." As a Zubr activist put it, "once we made the oath of allegiance, we will remain Zubr forever."[59]

Zubr, however, appeared to be less successful than Otpor in retaining new members. A Zubr activist suggested that the movement leadership devoted insufficient attention to the cultivation of members' commitment to nonviolent struggle:

> Zubr leadership underestimated the importance of human resources. People are not like robots; they can't function all the time as if they were wound up. A lot of young people inside Zubr considered themselves as patriots. Still, they needed a recurrent reinforcement of their motivation to stay involved [in the movement].[60]

Organizational Structure

Zubr leadership declared its commitment to the development of a horizontal organizational structure. Yet nonmembers perceived the deficit of democracy inside the movement. According to Belarusian civic activists Shalayka and Mackievich, "Zubr's structure … was scarcely democratic, based as it was on a vertical management structure more akin to a military organization than to democratic procedures."[61] The Zubr Council, composed of regional coordinators and heads of functional departments, made key strategic decisions.

The main office of Zubr was divided into several departments based on their functions. The press department was responsible for media relations. The marketing department dealt with the design of Zubr's print material. The legal department offered legal aid for movement participants. The university department coordinated movement activities at universities, whereas the high

59 Author's interview with Aleh, Minsk, Belarus, March 15, 2008. 60 *Ibid.*

61 Shalayka, Alaksandar, and Siarhiej Mackievich. 2002. "The First Step: NGOs and the Presidential Election in Belarus." *Centers for Pluralism Newsletter*, Winter (5–7), p. 7.

school department worked with high school students. Another department was charged with the task of organizing a GOTV campaign.

Zubr sought to strengthen the security of its members by promoting the rule of 10. Each person was supposed to know no more than 10 Zubr members. Each regional (*oblast*) coordinator, for example, was supposed to know no more than 10 people at the district (*raion*) level. In turn, district-level coordinators were supposed to reveal their identities to a limited number of people. The rule of 10, however, clashed with dominant social norms and compromised the security of movement leaders. According to a Zubr member:

> People got used to having a leader. In the past, there used to be a tsar. Then – the secretary of the Central Committee [of the Communist Party]. Even after the completion of some tasks during a probationary period, people wanted to see a leader. They wanted to give the oath of allegiance to the movement's leader.[62]

Another internal factor undermining the movement's strength was a monetary distinction between the movement leadership and rank-and-file members. There were rumors that a small cadre of youth activists, including regional coordinators and heads of functional departments, were placed on the payroll. The regional coordinator allegedly received a monthly allowance of $100. This amount of money, albeit miniscule by Western standards, was equivalent to the average monthly wage in Belarus in 2001. Percolating rumors about payments to the movement's leaders weakened unity within the movement.

Tactics vis-à-vis Opponents

The use of nonviolent methods was Zubr's strategic decision. Zubr spokesperson Alyaksandar Atroshchankau explained why movement participants were committed to nonviolent resistance. "The non-violent struggle has proved its effectiveness. Weapon and violence are means of authorities, if we want to defeat them we should act in the other way."[63] Like Otpor, Zubr deployed such nonviolent methods as stickers, graffiti, and street performances, but their use was riddled with some tactical missteps.

The dissemination of stickers became a popular method of nonviolent resistance on the eve of the elections. Within the framework of the GOTV campaign, Zubr stickers prompted citizens to choose between existence in a repressive political regime and life in a democratic state. To illustrate this choice, each sticker contained two images. An image on the left side stood for Belarus under Lukashenka and an image on the right side symbolized democratic Belarus in the European community. One sticker, for example, contrasted dim

62 Author's interview with Aleh, Minsk, Belarus, March 15, 2008.

63 Quoted from Charter 97. 2004. "French Media about Zubr." July 14. http://charter97.org/eng/news/2004/07/14/zubr.

lights in a prison cell with the bright flames of the Olympic torch. Another sticker contained images of a nuclear mushroom cloud on the left and a mushroom in the forest on the right. The third sticker contrasted a typewriter on the left with a desktop computer on the right. It is safe to conclude, though, that an intended interpretation of these visual symbols depended on shared political knowledge and high cognitive skills. Zubr might have connected with a larger number of ordinary citizens by presenting its ideas in a less abstract way.

Another tactical misstep on the part of movement leadership was the public display of a condescending attitude toward the Lukashenka electorate. One of Zubr stickers, for example, contrasted a pig on the left with a bison on the right, implying that only individuals with limited intelligence and questionable morals could plausibly support the incumbent. In reality, a large segment of the population bestowed electoral support on the incumbent government in exchange for welfare benefits. An opinion poll conducted in August 2001 showed that Lukashenka's approval rating stood at 52 percent.[64] Specifically, Lukashenka was popular in rural areas, where almost 32 percent of the population resided.[65] Elderly village inhabitants appreciated the preservation of collective farms (*kolkhozes*) in the post-Soviet period. According to a 70-year-old villager from the Hrodna region:

> Lukashenka takes care of the people, to let them live. You know, without Lukashenka the *kolkhozes* here would be destroyed; there would be no order, the land would not be plowed, and the hunger would come. Instead, we have the *kolkhozes* and they provide, and they feed, and they house, and everything is done.[66]

Furthermore, there appeared to be a tension between adherence to professional standards and the cultivation of a positive public image. On the one hand, Zubr leadership sought to display professionalism in nonviolent action and produce high-quality material. "We wanted to show in particular young Belarusians that being in the opposition was not a sign of weakness," stated a Zubr member. "Resistance could be cool too."[67] On the other hand, the professional quality of print material raised sensitive questions about the sources of the movement's financing. An Otpor activist provided the following insight into the situation:

> When you create such an organization [as Zubr], you need to keep in mind that you operate in an impoverished country. When you print a sticker, use black and white for two reasons: first, it is cheaper, you will be able to print more material; second, it builds up the brand. When people look at these stickers, they need to be convinced that it was cheap to print them. But Zubr printed a small quantity of stickers on high-quality paper.

[64] Independent Institute of Socio-Economic and Political Studies. 2001. *IISEPS Newsletter*. September Issue. www.iiseps.org/arhiv.html.

[65] Edgeworth, Linda, Richard Messick, and Jan Zaprudnik. 1994. *Pre-Election Technical Assessment*. Washington, DC: International Foundation for Electoral Systems, p. 2.

[66] Quoted from Engelking, Anna. 2001. "The Mentality of Kolkhoz Inhabitants: Research Notes from the Grodno Region of Belarus." *International Journal of Sociology* 31(4): 64–78, p. 76.

[67] Author's interview with Uladzimir (via Skype), March 11, 2012.

This print material left the impression that it came from such an organization as BMW, not an opposition movement.[68]

Graffiti was a less costly method of nonviolent resistance. A few movement participants with a can of paint could cover a large quarter of public space with Zubr's slogans. Compared with Serbia, however, the municipal government appeared to be more efficient in Belarus. Most Zubr graffiti was quickly wiped out by the cleanup teams. For example, Zubr's graffiti spray painted along Lukashenka's car route was swiftly removed before the president's passage, so only a handful of youth activists and journalists could catch sight of it.[69] In addition, Zubr disregarded the public's prevalent opinion of graffiti as a form of vandalism, assuming that "the fences could put up with it [graffiti] in a country where the well-known people disappear."[70]

The organization of street performances was another common method of nonviolent resistance against the regime. Like Otpor, Zubr targeted the incumbent president and, for example, used the president's birthday as an occasion for street action. On August 30, youth activists brought to the presidential residence such gifts as "the Statue of Liberty with a Lukashenka-style moustache; a rust-covered toilet pan; a bus ticket from Minsk to Shklou [Lukashenka's hometown]; and boiled eggs each bearing the inscription "normal egg" [Lukashenka once promised to supply the nation with "normal eggs" during an egg supply crisis]."[71] However, only a handful of ordinary citizens had a chance to observe this act of nonviolent resistance.

Tactics vis-à-vis Allies

Zubr sought to propagate movement ideas in a heavily controlled media environment by cultivating contacts with independent newspapers and online publications. The youth movement regularly invited journalists to cover its street actions. Moreover, one of the largest nonstate newspapers, *Narodnaia Volia*, placed copies of Zubr's stickers on its front page. These media outlets, however, reached a relatively small fraction of the electorate due to the government's restrictions on the distribution of independent media. Independent newspapers, for example, were unavailable at state-run kiosks selling local press. As an alternative strategy, Zubr set up the movement's website and distributed its newsletters via the web.

68 Author's interview with an Otpor member, Novi Sad, Serbia, January 24, 2008.

69 Zubr. 2001. "Today Zubr Asked Lukashenko a Question: 'Where is Zakharenko? Where is Gonchar? Where is Krasovsky? Where is Zavadsky?'" www.zubr-belarus.com/english/index.php?show=oldnews/march_oldnews001.

70 Charter 97. 2002. "Kanferetsyia Charter 97: Na pytanni adkazvali lidary rukhu Zubr." January 22. www.charter97.org/conf.htm.

71 Radio Free Europe/Radio Liberty. 2001. "Youth Opposition Activists Deliver Birthday Presents to Lukashenka." *(Un)Civil Societies Report*. September 6. www.rferl.org/content/article/1347329.html.

The human rights organization Charter 97 reportedly played an instrumental role in establishing and supporting the youth movement. Malady Front leader Seviarynets openly stated in his book that civic activists associated with Charter 97 were behind the creation of the youth movement Zubr.[72] In support of his claim, several interviewed activists pointed out that one of the founders of Charter 97 – 38-year-old Dzmitry Bondarenka – had a strong influence on the development of Zubr tactics, and another person was primarily responsible for designing Zubr's campaign material. Furthermore, the website of Charter 97 provided regular coverage of Zubr's activities and repressive actions against movement participants. This close relationship between the NGO and the youth movement, albeit beneficial in many ways, might have undermined the movement's capacity to establish rapport with young people.

Another alarming phenomenon was an unhealthy dose of competition among youth organizations in opposition to the regime. Some youth activists, for example, were willing to distribute Zubr's material only on the condition of the movement's invisibility. Nonmembers would occasionally pick up Zubr's stickers and tear away parts of the print material with Zubr's logo and contact information to minimize the promotion of the rival youth organization.[73] In turn, some representatives of the NGO community claimed that Zubr rarely coordinated its activities with other challenger organizations.[74] A Zubr activist provided the following perspective into this issue:

> Some organizations in Belarus disliked Zubr because we were so active. They complained to donor organizations that hardly anything could be done under such repressive political conditions. And we showed them what could be done.[75]

Zubr distanced itself from opposition political parties in the public eye. Any sort of cooperation between the youth movement and opposition political parties was strained by the fact that the party bosses "did not see Zubr as an equal partner."[76] Unlike Otpor, however, Zubr did not launch a large-scale public campaign to shame opposition political parties for lack of unity in the face of a common enemy. Instead, Malady Front addressed the old opposition with the slogan "*Khopits tarmazits*" ("Enough of Pushing on the Brakes"), urging them to nominate a presidential contender from the united opposition. The opposition politicians agreed on a single candidate from the opposition only a few weeks prior to the 2001 election. But it was not only the timing of this decision but also the choice of the presidential contender that damaged the GOTV campaigns of antiregime youth movements. The political opposition settled for the candidacy of 62-year-old Hancharyk, pressuring a more popular

72 Seviarynets, Paval. 2002. *Pakalennia Maladoga Frontu*, p. 52.
73 Author's interview with Aleh, Minsk, Belarus, March 2008.
74 Shalayka, Alaksandar, and Siarhiej Mackievich. 2002. "The First Step: NGOs and the Presidential Election in Belarus," p. 7.
75 Author's interview with Aleh, Minsk, Belarus, March 2008.
76 Author's interview with Alexei (vias Skype), January 25, 2013.

presidential contender, 51-year-old Domash, to withdraw from the race. Under these circumstances, Zubr faced the challenge of convincing youth to vote for an old, uncharismatic leader of a trade union.

Moreover, Zubr activists faced difficulty establishing a dialogue with the security apparatus. Like Otpor, Zubr used young women as messengers of movement ideas. Female activists, for example, went to police stations to present officers with copies of a book about Belarusian history, challenging a state-sanctioned version of Belarusian history and describing people's long-standing struggle for independence and democracy. Yet most police officers appeared to be immune to antiregime messages. In particular, OMON officers[77] were hostile to movement ideas:

> It was possible to have a conversation with policemen. But OMON officers refused to engage in a dialogue with us. They were so well-trained from the ideological perspective that they refused to accept anything else [that deviated from the official line].[78]

Finally, the youth movement secured some financial support from external actors. Compared with Malady Front, Zubr appeared to attract a larger amount of financial assistance from Western donors during the 2001 presidential election.[79] In addition, some local entrepreneurs sympathetic with the movement's cause offered in-kind support. For example, Dzmitry Borodko, Zubr coordinator in the city of Borisov, secured the backing of local businessmen:

> I don't know where the central office gets it [money]. I can only say where we get it. There are a lot of patriots in Borisov. They can't wear the T-shirts because their businesses would be dead. The T-shirts, stickers, and computers we get from the central office. The rest we get here.[80]

In sum, Zubr adopted a number of Otpor's tactics. The Belarusian youth movement organized a negative campaign targeting the incumbent president and a GOTV campaign to boost youth voter turnout on the eve of the 2001 presidential election. Yet movement leadership made a few tactical missteps that undermined the movement's capacity to mobilize a larger number of citizens. Furthermore, Zubr faced a popular incumbent who commanded considerable public support and pursued a variety of countermovement tactics.

77 OMON is a Russian acronym for *Otriad militsii osobogo naznachenia*, or "special purpose police unit."

78 Author's interview with Iryna, Minsk, Belarus, March 12, 2008.

79 On this point, see Wilson, Andrew. 2011. *Belarus: The Last Dictatorship in Europe*. New Haven, CT: Yale University Press, pp. 195, 215.

80 Wines, Michael. 2001. "Street Theater and Graffiti: Belarus Dissidents Make News by Making Noise." *New York Times*. August 19. www.nytimes.com/2001/08/19/world/street-theater-and-graffiti-belarus-dissidents-make-news-by-making-noise.html?pagewanted=all&src=pm.

STATE COUNTERMOVES

The government of Belarus adopted a wide range of tactics to decimate the youth movements in opposition to the regime. First, state-controlled media framed challenger organizations as puppets in a Western conspiracy against Belarus. Second, the government limited the movement's access to resources through state control of the educational system and legal constraints on political participation. Third, the coercive apparatus deployed overt repression against regime opponents. Finally, the government provided support for pro-regime youth organizations.

The state-controlled media demonized Zubr as a pawn in the geopolitical struggle for Belarus's resources. On September 5, 2001, less than a week before election day, most Belarusian households received a special issue of the state-run newspaper *Soviet Belarus*. A two-page article in this special issue exposed the alleged CIA operation under the code name "The White Stork."[81] Based on an analytical report allegedly prepared by the Moscow-based Center "Independent Political Expertise," *Soviet Belarus* claimed that the US government aimed to topple Belarus's constitutional order. To convince the electorate, the article supplied numerous examples of Western intervention in Belarusian politics and made references to Malady Front, Otpor, and Zubr. The newspaper, for example, reported that the IRI provided funding for participation of 120 young Belarusians in a workshop in Lithuania. *Soviet Belarus* also warned its readers that radical youth masterminded the deployment of extremist tactics to overthrow the incumbent government in the post-election period.

Another idea propagated by the state-controlled media was that challenger organizations were on the US payroll. *Soviet Belarus*, for example, claimed that opposition forces annually received between 5 and 7 million dollars in Western funding.[82] Likewise, the documentary *Zakulisy* (Behind the Scenes) produced by Azarenok allegedly traced financial connections between the Belarusian opposition and Western governments. These allegations undermined the legitimacy of challenger organizations in Belarusian society. In response, Zubr leaders advised movement participants to make claims about the movement's funding by Belarusians inside and outside the country.[83] Compared with Otpor, however, Zubr's response to a smear campaign appeared to be less persuasive.

The borrowing of the opposition's creative ideas was another state countermove. To confuse the electorate, Lukashenka's election campaign team borrowed Zubr's approach to the design of print material. One of Lukashenka's posters had the slogan "*Vremia vybora*" ("It's Time to Make a Choice") and the tagline "It is a crucial choice: escalation of hatred leading to poverty and refugees or happy childhood in a good country." Imitating Zubr's material, the poster was divided into two parts. To the left, there was a picture

[81] *Soviet Belarus*. 2001. "Operatsiia Belyi Aist – Inostrannye spetssluzby protiv Belorusi." September 5, pp. 2–3.

[82] *Ibid*. [83] On this point, see "Tsikl raboty s aktivistami."

of a begging woman with poorly clad children in the street. To the right, there was an image of smiling children in school uniforms. In part, the poster alluded to the NATO bombing of Belgrade and socioeconomic instability in Serbia. Voters were brought to the belief that only Lukashenka would prevent the repeat of this scenario in Belarus.

To deprive the opposition of symbolic resources, the government banned pre-Soviet symbols of statehood and launched an attack on Belarusian culture. Article 167 of the Administrative Code of the Republic of Belarus stipulated that the use of unsanctioned symbols, including the white-red-and-white flag and the old coat of arms (*Pahonia*), entailed administrative punishment ranging from administrative warning to a 15-day imprisonment.[84] Instead, the president restored Soviet-era state symbols. Furthermore, the government systematically inhibited use of the Belarusian language in the public sphere. In consonance with Lukashenka's assertion that "it's impossible to express anything great in Belarusian,"[85] the 1995 referendum made Russian the second official language in the country. In subsequent years, the government favored the predominant use of the Russian language in the public sector. The percentage of first graders taught in Belarusian dropped from 60 percent in 1994 to 18 percent in 1996.[86] Likewise, the share of all secondary school students who obtained an education in Belarusian declined from 58 percent in 1994 to 4 percent in 2000 in Minsk.[87] This steep decline in Belarusian-language instruction was in part achieved through the harassment and closure of regime-threatening educational institutions. Belarusian Humanities Lyceum, for example, regularly came under political pressure and eventually closed down in 2003.[88] This state-sponsored assault on Belarusian culture derived from the government's fear that the revival of national culture would provide a basis for citizens' rejection of Soviet-style methods of social control and prompt demands for greater respect of political rights and civil liberties. As noted by the Belarusian journalist Andrey Dynko, the government opposed the idea of Belarusian nationalism because it was "a kind of political nationalism that creates civic society in Belarus, that molds people into citizens."[89]

[84] For details, see the Administrative Code of the Republic of Belarus (originally adopted on 6 December 1984). Retrieved from www.levonevski.net/pravo/razdelb/text86/page11.html

[85] Quoted from Radio Free Europe/Radio Liberty. 2007. "Lukashenko – Father of the Nation or Loudmouthed Autocrat?" *Newsline*. February 8. www.rferl.org/content/article/1143808.html.

[86] Karbalevich, Valerii. 2001. "The Belarusian Model of Transformation: Alaksandr Lukashenka's Regime and the Nostalgia for the Soviet Past." *International Journal of Sociology* 31(4): 7–38, p. 16.

[87] Retrieved from the website of Society of the Belarusian Language. http://tbm.org.by/tbm_old/bel/stats_edu.html.

[88] Finn, Peter. 2004. "School of 'Partisans' Goes Underground in Belarus." *Washington Post*. October 17. www.washingtonpost.com/ac2/wp-dyn/A38755-2004Oct16.

[89] On the distinction between "Belarusian nationalism" and "Soviet Belarusian nationalism," see Maksymiuk, January 2003. "Soviet Nationalism as Lukashenka's Strategy of Survival." Radio Free Europe/Radio Liberty. December 9. www.rferl.org/content/article/1344055.html.

In reaction to student activism, the government of Belarus toughened control over the university system. In the aftermath of student engagement in antigovernment protests in 1996, the Ministry of Education amended the regulations for the transfer, reinstatement, and expulsion of university students.[90] The formal reasons for expulsion – "the systematic violation of educational discipline and the internal rules of the institute of higher education"[91] – were widely used to uproot regime-threatening student activism. Moreover, the university administration retained the Soviet-era practice of public shaming for engagement in unacceptable social behavior. Malady Front activist Maksim, for example, recalled how the deans at the Belarusian State Academy of Arts reacted to his participation in a street action on Freedom Day:

> The Academy held the so-called comrade's trial [*tovarishcheskii sud*] in my absence. I was not even informed about it, I found out about it later on from fellow students. At the meeting, the speakers repeatedly stated that "our student took morally unjustifiable action." And my absence was framed as "the inability to take responsibility for one's action." The students were divided. Some stealthily approached me and shook my hand. Others labeled me a fascist.[92]

More broadly, the legal environment obstructed unsanctioned forms of civic activism. The decree of January 1999 initiated the reregistration of all NGOs, opening the door for the closure of challenger organizations and harassment of youth activists. Given the denial of state registration for regime-threatening youth movements, any action by movement participants fell under Article 167 of the Administrative Code, prescribing administrative responsibility for acting on behalf of an unregistered organization. In addition, the legal system raised the costs of using certain protest tactics. As mentioned earlier, a presidential decree banned the use of masks in the wake of a Zubr's street performance.[93] By the same token, Article 341 of the Criminal Code penalized "vandalism of public buildings through graffiti of cynical content."

This legal environment enabled the security apparatus to harass and detain youth activists. At least 350 individuals were detained for spray painting graffiti in Minsk from May to August 2001.[94] Zubr members were also routinely arrested for the distribution of print material and participation in street performances. The inhumane treatment of detainees was another common type of state repression. Notably, the KGB of Belarus retained its Soviet-era name and deployed communist methods of social control. As in the Soviet

90 Ministry of Education of the Republic of Belarus, Decree No. 146, March 14, 1997. http://pravo.levonevsky.org/bazaby/org348/basic/text0676.htm.

91 Human Rights Watch. 1999. "Republic of Belarus: Violations of Academic Freedom."

92 Author's interview with Maksim, Kyiv, Ukraine, May 22, 2010.

93 Charter 97. 2001. "Lukashenko Bans Rallying in Masks." May 8. http://charter97.org/eng/news/2001/05/08/06.

94 Viasna Human Rights Center. 2002. *Obzor-Khronika narushenii prav cheloveka v Belarusi v 2001 godu*, p. 179.

times, the use of informants was a common state tactic against challenger organizations. Youth activists were subject to enormous pressure to collaborate with the regime. In December 2001, Zubr member Andrei Zaitsau allegedly committed suicide after the KGB's attempts to recruit him as an informant.

In response, Zubr tried to generate public outrage over state repression. The youth movement publicized information about the incidence of repression against movement participants. Zubr also designed a sticker with the slogan "Hands Off Our Children" and an image of the incumbent president whose hand looked broken after reaching for a little child. But this image did not resonate with Belarusians as strongly as the image of a beaten Otpor activist in Serbia a year ago. Another tactic borrowed from Otpor was the introduction of a rapid-response system to react to the detention of movement participants. The Belarusian police, however, were less inclined than their Serbian counterparts to release information about detainees or allow the entry of lawyers and journalists into police stations. Overall, Zubr was unable to generate a large-scale backlash against the incumbent government.

State Support for Pro-Regime Youth Organizations

The government of Belarus began to pay more attention to youth issues in the aftermath of antigovernment protests in spring 1996. In summer 1996, Lukashenka held a meeting with leaders of various youth organizations to secure their support for the political regime, but most youth leaders declined to collaborate with the government.[95] For example, the Belarus Youth Union (*Belarusskii soiuz molodezhi* [BSM]) confronted state authorities in a legal dispute over Komsomol property.[96] In these circumstances, the government of Belarus decided to confer its support on another newly formed youth organization.

The pro-regime youth organization Belarusian Patriotic Youth Union (*Belarusskii patrioticheskii soiuz molodezhi* [BPSM]) was set up in 1996 based on the youth organization *Priamoe Deistvie* ("Direct Action"), whose name was synonymous with the French terrorist group *Action Directe*.[97] Direct

[95] Michalevic, Ales. 1998. "A Short History of Youth Organizations in Belarus." In *Belarus: The Third Sector*, ed. Pawel Kazanecki. Warsaw, Poland: Institute for Democracy in Eastern Europe, pp. 40–44, p. 43.

[96] The Union of Belarusian Youth (*Soiuz molodezhi Belarusii*) was formed in December 1991 and renamed into the Belarus Youth Union (*Belarusskii soiuz molodezhi* [BSM]) in February 1995. BSM boasted membership of 22,000 people and used Komsomol property as a source of revenue. BSM leaders declared electoral support for Lukashenka in August 2001, but they did not organize a GOTV campaign in support of the incumbent president. See *NavinyBy*. 2001. "Belorusskii souiz molodezhi prizyvaet podderzhat na vyborakh kandidaturu Aleksandra Lukashenko." August 27. http://naviny.by/pda/material/?type=news&id=348068.

[97] Human Rights Watch. 1999. *Republic of Belarus: Violations of Academic Freedom*. Retrieved from www.hrw.org/reports/1999/belarus/Belrus99-06.htm#TopOfPage; Shpak, N. S., et al. 2004. *Molodezh Belorusi na sovremennom etape: Sostoianie, problemy i puti ikh reshenia*. Minsk: Independent Institute of Socio-Economic and Political Studies, p. 67.

Action advocated the use of violence against political opponents and was allegedly responsible for physical attacks on several civic activists in Belarus. In its pamphlet, *Why Are All Normal Youth Now Joining Direct Action?*, Direct Action declared the pursuit of three goals: "not to allow our own to be harmed, defend the interests of youth, and suppress opponents ruthlessly."[98] Specifically, the youth organization claimed that it did "not fear the ridiculous opposition, which lives on gifts from Western funds." Though the self-proclaimed goal of BPSM was the promotion of patriotism among the young generation, the youth organization clearly sought to mobilize youth in favor of the current regime. BPSM was dubbed the Lukamol in Belarusian society due to its overt support for Lukashenka.[99]

In turn, the government provided backing for the regime-friendly youth organization. The presidential decree of July 1997 declared government support for BPSM as "one of the priorities of state youth policy."[100] Though the Law on Education banned the presence of political parties on university grounds, BPSM freely set up branches at each university and placed its representatives on admissions committees. To boost the organization's appeal, the government delegated BPSM control over the youth radio station 101.2 previously closed down for the coverage of antigovernment protests and the promotion of Belarusian culture. Furthermore, BPSM membership was viewed as an instrument for career advancement in the public sector. BPSM leaders concurrently held positions in the municipal government (*ispolkom*). As a result of government backing, BPSM set up 170 branches nationwide, with a membership of 250,000 people in 2001.[101]

BPSM actively campaigned in support of the incumbent president during the 2001 election. As a political gesture, BPSM appealed to Lukashenka to run for the presidency and promised to collect signatures in support of his registration application. BPSM leader Usevalad Yanchewski stated that Lukashenka should stay in power because "in world politics he is a unique president who has followed his [electoral] program for all seven years."[102] To boost youth support for the incumbent president, BPSM launched a public campaign titled "*Ia za batku!* " ("I Am for the Daddy!"). Specifically, BPSM announced the formation of agitation groups involving a total of 20,000 people. Imitating

98 Human Rights Watch. 1997. *Republic of Belarus: Crushing Civil Society.* Retrieved from www.hrw.org/reports/1997/belarus/Belarus.htm#P83_2082.

99 The word "Lukamol" combines the first four letters of Lukashenka's last name and the last three letters of the Soviet-era youth organization Komsomol.

100 Decree of the President of the Republic of Belarus No. 380. "O gosudarstvennoi podderzhke Belorusskogo Patrioticheskogo Soiuza Molodezhi" [On state support for Belarusian Patriotic Youth Union]. July 9, 1997.

101 Raskolnikov, Rodion. 2001b. "Nabliudat za nabliudateliami: BPSM nashel sebe novoe zaniatie." *BelGazeta.* August 13. www.belgazeta.by/20010813.31/020080670/.

102 Quoted from Raskolnikov, Rodion. 2001a. "Vpered "Batki" v peklo." *BelGazeta.* June 18. www.belgazeta.by/20010618.24/020030672.

Zubr tactics, BPSM spray painted graffiti, distributed stickers, and organized concerts in support of the incumbent president. As an alternative to Belarusian-language rock concerts, BPSM organized free pop concerts for young people. In response to civic initiatives aimed at implementing an independent observation of the electoral process, BPSM promised to dispatch a total of 25,000 BPSM representatives, covering each polling station. Appropriating the opposition's discourse, Yuri Solovjov, Yanchewski's successor, stated, "The election monitoring should not be monopolized by the opposition that seeks to use monitoring for the falsification of results and the deceit of society."[103] Though Solovjov asserted in an interview with local journalists that BPSM carried out the GOTV campaign "without using a single penny from the state budget,"[104] the youth organization reportedly received $600,000 from the State Youth Affairs Committee to "boost patriotism" among Belarusian youth on the eve of the election.[105]

In addition to campaigning for the incumbent president, BPSM acted against regime opponents. At a press conference, Solovjov acknowledged that some BPSM activists might have removed Zubr's "filth" (graffiti) from public places.[106] Furthermore, BPSM was allegedly responsible for an attack on Nadezhda Zhukova, observer for the human rights organization Belarusian Helsinki Committee. The attackers introduced themselves as "young Belarusian patriots" and threatened her with further violence if she continued her human rights work in defense of Malady Front activists.[107]

On top, the government of Belarus allegedly backed the Belarus branch of the Russian National Unity Party (*Russkoe natsionalnoe edinstvo* [RNE]). For the propagation of neofascist ideas, RNE was banned in Moscow and found refuge in Belarus. Like the Red Guards in the People's Republic of China, RNE acted as a youth gang that assaulted regime opponents. In February 1999, for example, RNE members attacked Andrei Sannikau, leader of Charter 97 and organizer of the Congress of Democratic Forces, resulting in his hospitalization with three broken ribs and a broken nose.[108] Likewise, RNE members were allegedly responsible for violent attacks on Krai activists who opposed the current

[103] *NavinyBy*. 2001. "TsK BPSM budet prosit Lukashenko ballotirovatsia na post prezidenta." June 13. http://naviny.by/pda/material/?type=news&id=348675.

[104] Agency of Financial News. 2001. "BPSM budet agitirovat za Lukashenko s pomoshchjiu letuchikh piketov i obkhoda kvartir." August 20. http://afn.by/news/i/10715.

[105] Cole, Victor, ed. 2001. "Lukamol Gets Government Funding." In *Belarus Update*. New York: International League for Human Rights. Retrieved from www.ilhr.org/ilhr/regional/belarus/updates/2001/05.html.

[106] Raskolnikov, Rodion. 2001b. "Nabliudat za nabliudateliami: BPSM nashel sebe novoe zaniatie." *BelGazeta*. August 13.

[107] Amnesty International. 1997. "Belarus: Fear of Safety: Nadezhda Zhukova, Human Rights Defender." www.amnesty.org/en/library/asset/EUR49/015/1997/en/414ff2b3-e98a-11dd-8224-a709898295f2/eur490151997en.html.

[108] Hearing before the Commission on Security and Cooperation in Europe "Belarus – Back to the USSR?" April 27, 1999. P. 34. www.hose.gov/csce.

regime. The state-controlled media framed it as a scuffle between two youth gangs omitting any reference to intragroup political differences.

THE FAILED REVOLUTION

The outcome of the 2001 election was the reelection of the incumbent president. According to the official results released by the Central Election Commission, Lukashenka won 75.7 percent of the vote, while Hancharyk received 15.7 percent of the vote.[109] Shortly after the closure of polling stations, Lukashenka appeared on national TV and announced his "elegant victory."[110] In contrast, Hancharyk argued that the incumbent president failed to pass a 50 percent threshold, necessitating a run-off.[111] Based on the results of parallel vote tabulation, Hancharyk claimed 40 percent of the popular vote.

Emulating the Serbian example, the Belarusian opposition attempted to challenge the official election results through post-election protests. Despite heavy rain on election night, approximately 5,000 people turned to the street to demand a vote recount.[112] Zubr activists called for a permanent occupation of the city square and barricaded themselves inside Hancharyk's headquarters. Yet Hancharyk himself was unprepared to lead a post-election protest campaign.[113] The presidential candidate urged the protesters to disperse on September 9. The following day, Hancharyk did not show up at the protest site at all. Given the conspicuous absence of the presidential candidate, 80 Zubr activists who barricaded themselves inside Hancharyk's headquarters had to terminate their occupation of the building. Compared with the social turmoil in Serbia, these protest events captured little attention in the international community. The 9/11 terrorist attack on US soil further distracted the world's attention from local demands for the annulment of fraudulent election results.

On conclusion of the 2001 election, Zubr continued to wage nonviolent resistance against the regime. Zubr activists organized a large number of protest events from 2001 to 2006,[114] but Zubr formally self-dissolved in

[109] OSCE. 2001. *Republic of Belarus Presidential Elections (9 September 2001): OSCE/ODIHR Limited Election Observation Mission Final Report*. October 4. Warsaw: Office for Democratic Institutions and Human Rights, p. 26.

[110] *USA Today*. 2001. "Lukashenko Claims Victory in Belarus Election." September 10. www.usatoday.com/news/world/2001/09/09/belarus.htm.

[111] Birch, Douglas. 2001. "Belarus President Claims Victory in Vote, but Rival Alleges Fraud." *Baltimore Sun*. September 10. http://articles.baltimoresun.com/2001-09-10/news/0109100137_1_lukashenko-belarus-minsk.

[112] Charter 97. 2001. "Chronicle of Events." September 9. http://charter97.org/eng/news/2001/09/09.

[113] On this point, see, for example, Dashkevich, Dmitry. 2010. "Ne dozhidaias starosti." *PolitForums*. April 19. www.politforums.ru/belorussia/1253543827_2.html; Zelenkova, Anastasia. 2010. "Oppositsiia nachala bitvu za 'edinogo.'" *Belaruskaia Gazeta*. May 6. www.gazetaby.com/index.php?sn_nid=28524&sn_cat=32.

[114] For a summary of movement activities, visit the website of Zubr, www.zubr-belarus.com.

spring 2006.[115] By the time of the 2006 presidential election, Zubr turned into an "old, exhausted animal."[116] A slew of repressive methods, along with infiltration by government agents, put a heavy strain on the youth movement. Many Zubr members were driven out of the country and sought political asylum abroad. Some expelled youth activists, for example, continued their education at Polish universities thanks to the Polish government-funded Konstanty Kalinowski Scholarship Program. Still, some Zubr activists became engaged in new civic initiatives to erode the strength of the current regime.

Given youth's lukewarm support for Lukashenka, the effectiveness of BPSM agitation came into question. According to some reports, the government cut funding for the youth organization in the wake of the 2001 election.[117] Instead, a new youth organization – Belarusian Republican Youth Union (*Beloruskii respublikanskii souiz molodezhi* [BRSM]) – was formed through the merger of BSM and BPSM in 2002. To date, BRSM fulfills the role of Lukamol in domestic politics and campaigns in support of the incumbent. Since Lukashenka has been in office for more than two decades, "a young generation of people who have grown up in Belarus does not remember anything except Lukashenka's regime."[118]

CONCLUSION

This chapter examined tactical interactions between a challenger organization and the incumbent government during the 2001 presidential election in Belarus. Within a few months of Milosevic's downfall, youth activists formed the social movement Zubr and modeled it on Otpor. Movement participants, however, committed a few tactical missteps. Zubr leadership, for example, might have been more discreet about its use of resources and more outspoken about its alleged ties with the international donor community to burnish its public image. Compared with Otpor, Zubr generated a smaller-scale public backlash against the regime. On top, the state of the national economy diminished the odds of a popular uprising. Public opinion data indicated that the plurality of the electorate were willing to back the incumbent in exchange for socioeconomic stability.[119] Had the national economy been in worse shape in Belarus in the early 2000s, the political opposition would have stood a better chance of winning over Lukashenka's electorate.

115 Zubr. 2006. "Belarus' Zubr Dissolves to Join a Wider Pro-Democracy Movement in the Future." May 5. www.zubr-belarus.com/english/index.php?show=news512.

116 Author's interview with Iryna, Minsk, Belarus, March 12, 2008.

117 Andreeva, Ekaterina. 2005. "Za batku. Epizod vtoroi." *EuraMost*. October 11. www.euramost.org/?artc=3783; Martinovich, Viktor. 2002. "Ia za batku. Teper besplatno." *BelGazeta*. April 15. www.belgazeta.by/20020415.15/290110142.

118 Author's interview with Alexei (via Skype), January 25, 2013.

119 On the results of public opinion polls in Belarus, visit the online archive of the Independent Institute of Socio-Economic and Political Studies, www.iiseps.org/arhiv.html.

Furthermore, the incumbent's tactics affected the level of youth engagement in civil resistance. President Lukashenka drew lessons from Milosevic's defeat and introduced a wide range of countermoves to prevent a repeat of the Yugoslav scenario. The government of Belarus quickly reacted to any manifestation of dissent, inhibited the cross-national diffusion of ideas, and supported the establishment of regime-friendly youth organizations. Meanwhile, the president courted the electorate by championing populist policies. Overall, the incumbent's popularity reduced the likelihood of mass mobilization against the regime.

The case of the Belarusian youth movement shows both the importance and the limits of innovative tactics in a repressive political environment. On the one hand, the use of savvier protest tactics might have increased the level of mass mobilization against the regime. A better-executed outreach to Lukashenka's electorate, for example, might have increased popular support for the youth movement. On the other hand, the degree of the movement's success, measured as the level of civil resistance, was severely constrained by unfavorable structural conditions. The government's provision of Soviet-style welfare benefits undermined the movement's call for a turnover of power. The case of Zubr also demonstrates how the performance of the youth movement depends, to some extent, on the behavior of the old opposition. The opposition political parties in Belarus settled for a much less charismatic leader from the opposition than their counterparts in Serbia, Georgia, or Ukraine, thwarting Zubr's push for political change.

6

Kmara! Enough of Corruption and Poverty in Georgia

On April 14, 2003, approximately 500 university students marched from Tbilisi State University (TSU) to the presidential administration chanting the slogan "*Kmara*," which means "enough" in Georgian.[1] Once young people reached the chancellery, they burned the red flags of the Georgian Soviet Socialist Republic embellished with the Soviet-style images of the country's political leaders. Through such provocative street action, youth activists delivered their demand for genuine political change in the country ruled by former communist apparatchiks. The date of this protest march harkened back to memories of another protest event held in Tbilisi on April 14, 1978. Back then, university students protested against a revision of the republic's constitution abolishing the status of Georgian as the sole state language.[2] What remained unchanged since the Soviet times was that students confronted the same politician – Shevardnadze – as their main opponent. In 1978, Shevardnadze yielded to public pressure and renegotiated with the Moscow-based party bosses the retention of Georgian as the sole state language. Since 1990, April 14 has been designated in Georgia as the Day of the Georgian Language, celebrating the country's rich cultural heritage and honoring the popular resistance to the Soviet oppression.[3] Now youth activists aspired to bring about more drastic reforms and oust the incumbent president from office.

1 Kandelaki, Giorgi. 2006. "Georgia's Rose Revolution: A Participant's Perspective." *USIP Special Report 167*. Washington, DC: United States Institute of Peace, p. 6.

2 Bigg, Claire. 2008. "Georgia: Tbilisi Marks 30th Anniversary of Language Protests." Radio Free Europe/Radio Liberty. April 14. www.rferl.org/content/article/1109567.html; Rayfield, Donald. 2012. *Edge of Empires: A History of Georgia*. London: Reaktion Books, p. 376.

3 See, for example, Jamestown Foundation. 1998. "Language Day Celebration Highlights Shevardnadze's Role." *Monitor*. April 16. https://jamestown.org/program/language-day-celebration-highlights-shevardnadzes-role/; Megeneishvili, Tatia. 2016. "Georgia Celebrates Language Day." *The Messenger*. April 15. www.messenger.com.ge/issues/3608_april_15_2016/3608_tatia.html.

In turn, the incumbent dismissed the importance of the nascent youth movement. In media interviews, President Shevardnadze revealed his irritation with Kmara's action, but state authorities treated youthful regime opponents as hooligans rather than terrorists. The local police hardly ever detained youth activists for their political action. Moreover, the Georgian government did not systematically inhibit the cross-national diffusion of ideas or invest resources into creating a regime-friendly youth organization.

This chapter explains the relatively high level of youth mobilization in favor of political change by examining the interplay between the youth movement and the incumbent government. The chapter begins with an overview of protests and repression in the former Soviet republic. Next, the chapter traces the cross-national diffusion of nonviolent methods in the region. The remainder of the chapter is devoted to an analysis of movement tactics and state countermoves.

PROTESTS AND REPRESSION IN POST-SOVIET GEORGIA

State-society relations in post-Soviet Georgia were affected by the civil war that ravaged the country in the 1990s. The consensus was that the nation should make every effort to prevent another outbreak of violence against coethnics. Against this backdrop, Shevardnadze's tenure was spared of large-scale antigovernment protests. In particular, Georgia lacked a history of post-election protests. At the start of Shevardnadze's second presidential term, however, some Georgians turned to the street to defend press freedom. Moreover, a group of students organized a public campaign to push for institutional change at TSU. Participants in these two protest campaigns later assumed leadership roles in the youth movement Kmara.

2001 Protests in Support of Rustavi-2

The TV channel Rustavi-2 established itself as an outspoken critic of the incumbent government. The TV program "60 Minutes," for example, exposed cases of high-level corruption in the country. In particular, Rustavi-2 journalists investigated opaque business deals involving the Minister of Interior Kakha Targamadze.[4] An investigative report on the TV show "The Night Courier" suggested that Targamadze might be involved in drug trafficking.[5]

For its exposure of corruption in the high echelons of power, Rustavi-2 was repeatedly a target of state repression. Political pressure on the broadcasting

[4] Loria, Ephemia, and Levan Gegeshidze. 2006. "Georgia Cautiously Hopes for Better Times." *Insight: Post-Soviet Armies Newsletter*. http://psan.hypotheses.org/insight/insight-archives-2001–2006.

[5] Steavenson, Wendell. 2001. "Letter from Tbilisi: Protests Are Forcing Change in Georgia's Government, but the People Want More." *Johnson's Russia List*. December 3. www.russialist.org/archives/5566–11.php.

company reached a high point in 2001. It was widely upheld that the Rustavi-2 journalist Giorgi Sinaia was murdered for his professional activity in July 2001. Several staff members also received death threats in October 2001.[6] Furthermore, the broadcasting company faced the threat of closure in the fall of 2001. The company's Tbilisi office was raided by law enforcement agents in an alleged attempt to investigate the incidence of tax evasion and seize its financial records. Journalists broadcast live the police raid on the station, causing public outrage against the incumbent government.

The government's attack on Rustavi-2 spurred citizens to action. Protesters gathered in front of the national parliament on October 30, 2001, and the size of the protest rally grew in the next two days. Between 5,000 and 10,000 people participated in a protest event on November 1, 2001. Many of them were students.[7] "They were so against the government that the attack against Rustavi 2 was the last straw that forced them to go into the streets," said Nika Tabatadze, the station's chief executive. "It's almost like Yugoslavia after Milosevic."[8] This protest campaign also bore resemblance to the Ukraine without Kuchma Movement formed in the winter of 2001. Following the example of Ukrainian protesters, Georgian youth carried posters with the slogan "Georgia without Shevardnadze."

To appease protesters, Shevardnadze fired his cabinet of ministers. But his action did not signify genuine turnover of power. Targamadze was replaced with another party loyalist, Koba Narchemashvili. Furthermore, Shevardnadze declared that he would not step down. The political standoff led to the emergence of new factions in the national parliament and more forceful vocalization of demands for institutional change. Most participants in this protest campaign felt that the resignation of the incumbent president and the introduction of institutional reforms were necessary to propel democratization processes in the country.

Anti-Corruption Campaign at TSU

Lack of institutional reforms and proliferation of corruption crippled TSU, one of the most prestigious and largest national universities in the country, with a student population of over 20,000. Bribery was an endemic problem at the university. According to some estimates, admission to the TSU Law School cost between $15,000 and $20,000 in a bribe.[9] These illicit revenues were pocketed

[6] Internews. 2001. "Victory for Independent Media in the Former Soviet Republic of Georgia." November 5. www.internews.org/news/2001/110201_georgia/110201_georgia.htm.

[7] *Civil Georgia*. 2001. "Protests Widen as More Students Hit the Street." October 31. www.civil.ge/eng/article.php?id=543.

[8] Quoted from Baker, Peter. 2001. "Georgian Political Crisis Sparked by Raid on Independent TV." *Washington Post*. November 1.

[9] There was a quota for tuition-free admission to the university, but the university administration extracted bribes from applicants to get admitted to such a program. For an overview of corrupt

by the university administration, while paltry funding was available for development of the university infrastructure. Some TSU students saw the rector, Roin Metreveli, as a major obstacle to institutional change. Metreveli had held the post since 1992, showing no intent to step down at the end of his second term. With the support of a special presidential decree, he unilaterally amended the university's statute so that he could run for a third term in office. Overall, Metreveli ruled in the so-called white temple, neglecting students' needs and violating their rights.

A group of TSU students attempted to counteract Metreveli's management style by establishing an independent student government. It all began with a couple of female undergraduate students inquiring about the university's statute:

> My friend and I were second-year students in the Department of International Law at TSU when we began to question how things were done at the university. In 1999 we had a CEP [Civic Education Project] Lecturer. A professor from Germany taught us comparative politics. He did not teach us anything about student self-government, but he spoke about democracy and autonomy. So we decided to find out what was written in the Constitution of the University and how student rights were defined. We went to various departments, and everywhere we were referred to another place. In the long run, we went to 15 different departments, and we couldn't find the text of the University's Constitution anywhere. We also went to the student union, and they could not help us either. Shortly afterwards, our rector held a public meeting with students. Various NGO representatives also came to this public event. And I stood up and asked the rector where the University's Constitution was kept and how students could find out about their rights ... Soon a group of like-minded students emerged, and we came regularly to the Liberty Institute and discussed various ideas. We decided to set up an independent student government as a structure parallel to the official student union.[10]

The student government was envisioned as a counterweight to the student union controlled by the university administration, so it was met with the rector's resistance.[11] The deans conducted so-called informal conversations with reform-minded students, threatening them with low grades and expulsion from the university. Furthermore, the student union deliberately scheduled its own election for April 25, 2001, one day prior to the election of the independent student government, to cause confusion among students. Nonetheless, most students backed up the establishment of the student government and voted in the election on April 26.

practices in the university sector, see Orkodashvili, Mariam. 2010. "Corruption in Higher Education: Causes, Consequences, Reforms – The Case of Georgia." MPRA Paper No. 27679. http://mpra.ub.uni-muenchen.de/27679/.

10 Author's interview with Nini Gogiberidze, Tbilisi, Georgia, February 14, 2008.

11 Devdariani, Jaba. 2001. "Running in Place: Tbilisi State University Is Proud of Its Traditions, but the Students Are Demanding an Outlook toward the Future, not the Past." *Transitions Online*. July 25. www.tol.cz/look/TOLrus/article.tpl?IdLanguage=1&IdPublication=4&NrIssue=24&NrSection=3&NrArticle=1695.

The rector's election, held on April 21, 2003, was seen as another critical step toward bringing about reforms at TSU. According to the university's statute, the University Council was responsible for electing a rector. But the electoral outcome seemed to be predetermined. Only the incumbent rector was running for office. Members of the University Council were appointed by the rector. Furthermore, the Council's deliberations occurred in a nontransparent manner, with Metreveli's opponents and journalists banned from the auditorium. Not surprisingly, the University Council declared Metreveli as the TSU rector for the next six years.

In response, a faction of TSU students filed an appeal in the Tbilisi District Court disputing Metreveli's reelection.[12] In particular, students challenged the 2001 presidential decree that enabled Metreveli's run for a third term in office and demanded annulment of the Council's vote. TSU students also called on the Minister of Education to provide a set of common standards for the development of a university's statute. This student initiative, however, did not result in Metreveli's resignation owing to the moribund political system. As Gigi Tevzadze, former TSU lecturer, put it, "This system and the rector would vanish only after this government is gone."[13] So this experience brought the minority of university students to the realization that the whole political regime needed to be dismantled to bring about drastic reforms in the education sector.

CROSS-NATIONAL DIFFUSION OF IDEAS

Civic activists scrutinized multiple cases of nonviolent resistance to the regime, but Otpor's example was the most inspiring to Georgian youth:

> In 2001 we were looking for fresh examples of changing the political system. Gandhi was too old and too remote from Georgian reality. It was not too appealing to our youth. Likewise, velvet revolutions of the 1980s occurred a while ago. The most recent example of nonviolent resistance came from Serbia.[14]

A group of Georgians visited Serbia in spring 2003. Among them were a leader of the National Movement Giorgi Ugulava, GYLA chairman Tinatin Khidasheli, and director of the Liberty Institute, Levan Ramishvili. They came back with a more solid understanding of how to challenge the power of the incumbent government. "On the Internet you can find a lot of manuals on how to do this or that," noted Ramishvili. "But to have a text is one thing, and to have a real conversation with somebody involved in the process is another thing ... we met several former Otpor activists and identified a set of skills that we needed to

[12] *Civil Georgia*. 2003. "Enough of Having the Same Rector for 11 Years." April 24. www.civil.ge/eng/article.php?id=7311.

[13] Gularidze, Tea. 2003. "Tbilisi State University Elects the Rector Amid Charges of Illegality." *Civil Georgia*. April 23, www.civil.ge/eng/article.php?id=4092.

[14] Author's interview with Levan Ramishvili, Tblisi, Georgia, February 13, 2008.

develop."[15] Georgian activists attended a training session organized by CeSID to learn about the organization of an election observation mission and a GOTV campaign.[16] Another major lesson learned from Otpor was "the importance of creating a sense of moral superiority over the autocratic regime."[17] Kmara's leadership anticipated that repressive methods against the youth movement would signify its advancement in the right direction.

Adoption of the clenched fist as Kmara's symbol was another example of Otpor's impact on the Georgian youth movement. "We succeeded in creating some sort of myth around us – that we were crazy kids who knew how to subvert a dictator. This really helped us," said Kmara member Giorgi Kandelaki.[18] Another Kmara member, Nini Gogiberidze, recalled how movement participants deliberated the choice of the movement's symbol and settled on the image of the clenched fist in the long run:

> We were brainstorming various symbols. We were thinking about having the fist with a thumb up, but it appeared to be stupid. We considered having as a symbol a palm pierced with the knife and blood dripping out of the palm, but it would scare off people. It was too depressing. In the long run, we decided to adopt Otpor's symbol. The symbol had a history.[19]

In addition to its connection with Otpor, the image of the clenched fist was rooted in Georgian history. "When our independence was proclaimed, people stood holding their fists as a symbol of unity," recalled Gvantsa Liparteliani, a Kmara member. "We chose the fist as a symbol of unity and victory."[20]

The youth movement used both direct and indirect channels of diffusion to deepen youth familiarity with nonviolent tactics. Kmara organized a summer camp to train youth activists from the provinces. At the summer camp, Kmara used a copy of Otpor's manual previously translated into Russian for the youth movement Zubr. Another channel of cross-national diffusion was York's documentary, *Bringing Down a Dictator*. Kmara showed this documentary to its new recruits to boost their enthusiasm about nonviolent resistance. Moreover, Rustavi-2 aired this documentary on the eve of the 2003 parliamentary elections in an attempt to strengthen public confidence in the people's power.

15 Author's interview with Levan Ramishvili, Tblisi, Georgia, February 13, 2008.

16 Author's interview with Marko Blagojevic, Belgrade, Serbia, February 6, 2008.

17 Quoted from Kandelaki, Giorgi. 2004. "An Inside Look at Georgia's "Rose Revolution," or How I Became a Revolutionary." *Scholar Forum: The Journal of the Open Society Institute's Network Scholarship Program*, Fall Issue, pp. 3–5.

18 *Ibid.*, p. 4.

19 Author's interview with Nini Gogiberidze, Tbilisi, Georgia, February 14, 2008.

20 Author's interview with Gvantsa Liparteliani, Tbilisi, Georgia, February 18, 2008.

NONVIOLENT ACTION AGAINST THE REGIME

Kmara burst onto the political scene in spring 2003. The youth movement called for democratic change and the eradication of corruption in Georgian society. Many Georgians supported the movement's demands but disapproved of its methods. According to a Georgian scholar, "Kmara was too radical. Like a typical revolutionary, it was against any compromise with the incumbent government."[21] These mass attitudes did not deter Kmara from using subversive tactics against the incumbent. "To be hated is better than to be ignored," explained Ramishvili. "We did not try to win everybody's heart. The idea was to be visible."[22] As illustrated by various accounts of the Rose Revolution,[23] Kmara succeeded in becoming a prominent civil society actor during the parliamentary elections.

Recruitment

The recruitment of political novices posed a challenge to the youth movement. In particular, most urban youth in the capital city were reluctant to participate in provocative street action. A large share of students at such prestigious universities as TSU represented children of the ruling elite. As beneficiaries of the current political system, these offspring enjoyed a luxurious lifestyle and were more preoccupied with fashion and entertainment than politics. "If you are not a Gucci girl, you are not cool," a female youth activist said, summing up the prevailing view at TSU. "To many, Kmara was a movement of radical junkies."[24] Another possible explanation for Kmara's low appeal in the capital city was widespread skepticism about the effectiveness of mass protests.

> In Tbilisi, people were tired of politics. There were big demonstrations in 2001, but nothing changed. In [the] provinces, people were less disillusioned and hungrier for politics.[25]

Rural youth became a more receptive audience for Kmara's political message than college-educated urbanites. Ketevan Kobiashvili, member of Kmara's training and recruitment team, provided the following insight into Kmara's popularity in the provinces:

[21] Author's interview with Gocha Lordkipanidze, New York City, October 16, 2009.

[22] Author's interview with Levan Ramishvili, Tblisi, Georgia, February 13, 2008.

[23] Hash-Gonzalez, Kelli. 2013. *Popular Mobilization and Empowerment in Georgia's Rose Revolution*. Lanham, MD: Lexington Books; Angley, Robyn. 2010. "NGOs in Competitive Authoritarian States: The Role of Civic Groups in Georgia's Rose Revolution." Ph.D. dissertation, Boston University; Wheatley, Jonathan. 2005. *Georgia from National Awakening to Rose Revolution: Delayed Transition in the Former Soviet Union*. Aldershot, UK: Ashgate.

[24] Author's interview with Nini Gogiberidze, Tbilisi, Georgia, February 14, 2008.

[25] Author's interview with Levan Ramishvili, Tblisi, Georgia, February 13, 2008.

For a long time, they cultivated land and stayed at home. But they wanted to feel useful. They wanted to feel that they were needed. It was clear from their faces that they wanted some change.[26]

Organizational Structure

Kmara's leadership was a closely knit group of young people who sought to build a horizontal organizational structure. Like Otpor, Kmara instituted a division of labor whereby activists were responsible for different tasks within the movement. Notably, several female activists were represented in the movement's leadership. Tea Tutberidze, a TSU law student, acted as Kmara's spokesperson, and another TSU student, Nini Gogiberidze, was heavily involved in Kmara's logistics and fund-raising efforts. Gvantsa Liparteliani was on the public relations team, while Ketevan Kobiashvili was responsible for training and recruitment of new members. Among other things, the presence of young women in the movement's leadership strengthened public confidence in the movement's commitment to nonviolent action, given widespread beliefs in women's aversion of violence.

Emulating Otpor's example, Kmara's leadership granted a lot of autonomy to local branches in the provinces. "They had their own [local] problems, so we let them do what they felt was necessary. When there was a particular event we wanted to be held on the same day, we coordinated our activities," a Kmara member explained.[27]

Tactics vis-à-vis Opponents

Kmara focused its efforts on a negative campaign against the incumbent president and adopted Otpor's repertoire of nonviolent action. Movement participants covered the capital city with graffiti and staged street performances. According to Kmara member Giorgi Meladze, the youth movement did not have sufficient time and resources to organize a large-scale positive campaign on its own.[28] Instead, youth activists contributed to a GOTV campaign encompassing multiple civil society actors.

Like Otpor, Kmara decided to establish its presence in the capital city by spray painting its main slogan, "Enough!." Kmara's first graffiti appeared shortly after the movement's march in Tbilisi on April 14. And the incumbent president himself made the best publicity for Kmara's action. In response to a journalist's question about Kmara on May 12, 2003, Shevardnadze stated, "If somebody writes something on the sidewalk or on the wall, it does not affect me. I do not think that the authorities are going to tremble and pale at the sight

[26] Author's interview with Ketevan Kobiashvili, Tbilisi, Georgia, February 15, 2008. [27] *Ibid.*
[28] Author's interview with Giorgi Meladze, Belgrade, Serbia, February 7, 2008.

of it."[29] Shevardnadze further attempted to dismiss the significance of Kmara's protest tactics by stating on June 16, 2003 that he had spotted Kmara's graffiti from his limousine and "nobody seemed to be reading it."[30] In fact, Kmara's slogan captured the dominant mood in society. According to an opinion poll conducted in May 2003, 69 percent of citizens were dissatisfied with "the way democracy was developing in Georgia."[31]

The street performance was another type of nonviolent action directed against the incumbent president. In one of the street actions, for example, youth activists offered passers-by an opportunity to be photographed flushing the toilet. Close-up images of the country's leaders were portrayed popping out of the toilet, signifying society's need for their disposal. Another street action – a mock funeral – was staged on the day the government unveiled a new economic program, underscoring the dismal state of the national economy. Notably, the creative use of low-cost props was sufficient to deliver a compelling message to the general public. In November 2003, for example, 35 Kmara activists wrapped in plastic sheeting stood for half an hour in downtown Tbilisi to symbolize the suffocating political environment in the country.[32]

Despite Kmara's scathing criticism, Georgian universities were much more open to political deliberations than Azerbaijani institutions of higher education. For example, the National Debate Tournament sponsored by the Soros Foundation and held at TSU in October 2003 provided a platform for heated political discussions.[33] Forty-eight teams from universities across the country debated a variety of issues related to that year's theme of democracy. Youth activists clad in Kmara T-shirts used this venue to boost the movement's image and raise the issue of authoritarian entrenchment in Adjara. In another move, Kmara activists placed a portable wall in a TSU yard, inviting students to scribble their messages to the incumbent president.[34]

Emulating Serbia's Otpor, Kmara produced TV spots calling for Shevardnadze's resignation. One TV spot showing images of crumbling buildings and the poverty-stricken population concluded with the slogan, "*Kmara vardnas!*" ("Enough of Falling!"). Another Kmara ad subsequently aired on TV replaced the previous slogan with "Enough of Shevardnadze!" ("*Kmara she-vardnadzes*"). According to a participant in post-election protests, these TV spots changed citizens' expectations about the possibility of change:

[29] Quoted from Namtalashvili, Gabriel. 2003. "Protsess stabilizatsii neobratim." *Svobodnaia Gruzia*. May 13.

[30] Gularidze, Tea. 2003. "Youth Protest – A Painful Sting to the Government." *Civil Georgia*. June 18. www.civil.ge/eng/article.php?id=4409.

[31] International Republican Institute. 2004. *Georgian National Voter Study* [PowerPoint presentation].

[32] Gvalia, Nino. 2003. "Protest Art Livens Up in Tbilisi." *The Messenger*. November 21. P. 8.

[33] Gorgodze, Sopho, and Warren Hedges. 2003. "Heads Turn at National Debate Tournament." *The Messenger*. October 23. P. 5.

[34] Gvalia, Nino. 2003. "Protest Art Livens Up in Tbilisi." *The Messenger*. November 21. P. 8.

> They [TV spots] influenced people's mentality. The older generation didn't believe a change of government was possible through protest. They still had, or have, a Soviet mentality and were afraid of protest because of 1956 and 1989. But when they saw Kmara spots on TV, which would never have happened during the USSR, and they saw that there was no punishment, their thinking changed.[35]

As in Serbia, rock concerts were seen as a mechanism for galvanizing mass support for political change. Rock musicians performed in such big cities as Batumi, Gori, Kutaisi, and Tbilisi. Among them was 29-year-old Zaza Korinteli, better known by his stage name, Zumba. Calling for *EuroRemont* (dramatic overhaul of society and integration with Europe), Zumba wrote a song that became popular with regime opponents for its blunt summary of their demands. The lyrics stated, "Listen, you, guy! Have you gone crazy? Go away, otherwise you may get hurt." As Liparteliani noted, "[T]he spirit of the youth movement and the spirit of rock music converged."[36]

Moreover, a GOTV campaign launched by civic activists included a bus tour around the country. Georgian artists, poets, and writers visited small towns and cities to mobilize the electorate in favor of political change. They distributed books and held meetings with local intelligentsia and youth. Civic activists also invited local artists to get involved in this project. Female poets in the city of Poti, for example, read their work in an attempt to boost mass support for political change. On election day, Kmara members toured Tbilisi in a painted truck, waiving their flags with the image of the clenched fist, and calling on voters to cast a ballot.[37]

In general, Kmara routinely used the public space as an opportunity for direct contact with citizens. Kmara activists would attempt to convince ordinary citizens of the need for action by striking a conversation and getting into a political debate with pedestrians on the street or passengers on public transportation. In contrast, the use of digital technology as a voter mobilization device was minimal in Georgia. According to a Kmara member, the youth movement also rarely used SMS to bring young people into the street. "In Georgia, if you do not personally invite an individual, he won't come."[38]

It is also noteworthy that the use of political humor was quite popular in Georgia. One of the most popular entertainment shows on Georgian TV was "Dardubala," a political satire cartoon series produced by Shalva Ramishvili. This animated TV series featured Shevardnadze and his ministers as main characters, and it was broadcast on Rustavi-2 from 1999 to 2001. Student protesters carried posters with Dardubala-esque images of the incumbent president during

[35] Quoted from Hash-Gonzalez, Kelli. 2013. *Popular Mobilization and Empowerment in Georgia's Rose Revolution*. Lanham, MD: Lexington Books, p. 53.

[36] Author's interview with Gvantsa Liparteliani, Tbilisi, Georgia, February 18, 2008.

[37] Gorgodze, Sopho. 2003. "Tbilisi's Youth Skip the Vote." *The Messenger*. November 3. P. 5.

[38] Author's interview with Ketevan Kobiashvili, Tbilisi, Georgia, February 15, 2008.

antigovernment protests in the fall of 2001.[39] Similarly, Kmara's street actions mocked the incumbent president. As preceding cases of nonviolent resistance illustrate, humor was important to erode the strength of the current regime.

Tactics vis-à-vis Allies

Kmara's leadership seemed to be cognizant of pitfalls associated with close association with different civil society actors. Kmara sought to downplay its ties with opposition political parties. Like Zubr, however, Kmara was closely linked with a civic organization. The Liberty Institute was widely perceived as the movement's guardian. In addition, Rustavi-2 was Kmara's influential ally in the media sector.

Kmara's first protest march was an outcome of savvy negotiations with opposition political parties. As a small youth movement, Kmara aspired to create an illusion of a powerful social force, and Kmara activists turned to politicians for assistance. The movement's leadership asked politicians to bring young people for participation in the protest march without revealing their partisan ties. Nini Gogiberidze recalled how Kmara activists negotiated with the opposition political parties:

> We needed people to hold a large rally. So a few of us went to different political parties, asking for assistance. First, we went to Zhvania's party and told him that we needed young people for street action. We stated that Saakashvili promised us to bring 200 people. And we asked Zhvania, "How many could your party bring to the rally?" He told us, "500." Then we went to Saakashvili's Movement and told his party members that Zhavnia had promised us to bring 500 young people. They told us that they would bring 1,000 young people ... When we approached political parties, we asked them to bring young people who are not directly affiliated with the political party. We did not want party activists to represent Kmara.[40]

In media interviews, however, the opposition political parties denied any connection with the youth movement. Saaskashvili and Zhvania, for example, brushed away allegations that they had been behind Kmara's protest march on April 14.[41] This tactic helped Kmara to attract youth disinterested in party politics.

Among local NGOs, the Liberty Institute was Kmara's strongest ally. As Ramishvili noted, the Liberty Institute staff were representative of the older generation of the student movement; they participated in anticommunist protests in 1989 and wanted to pass on the torch to the young generation. From this perspective, Kmara was "a natural continuation of earlier student

[39] For details, see Manning, Paul. 2007. "Rose-Colored Glasses? Color Revolutions and Cartoon Chaos in Postsocialist Georgia." *Cultural Anthropology* 22(2): 171–213.

[40] Author's interview with Nini Gogiberidze, Tbilisi, Georgia, February 14, 2008.

[41] Gorgodze, Sophia. 2003. "Who Was Behind the Students?" *The Messenger*. April 17. P. 4.

struggles for more rights and freedoms."[42] The Liberty Institute provided Kmara with office space and computer equipment. "We would spend days and nights there discussing various ideas and planning street actions," recalled a Kmara member.[43]

The regime-friendly media also drew a link between the youth movement and the Open Society Georgia Foundation (OSGF). State officials and political pundits claimed that Soros sought to destabilize the political situation in the country and provided funding for Kmara.[44] It was rumored that the youth movement received a $500,000 grant from the OSGF.[45] For example, an article in the Russian-language newspaper *Svobodnaia Gruziia* ("*Free Georgia*") alleged that Soros allocated money for the purchase of 30,000 T-shirts and 30,000 caps with Kmara's logo.[46] Both Kmara members and OSGF staff denied these allegations. "We do not need big money to do what we do – buy some paint and write the word 'enough' on the walls," Kmara activist Levan Ekhvaia stated. "We can afford this on our own."[47] As young professionals, several Kmara activists based in Tbilisi acknowledged that they contributed a fraction of their personal income to buy some low-cost supplies for their street actions.

Rustavi-2 was another Kmara's influential ally. The TV channel regularly covered Kmara's actions, raising public awareness of the movement's interactions with state authorities. The Rustavi-2 crew, for example, captured on camera a police raid against Kmara members on the eve of Shevardnadze's visit to Poti in October 2003. Moreover, the TV channel aired Kmara's ad admonishing election commission officials to comply with electoral procedures and uphold the integrity of the parliamentary elections. Rustavi-2 kept on broadcasting Kmara's ad even after the Central Election Commission deemed it as intimidating to election officials and requested its removal off the air. In response, the Central Election Commission withdrew Rustavi-2's accreditation, constraining the channel's access to election-related information. On the start of post-election protests, Rustavi-2 aired TV spots urging people to turn to the street in support of the political opposition.[48] In turn, pro-regime forces branded Rustavi-2 as a violence-inciting TV channel, holding it responsible for "possible bloodshed in front of the parliament."[49]

42 Author's interview with Levan Ramishvili, Tblisi, Georgia, February 13, 2008.

43 Author's interview with Gvantsa Liparteliani, Tbilisi, Georgia, February 18, 2008.

44 Beridze, David. 2003. "Manifestatssiia protesta – samotsel." *Svobodnaia Gruziia*. June 4.

45 MacKinnon, Mark. 2003. "Georgia Revolt Carried Mark of Soros." *Globe and Mail*. November 26. www.theglobeandmail.com/servlet/story/RTGAM.20031126.wxsoros1126/.

46 Lomsadze, Tamaz. 2003. "Deti kapitana Granta." *Svobodnaia Gruziia*. November 11.

47 Quoted from Gularidze, Tea. 2003. "Youth Protest – A Painful Sting to the Government." *Civil Georgia*. June 18. www.civil.ge/eng/article.php?id=4409.

48 *The Messenger*. 2003. "Protests Continue." November 10. P. 7.

49 Rennau, Marina. "Georgia in Pivotal Standoff with Independent Media." *EurasiaNet*. November 17. www.eurasianet.org/departments/rights/articles/eav111703.shtml.

STATE COUNTERMOVES

The government's response to Kmara involved a conventional set of repressive methods ranging from a smear campaign in the media to police harassment of youth activists. In turn, Kmara members developed tactics to counteract state repression and amplify public support for their political demands.

State-controlled media framed Kmara as a gang of uneducated, aggressive youth. Another discursive strategy was to discredit civic activism by spreading allegations about monetary rewards for participants in Kmara's actions.[50] In addition, the government's spokespeople attempted to frame Kmara either as an agent of the Russian government or as a youth branch of Saakashvili's National Movement.

In response, Kmara took several steps. First, Kmara carefully selected its spokespeople to dispel the movement's negative image in the mainstream media. For example, Kmara accepted an invitation from a state-controlled TV channel to appear on air and comment on its actions:

> We tried to show people that we were normal, average students. We were ordinary citizens who wanted to live in a normal country. That's why we carefully selected our public faces. They had to be convincing and "ours."[51]

Furthermore, Kmara sought to burnish its image as a positive social force by organizing cleanup and book drives. Kmara, for example, organized a charity concert "Enough for Educated Future Generations" to collect books for Tbilisi-based school libraries. The added value of such community events was that they were infused with political overtones. For example, a cleanup drive, titled "Throw Out Your Garbage Yourself," had a double meaning. Kmara explicitly invited citizens to clean up their neighborhoods. The implicit message was that citizens should also turn to the street to rid the country of its rotten political elite. By the same token, the organization of cleanups provided an opportunity for recruitment. "I remember how we went to a small town to meet local youth. They were complaining of not having a well-functioning city park or a soccer field. So we went together to a local park and cleaned it up. Afterwards, we played soccer together."[52] To further stress the movement's concern with the country's national interests, Kmara designed a public campaign, "Because I Love Georgia!"

Compared with Azerbaijan, the level of administrative pressure on youth activists was quite moderate. A few university students claimed that their grades had been lowered in retaliation for their civic position. Nobody, however, was

[50] Kandelaki, Giorgi, and Giorgi Meladze. 2007. "Enough! Kmara and the Rose Revolution in Georgia." In *Reclaiming Democracy: Civil Society and Electoral Change in Central and Eastern Europe*, eds. Joerg Forbig and Pavol Demes. Washington, DC: German Marshall Fund, pp. 101–25, p. 110.

[51] Author's interview with Gvantsa Liparteliani, Tbilisi, Georgia, February 18, 2008.

[52] Author's interview with Akaki Minashvili, Tbilisi, Georgia, February 17, 2008.

expelled from university on political grounds. And most Tbilisi-based faculty appeared to be tolerant of youth activism. With the start of post-election protests, some professors did not conceal their disapproval of the incumbent government and freely permitted their students to skip classes to participate in protest events, while others assigned extra coursework, which was a mild form of punishment for politically motivated absences.[53] In addition, the threat of eviction from the dormitory did not hang like Damocles' sword over Georgian students because the state did away with subsidized student housing awhile ago.

Psychological harassment of youth's relatives was used as a demobilization tactic. Several interviewed Kmara members stated that their parents were shamed at work for the deviant behavior of their children. "A relative working in a state agency might come to parents and tell them that their kid should stop his involvement in Kmara," said Ramishvili.[54] Parents were admonished that youth's primary responsibility was to excel in academic performance and set high career goals. More broadly, the ruling elite tried to link respect for state authorities with respect for the elderly.

Police harassment of youth activists was more common in the provinces than in the capital city. A police officer, for example, dumped a can of paint on the head of a Kmara member who spray painted graffiti in the Kakheti region. The local police also interfered with the free movement of Kmara members on the eve of a public rally in the city of Borjomi in July 2003. Taking a cue from Otpor, Kmara sought to deescalate the situation and treat the police as a victim of the regime. According to Kmara member Akaki Minashvili:

> We tried to send the policemen the message that we were fighting for them too. We didn't blame them for being corrupt. We were giving flowers and *khachapuri* [Georgian cheese pastry] to the policemen standing in the street in November 2003 ... If people are sitting in a conference room underground, it does not matter who is the president. It matters who makes the ventilation. Without air, everybody can get suffocated.[55]

Detention of youth activists was less widespread in Georgia than in Azerbaijan. For example, seven youth activists were detained for two hours and released without being charged after their participation in a picket in front of the presidential administration in October 2003.[56] One of the most widely publicized arrests of Kmara members happened on June 12, 2003. When young people attempted to spray paint graffiti on the building of the Ministry of Interior, Narchemashvili himself came out to speak with the Kmara members, describing their action as hooliganism. On the minister's order, nine Kmara members were initially detained but subsequently released without any criminal

[53] Rioneli, Gio. 2003. "Glas naroda." *Kavkazskii aktsent* 22, p. 5.
[54] Author's interview with Levan Ramishvili, Tblisi, Georgia, February 13, 2008.
[55] Author's interview with Akaki Minashvili, Tbilisi, Georgia, February 17, 2008.
[56] Human Rights Information and Documentation Center. 2003. "Kmara Meetings Are Dispersed, Participants Assaulted." *Monthly Bulletin "Human Rights in Georgia,"* October Issue, p. 2. Retrieved from www.hridc.org.

charges. Still, Kmara managed to turn this seven-hour detention into a media event showcasing the repressive character of the current regime.

Traditionally, pop music served as the government's voter mobilization tool. A large musical show, for example, was held in Tbilisi on October 31 to mark the founding of the city by King Vakhtang Gorgasali in the fifth century. It was the government's response to the opposition's organization of rock concerts during the election period.

As a counterweight to Kmara, state authorities backed the formation of the youth organization Student Movement – Future of Georgia in May 2003. The Student Movement was framed as a depoliticized student organization made up of student unions from 13 universities around the country. According to Irakli Murtzkhvaladze, president of the rector-backed student union at TSU, the movement's main aim was "to work upon the development and improvement of youth policy in the country."[57] The union leader, however, did not conceal his disapproval of Kmara's action. Siding with the government's position on Kmara, Murtzkhvaladze stated that its members should attend classes rather than run around in the street.[58] Beyond media interviews, the state-sponsored Student Movement carried out few activities during the parliamentary elections, posing no real challenge to the opposition forces.

THE ROSE REVOLUTION

The parliamentary elections held on November 2, 2003 were widely regarded as a precursor to the 2005 presidential election. Kmara activists themselves pointed out that they viewed the 2003 parliamentary elections as a trial-run before the expiration of Shevardnadze's second term in office. Yet the political standoff culminated in the incumbent's resignation and became known as the Rose Revolution.

The validity of official electoral results was challenged by the opposition political parties. According to the official results released by the Central Election Commission on November 13, the electoral bloc For New Georgia received the largest share of votes (21.32 percent), followed by the Union of Democratic Revival (18.84 percent) and the National Movement (18.08 percent).[59] In contrast, the results of parallel vote tabulation conducted by the ISFED-led domestic election observation mission showed that the National Movement was ahead of the pro-regime bloc For New Georgia with 26.26 versus 18.92 percent of the popular vote.[60] Furthermore, ISFED filed over 400 appeals regarding electoral irregularities observed during the voting process and vote count. Based on an analysis of electoral procedures in the country, the OSCE

[57] Zviadauri, Tina. 2003. "My khtotim peremen." *Svobodnaia Gruziia*. August 12. [58] *Ibid.*

[59] OSCE. 2003. *Georgia Parliamentary Elections: Post-Election Interim Report (3–25 November 2003)*. Warsaw, Poland: Office for Democratic Institutions and Human Rights, p. 5.

[60] *ISFED Preliminary Statement on the Parliamentary Elections of November 2, 2003.*

election observation mission concluded that "inflated turnout and fraudulently garnered votes for particular parties had a significant effect on the national election results."[61]

Starting November 4, protest rallies were held in Tbilisi to demand the annulment of the election results. Saakashvili eloquently called on people to join this protest campaign. "If you stay by your television now, you will remain slaves for the next four years," he stated in a public address.[62] As the number of protesters swelled, opposition political parties radicalized their demands and began to call for Shevardnadze's immediate resignation. Succumbing to public pressure, Shevardnadze stepped down on November 23 and opened the door for drastic reforms.

On Shevardnadze's downfall, Kmara reignited its campaign against Metreveli as a remnant of the old regime. Kmara members organized protest events and collected signatures petitioning the rector's resignation, while some TSU students sided with the incumbent rector.[63] Metreveli stepped down in October 2004, almost a year after the Rose Revolution, and the former Ambassador to Italy, Rusudan Lortkipanidze, replaced him as the rector.[64]

Another remaining target of Kmara's action in the post-election period was Abashidze, autocratic ruler of the Autonomous Republic of Ajara. This regional leader provided political backing for Shevardnadze and prevented the opposition political parties from campaigning in the republic during the parliamentary elections.[65] In turn, Kmara called for the end of his arbitrary rule and distributed posters with the slogan, "Enough of Abashidze's Dictatorship."[66] A few Kmara members went on a 23-day hunger strike to put pressure on the local government, but to no avail.[67] Abashidze deployed more repressive methods against his opponents than the ousted president to hold on to power.[68] But the governor eventually resigned and moved to Russia. The youth movement subsequently disappeared from the political scene, while a few Kmara members developed contacts with youth activists in Azerbaijan, Belarus, and Ukraine to share their expertise in nonviolent resistance.

[61] OSCE. 2003. *Georgia Parliamentary Elections: Post-Election Interim Report (3–25 November 2003)*, p. 5.

[62] *The Messenger*. 2003. "Protests Continue." November 10. P. 7.

[63] Gorgodze, Sophia. 2003. "Kmara! Versus University." *The Messenger*. November 26. P. 1; Tonakanian, Liza. 2003. "Kmara 'Kmara'!" *Svobodnaia Gruziia*. November 26.

[64] *Civil Georgia*. 2004. "Tbilisi University Rector Resigns." October 1. www.civil.ge/eng/article.php?id=7951.

[65] On electoral malpractices in Ajara, see OSCE. 2003. *Georgia Parliamentary Elections: Post-Election Interim Report (3–25 November 2003)*.

[66] *Svobodnaia Gruziia*. 2004. "Kmara ukhodit v podpolje." March 2.

[67] *Svobodnaia Gruziia*. 2004. "Aktivisty Kmara prekratili golodovku." December 18.

[68] *Svobodnaia Gruziia*. 2004. "Nasha Adzharia ne mozhet poekhat v Batumi." March 24.

CONCLUSION

This chapter examined protest tactics and state countermoves during the 2003 parliamentary elections in Georgia. The youth movement Kmara gained name recognition in Georgian society through the use of such unconventional protest tactics as graffiti, street performances, and rock concerts. Furthermore, the Georgian youth movement effectively addressed the challenge of recruiting political novices in the cities by reaching out to the rural youth. In turn, the incumbent government miscalculated the power of civil society and dismissed Kmara's action as juvenile hooliganism. Furthermore, the Georgian government did not invest substantial resources into building a pro-regime youth organization.

The case of the Georgian youth movement illustrates how novel tactics can produce a detectable impact on mass mobilization in a rather weak state. As discussed in Chapter 3, there appeared to be favorable conditions for political change on the eve of the parliamentary elections, including the unification of opposition political parties and the development of independent media. In addition, the level of state repression was lower in Georgia than in Azerbaijan under the Aliyevs and Belarus under Lukashenka. Nonetheless, the regime's weakness by itself is an insufficient condition for mass mobilization. Kmara played an important role in propagating the notion of revolutionary change and urging citizens to act on their grievances. Moreover, there emerged a charismatic political leader championing the idea of democratic change. A partial convergence of goals pursued by the youth movement and the opposition political parties was conducive to youth's engagement in civil resistance. It is safe to conclude that President Shevardnadze would have stayed in office until the next presidential election in the absence of strong public pressure for early resignation.

7

Pora! Youth's Mobilization in Ukraine

A group of young people wearing striped caps walked in a circle in downtown Kyiv in the summer of 2004. Youths bent their heads and folded their arms behind their backs to imitate a prison walk. This street action was conceived to warn citizens against the looming threat of authoritarianism as a result of the political ascendancy of the president's handpicked successor. In particular, Yanukovych's criminal record, as well as his connections with the Donetsk mafia and his pro-Russian foreign policy, was a major source of concern for movement participants. Most youths felt that it was time to act in defense of the country's democratic future.

Thousands of young Ukrainians revolted against the current regime during the Orange Revolution. More than 80 percent of 18–29-year-old Ukrainians reported voting in the presidential election, with approximately 60 percent of youth votes cast for Yushchenko, a candidate from the united opposition.[1] Once the voting process was over, thousands of young people turned to the street to defend their votes. Approximately 8 percent of 18–29-year-old Ukrainians participated in Kyiv protests against vote rigging, and 17.8 percent of Ukrainian youths were engaged in protest events in their hometowns or other locales outside the capital city. Moreover, thousands of young people stayed in the tent city installed in Kyiv's main square to demand political change. The two youth movements, later labeled as "black Pora" and "yellow Pora" for the colors of their insignias, played a prominent role in mobilizing youth against the regime. For seven months prior to the elections, movement participants leveled criticism at the ruling elite and called for free and fair elections.

In turn, the incumbent government deployed a conventional set of demobilization tactics, exerting political pressure on the mass media, NGOs,

[1] Institute of Sociology. 2005. *Ukrainian Society 2005: Social Monitoring [data file]*. Kyiv, Ukraine: National Academy of Science of Ukraine. On the survey findings, see Panina, Natalia. 2005. *Ukrainske suspilstvo 1994–2005: Sotsiologichnyi monitoring*. Kyiv, Ukraine: Institute of Sociology of the National Academy of Science of Ukraine and the Foundation "Democratic Initiatives."

and universities. The state-controlled media portrayed nonviolent youth movements as a puppet of the West or a home-growth product of right-wing nationalists. In addition, the security services framed Pora as a terrorist organization by spreading allegations about the movement's storage of explosives. More broadly, the government targeted the student population as a threat to political stability. The state countermoves, however, were ineffective in checking the growth of youth movements in opposition to the regime.

This chapter explains a high level of youth mobilization in Ukraine through the analysis of tactical interactions between the youth movements and the incumbent government. The chapter begins with a discussion of two major protest campaigns that set the backdrop for the development of Pora's tactics: the student hunger strike (October 1990) and the Ukraine without Kuchma Movement (2000–01). Next, the chapter traces youth's cross-national exchange of ideas in anticipation of the fraudulent elections. The remainder of the chapter is devoted to an analysis of movement tactics and state countermoves, demonstrating the resourcefulness of Ukrainian youth activists in challenging the incumbent government and the use of conventional demobilization tactics by state authorities.

MAJOR PROTEST CAMPAIGNS IN UKRAINE

Since the early 1990s, Ukrainian youth participated in two major protest campaigns: the student hunger strike and the Ukraine without Kuchma Movement. The hunger strike organized by university students during the late Gorbachev period marked a turning point in Ukraine's struggle for national independence. The protest campaign exposed weaknesses of the communist regime and produced a new cohort of civic activists pushing for the revival of Ukrainian culture and the introduction of democratic reforms in the post-Soviet period. A number of former strike participants played a leading role in the protest campaign against the incumbent government in 2000–01. The political opposition held protest rallies and pitched tents to demand the president's resignation. Though these protest campaigns failed to dismantle the nondemocratic regime, they laid the groundwork for a subsequent organization of antigovernment protests.

Student Hunger Strike of 1990

The student hunger strike, also known as the Granite Revolution, was held in the Ukrainian Soviet Socialist Republic in October 1990, a few weeks after the adoption of the Declaration of State Sovereignty of Ukraine.[2] The striking students declared, "It's time to choose: either we achieve independent democratic

[2] For an overview of the student strike, see Donii, Oles. 1995. *Studentska revoluitsia na graniti: Fotoalbom pro studentske goloduvannia 1990 roku*. Kyiv: Smoloskyp; Ostrovskii, Ihor, and

Ukraine or we remain an empire's colony, a spiritually poor denationalized nation."[3] To propel regime change, students advanced five demands: (1) the administration of multiparty parliamentary elections no later than spring 1991, (2) the rejection of a union treaty preserving the Soviet Union, (3) the nationalization of Communist Party property, (4) the return of Ukrainian draftees to the territory of Ukraine, and (5) the resignation of Vitaly Masol, chair of the Council of Ministers of Ukraine. Nonviolent methods were used to attain these goals. In particular, the tent city became a symbol of resistance to the regime.

Approximately 100,000 Ukrainian students, comprising one-fifth of the republic's student population, participated in this protest campaign.[4] On the first day of the hunger strike on October 2, forty university students set up tents on granite-covered October Square, later renamed Independence Square (*Maidan Nezalezhnosti*) or simply the Maidan.[5] An additional 100 students went on a hunger strike the next day. Moreover, at least 131 nonstarving students volunteered to maintain public order, provide first aid, and communicate with the mass media,[6] while thousands of students participated in protest events in support of the hunger strikers. The core of protesters came from two student organizations: the Student Brotherhood and the Ukrainian Student Union. Strike leadership included 20-year-old Oleh Barkov from the city of Dnirpodzerzhinsk in eastern Ukraine, 21-year-old Oles Donii from Kyiv, and 24-year-old Markian Ivashchshyn from the city of Lviv in western Ukraine. Undergraduate student Taras Korpalo was designated as the tent city commandant to oversee its daily operations.

The presence of democratic forces in the local government, along with the tense political situation in the Soviet Union, reduced the likelihood of police violence against students. As a result of an emergency meeting on October 2, the Kyiv City Council issued a permission to hold public events in downtown Kyiv, which bestowed legitimacy on the student strike. Neither did the local police nip the protest campaign in the bud. Kyiv residents, for example, were allowed to bring warm clothes and blankets to the striking students. Nonetheless, party officials attempted to delegitimize the protest campaign by framing it as an initiative of radical youth from Halychyna, a region in the western part of Ukraine. Moreover, the security officers tried to discredit the hunger strike by placing food in the tent city and provoking an outbreak of violence. In response to percolating rumors about government provocations, approximately 50,000 Kyivites came to the Maidan on October 5 with the aim to defend students against possible assailants.[7] By that time, the Soviet Army had deployed violence and killed

Serhiy Chernenko. 2000. *Velykyi zlam: Khronika 'revoluitsii na graniti' 2–17 zhovtnia 1990 roku*. Kyiv: Agentsvo Ukraina.

[3] Ostrovskii, Ihor, and Serhiy Chernenko. 2000. *Velykyi zlam*. P. 20. [4] *Ibid.*, p. 77.

[5] Melnyk, Ihor. 2005. "Goloduvannia na Maidani." *Postup*. October 3. http://postup.brama.com/usual.php?what=45693.

[6] Ostrovskii, Ihor, and Serhiy Chernenko. 2000. *Velykyi zlam*. P. 26. [7] *Ibid.*, p. 32.

participants in anticommunist protests in Tbilisi on April 9, 1989 and in Baku on January 20 1990.[8] Remarkably, the two-week protest campaign held in Kyiv remained peaceful, which had a profound impact on political developments in post-Soviet Ukraine. The peaceful transition from communism occurred without lustration in the high echelons of power.

> Initially, everyone was proud of our hunger strike: Ukraine became independent bloodlessly and peacefully thanks to it. However, it turned out that absence of bloodshed also brought about continuity: Soviet Ukraine remained Soviet, and eclecticism has also remained eclecticism.[9]

Overall, this protest campaign affected Ukrainian politics in several ways. In the short run, the strike led to Masol's resignation and the passage of a legislative act promising to satisfy the remaining political demands. Moreover, the student strike symbolized a revolution in popular consciousness. As Kost Bondarenko states, "[P]eople realized that . . . the regime was not so strong and monolithic as it appeared to be if it retracted in front of 17–20-year-old youngsters."[10] Ukrainian students, however, were unable to bring about a revolutionary break with the communist regime. Contrary to the protesters' demands, the new parliamentary elections were delayed until 1994, which hampered the overhaul of the political system in the post-Soviet period. Like Serbian protesters in the 1990s, Ukrainian civic activists felt that they had failed to accomplish their main goal and bring about regime change. Veterans of the 1990 student strike became heavily involved in subsequent protest campaigns, repeatedly calling for genuine democratic reforms.

The Ukraine without Kuchma Movement

The murder of investigative journalist Georgiy Gongadze triggered a major protest campaign in Ukraine in 2000–01. The 31-year-old journalist who founded the online publication *Ukrainska Pravda* ("*Ukrainian Truth*") and published a series of investigative reports about high-level corruption disappeared on September 16, 2000.[11] His beheaded body was found in the woods south of Kyiv on November 2. Shortly afterwards, leader of the Socialist Party of Ukraine Oleksandr Moroz presented in the national parliament the tapes allegedly recorded in the president's office by security guard Mykola Melnychenko. According to the wiretapped conversation, Kuchma ordered the Minister of Interior to "drive him [Gongadze]

[8] On protest events in the late Gorbachev period, see Beissinger, Mark. 2002. *Nationalist Mobilization and the Collapse of the Soviet State*. New York: Cambridge University Press.

[9] Onyshkevych, Roman. 1998. "A Revolution of Lost Illusions and Gained Opportunities." *Den*. October 27. www.day.kiev.ua/290619?idsource=270283&mainlang=eng.

[10] Bondarenko, Kost. 2000. "Dvi revoluitsii." *Postup*. September 28. http://postup.brama.com/000928/160_2_3.html.

[11] For a thorough analysis of this case, see Koshiw, Jaroslaw. 2002. *Beheaded: The Killing of a Journalist*. Reading, UK: Artemia Press.

out, throw him, give him to the Chechens."[12] In addition to the president's assault on investigative journalism, the Melnychenko tapes revealed multiple cases of the abuse of power, triggering demands for the president's impeachment. In turn, Kuchma denied his involvement in the journalist's murder and described the exposé as a foreign-sponsored "provocation."[13]

A group of former participants in the 1990 student strike launched a protest campaign against the incumbent president on December 15, 2001, three months after Gongadze's disappearance. In part, this date was chosen because a corps of foreign journalists was expected to arrive in the city to report the formal closure of the Chernobyl nuclear power plant. Volodymyr Chemerys recalled how this idea was born:

> Mykhailo Svystovych's birthday fell on December 11. Oleh Levitsky, Andriy Pidpalyi, and he stopped by the office of the Institute "Republic" on Gorkii Street. Not so much to celebrate, but to discuss the idea that something needs to be done. We decided that we should go to the Maidan and pitch tents, as we had done during the student hunger strike in 1990. We made the count and assumed that we could gather between 100 and 150 friends ... At night I called Moroz's press secretary Yuri Lutsenko. The idea that something needs to be done turned out to be floating among socialists too.[14]

Approximately 100 protesters gathered in front of the concert hall in which Kuchma presided over the honorary ceremony on the occasion of the plant's closure.[15] In addition, civic activists set up five tents on the Maidan, the site of the 1990 student hunger strike. The main demand of the protesters was resignation of the incumbent president. In addition, civic activists called for the resignation of top officials responsible for obstruction of the criminal investigation into Gongadze's murder: Minister of Interior Yuriy Kravchenko, head of the State Security Services Leonid Derkach, and Prosecutor General Mykhailo Potebenko. The event organizers, however, did not anticipate that the protest event would grow into a three-month-long protest campaign.

The Ukraine without Kuchma (*Ukraina bez Kuchmy* [UbK]) Movement was formed based on an alliance of several political parties and civic organizations, including the Sobor Party, the Socialist Party of Ukraine, and the Ukrainian National Assembly–Ukrainian National Self-Defense (UNA-UNSO). According to Chemerys, it was "the first mass movement in independent Ukraine for citizens' rights, democracy, and against the system of oligarchic capitalism."[16]

[12] Gongadze, Myroslava, and Serhiy Kudelia. 2004. *Rozirvanyi nerv*. Kyiv: Open Society Institute, p. 36.

[13] Kuzio, Taras. 2001. "Kuchmagate Continues to Dominate Ukrainian Politics." *Prism* 7(1). January 30. www.jamestown.org/archives/prism/p2001/?tx_publicationsttnews_pi2[issue]=1.

[14] Chemerys, Volodymyr. 2010. "Grudnevi tezy do 10-richchia masovykh protestiv v Ukraini." *Ukrainska Pravda*. December 15. www.pravda.com.ua/articles/2010/12/15/5675106/.

[15] *Ukrainska Pravda*. 2000a. "Militsiia i osoby v shtatskomu sklaly kompaniiu aktsii 'Try misiatsi bez Pravdy.'" December 15. www.pravda.com.ua/news/2000/12/15/2981483/.

[16] Chemerys, Volodymyr. 2010. "Grudnevi tezy do 10-richchia masovykh protestiv v Ukraini." *Ukrainska Pravda*.

In challenging the incumbent government, the UbK Movement used a traditional repertoire of contention, including protest rallies, marches, and the occupation of public space via installment of the tent city. To counterbalance state propaganda and provide daily coverage of protest events, Svystovych launched the website Maidan (http://maidan.org.ua), which remains, to this date, a major source of news about civil resistance in the country.

The UbK Movement, however, attracted a relatively small number of people. According to most media reports,[17] the number of protesters ranged from a few hundred to a few thousand people. As an eyewitness of protest events, Wilson, for example, estimates that no more than 30,000 people participated in antigovernment demonstrations in the winter of 2001.[18] In particular, only a small fraction of university students became engaged in these antigovernment protests. Nonetheless, an important outcome of the protest campaign was the transmission of nonviolent expertise from the veterans of the 1990 student strike to a younger cohort of civic activists.

A group of Lviv-based youth activists initiated establishment of the National Civic Resistance Committee "For Truth" (*Vseukrainskii gromadskii komitet oporu "Za pravdu"*). Lviv students were known for their high protest potential, and they frequently turned to the street. In 1999, for example, Lviv students protested against the removal of student discounts for domestic travel. This time students advanced more radical demands. The newly formed committee called for "complete change of the political system and the return of rights and freedoms to Ukrainian society."[19] As in the early 1990s, the Student Brotherhood and the Ukrainian Student Union played a vital role in mobilizing students in opposition to the regime. In addition, members of the youth organization *Moloda Prosvita* ("Youth Education"), primarily concerned with cultural issues, decided to join the protest campaign en masse. The committee's Founding Assembly, held in Kyiv on March 9, 2001, brought together 300 youth activists from different parts of the country to discuss a future course of action. In addition, the 14-member Presidium, composed of well-known civic activists and politicians, assumed the decision-making powers to channel youth energy in a certain direction. Among them were Oles Donii, Markian Ivashchshyn, Vladyslav Kaskiv, Oleksandr Kryvenko, Taras Stetskiv,

[17] Bishop, Kevin. 2001. "Eyewitness: Among the Kiev Protesters." BBC World Service. February 11. http://news.bbc.co.uk/2/hi/europe/1165168.stm; *Kyiv Post*. 2001. "Ukraine without Kuchma Plans Two Quiet Days." February 7. www.kyivpost.com/content/ukraine/ukraine-without-kuchma-plans-two-quiet-days.html; Tyler, Patrick. 2001. "A Grisly Mystery in Ukraine Leads to a Government Crisis." *New York Times*. January 30. www.nytimes.com/2001/01/30/world/a-grisly-mystery-in-ukraine-leads-to-a-government-crisis.html?pagewanted=all&src=pm; *Ukrainska Pravda*. 2001. "Aktsia Ukraina bez Kuchmy." February 1. www.pravda.com.ua/news/2001/02/1/2981775/.

[18] Wilson, Andrew. 2005. *Ukraine's Orange Revolution*. London: Yale University Press, p. 58.

[19] Za Pravdu. 2001. "Zvernennia Vseukrainskogo gromadskogo komitetu oporu Za Pravdu u zviazku z rozpravoiu nad myrnymy demonstrantamy ta rizkym zagostrenniam politychnoi kryzy." March 10 [press release]. www.brama.com/news/press/010310zapravdu.html.

and Mykhailo Svystovych. *Za Pravdu*'s Presidium, however, lacked a student representative. As a result, youth involvement in the protest campaign was often limited to participation in protest rallies organized by opposition political parties. Nonetheless, a few protest events were held to appeal to the youth population. For example, *Za Pravdu* organized a rock concert, "Rock for the Truth," in Kharkiv, Kyiv, and Lviv in spring 2001.

In turn, the incumbent government deployed a mix of legal, covert, and violent repressive methods. The city administration obstructed the organization of antigovernment protests by hampering access to the main protest site. City officials initially scheduled construction work on the Maidan and later labeled the tent city as "a danger to pedestrians and a health hazard."[20] Acting on the court's order, the police violently dismantled the tent city on March 1. In response, civic activists pitched tents in a city park near the monument to the Ukrainian poet Taras Shevchenko. On March 7, the tent city was again dismantled, but men in plain clothes folded the tents with greater care this time.[21] Another state countermove was the installation of an alternative tent city in downtown Kyiv and the organization of pro-Kuchma rallies with the coerced participation of public-sector employees and university students.[22]

The framing of protesters as extremists was another state countermove. President Kuchma dismissed his critics as a "destructive force comprising the extreme left and extreme right – semi-fascists and anti-Semites who go to these demonstrations with swastikas."[23] Toeing the official line, the state-controlled media portrayed protesters as violent. The state-owned TV channel UT-1, for example, reported the prevalence of "aggressive youth" and "destructive forces" among protesters.[24] To demonstrate the validity of these claims, the security services sought to provoke a scuffle between regime opponents and political conformists housed in the two adjacent tent cities. Moreover, provocateurs allegedly planted in the protest crowd shouted, "Beat the Cops," to instigate violence against the police.[25]

[20] Woronowycz, Roman. 2001. "Police Forcefully Dismantle Tent City." *Ukrainian Weekly*. March 1. P. 1.

[21] *Ukrainska Pravda*. 2000a. "Militsiia i osoby v shtatskomu sklaly kompaniiu aktsii 'Try misiatsi bez Pravdy.'" December 15. www.pravda.com.ua/news/2000/12/15/2981483/.

[22] *Ukrainska Pravda*. 2000b. "Khronika mityngu." December 20. www.pravda.com.ua/news/2000/12/20/2981513/.

[23] CNN. 2001. "Ukraine's Kuchma Dismisses Protests." February 24. http://articles.cnn.com/2001-02-24/world/ukraine.kuchma_1_ukraine-and-russia-ukraine-s-kuchma-political-crisis?_s=PM:WORLD.

[24] *Ukrainska Pravda*. 2000c. "Kryve dzerkalo ukrainskogo telebachennia." December 20. www.pravda.com.ua/news/2000/12/20/2981518/.

[25] Kapliuk, Galina. 2006. "Rokovoe 9 marta ili piat let spustia." *Glavred*. March 6. www.glavred.info/archive/2006/03/09/212045-7.html.

The protest campaign culminated in violent clashes with the police on March 9, 2001. According to numerous eyewitness accounts,[26] a handful of provocateurs attempted the takeover of the presidential administration during a peaceful march and provoked police violence. As UNA-UNSO member Ihor Mazur put it, "[W]e [UbK] did not plan a violent action; their [government's] plan worked."[27] In addition to protesters, approximately two-thirds of participants in *Za Pravdu's* Founding Assembly were arrested that day.[28] Legal repression manifested itself in the criminal proceedings against 19 UNA-UNSO members. Invoking Article 61 of the Criminal Code (infliction of physical injuries on police officers), the Kyiv court sentenced young men to two to four years in prison. The incumbent government also instructed rectors to stifle student participation in antipresidential protests, threatening noncomplying institutions with unscheduled tax audits.[29]

In sum, the 2000–1 protest campaign failed to mobilize a large number of protesters and oust the incumbent president from power. The heads of the Ministry of Interior and the State Security Service were forced to resign, but Kuchma stayed in office until expiration of his second presidential term. Furthermore, the current regime remained intact. On the demise of the UbK Movement, the ruling elite focused its attention on the 2002 parliamentary election. Meanwhile, civic activists deliberated on the development of more effective protest tactics. In particular, informal groups of former participants in antigovernment protests brainstormed ideas about novel street actions and staged small acts of resistance to the regime.[30]

Lessons Learned from the Previous Protest Campaigns

A key lesson that the political opposition learned from the previous protest campaigns was the significance of nonviolent action. One of the often-cited reasons for the demise of the UbK Movement was its breach of nonviolent discipline. In particular, violent clashes with the police on March 9 delivered a debilitating blow to the movement, which motivated youth activists to examine

[26] *Ibid.*; Solodko, Pavlo. 2006. "9 bereznia 2001 roku: Spogady i prognozy vid initsiatoriv 'Ukrainy bez Kuchmy.'" *Ukrainska Pravda*. March 9. www.pravda.com.ua/articles/2006/03/9/3074768/; Tkachuk, Maryna. 2011. "Odynadtsiata zapovid Khrysta – Ne biisia." *Ukraina Moloda*. March 4. www.umoloda.kiev.ua/number/1845/180/65535/.

[27] Quoted from Tkachuk, Maryna. 2011. "Odynadtsiata zapovid Khrysta – Ne biisia."

[28] Lykhovii, Dmytro. 2001. "Ustanovchui z'izd Komitetu Za Pravdu zavershuvsia za gratamy." *Ukrainska Pravda*. March 11. www.pravda.com.ua/news/2001/03/11/2982094/.

[29] Kuropas, Myron. 2001. "Is Ukraine Europe's Black Hole?" *Ukrainian Weekly*. April 29. www.ukrweekly.com/old/archive/2001/170115.shtml.

[30] Pavlo Zubiuk, for example, recalled how he was a member of an informal group of youth activists who distributed leaflets with the slogan "People, Stop Sleeping!" on the subway in the fall of 2001. Author's interview with Pavlo Zubiuk, Kyiv, Ukraine, March 23, 2010.

unarmed insurrections around the globe and apply novel methods of civil resistance in Ukraine.

Another major lesson youth activists drew from the 2000–1 protest campaign was that they should clearly establish independence from the opposition political parties. Many youth activists shared the view that the domination of party interests over national ones contributed to the decline of the UbK Movement.[31] Moreover, some youth activists were appalled by the lack of professionalism on the part of the old opposition. In response, Pora declared its adherence to the principle of nonpartisanship (*pozapartiinist*).[32]

> Above all, we realized that Ukrainian political leaders were inept. They carried out an ill-conceived information campaign. They printed large-size leaflets with a lot of small-print text. Nobody would read such leaflets. We realized that leaflets should be smaller in size and contain less information … The political parties exerted monotonous pressure on Kuchma. People would stand in the street and demand the president's resignation. We realized that we should diversify forms of political pressure on the regime.[33]

A related reason for youth's distance from the opposition political parties was the realization that nonviolent action should not look boring to young people.

> The civic resistance committee organized trips of Lviv students to Kyiv. At first, it was very interesting. We went to protest rallies and chanted "Away with Kuchma!" But then the UbK began to lose its spark. The same thing happened over and over again. Yury Lutsenko was a regular speaker at these protest rallies. He would chant "Away with Kuchma!" and we would chant back this slogan again and again.[34]

Furthermore, these protest campaigns laid the groundwork for the development of a social network in opposition to the regime. In February 2001, Oles Donii, a leader of the 1990 student strike, wrote an open letter "From the Survivors of Young Ukrainian Intelligentsia" in which he urged Ukrainians to exercise their right to resistance (*pravo na opir*) and demand the turnover of power.[35] The text of this letter was circulated via a list-serv of Ukrainian students studying in North America and Western Europe. "I signed the letter, and I found out about other like-minded individuals by looking at the list of signatories," said Dmytro Potekhin, participant in the 2000–01 protests and founder of the civic campaign *Znaiu!* ("I Know") in 2004.[36] Overall, more

[31] Shevtsiv, Andriy. 2005. "Konflikty dovkola Pory: Moia pozytsiia." Maidan. July 15. http://maidan.org.ua/static/mai/1121422197.html.

[32] Pora. 2004. "Pora pochynaje gromadiansku kampaniu." March 31 [press release]. http://kuchmizm.info/weblog/archives/2004_03.html.

[33] Author's interview with Oleksiy Tolkachov, Kyiv, Ukraine, April 22, 2010.

[34] Author's interview with Volodymyr Viatrovych, Kyiv, Ukraine, March 2, 2010.

[35] Donii, Oles. 2001. "Vidkrytyi lyst: Vid nedobytkiv molodoi ukrainskoi inteligentsii." *Ukrainska Pravda*. February 16. www.pravda.com.ua/news/2001/2/16/16135.htm.

[36] Author's interview with Dmytro Potekhin, Kyiv, Ukraine, April 10, 2008.

than 1,500 Ukrainians signed Donii's petition demanding the president's resignation.[37]

CROSS-NATIONAL DIFFUSION OF IDEAS

By the time of the 2004 election, Ukrainian youth could tap into a large reservoir of nonviolent expertise and learn from graduates of several electoral revolutions. The diffusion of Otpor's ideas began shortly after Milosevic's downfall and the decline of the UbK Movement. The first workshops involving former Otpor activists were held in Ukraine in spring 2001, while a few young Ukrainians visited Serbia in April 2004. The content of workshops focused on a few major issues, including fund-raising, public relations, security, and nonviolent methods. Some youth activists, however, felt that they had plenty of prior protest experience to organize street actions. Volodymyr Lesyk, for example, stated that he did not need any Otpor's manual to develop a mechanism for the movement's response to the arrest of youth activists, since he could draw on his previous engagement in protest campaigns in Ukraine.[38] The interviewed activists stressed the example of prior success as the most important facet of their interactions with graduates of earlier electoral revolutions.

> When we debated the development of a resistance movement, we realized that the blunt copying of the Serbian experience would not work or would not produce the best results. We knew that we had to get rooted into our own conditions. We invited Otpor and Zubr activists to participate in our seminars, introduced them to our youth, and said, "If they could do it, you can do it too." It was a motivational factor.[39]
>
> In Novi Sad it was interesting to hear directly from people who had firsthand experience with organizing nonviolent resistance. Each seminar started with a series of slides. But then there was an opportunity to ask questions . . . We could feel that they had built a team and understand better what they had gone through.[40]

Similarly, the example of prior success was central to face-to-face interactions with Georgian activists. Pora activist Volodymyr Viatrovych recalled the impact of emotions on the cross-national diffusion of ideas:

> Young small-frame girls came to Kyiv, but I saw fire in their eyes. It was clear that these people had gone through something special. Serbs have already digested everything and developed a methodology of nonviolent resistance. But the Georgians had raw emotions. This emotional recharge that we received from them was the most important thing. It was an example of success.[41]

[37] For a full list of names, see Donii, Oles. 2002. *Sproba Buntu*. Kyiv, Ukraine: [s.n].
[38] Author's interview with Volodymyr Lesyk, Kyiv, Ukraine, April 11, 2008.
[39] Author's interview with Andriy Kohut, Kyiv, Ukraine, March 19, 2010.
[40] Author's interview with Yaryna Yasynevych, Kyiv, Ukraine, April 16, 2008.
[41] Author's interview with Volodymyr Viatrovych, Kyiv, Ukraine, March 2, 2010.

The Belarusian resistance against the regime also caught the attention of Ukrainian youth. Some Ukrainian activists, for example, borrowed Zubr's ideas regarding the symbolic portrayal of civil resistance. Yaroslav Zen, a designer at yellow Pora, explained how activists came up with the design for a movement sticker:

Pora had a poster with [a] boot stamping on [a] bug. We borrowed this image from Zubr. But we made a few changes. First, Zubr used a picture of some office-style shoes. We replaced them with military boots to deliver a stronger message. Second, we changed the type of insect to be squashed by the boot. Ours was a brownish spider. In this way, we made a reference to Kuchma nicknamed as the brown spider.[42]

Other Pora activists, on the contrary, favored a conceptually different approach to the design of the movement's stickers. Olha Salo, a designer at black Pora, summarized her position as follows:

Zubr's posters referred to the phenomenon, rather than specific events. For example, "It Is Time to Choose" stickers contained images of abstract concepts. We centered our design around specific events or facts. A lot of our material focused on Yanukovych's criminal past.[43]

Another inspiring example of nonviolent resistance came from neighboring Poland.[44] Ukrainian activists scrutinized how the Solidarity movement pressed for political change in the 1980s.

When politicians think of a protest rally in Ukraine, they usually imagine a stage, several speakers, and a lot of people in the crowd. But the Poles organized very short rallies. The protesters would come, somebody would make a brief speech, and they would disperse within half an hour. The Serbian movement Otpor did the same thing: rapid, but memorable action.[45]

The case of the 1998 Slovak election provided another powerful example for the organization of voter mobilization and voter education campaigns in Ukraine. According to Demes, coordination of action among various civil society actors was critical to the success of a civic campaign:

I think what we [Slovaks] showed them was a variety of people, of programs, and opinions but at the same time something that was unifying all these under the same logo and the same commitment to the goals . . . I think that this capacity to form a broad coalition within the third sector and other democratic players is something that they have to start to do.[46]

42 Author's interview with Yaroslav Zen, Kyiv, Ukraine, April 18, 2008.

43 Author's interview with Olha Salo, Kyiv, Ukraine, April 16, 2008.

44 On the role of Polish civil society during the 2004 presidential election in Ukraine, see Petrova, Tsveta. 2014. *From Solidarity to Geopolitics: Support for Democracy among Postcommunist States*. New York: Cambridge University Press, pp. 107–9.

45 Author's interview with Mykhailo Svystovych, Kyiv, Ukraine, March 27, 2010.

46 Shadbolt, Peter. 1999. "OK'98: Slovak NGOs Efforts Help Boost Election Turnout." *Mott Now* 2(4), p. 3, a publication of Charles Mott Foundation.

The first attempt to use OK'98 tactics was made by Ukrainian civil society during the 1999 presidential election. But the political conditions in the country constrained the effectiveness of these innovative tactics. According to Kapusta, "[I]t was a difficult case because Ukraine at that time did not have very good prospects for change or any good candidates, so from the beginning we understood that those elections were a lost cause."[47] Nonetheless, Ukrainian NGOs learned how to build a coalition to conduct a voter education campaign and monitor the electoral process. As a leader of the NGO coalition Freedom of Choice, Kaskiv developed various contacts inside and outside Ukraine, and yellow Pora attempted to reactivate these networks during the movement's embryonic stage. In an interview with Radio Svoboda, Kaskiv described Pora's interactions with Slovak civic activists as "personal contacts in the context of solidarity of East European democratic movements."[48] Specifically, Kaskiv recalled Demes's role in supporting the Ukrainian youth movement:

> Speaking of the George Marshall Fund, it provided invaluable assistance that could not be actually measured in monetary terms. The thing is that the Fund is chaired by Pavol Demes, former Minister of Foreign Affairs of Slovakia, our old friend with whom we have been working for several years. We discussed with him our plans and formulated the logic of our organizational structure. He participated in Pora's founding assembly held in Uzhhorod in April prior to the Mukachevo elections.[49]

Sharp's book was translated into Ukrainian and distributed among movement participants prior to the Orange Revolution, but few interviewed activists admitted reading it from cover to cover.

> Myself, I have read the book on the seventh or eighth month of my involvement in the civic campaign. I did it on the train. Maybe, I didn't have anything else to do. That book is useful at the stage of brainstorming ideas and planning. It is too late to read it when the revolution is in full swing.[50]

With the growing access to the Internet, the web has become a major channel for the diffusion of ideas in Ukraine. The website Maidan contained an electronic collection of publications on civic activism in different political settings. Youth activists, for example, posted a Ukrainian-language copy of the *Nonviolence Training Manual* prepared by the US organization American

[47] Arias-King, Fredo. 2007. "Revolution Is Contagious: Interview with Marek Kapusta." *Demokratizatsiya: Journal of Post-Soviet Democratization* 15(1): 133–37, p. 133.

[48] Drach, Mariana. 2005. "Lider Pory Vladyslav Kaskiv zustrivsia u Bratyslavi z prezydentom Spoluchnykh Shtativ." Radio Svoboda. February 24. www.radiosvoboda.org/content/article/927443.html.

[49] Shust, Iryna. 2005. "Vladyslav Kaskiv: Treba bulo bachyty oblychia liudei, iaki pishly na administratsiiu Kuchmy." *Ukrainska Pravda*. April 5. www.pravda.com.ua/articles/2005/04/5/3008540/.

[50] Author's interview with Oleksandr Solontay, Kyiv, Ukraine, April 11, 2008.

Peace Test during its campaign against nuclear warhead testing in the late 1980s.[51] By the same token, Ukrainian activists examined how the Muslim Brotherhood built a nationwide network of supporters in Egypt under Hosni Mubarak.[52]

To advance youth's understanding of nonviolent methods, Pora organized workshops for youth activists, although the leaders of yellow and black Pora differed in their execution of this idea. Yellow Pora organized a well-publicized summer camp for 300 activists in the Crimea in August 2004.[53] Among 15 guest speakers were Slovak civic activists Pavol Demes and Balazs Jarabik, as well as a leader of the 1990 student strike, Markian Ivashchshyn. Youth activists discussed how to develop a network of volunteers, interact with the mass media, and educate voters. In contrast, black Pora organized a much less publicized summer camp in the Carpathian Mountains. Ironically, a sanatorium owned by the Ministry of Interior served as a hideout for Pora activists due to a cash payment to the facilities manager.

> On the first day of the summer camp, a few young people assumed that there would be political consultants teaching us what to do. But we didn't invite any foreign speakers. We invited young people to come up with their own ideas. At first, people were puzzled. But then a heated discussion on our course of action started.[54]

The detention and deportation of a foreign trainer were the government's belated response to the cross-national diffusion of ideas. Aleksandar Maric, former Otpor member and trainer for a US-funded voter education program, was detained in the Boryspil airport and deported to Serbia in mid-October, two weeks prior to election day.[55] It was a single known case of a trainer's deportation on a government's order. A more common predicament for foreign trainers was petty corruption in the local police. Otpor activist Nenad Belcevic recalled how he tried to avoid an encounter with the police immediately on his entry to Ukraine:

> My Ukrainian friends instructed me to hop on the train to Kyiv at the last moment, just a minute or two before its departure. Otherwise, I could have been detained by the local police. They could take me off the train and keep me in the police station until the train departed in an effort to extract from me some money.[56]

[51] For the Ukrainian-language copy of the *Nonviolence Training Manual*, visit www2.maidan.org.ua/n/lib/1041117922.

[52] Maidan. 2003. "Uspishnyi sotsialnyi rukh iak dobre pobudovannyi mesidzh." May 14. www.maidan.org.ua/news/view.php3?bn=maidan_lib&key=1052920458&first=1259537591&last=1038336381.

[53] Pora. 2004. "Tabir Pora pochynaty: Iak my navchalys?" August 8. www.pora.org.ua.

[54] Author's interview with Yaryna Yasynevych, Kyiv, Ukraine, April 16, 2008.

[55] Freedom House. 2004. "Concern over Trainer's Deportation from Ukraine." Press release. October 14. www.freedomhouse.org/media/pressrel/101404b.htm.

[56] Author's interview with Nenad Belcevic, Belgrade, Serbia, February 7, 2008.

In sum, the cross-national diffusion of ideas advanced youths' knowledge of nonviolent methods. A number of Ukrainian activists contemplated the application of Otpor's tactics during the 2004 presidential election. The emergence of two youth movements with the same name was a product of such long-term deliberations.

THE EMERGENCE OF PORA

The emergence of the youth movement Pora is ridden with controversy. Some Pora activists claim that there was one movement with two wings. Others point out that there were actually two youth movements with the same name. A number of Lviv and Kyiv activists formed the backbone of what later became known as black Pora, whereas another group of Kyiv and Kharkiv activists coalesced around the so-called yellow Pora. As a mediator between the two groups, Dmytro Potekhin provided the following summary of what had happened:

> Svystovych and his associates had for a long time planned to create such a movement, but didn't have the time, resources or understanding of how to organize the operation themselves ... Following the creation of the Pora "brand," replete with its black emblem, logotype, etc., the strategic goal of the campaign was defined: to fight against the system of power under Kuchma ... A copycat Pora movement appeared in Kyiv, replete with their own (yellow) logo and campaign in April 2004. The group, led by 31-year-old Ternopil native Vladyslav Kaskiv, appeared out of nowhere and began making the rounds of foreign donors.[57]

The two youth movements made their first public appearance in spring 2004. Black Pora launched the public campaign "What Is Kuchmism?" on March 28. Pora activists in 17 regions (*oblasts*) distributed black-and-white stickers with the symbol of the rising sun on the night Ukrainians turned their clocks forward for daylight savings. To the surprise of many, yellow Pora emerged in the city of Mukachevo during the local elections a few weeks later. As late as April 5, Kaskiv spoke at a press conference about the voter education campaign "Wave of Freedom" (*Khvylia svobody*). Volunteers for this campaign, however, were seen in mid-April wearing yellow T-shirts with the symbol of the ticking clock. According to several firsthand accounts of Pora's origins,[58] Kaskiv deliberately changed the campaign's name to capitalize on the idea of black Pora. Some

[57] *Kyiv Post*. 2005. "Q&A: Dmytro Potekhin." February 24. www.kyivpost.com/content/ukraine/qa-dmytro-potekhin-22378.htm.l.

[58] Shevtsiv, Andriy. 2005. "Konflikty dovkola Pory: Moia pozytsiia." Maidan. July 15. http://maidan.org.ua/static/mai/1121422197.html; Solontay, Oleksandr. 2005. "Pravda pro Poru ochuma zseredyny." *Ukrainska Pravda*. April 15. www.pravda.com.ua/news/2005/4/15/3505.htm; Tolkachov, Oleksii. 2009. "Nevidomi istorii Maidanu." *Ukrainska Pravda*. November 18. www.pravda.com.ua/articles/2009/11/18/4321456/?attempt=1; Yurochko, Bohdan. 2005. "Interview with Mykhailo Svystovych: My ne proty, shchob aktyvisty ishly v polityku, mu proty, shchob tse vidbuvalos vid imeni Pory." *Lvivska gazeta*. February 1. www.gazeta.lviv.ua/articles/2005/02/01/2216/.

reports suggest that Oleh Yatsenko, leader of the Student Brotherhood, shared information about the nascent movement's branding with Kaskiv.[59]

The ownership of the movement's name was a major point of contention among movement leaders. Most interviewed youth activists concurred that the leader of yellow Pora did not behave in an ethical manner. In his defense, Kaskiv dismissed the fixation on the movement's name and pointed out that the idea of "creating a structure that would defend elections and would convey the truth to people" existed from the very beginning. "And even if it [the movement] were named *Taburetka* (stool), it would have been popular as Taburetka today because this organization defended elections."[60]

One of the often-cited reasons for the choice of the movement's name is the fact that it is spelled the same way in Russian and Ukrainian. This was an important factor, given the extensive use of the Russian language in contemporary Ukraine. Alternative names considered by youth activists included *Opir* ("Resistance") and *Vpered* ("Forward"). An additional reason for the choice of the movement's name is that it provided a symbolic connection between youth's resistance against the regime and long-standing struggle for national independence. In his well-known poem "*Ne Pora*" ("Now Is Not the Time"), written in 1880, the Ukrainian poet Ivan Franko proclaimed that "Now is not the time to serve the Muscovites and the Poles ... It's time to live for Ukraine."[61]

The emergence of two civic campaigns with the same name was confusing for many activists, so there was an attempt to unite these groups into a single organizational structure. Several youth activists organized a forum to agree on the details of the merger in August 2004. The proposed symbol of the joint civic campaign incorporated the images of a rising sun and a ticking clock. But personal ambitions at the leadership level reportedly hampered realization of the full merger. In particular, movement leaders were reluctant to share information about the movement's finances. To the credit of movement leaders, they decided to mute their differences in the public eye to wage nonviolent resistance against the regime more effectively. By the same token, Kyiv-based activists in both movements maintained informal contacts with each other, and youth activists throughout Ukraine regularly participated in activities of both movements without getting enmeshed in the tensions at the leadership level. Most information about the split surfaced only after the Orange Revolution, in the midst of heated debates about Pora's future.

Both youth movements were driven by concerns about systematic violations of democratic procedures in the course of the election season. In campaigning

[59] Zakhidna informatsiina korporatsiia. 2007. "Khrest na Pori." April 24. http://zik.ua/news/2007/04/24/71901.

[60] Shust, Iryna. 2005. "Vladyslav Kaskiv: Treba bulo bachyty oblychia liudei, iaki pishly na administratsiiu Kuchmy." *Ukrainska Pravda*. April 5. www.pravda.com.ua/articles/2005/04/5/3008540/.

[61] The full text of the poem is available in Ukrainian at http://ukr-lit.net/franko/297-virshi/891-ne-pora-ne-pora-ne-pora.html.

for free and fair elections, the two youth movements appeared to complement each other well. Yellow Pora focused on voter education and voter mobilization campaigns, whereas black Pora organized a large number of street actions against the current regime. In anticipation of electoral fraud, youth activists geared up for the defense of stolen votes. "We realized from the very beginning that we would have to defend our vote, not just vote," said Pora activist Yaryna Yasynevych.[62] The remainder of this section discusses tactics of both movements, whenever necessary, making a distinction between them.

Recruitment Tactics

The core of Pora membership was made up of students and young professionals, but the two youth movements adopted different approaches to recruitment. Yellow Pora sought to build on a preexisting network of NGOs, whereas black Pora made a greater effort to recruit individual members and draw into nonviolent resistance politically inactive youth.

The leadership of yellow Pora sought to reactivate organizational ties built during previous election campaigns. The coalition Freedom of Choice, composed of 292 NGOs, was "the largest contributor to voter and civic education programs" during the 1999 presidential election.[63] This coalition continued to monitor elections and implement voter education programs during the 2002 parliamentary election. For example, Freedom of Choice monitored media advertising by major political parties.[64] As a former coordinator of this civic coalition, Kaskiv tried to revive earlier institutional ties to carry out a civic campaign in 2004. In addition, Oleksandr Solontay, leader of the Foundation of Regional Initiatives (*Fundatsiia Regionalnykh Initsiativ* [FRI]), sought to bring disconnected youth into existing civic organizations.

> I wanted youth organizations to come out stronger after the Orange Revolution. That's why I strongly objected to taking people off the street. I told them, "Join some youth organization and then come back to us." But my approach didn't appeal to everybody in yellow Pora. I wasn't responsible for recruiting new members after September 2004.[65]

In contrast, Black Pora seemed to place greater emphasis on the recruitment of individuals rather than the cultivation of organizational ties. Many Pora members were political novices. For example, 20-year-old student Oleksandr Lomako became a Pora coordinator in the city of Chernihiv. Seminars on nonviolent

[62] Author's interview with Yaryna Yasynevych, Kyiv, Ukraine, April 16, 2008.

[63] Organization for Security and Cooperation in Europe. 2000. *Ukraine Presidential Elections: 31 October and 14 November 1999 (Final Report)*. Warsaw, Poland: Office for Democratic Institutions and Human Rights, p. 24.

[64] Organization for Security and Cooperation in Europe. 2002. *Ukraine Parliamentary Elections: 31 March 2002 (Final Report)*. Warsaw, Poland: Office for Democratic Institutions and Human Rights, p. 14.

[65] Author's interview with Oleksandr Solontay, Kyiv, Ukraine, April 11, 2008.

resistance provided an opportunity for the recruitment of young people in the provinces. Liubov Yeremycheva, for example, started a Pora cell in the city of Kherson after her attendance of such a seminar in March 2004. "At that time, I was not very interested in politics. I was the chair of the Kherson branch of *Moloda Prosvita* [a cultural youth organization]. But having watched the documentary *The Face of the Protest*, I realized that many things had gone wrong in the country. I took off the rosy glasses."[66]

Moreover, the youth movements sought to broaden their appeal beyond student population. According to yellow Pora's leader Kaskiv,

> It would be wrong to say that Pora is a solely student organization. There are a lot of young people in it who are not students, but college students were and are the most active force of the Pora movement. They propagate Pora ideas and ideals.[67]

As in Serbia, some youngsters in Ukraine drew their parents into the nonviolent struggle against the regime. In Lviv, for example, a 16-year-old daughter and her middle-aged mother jointly plastered Pora stickers at night.[68] Meanwhile, Pora sought to mitigate the effects of possible informants inside the movement.

> Even if there was an informant among our new recruits, he had to work hard and do a lot of good things for the organization before getting access to any information. We introduced several rules to fight the paranoia of informants. Nobody was supposed to discuss his or her current project with friends. It was viewed as inappropriate to ask, "What are you working upon right now?" An activist might say that he had been sending faxes, while in reality he wrote press releases.[69]

Organizational Structure

This study finds that yellow Pora was more hierarchical than black Pora. While the Coordinating Council composed of a dozen people discussed protest tactics, Kaskiv appeared to play a decisive role in determining the movement's course of action. In part, his power derived from the fact that he managed the movement's finances and served as a primary contact for donors. As a youth activist put it, "There wasn't even a hierarchy in yellow Pora. There was just one dot – Vlad Kaskiv. He made all the major decisions."[70] Another youth activist concurred, "Kaskiv made all the financial decisions ... But he managed to assemble an excellent team of

[66] Author's interview with Liubov Yeremycheva, Kyiv, Ukraine, May 14, 2010.

[67] Quoted from Kutsenko, Zinayida. 2005. "Pora – It's High Time!" *Welcome to Ukraine Magazine*. www.wumag.kiev.ua/index2.php?param=pgs20052/52.

[68] Shcherbaty, Mykola. 2004. "Tsia zagadkova Pora." Maidan. May 31. http://maidan.org.ua/static/mai/1085995215.html.

[69] Author's interview with Yaryna Yasynevych, Kyiv, Ukraine, April 16, 2008.

[70] Author's interview with a youth activist, Kyiv, Ukraine, April, 2008.

professionals."[71] In contrast, the leadership of black Pora made a genuine effort to build a horizontal organizational structure.

We borrowed a few ideas from the Serbs. One of them was a leaderless structure. A completely leaderless structure does not exist, but at least there should not be a single leader. We also encouraged communication of all with all. Communication in a hierarchical structure occurs exclusively through the center. We had autonomous cells across the country. Activists from Poltava could get in touch with activists from Chernihiv and agree upon the organization of a joint action. We just asked activists to inform us about their action, but we never prohibited a street action at the local level.[72]

We didn't impose any leaders. If a person could bring 500 people to a protest rally, such a person could be considered a leader. Indeed, he proved to be capable of making a big accomplishment. Nobody asked why a certain individual became a coordinator. There was some level of interpersonal trust.[73]

The headquarters of the two youth movements were based in Kyiv. Each main office was divided into various departments responsible for finances, logistics, marketing, public relations, and security. These departments were staffed with youth activists with relevant professional skills. Olha Salo, for example, studied design at the Academy of Arts before becoming a designer at black Pora. Likewise, Ostap Kryvdyk received a master's degree from the National University of Kyiv–Mohyla Academy and worked at the national TV channel 1+1 before joining a team of copyrighters and designers at yellow Pora.[74] Youths' professional skills, along with their prior protest experience, strengthened the movement's capacity to campaign against the regime.

Tactics vis-à-vis Opponents

Pora's repertoire of contention included a mix of old and new protest tactics. Youth activists supplemented the distribution of leaflets and the organization of pickets with such innovative tactics as the production of stickers and the organization of street performances. Moreover, youth injected creativity into nonviolent action. "We didn't have any barriers in our creative thinking. We tried to come up with unconventional approaches to addressing societal problems," said a Pora activist.[75] Even the most routine activity was a subject of extensive deliberation among movement participants.

[71] Author's interview with Ostap Kryvdyk, Kyiv, Ukraine, April 16, 2008.
[72] Author's interview with Mykhailo Svystovych, Kyiv, Ukraine, March 27, 2010.
[73] Author's interview with Yaryna Yasynevych, Kyiv, Ukraine, April 16, 2008.
[74] Retrieved from www.ostap.name/kryvdyk.html.
[75] Author's interview with Tetyana Boyko, Kyiv, Ukraine, April 14, 2008.

Activists thought out and discussed various methods of nonviolent resistance. Even such a mundane task as the distribution of leaflets in the street generated an online discussion. People exchanged ideas on how to approach pedestrians. Then they compiled guidelines on how to do it in the most effective way.[76]

Unlike the distribution of leaflets, the dissemination of stickers was a relatively novel protest tactic in Ukraine. According to Kaskiv et al., Pora distributed a total of 40 million copies of print material in 2004,[77] although the actual number is likely to be lower.[78] Youth activists designed stickers to correspond to different phases of nonviolent struggle during an election year. The recruitment campaign, for example, was accompanied by the production of stickers with the slogans, "It's Time to Rise!" (yellow Pora) and "Be Yourself! Be Free! Be with Us – It's Your Time!" (black Pora). A sticker designed by yellow Pora showed the profile of a young man against the backdrop of Taras Shevchenko's portrait, reminding youngsters of earlier struggles for Ukraine's independence. Another sticker produced by yellow Pora on the eve of the second round of the presidential election carried an image of Che Gevara in an embroidered Ukrainian shirt, reflecting a mix of local and global symbols of resistance. In contrast, black Pora used a few photographs of ordinary Ukrainians for its recruitment campaign, implying that Pora consisted of youth like them.

The organization of street performances was another innovative method of nonviolent resistance. Yanukovych's criminal record was a popular subject of street action, while some actions targeted the outgoing president. For example, young Ukrainians staged a street performance in which they sent the head of state into outer space.

We organized a street action "Kuchma – to the Moon" in Kharkiv. In his book *Ukraine Is Not Russia*, Kuchma promised that Ukrainians would fly to the Moon. And we decided to send him to the Moon in a washing machine. For this purpose, I borrowed from my mom the washing machine "Riga" that looked like a rocket. We also played the song "One-Way Ticket" by the British band Eruption ... We overcame the problem of fear via street action with elements of humor.[79]

Pora's civil resistance was infused with humor. In particular, the alleged attempt on Yanukovych's life in the city of Ivano-Frankivsk engendered a host of political jokes in fall 2004. The state-controlled media framed the incident as an act of violence and reported Yanukovych's temporary

[76] Author's interview with Yaryna Yasynevych, Kyiv, Ukraine, April 16, 2008.

[77] Kaskiv, Vladyslav, Iryna Chupryna, and Yevhen Zolotariov. 2007. "It's Time! Pora and the Orange Revolution in Ukraine." In *Reclaiming Democracy: Civil Society and Electoral Change in Central and Eastern Europe*, eds. Joerg Forbig and Pavol Demes. Washington, DC: German Marshall Fund, pp. 127–51, p. 127.

[78] Solontay, Oleksandr. 2005. "Pravda pro Poru ochuma zseredyny." *Ukrainska Pravda*. April 15. www.pravda.com.ua/news/2005/4/15/3505.htm.

[79] Author's interview with Yevhen Zolotariov, Kyiv, Ukraine, March 30, 2010.

hospitalization due to an "attack with a heavy blunt object."[80] But local journalists clearly captured on camera how the presidential candidate fell to the ground immediately after a student had thrown an egg at him. To ridicule Yanukovych's behavior on the campaign trail, Pora activists picketed the building of the Cabinet of Ministers with a makeshift version of the chicken egg. In addition, a Pora sticker depicted the yellow chick with Pora's bandana, naming the fluffy animal a national hero for bringing down the heavy-weight politician.

Moreover, Ukrainian-language music was seen as a symbol of resistance to the current regime.[81] Many well-known Ukrainian musicians, including Maria Burmaka, the 2004 Eurovision winner Ruslana, the rock band Okean Elzy, and Vopli Vodopliasova, performed on the Maidan's stage in November – December 2004 to demonstrate their solidarity with protesters and express their opposition to the regime via art. Burmaka's songs "*Ne Biisia Zhyty*" ("Don't Be Afraid to Live") and "*My Idemo*" ("We Are Coming"), for instance, conveyed people's resolve to fight for political change. Most songs performed on the Maidan did not explicitly deal with electoral politics, but they took on a new meaning in the thick of antigovernment protests. For example, Okean Elzy's hit "*Maizhe Vesna*" ("It's Almost Spring") narrated a love story, but the rebellious audience reinterpreted its lyrics to cherish hopes for a better future of their country and their compatriots. Nonetheless, it was the Ukrainian-language version of the Chilean protest song "*El pueblo unido jamas sera vencido*" that became an informal hymn of the Orange Revolution. Protesters in the street chanted the refrain "Together we are many; we cannot be defeated," stressing their power in numbers.

Finally, youth activists built on the local tradition of the tent city as a symbol of resistance. The main tent city was located in Kyiv's main square, but smaller tent cities mushroomed up throughout the country. Lviv students, for example, set up tents near the monument to Ivan Franko. "After classes students would come to the tent city and ask about happenings in the country," recalled Pora activist Nazar Matkivsky.[82] Pora activists also attempted to pitch tents in downtown Donetsk, but a group of 50 young men violently dismantled this tent city less than an hour after its installation.[83] The subnational differences in the political conditions affected the extent to

80 *Ukrainska Pravda*. 2004. "V Ianukovycha kynuly tverdym predmetom, vin u likarni." September 24. www.pravda.com.ua/news/2004/09/24/3002689/; Viktorovych, Iana. 2004. "Operatsia 'Iajeshnia,' abo 'Terakt' proty Ianukovycha." *Ukrainska Pravda*. September 24. www.pravda.com.ua/news/2004/09/24/3002704/.

81 For an overview, see Klid, Bohdan. 2007. "Rock, Pop, and Politics in Ukraine's 2004 Presidential Campaign and Orange Revolution." *Journal of Communist Studies and Transition Politics* 23(1): 118–37.

82 Author's interview with Nazar Matkivsky, Kyiv, Ukraine, April 14, 2008.

83 Garmash, Sergei. 2004. "Pora v Donetske ne pora." Ostro. December 22. www.ostro.org/general/politics/articles/477/#.

which youth activists could apply the same nonviolent methods against the regime. State authorities in the Donetsk region more ruthlessly suppressed dissent than their counterparts in western Ukraine.

Tactics vis-à-vis Allies

The mass media was one of the movement's influential allies. The two youth movements, however, adopted different approaches to their interactions with journalists. Yellow Pora sought to establish good working relations with the media by promptly answering media queries and regularly supplying journalists with information about movement activities. As a Pora spokesperson, Anastasiia Bezverkha did a tremendous amount of work dealing with local media and explaining to foreign journalists the nuances of Ukrainian politics and youth's struggle for political change. Moreover, movement leaders came up with various ideas to keep Pora in the media spotlight during periods of lull.

> There were 2–3 days in December when nothing was happening. Then we came up with a media event for Pora. We found out that Kuchma frequently dined at the restaurant "Caravella." Pora brought a box of oranges to the restaurant and gave it to the management as a gift for Kuchma. I don't know whether Kuchma was at the restaurant that day. But journalists ran a story about our action.[84]

In contrast, black Pora activists were less easily available for interviews and more secretive about the movement. Black Pora members, for example, gave interviews on the condition of anonymity. This tactic was adopted to minimize the presence of career-minded individuals who might capitalize on the movement's reputation for self-promotion.

Compared with youth activists in the preceding cases, Ukrainian youth used the Internet more extensively.[85] As Serhiy Taran, former director of the Institute of Public Information, put it, "The online audience is a critical mass. One Internet user is worth ten factory workers because he is a critically thinking person."[86] To reach this audience, the two youth movements set up the following websites: (1) the website http://kuchmizm.info, named after black Pora's public campaign "What Is Kuchmism?," and (2) the website www.pora.org.ua registered by yellow Pora. Moreover, Pora activists regularly contributed to the website Maidan launched by veterans of the 1990 student strike at the start of the 2000–01 protest campaign.

[84] Author's interview with Serhiy Taran, Kyiv, Ukraine, April 28, 2008.

[85] On the use of the Internet, see Goldstein, Joshua. 2007. "The Role of Digital Networked Technologies in the Ukrainian Orange Revolution." Working Paper No. 2007–14. Berkman Center for Internet and Society, Harvard University, Cambridge, MA. Retrieved from http://cyber.law.harvard.edu/publications/2007/The_Role_of_Digital_Networked_Technologies_in_the_Ukranian_Orange_Revolution.

[86] Author's interview with Serhiy Taran, Kyiv, Ukraine, April 28, 2010.

Another Pora's challenge was alliance with the opposition political parties without compromising the movement's independence. Like the opposition leaders in other former Soviet republics, Yushchenko initially "viewed Pora as his Komsomol,"[87] assuming that the youth organization would blindly follow instructions from senior political figures. But the youth movements resisted the old opposition's efforts to assert control over them. In particular, black Pora tried to distance itself from the opposition political parties.

According to a Pora activist, lack of professionalism on the part of Yushchenko's election campaign team eventually provided an impetus for opening up some lines of communication with the old opposition:

> We were appalled at the results of the first round of the presidential election and the unprofessionalism of Yushchenko's election campaign team. We had to cooperate with them after the first round. Our cooperation was based on the principle "we continue to do what we are doing now. If you provide us with financial assistance, we will print two million instead of one million of leaflets. But the texts and the design of these leaflets will be ours." Nobody outside the movement should influence our strategic action. People in Yushchenko's headquarters were stunned by our approach.[88]

Compared with black Pora, yellow Pora established deeper ties with the Yushchenko bloc.[89] Taras Stetskiv, participant in the student hunger strike of 1990, was reportedly designated as Yushchenko's main contact person with yellow Pora. Rumor also had it that Ukrainian businessman of Georgian descent David Zhvania provided substantial financial assistance to yellow Pora.[90] But most meetings between movement leaders and Yushchenko's team occurred behind closed doors. Only a handful of public events disclosed this alliance. Yushchenko wore a sticker with yellow Pora's symbol during the movement's first public appearance in Mukachevo in April 2004. In turn, yellow Pora waved its flags at the Student Assembly organized by Yushchenko's bloc in October 2004. The media coverage of yellow Pora activities on Channel 5, a TV channel closely associated with Yushchenko's bloc, was another indicator of the movement's alliance with the political opposition.[91] Yet Kaskiv's secret dealings with party bosses had a rather limited impact on the movement's standing in Ukrainian society during the 2004 elections. Media reports about Kaskiv's alleged misappropriation of the movement's resources came out in the post–Orange Revolution period.

[87] Author's interview with Evhen Zolotariov, Kyiv, Ukraine, March 30, 2010.

[88] Author's interview with Yaryna Yasynevych, Kyiv, Ukraine, April 16, 2008.

[89] On this point, see, for example, Dovzhenko, Otar. 2005. "Uroki Pory" [Lessons from Pora]. *LiveJournal*. September 9. http://otar.livejournal.com/112685.html.

[90] CensorNetUa. 2005. "Kaskiv: Yushchenko predostavil svoim soratnikam neogranichennye polnomochia, a oni pod sebia nasozdavali raznykh struktur." September 16. http://censor.net.ua/resonance/1932/kaskiv_yuschenko_predostavil_svoim_soratnikam_neogranichennye_polnomochiya_a_oni_pod_sebya_nasozdavali.

[91] Telekrytyka. 2006. "Svystovych vs. Pjiatyi." April 12. http://telekritika.kiev.ua/process/2006-04-12/6838?theme_page=220&.

In anticipation of police violence, the youth movements sought to build rapport with the police. As in Serbia, female activists went to police stations with flowers. But most youth activists refrained from getting into political debates with police officers. "Activists didn't try to change political attitudes of the police officers; they just wanted to make sure that they would be beaten, rather than killed, at the time of the arrest."[92] The phrase "Police Are with the People!" became a popular chant at protest events to deter police violence against peaceful protesters.

Moreover, Pora fostered ties with domestic and international donors to secure funding for its activities. Compared with Serbia, Ukraine had a sizable middle class in the mid-2000s. As a result, the Ukrainian youth movements garnered considerable in-kind support from local entrepreneurs. According to Kaskiv, Pora secured financial support from "hundreds of businessmen."[93] In addition, Pora benefited from a long-term flow of Western funding for civil society development in Ukraine. Between 2001 and 2003, the Alfred Mozer Foundation (Netherlands) supported the organization of approximately 20 training seminars with the participation of Otpor and Zubr activists.[94] Many times, however, Ukrainian activists had to learn how to reconcile their needs with the donor's agenda. Solontay, for example, recalled how he used his participation in Western-funded seminars to build a nationwide network of youth activists:

> Donors were willing to spend money on seminars and workshops dedicated to the issues of democracy and the rule of law. European parliamentarians and other Western officials were invited as guest speakers at these seminars. It was all done under the banner of "Dialogue for the Sake of Democracy." At the same time, Western donors refused to support our grant proposals for building a network of activists. Donors would not give us money to set up meetings or training sessions with Belarusian, Georgian, or Serbian activists either. The donors didn't want to make a public impression that they were sponsoring a revolution ... We attended these [Western-funded] workshops, but the most important and useful thing was happening in the evenings. When the workshop sessions were over, we could meet people from different regions and discuss the possibility of joint action.[95]

In sum, Otpor's ideas of nonviolent resistance were planted in fertile ground in Ukraine. The youth movements built on the national history of civic activism to challenge the current regime. In particular, youth activists developed an extensive network of movement participants and came up with creative ideas to wage a nonviolent struggle against the ruling elite.

[92] Author's interview with Oleksandr Solontay, Kyiv, Ukraine, April 11, 2008.

[93] Kutsenko, Zinayida. 2005. "Pora – It's High Time!" *Welcome to Ukraine Magazine*. www.wumag.kiev.ua/index2.php?param=pgs20052/52.

[94] Solodko, Pavlo. 2006. "Liudy, iaki stvoryly revoluitsiu: Chastyna druga." *Ukrainska Pravda*. January 26. www.pravda.com.ua/articles/2006/01/26/3056735/.

[95] Author's interview with Oleksandr Solontay, Kyiv, Ukraine, April 11, 2008.

STATE COUNTERMOVES

As in previous cases, the government's discursive strategy was to frame nonviolent youth movements as extremist right-wing groups, puppets of a foreign government, or foot soldiers of opposition political parties. One of the largest Ukrainian dailies, *Fakty i Kommentarii*, for example, propagated the idea that Western foundations paid for the training of Ukrainian movement participants to destabilize the political situation in the country.[96] Likewise, the Kyiv-based weekly *2000* claimed that Pora "is looking for a niche in Ukrainian politics, specializing in extreme radicalism."[97] Moreover, state-controlled media attempted to link the antiregime youth movements with a presidential contender from the united opposition. For example, Taras Chornovil, Yanukovych's campaign manager, described Pora as follows:

> Members of Pora – real gangsters (former members of special military units) – have not yet appeared. They are waiting for their moment. They are armed. Among them are snipers, experts in explosives, instructors on the violent seizure of buildings.[98]

Pora activists looked on any media coverage of movement activities as a form of free advertising. Pora observed increasing interest in the youth movement in the aftermath of negative media reports, although the movement's misrepresentation in the media had scared off some people. In response, youth activists criticized state-controlled media for their biased coverage of challenger organizations. Yellow Pora carried out the public campaign "They Lie," shaming national TV channels and major newspapers for their blatant lies. To this end, Pora activists designed several stickers:

> At first, we inserted the TV channel's logo and put the tagline "They Lie!" on the sticker. But we realized that some people might glance at the sticker without reading the tagline and conclude that it was some sort of promotional material by the TV channel. So we printed another batch of stickers and crossed the channel's logo with a red line. Visually, it became clearer what we meant to say.[99]

Another state countermove was intimidation of voting-age students in general and movement participants in particular through the use of administrative resources. The administration at most universities pressured students to vote for the incumbent's handpicked successor. Furthermore, deans organized so-called preventive conversations with university students to deter their participation in antiregime protests. Students were threatened with expulsion from the university or eviction from student housing for their civic activism. In addition, the regional

[96] Fakty. 2004. "Za obuchenie aktivistov ukrainskoi molodezhnoi organizatsii 'Pora' platiat zapadnye fondy.... " October 27. www.facts.kiev.ua/archive/2004-10-27/37684/index.html.

[97] Bessmertnyi, Ivan. 2004. "Pora, brat, Pora!" *2000*. August 13–19. http://2000.net.ua/2000/forum/5689-pora-brat-pora.

[98] Quoted from Bezverkha, Anastasiya, ed. 2005. *Ukraine's Orange Revolution: A Chronicle in Pora Newsletters*, p. 40. Retrieved from www.gmfus.org/doc/PORA%20Newsletter.pdf.

[99] Author's interview with Yaroslav Zen, Kyiv, Ukraine, April 18, 2008.

appointees of the Ministry of Interior pressured university rectors to submit lists of student participants in antigovernment protests. However, some rectors, including Viacheslav Briukhovetsky of the National University of Kyiv–Mohyla Academy, Reverend Borys Gudziak of the Ukrainian Catholic University, and Ivan Vakarchuk of the Lviv National University, publicly refused to comply with this state directive. Furthermore, the faculty, staff, and students at the National University of Kyiv–Mohyla Academy went on strike from November 23 to December 8 to protest against electoral fraud during the presidential election.[100]

The organization of a national student assembly (*studentske viche*) by the civic campaign *Studentska Khvylia* ("Student Wave") clearly demonstrated how different political forces competed for student votes. On the one hand, university rectors received instructions from the Ministry of Education and Science to schedule extra classes on the day of the student assembly and compile lists of student absentees. On the other hand, the event organizers backed by the youth wing of Yushchenko's electoral bloc Our Ukraine "wanted to demonstrate the power of students to the incumbent government and test how quickly we could mobilize people."[101] Despite state repression, hundreds of students from all over the country arrived in Kyiv to attend the student assembly and display their electoral support for Yushchenko.

The attempted merger of three Sumy universities is another telling example of how state authorities sought to coerce university students into supporting the current regime. According to a presidential decree, the Sumy National University was supposed to be formed on the basis of the Sumy National Agrarian University, the Sumy National Pedagogical University, and the Sumy State University, with an overall student body of 30,000 people.[102] As the rector of the newly formed university, Kuchma's political appointee Oleksandr Tsarenko was expected to deliver youthful electoral support for Yanukovych. The majority of Sumy voters, however, were inclined to vote for Yushchenko, a native of Sumy oblast. Moreover, there was strong public opposition to the merger of local universities due to Tsarenko's reputation as a corrupt university administrator. Sumy students organized a protest campaign to demand the preservation of their academic institutions.[103] Oleksandra Vesnich, spokesperson for the resistance campaign and a sophomore at the Sumy State University, recalled how the organization of the tent city in Sumy was modeled on the experience of participants in 1990 student hunger strike:

[100] On the start of the political strike, see "Declaration of the Students, Faculty, and Staff Members of the National University of Kyiv Mohyla Academy," November 23, 2004. Retrieved from www.dfc.ukma.kiev.ua/index.php?page=10&id=52.

[101] Author's interview with Taras Shamaida, Kyiv, Ukraine, April 14, 2008.

[102] Presidential Decree No. 453/2004, "Pro utvorennia Sumskogo natsionalnogo universitetu." April 20.

[103] For a thorough discussion of the protest campaign, see Melnik, Leonid, Sergei Iliashenko, and Natalia Iliashenko. 2006. *Vivat alma mater, ili khronika Palatochnoi revolutsii v Sumakh-2004*. Sumy: Universitetskaia kniga.

Oleh Medunitsa, a participant in the Granite Revolution, was one of the organizers of the tent city. The territory of the tent city was clearly demarcated. There was a registration of everybody who entered and left the tent city because we worried about provocateurs. Approximately 1,000 students daily came to the tent city. Initially, we had only three tents. By the fifth day of the protest, there were 19 tents.[104]

Meanwhile, the youth movements launched public campaigns titled "It's Time to Study Freely!" (yellow Pora) and "Student Solidarity" (black Pora) in support of Sumy students. Pora activists picketed the Ministry of Education to denounce the government's interference in academic affairs.[105] Moreover, a few Pora activists traveled to Sumy to share their expertise in nonviolent action. Svystovych, for example, warned student leaders that protesters might get bored sitting in the tent city, so Sumy students organized a rock concert with a local band. Another Pora activist – Volodymyr Lesyk – advised Sumy students to embark on a multiday pedestrian march to Kyiv to demand the preservation of their universities.[106] In view of unabated student protests on the eve of national elections, the incumbent president decided to diffuse social tensions through the annulment of the controversial decree in August 2004.

The incumbent government also sought to limit the movement's access to resources by hunting down private printing houses that provided their services for the political opposition. Pora, for example, lost the possibility to print material at the Lviv-based printing house *Papuga* ("Parrot") when its owner, Taras Hataliak, was arrested on trumped-up charges in April 2004. The Odesa security services claimed that Hataliak printed fake Moldovan currency at the behest of the Moldovan political opposition and held him in the detention center for half a year.[107]

Turning to repression, the police regularly harassed and arrested movement participants.[108] Some youth activists were summoned to police stations for so-called informative interviews with the police. Many others were detained for their participation in street performances, distribution of stickers, or simply affiliation with the movement. Police officers also planted fake money or explosives on Pora activists as a pretext for their arrests. Policing, however, was crippled by low professionalism anda shortfall of state funding for the law enforcement agency. Pora activist Volodymyr Viatrovych observed the dismal state of the police force during his detention in the capital city:

104 Author's interview with Oleksandra Vesnich, Sumy, Ukraine, March 19, 2008.

105 Bezverkha, Anastasiya. 2004. "Kremeniu PORA u agronomy." July 5. http://sd.org.ua/news.php?id=4136.

106 Vesnych, Oleksandra. 2006. "Vichnyi Revoliutsioner." *Panorama*. October 20. http://rama.com.ua/AMS+article.storyid+1677.htm.

107 Mykhailuk, Volodymyr. 2006. "Dyrektora Papugy zaliakuiut." Postup. March 10. http://postup.brama.com/usual.php?what=50606.

108 On state repression against Pora activists, see Kharkiv Human Rights Group. 2005. *Prava liudyny v Ukraini-2004*. Retrieved from http://khpg.org/index.php?id=1124786228.

Once I was detained for participation in an unsanctioned rally. I was taken to the police station. It was necessary to fill out a police protocol. But they had a very old computer, and the police officer tried to type the text with one finger. To speed up my release, I volunteered to type the text of the protocol myself. Then it turned out that the police officer did not have any office paper left. I called my friends and asked them to bring a pack of print paper to the police station.[109]

Like Otpor, Pora drafted a code of behavior in case of arrest and developed a response system aimed at facilitating the rapid release of detained activists. Usually a few members of the movement's security department mingled with the crowd during a street action so that they could quickly react to the detention of Pora activists. Moreover, parliamentarians affiliated with opposition parties used their mandate to put some pressure on the police and speed up the release of certain activists.

Repressive action against the youth movements escalated two weeks prior to election day. The police allegedly found 5.3 pounds of explosives in yellow Pora's main office on October 15, providing a basis for the official framing of Pora as a terrorist organization. Police officers also confiscated the movement's campaign material, whose content was "even more terrifying than the explosives," according to Mayor Omelchenko.[110] The police fabrication of criminal cases against Pora, however, was ill conceived. "The state's action to discredit Pora bordered on the ridiculous," remarked a Pora activist. [111] For example, the police found explosives inside the kitchen stove of a Pora activist in Chernihiv. In response, Pora organized a street action in which female activists sat on the sidewalk with signs saying, "I am not a terrorist." More importantly, movement participants challenged the credibility of state-sponsored media messages through their systematic enforcement of nonviolent discipline.

Youth for Y

The Party of Regions of Ukraine, closely associated with Yanukovych, built on the communist experience of state-sponsored mass mobilization to co-opt youth in favor of the ruling elite. Since its inception in March 2001, the party had a youth wing. The Union of Youth from the Regions of Ukraine (*Souiz molodi regioniv Ukrainy* [SMRU]) de jure transformed itself from the youth wing of the political party into a national youth organization in April 2002, but SMRU officially defined the Party of Regions as its "strategic partner."[112] According to SMRU's statute, the organization's main goal was to facilitate "the realization and protection of social, economic, artistic, spiritual, cultural,

109 Author's interview with Volodymyr Viatrovych, Kyiv, Ukraine, March 2, 2010.

110 *Ukrainska Pravda*. 2004. "U Pori sobaka znaishov vybukhivku: Dostatniu pidirvaty dva sudy." October 16. www.pravda.com.ua/news/2004/10/16/3003259/.

111 Author's interview with Andriy Yusov, Kyiv, Ukraine, April 17, 2008.

112 On the history of SMRU (in Russian), see http://mo-re.org/ru/o/istorija.htm.

and other interests of its members."[113] Based on official statistics, SMRU was one of the largest youth organizations in the country. The movement's growth, however, heavily depended on the use of administrative resources by the ruling party, especially in eastern Ukraine. At the end of the 2003–4 academic year, for example, 1,885 graduating high school students received SMRU membership cards in the city of Donetsk, the home base for the Party of Regions.[114] A native of Donetsk oblast – Vitaliy Khomutynnyk – chaired the youth organization from 2003 to 2009.[115] At the age of 26, Khomutynnyk became one of the youngest deputies to the national parliament elected from the Party of Regions list in March 2002. Furthermore, the young politician exploited his position as head of the National Union of Youth Organizations of Ukraine to set up a multiorganizational coalition in support of Yanukovych.

The National Forum of Ukrainian Youth held in Kyiv in July 2004 unveiled the creation of the coalition Youth Chooses Yanukovych. A total of 52 youth organizations, including SMRU, reportedly joined the coalition and endorsed Khomutynnyk as its coordinator.[116] Some media reports, however, indicate that the Ministry of Family, Youth, and Sports pressured youth activists to participate in the forum and endorse Yanukovych's candidacy.[117] In addition, the Party of Regions issued quotas for university rectors to bring a certain number of students for participation in public rallies held under the slogan, "Youth – for Peace, Youth – for Stability, Youth – for Yanukovych."[118] In another move, the Party of Regions launched a public campaign, titled "Youth – Against; Youth – For." A hallmark of this vote drive was the organization of concerts with a lineup of Russian and Ukrainian performers.[119] The musical repertoire for these events mostly consisted of Russian-language pop songs.

As another counterweight to Pora, the Party of Regions allegedly set up the youth movement *Dosyt* ("Enough"). Borrowing its name from the Georgian

113 For details, see "Statut Vseukrainskoi molodizhnoi gromadskoi organizatsii Molodi regiony." Retrieved from http://mo-re.org/ru/o/ustav.htm.

114 Skhid. 2004. "Donetskie shkolniki popolnili riady 'Soiuza regionov Ukrainy.'" June 1. http://cxid.info/11346.html.

115 For an official biography of Vitaliy Khomutynnyk, see www.partyofregions.org.ua/ua/person/4fef3f08c4ca42c62900000d5.

116 Press Service of the Cabinet of Ministers. 2004. "Na forumi molodi Ukrainy v Kujevi stvoreno koalitsiiu 'Molod obyraje Yanukovycha'" [press release]. July 23. www.kmu.gov.ua/control/publish/article?art_id=7530084.

117 *Ukrainska Pravda*. 2004. "Na forum Yanukovycha molod zvozytymut 'etapom,' a v oblasti SDPU(o) zakryvaiut gazety." July 22. www.pravda.com.ua/news/2004/07/22/3001347/.

118 Chysta Ukraina. 2004. "Studentiv zganiaiut pidtrymuvaty 'proffesora' Ya." September 24. www.chysto.com/index.php?item=news&sub=msg267.

119 Strikzhak, Alina. 2004. "Torgivtsi sovistiu: Iak vygidno prodaty svoiu slavu na prezydentskih vyborah, znaiut uchasnyky turu 'Molod proty, molod za.'" Ukraina Moloda. September 10. www.umoloda.kiev.ua/number/261/175/9311/.

youth movement Kmara, this Ukrainian youth movement demanded the eradication of "aggression, confrontation, and radicalism."[120] Dosyt targeted Yushchenko as the main instigator of extremism and actively campaigned against him on the eve of the second round of the elections. Imitating Pora's tactics, for example, Dosyt members staged a street performance in front of Yushchenko's headquarters on November 13.[121] Approximately 60 young people wearing white robes and face masks called for the end of political unrest and distributed tranquilizers to passers-by. This newly formed youth organization, however, did not appear to pose a serious challenge to the youth movements in opposition to the regime due to its small size and heavy-handed control by the ruling party.

THE ORANGE REVOLUTION

As anticipated, the 2004 presidential election was fraught with electoral fraud. The two presidential contenders with the largest share of votes faced each other in the second round of the election. According to the official results, Yanukovych received 49.5 percent of the votes and Yushchenko 46.6 percent of the votes. In contrast, an exit poll conducted by the Kyiv International Institute of Sociology and the Razumkov Center on November 21 found that 52.9 percent of voters cast the ballot for Yushchenko and 44.2 percent voted for Yanukovych.[122] This discrepancy between the official results and the exit poll findings exposed the magnitude of electoral fraud in favor of Yanukovych and provoked public outrage. To the surprise of the ruling elite and the political opposition, thousands of ordinary citizens turned to the street to protest against vote rigging in November 2004.[123] Overall, approximately one-fifth of the Ukrainian population participated in post-election protests,[124] dubbed as the "Orange Revolution" due to the ubiquitous use of Yushchenko's campaign color.

Pora activists were among the first to pitch tents on the Maidan on November 22. According to Kaskiv et al., Pora set up 1,546 tents with more than 15,000

[120] Novosti Donbassa. 2004. "V Ukraine poiavilas novaia organizatsia Dosyt. Protiv Yushchenko." November 9. http://novosti.dn.ua/details/8406/.

[121] ProUa. 2004. "Organisatsiia 'Dosyt!' provela 'zaspokiilyvu aktsiiu bilia pres-tsentru 'Tak.'" November 14. http://ua.proua.com/news/2004/11/14/140333.html.

[122] Kharchenko, Natalia, and Volodymyr Paniotto. 2010. "Exit Polling in an Emerging Democracy: The Complex Case of Ukraine." *Survey Research Methods* 4(1): 31–42, p. 36.

[123] For a thorough analysis of protest activism, see Beissinger, Mark. 2011. "Mechanisms of Maidan: The Structure of Contingency in the Making of the Orange Revolution." *Mobilization* 16(1): 25–43.

[124] Panina, Natalia. 2005. *Ukrainske suspilstvo 1994–2005: Sotsiologichnyi monitoring*. Kyiv: Institute of Sociology of the National Academy of Sciences of Ukraine and the Foundation "Democratic Initiatives," p. 148.

tent residents in Kyiv.[125] Most movement participants stayed in the tent city until the Supreme Court canceled the election results and ordered a rerun of the second round of the presidential election in December 2004.

CONCLUSION

This chapter analyzed tactical interactions between the youth movements and the incumbent government in Ukraine, which contributed to a high level of youth mobilization against the regime. Like Serbia's Otpor, Pora developed a negative campaign targeting the current regime and a positive campaign aimed at voter mobilization. Movement participants displayed a great deal of resourcefulness to galvanize youth into political action. The use of humor, for example, enabled the youth movements to combat apathy and fear, leading to a higher level of citizen participation in protest events. Furthermore, youth activists made a critical decision regarding their internal divisions. Movement participants tried to put aside intraleadership tensions so that they could focus on the common goal of bringing about political change. Had they become embroiled in an acrimonious public exchange over the movement's origins, they would have mirrored the behavior of opposition party leaders and thus have alienated a significant portion of young people.

In response to the rise of nonviolent youth movements, the incumbent government deployed a conventional set of repressive methods. State-controlled media branded nonviolent youth movements as extremist organizations formed with the sole aim to sow chaos and instigate bloodshed in the country. The police harassed youth activists, and the university administration threatened movement participants with expulsion from university or eviction from student housing. Furthermore, the Party of Regions' attempt to set up a copycat movement in support of Yanukovych was made late in the election cycle and did not gain genuine popularity with most youngsters.

Another finding to be gleaned from this analysis is that Pora activists pursued a variety of tactics to counteract state repression. The youth movement launched a public campaign to expose a biased coverage of current events in the state-controlled media. Another public campaign defied the government's allegations that Pora was a terrorist organization. The youth movement also enlisted the support of several university rectors to denounce political pressure on students. In the absence of these countermoves, the size of the youth movement would have been smaller.

As discussed in Chapter 3, there appeared to be a favorable political environment for antigovernment protests. The unification of opposition political

[125] Kaskiv, Vladyslav, Iryna Chupryna, and Yevhen Zolotariov. 2007. "It's Time! Pora and the Orange Revolution in Ukraine." In *Reclaiming Democracy: Civil Society and Electoral Change in Central and Eastern Europe*, eds. Joerg Forbig and Pavol Demes. Washington, DC: German Marshall Fund, pp. 127–51, p. 127.

parties around a charismatic candidate, along with the emergence of a private TV channel and eventual defections within the security apparatus, were conducive to mass mobilization against the regime. Thousands of people dissatisfied with brazen vote rigging, rampant corruption, and political violence turned to the street despite a streak of positive economic growth. Most elite defections happened only when the number of protesters swelled to tens of thousands. The ruling elite did not anticipate that the government's wrongdoings would produce such a backlash in Ukrainian society. The significance of the youth movements lies in the resourceful deployment of nonviolent methods to spur citizens to action.

8

The Emergence of Youth Movements in Azerbaijan

In May 2005, Emin Huseynov, leader of the newly formed Azerbaijani youth movement Maqam, traveled to Tbilisi to deliver a message to the US president.[1] The youth activist seized an opportunity to be heard during President George Bush's public address in Freedom Square, main site of the Rose Revolution. As President Bush was speaking about the advancement of freedom "from the Black Sea to the Caspian, and to the Persian Gulf and beyond,"[2] Huseynov was standing in the crowd with large orange-colored posters. One poster said in English, "President Bush, please help democracy in Azerbaijan." Another poster declared, "Youth of Azerbaijan for Free and Fair Elections!" These slogans reflected youth's aspirations to bring about political change in the former Soviet republic.

Azerbaijan witnessed the emergence of several youth movements on the eve of the 2005 parliamentary elections.[3] Yeni Fikir was founded by a group of Baku students in April 2004. Another group of students based at the National Economic University formed *Dalga* ("Wave") in February 2005. Both youth movements started out by exposing corruption in the education sector, but Yeni Fikir expanded the scope of its demands to push for political change during the parliamentary elections.[4] In addition, Maqam and Yokh were founded in February 2005 to call for free and fair elections. Compared with Georgia's Kmara, these youth movements mobilized a smaller fraction of the youth

[1] Huseynov, Emin. 2006. "Open Letter to US President George Bush." April 26. www.idee.org/Azerbaijan%20Youth%20Appeal%202006.html.

[2] BBC. 2005. "Bush's Speech in Georgia." BBC Online. May 10. http://news.bbc.co.uk/go/pr/fr/-/2/hi/europe/4527233.stm.

[3] For a detailed overview of the Azerbaijani youth movements, see Huseynov, Emin. 2007. "Molodezhnye dvizhenia Azerbaidzhana: Obzor za 2005–2007 gody." In *Azerbaijan and Uzbekistan: Human Rights and Democratic Freedoms in 2006*. Baku: Institute of Peace and Democracy (Azerbaijan) and Legal Aid Society (Uzbekistan).

[4] The case of Dalga is excluded from this study because the movement's public campaigns focused on the issue of corruption in the university sector in 2005.

population against the regime. Nearly half of Azerbaijani youth did not vote in the 2005 election, and the overwhelming majority of youngsters refrained from participation in protest events.

President Aliyev, compared with Shevardnadze, responded more forcefully to the rise of youth movements in opposition to the regime. The government of Azerbaijan smeared the reputation of youth activists by framing them as collaborators with the Armenian intelligence services. Moreover, the coercive apparatus built a climate of fear through police arrests of movement participants and psychological harassment of their families. State authorities also threatened students with expulsion from university or loss of employment for participation in protest events. Finally, the government set up a regime-friendly youth movement to induce compliant activism.

This chapter provides a partial explanation for a low level of antiregime mobilization by examining tactical interactions between the youth movements and the incumbent government. The chapter begins with an overview of protests and repression in the post-Soviet period. Next, the chapter traces the cross-national diffusion of nonviolent methods. The chapter proceeds with an analysis of movement tactics and state countermoves. In particular, the chapter investigates how the government allegedly sponsored the establishment of a pro-regime youth movement *Ireli* ("Forward") to counteract youth mobilization against the regime.

PROTESTS AND REPRESSION UNDER THE ALIYEVS

Since the start of Heydar Aliyev's presidency, there were several episodes of contentious collective action against the incumbent government. As in the preceding cases, the government's crackdown on the mass media ignited acts of nonviolent resistance. Regime opponents organized protest events in the wake of a repressive law on the mass media in December 2001 and in the aftermath of the murder of an investigative reporter in March 2005. Furthermore, unlike Georgia, several post-election protests broke out in Azerbaijan in the early 2000s. Protest rallies were held in Baku and several large cities to contest electoral malpractices during the 2000 parliamentary elections. Another protest campaign against electoral fraud was organized in the wake of the 2003 presidential election. A brief overview of these protest events is provided in chronological order to illuminate the dynamics of state-society relations prior to the 2005 parliamentary election.

Elections and Protests in November 2000

The 2000 parliamentary elections "marked some progress over previous occasions" but "fell short of international standards for democratic elections."[5] The Central Election Commission registered 13 parties and coalitions for participation in the elections, signaling political pluralism in Azerbaijani society.[6] Yet the OSCE observation mission found a plethora of election irregularities, including lack of fairness during the election campaign and lack of transparency during the vote count and tabulation of the results.[7] To challenge the fraudulent election results, the opposition political parties organized protest rallies in Baku and large cities nationwide.

One of the largest antigovernment protests broke out in the city of Sheki, located 120 miles northwest of Baku.[8] According to some estimates, approximately 1,500 people participated in a protest rally held on November 18, 2000.[9] The Minister of Interior claimed that protesters set police vehicles on fire and attacked the police station to free detainees.[10] One of the triggers for this outburst of political discontent was the cutoff of the electricity supply immediately at the end of the election campaign. The disgruntled population demanded the regular supply of electricity. In addition, the opposition political parties called for the annulment of fraudulent election results.

These post-election protests were met with state repression. The national government dispatched internal troops to suppress protests in the provinces. According to the Baku-based NGO Institute of Peace and Democracy, 350 people were arrested in the aftermath of the protest rally in Sheki.[11] Human rights groups also reported the inhumane treatment of detainees at police stations. Furthermore, the government effectively applied the divide and rule principle by ordering the rerun of elections in several precincts. APFP decided to participate in repeat elections, whereas the Musavat Party called for boycotting the elections. These divisions within the opposition camp weakened the capacity of the opposition forces to continue post-election protests.

Protests in Defense of Press Freedom in December 2001

The government's crackdown on independent media escalated in the winter of 2001. In the course of a parliamentary debate on changes to the law on media on December 4, 2001, YAP member Calal Aliyev articulated the government's

[5] OSCE. 2001. *Republic of Azerbaijan: Parliamentary Election 5 November 2000 and 7 January 2001: Final Report*. Warsaw, Poland: Office for Democratic Institutions and Human Rights, p. 1.

[6] *Ibid.*, p. 6. [7] *Ibid.*

[8] For an account of this protest event, see Lepisto, Eric. 2008. "Unraveling Youth: Social Ties and Structural Adjustment in Azerbaijan." Ph.D. dissertation, Columbia University, New York, pp. 1–2.

[9] *Hurriyet Daily News*. 2000. "Police Nab Organizer of Azerbaijan Protest." November 20. www.hurriyetdailynews.com/default.aspx?pageid=438&n=police-nab-organizer-of-azerbaijan-protest-2000-11-20.

[10] *Ibid.*

[11] Institute of Peace and Democracy. 2005. *The Report of the Institute of Peace and Democracy on the Facts of Police Violence and Brutality against Women and Girls*. Baku, Azerbaijan, p. 2.

opinion of media outlets associated with the main opposition parties. "These are the most vicious papers and they are defaming the nation ... Such people should be annihilated in every society. They are a danger to society. They are parasites."[12] These public statements made by the incumbent president's brother rubberstamped violence against independent media. *Yeni Musavat* journalist Shahnaz Metlebqizi was attacked in the street two days after Aliyev's speech.[13]

In response, media professionals organized several protest events. A few *Yeni Musavat* journalists went on a hunger strike, whereas three opposition dailies – *Azadlyq, Hurriyet*, and *Yeni Musavat* – held a protest rally in front of the YAP headquarters on December 12. A larger protest rally held on December 20 was attended by approximately 2,000 people. The aim of these protest events was to demand the protection of press freedom and prevent the introduction of new legal constraints on the mass media.

These protest events produced mixed reactions from state authorities. The police applied violence against protesters. At least 20 journalists were heavily beaten at the rally held on December 12.[14] One of the protesters was taken to the hospital with a cerebral concussion. In another move, the government attempted to appease media professionals by adopting a rather liberal law on the mass media. The new law removed numerous restrictions on press freedom and liquidated a requirement for state registration of newspapers.[15] Nonetheless, independent media continued to suffer from the government's encroachment on press freedom.

Elections and Protests in October 2003

The 2003 presidential election, compared with the 2000 parliamentary election, was marred by a higher level of electoral malpractices, enabling the transfer of power from the incumbent president to his son. On October 2, 2003, two weeks prior to election day, the ailing incumbent formally withdrew from the presidential race and urged citizens to vote for his son Ilham. In addition to Aliyev, seven presidential contenders were placed on the ballot. Yet the political competition was skewed in favor of the president's son due to multiple pre- and

[12] International Freedom of Expression Exchange (IFEX). 2001. "President's Brother Levels Serious Accusations against Opposition Media." December 5. www.ifex.org/azerbaijan/2001/12/05/president_s_brother_levels_serious/.

[13] IFEX. 2001. "Journalist Attacked and Threatened." December 7. www.ifex.org/azerbaijan/2001/12/07/journalist_attacked_and_threatene/.

[14] IFEX. 2001. "Journalists Arrested, One Seriously Injured during Demonstration." December 12. www.ifex.org/azerbaijan/2001/12/12/journalists_arrested_one_seriously/.

[15] IFEX. 2002. "Law on Mass Media Revised: A Number of Restrictions on Media Freedom Removed." April 8. www.ifex.org/azerbaijan/2002/04/10/law_on_mass_media_revised_a_number/.

post-election abuses. The OSCE observation mission documented lack of transparency in the tabulation process and "implausible results" in many precincts.[16] The Central Election Commission, for example, reported that all valid votes in 135 precincts were cast in support of Aliyev.[17] According to the official results, Ilham Aliyev won 76.8 percent of the vote, and Isa Gambar came in second with 13.9 percent.[18] In contrast, an exit poll found that Gambar led with 46 percent of the vote, and Aliyev trailed behind with 24 percent of the vote.[19] Based on exit poll results, Gambar called for post-election protests against vote rigging. At that time, a youth movement championing the idea of free and fair elections was nonexistent in Azerbaijan.

The opposition political parties were behind post-election protests in October 2003. On election night, Gambar's supporters gathered in front of the party headquarters to challenge the fraudulent election results, but the riot police violently dispersed the peaceful rally.[20] In response, some Musavat supporters armed themselves with metal bars and rocks at the next protest rally.[21] A violent clash between the police and the protesters resulted in the arrest of more than 400 people, including opposition politicians, election commission officials, and journalists.[22] The leader of the Musavat Party was placed under house arrest for almost a month.

The outcome of the 2003 election signified the durability of the nondemocratic regime and an escalation in state repression. According to local human rights groups, the police torture of detainees was carried out at an unprecedented level in the fall of 2003.[23] The leader of the Umid Party, for example, was allegedly tortured before he made a public confession and blamed the Musavat Party for unrest in Baku.[24] These repressive measures had a chilling effect on civil society.[25] Human rights defender Peter Bouckaert, for example, argued that "there won't be an opposition left in Azerbaijan by the end of this month if

[16] OSCE. 2005. *Republic of Azerbaijan: Presidential Election 15 October 2003: OSCE/ODIHR Election Observation Mission Report*, p. 25.

[17] *Ibid.* [18] *Ibid.*

[19] Weir, Fred. 2003. "As Soviet-era Strongmen Fade, Caspian Unrest Grows." *Christian Science Monitor*. October 22. www.csmonitor.com/2003/1022/p07s02-wosc.html.

[20] Radio Free Europe/Radio Liberty. 2005. "Azerbaijan: Clash Breaks Out in Baku after Polls Close." October 15. www.rferl.org/features/2003/10/15102003185111.asp.

[21] Radio Free Europe/Radio Liberty. 2005. "Azerbaijan: Violent Protests in Baku in Wake of Election." October 16. www.rferl.org/features/2003/10/16102003103413.asp.

[22] Csongos, Frank. 2005. "Azerbaijan: Washington Warns Aliyev against Wholesale Arrests." Radio Free Europe/Radio Liberty. October 23. www.rferl.org/features/2003/10/23102003165531.asp.

[23] Peuch, Jean-Christophe. 2005. "Azerbaijan: Rights Groups Say Post-Election Detainees Tortured." Radio Free Europe/Radio Liberty. October 24. www.rferl.org/features/2003/10/24102003165107.asp.

[24] *Ibid.*

[25] Ismailzade, Fariz. 2003. "Disillusionment Defines Azerbaijan's Opposition." EurasiaNet. November 12. www.eurasianet.org/departments/insight/articles/eav111303.shtml.

this crackdown continues."[26] State repression also deepened citizens' alienation from the current regime. In an interview with BBC film makers, Huseynov pointed out the significance of the 2003 election and the ensuing political violence:

> The very fact that me and countless others were beaten or even killed on the sixteenth of October 2003 made many understand that the present regime has no right to rule Azerbaijan and that sooner or later this regime would be forced to go.[27]

Protests in the Aftermath of Elmar Huseynov's Murder in Spring 2005

The murder of 38-year-old Elmar Huseynov, founder and editor of the weekly magazine *Monitor*, exposed the severity of press freedom violations in Azerbaijan. On March 2, 2005, Huseynov was gunned down in his apartment building, and most analysts believe that his assassination was related to his professional work as an editor.[28] Huseynov was known for his critical stance toward the incumbent government and his commitment to investigative journalism. *Monitor* published a series of reports exposing the incidence of high-level corruption, and Huseynov subsequently received multiple work-related threats. The editor's murder provoked a backlash.

Despite warnings from the government, Huseynov's funeral turned into a protest event with speeches by prominent journalists and opposition politicians. Approximately 3,000 people participated in the funeral procession and attended a public rally.[29] Some civic activists entertained the idea that Huseynov's murder might serve as a catalyst for the emergence of a broad-based social movement against the incumbent government. "I hope this murder will become for Azerbaijan what Gongadze's case was for Ukraine. It is time for us to stand up for our rights," said a participant in the funeral procession.[30] The Azerbaijani opposition, however, was unable to organize a protest campaign on par with the UbK Movement in Ukraine.

[26] Bouckaert, Peter. 2003. "Stolen Election and Oil Stability." *International Herald Tribune*. October 20. www.hrw.org/news/2003/10/19/azerbaijan-stolen-election-and-oil-stability.

[27] Quoted from BBC. 2006. *How to Plan a Revolution* [documentary]. London, UK: BBC. Directed by Ivan Mahoney.

[28] Gojayev, Vugar. 2010. "Remembering a Brave Journalist in Azerbaijan." *Human Rights House Report*. March 2. http://humanrightshouse.org/noop/page.php?p=Articles/13614.html&d=1; IFEX. 2005. "Editor of Opposition Weekly Gunned Down." March 2. www.ifex.org/azerbaijan/2005/03/02/editor_of_opposition_weekly_gunned/; Mite, Valentinas. 2005. "Azerbaijan: Editor's Killing Sparks Accusations of Political Motives." Radio Free Europe/Radio Liberty. March 3. www.rferl.org/featuresarticle/2005/03/710d619d-d62e-4359-b7f5-4f29f2075a83.html.

[29] BBC. 2005. "Thousands Mourn Azeri Journalist." March 4. http://news.bbc.co.uk/2/hi/europe/4317221.stm.

[30] Quoted from Antelava, Natalia. 2005. "Rage and Tears at the Editor's Funeral." *BBC News*. March 5. http://news.bbc.co.uk/2/hi/europe/4320303.stm.

A central conclusion to be drawn from the survey of major protest campaigns in the early 2000s is that Azerbaijani youth played a secondary role in antigovernment protests. Though some young people participated in protest rallies organized by opposition political parties, youth lacked an independent challenger organization representing its own interests. According to an interviewed youth activist, Azerbaijani youth appeared to pin a lot of hopes on the opposition political parties. "We had so much hope for the old opposition in 2003. We did not feel that we needed a youth movement."[31] Given the absence of youth-led challenger organizations, youth activists lacked the organizational skills necessary to build a viable youth movement. Another weakness of Azerbaijan's civil society in the early 2000s was the underdevelopment of a nationwide network of civic activists. Most protest events were held in Baku without spreading into the provinces. This analysis suggests that Azerbaijani youth were less prepared than graduates of earlier electoral revolutions to carry out a protest campaign during the national elections.

CROSS-NATIONAL DIFFUSION OF IDEAS

Notwithstanding the weaknesses of Azerbaijan's civil society, the prior success of nonviolent action in the post-communist region served as inspiration for regime opponents and as a warning for the incumbent government. The opposition political parties cherished "the Yugoslavian dream,"[32] that is, removal of the incumbent president from power through post-election protests. By the same token, prior success of nonviolent youth movements in Georgia, Serbia, and Ukraine eventually provided an impetus for the establishment of similar youth groups in Azerbaijan. Meanwhile, the incumbent government took preemptive action to inhibit the cross-national diffusion of ideas and to bolster the strength of the current regime.

The toolkit of voter mobilization techniques previously used in Slovakia and Serbia became a diffusing item during the 2003 presidential election. The Open Society Institute brought six Serbian civic activists to Azerbaijan to participate in workshops on election-related issues.[33] Specifically, Serbian activists planned to share with their Azerbaijani counterparts their expertise on youth voter mobilization. Yet the incumbent government deemed such workshops as threatening to the current regime. Shortly before the arrival of the Serbian delegation to the city of Nakhchivan, the Nakhchivan Human Rights Center came under attack. A mob of 50 women assaulted workshop organizers with tomatoes and eggs. Moreover, the Serbian activists were ordered by the police

[31] Author's interview with Said Nuri (via Skype), October 17, 2014.

[32] Pedziwol, Aureliusz. 2005. *Azerbaijan: A Yugoslavian Dream*. Washington, DC: Institute for Democracy in Eastern Europe. Retrieved from www.idee.org/Azerbaijan_2000Pedziwol.html.

[33] Human Rights Watch. 2003. "Azerbaijan: Presidential Elections 2003." Human Rights Watch Briefing Paper. October 13, pp. 18–19.

to leave the country. In contrast, Otpor activists could travel freely to Georgia and interact with Kmara members without police interference.

In the aftermath of the Rose Revolution, Azerbaijani activists examined the case of Georgia's peaceful turnover of power. There was, however, relatively little direct interaction between Georgian activists and their Azerbaijani counterparts. According to Kmara member Giorgi Meladze, the initial cross-national contacts "did not develop into close connections because they [the youth organizations in Azerbaijan] were not well organized and lacked a clear strategy."[34] In turn, Azerbaijani youth activists felt that Kmara members were not enthusiastic about sharing their knowledge and skills.[35] Rumors circulating in Azerbaijani civil society suggested that Georgian civic activists did not become heavily involved in the diffusion of nonviolent methods to the neighboring state due to domestic political pressures. Numerous reports indicate that President Saakashvili strove to build friendly relations with the incumbent government of Azerbaijan and deepen economic ties between the two countries.[36] At the opening ceremony of the Georgian section of the Baku-Tbilisi-Ceyhan oil pipeline in October 2005, Saakashvili described Ilham Aliyev as "a great hope for his people ... whose achievements are obvious, but who is also a man very close to Georgia."[37] This close economic partnership, along with growing criticism of Saakashvili's leadership style, dashed popular expectations about the role of Georgia as a beacon of democracy in the South Caucasus.[38]

To the Azerbaijani opposition forces, the most powerful example of nonviolent resistance came from Ukraine. On Gambar's visit to Kyiv during the Orange Revolution, the Musavat Party invited a few Ukrainian activists to Azerbaijan.[39] For example, Pora member Serhiy Yevtushenko received an invitation to participate in an international conference titled, "Azerbaijan and Belarus during the Second Phase of Democratization in the Post-Soviet Region," jointly organized by the Musavat Party and the Popular Front Party (Belarus) in Baku in September 2005.[40] Yet the immigration services of Azerbaijan denied

[34] Quoted from Aliyeva, Jahan. 2005. "Georgia Pushes Friendship, Not Revolution with Azerbaijan." EurasiaNet. October 31. www.eurasianet.org/azerbaijan/news/friendship_2005 1031.html.

[35] Author's interview with Said Nuri (via Skype), October 17, 2014.

[36] Anjaparidze, Zaal. 2005. "Will Tbilisi Facilitate an Anti-Aliev Revolution in Azerbaijan?" *Eurasia Daily Monitor*. September 12; *Civil Georgia*. 2005. "Saakashvili, Aliyev Discuss Cooperation, Energy Projects." April 23. www.civil.ge/eng/article.php?id=9682.

[37] Aliyeva, Jahan. 2005. "Georgia Pushes Friendship, Not Revolution with Azerbaijan." EurasiaNet.

[38] On this point, see Matsaberidze, Malkhaz. 2005. "The Rose Revolution and the Southern Caucasus." *Central Asia and the Caucasus* 2(32): 7–15.

[39] Valiyev, Anar. 2004. "Baku Balances the Ukrainian Revolution." *Central Asia-Caucasus Analyst*. December 15. www.cacianalyst.org/?q=node/2650.

[40] TrendAz. 2005. "Ukrainskaia 'Partia Reformy i Poriadok' shchitaet zaderzhanie Sergeia Yevtushenko grubym narusheniem prav cheloveka." September 17. http://ru.trend.az/news/politics/foreign/759533.html.

Yevtushenko entry into the country. Likewise, Pora activists Serhiy Taran and Yevhen Zolotarev were denied entry to Azerbaijan in November 2005.[41] One of the tactical errors committed by the Musavat Party was advance advertising of the Pora activists' arrival, enabling the security apparatus to take preemptive action.

In addition to party functionaries, local youth sought to learn from their Ukrainian peers about the use of nonviolent methods. The leaders of all three youth movements acknowledged their direct contacts with Pora activists.[42] Maqam leader Huseynov, for example, spoke with Ukrainian youth activists and ordinary citizens during his visit to Ukraine in the wake of the Orange Revolution:

> I was heavily beaten in October 2003, and I went to Ukraine to get some medical treatment in the winter of 2005. I arrived in Kyiv in January 2005, shortly before Yushchenko's inauguration. For three days, I've met a lot of people, including Pora activists. Then I traveled to Ternopil [a city in western Ukraine] and spoke with young nurses there. They told me how they had gone to the capital city to protest, and this experience inspired me to form a youth movement in Azerbaijan.[43]

According to some Yeni Fikir activists, "80 percent of their knowledge came from Pora via one of their members who had experience in Ukraine."[44] In particular, Pora discussed with Azerbaijani youth activists the importance of having backup plans in case of state repression of the movement. On Pora's advice, Yeni Fikir divided up movement participants into echelons.[45] The first echelon consisted of publicly visible movement participants. Once this segment of the movement fell victim to state repression, the second echelon of movement participants was supposed to come forward to signal the movement's continuous strength. Subsequently, the third echelon of movement participants was supposed to be activated.

The Belarusian youth movement Zubr provided another example of how to survive in a repressive political environment. Maqam activists, for example, downloaded from Zubr's website a copy of *The Little Conspirator*, written by Polish dissidents and later translated into Russian by Belarusian activists.[46] Moreover, the Tirana Activism Festival organized by the Albanian youth movement *Mjfat* ("Enough") provided a platform for the cross-national

[41] *Ukrainska Pravda*. 2005. "Aliyev pered vyboramy ogolushuje ukraintsiv personoiu non grata." November 5. http://pravda.com.ua/ukr/news/4b1a9a03c11bb/.

[42] Author's interview with Said Nuri (via Skype), October 17, 2014; *Nonviolent Journal*. 2005. "Excerpts from a Letter on the Yox Movement in Azerbaijan by Razi Nurullayev." February 15. www.nonviolentchangejournal.org/nc10dialog.html.

[43] Author's interview with Emin Huseynov, Baku, Azerbaijan, February 22, 2008.

[44] Quoted from Bunce, Valerie, and Sharon Wolchik. 2011. *Defeating Authoritarian Leaders in Post-Communist Countries*, p. 190.

[45] Author's interview with Said Nuri (via Skype), October 17, 2014.

[46] Author's interview with Emin Huseynov, Baku, Azerbaijan, February 22, 2008.

diffusion of nonviolent methods in June 2005. This festival brought together representatives of nearly 100 youth organizations, including Kmara, Otpor, Pora, Yokh, and Zubr.[47] One of the main outcomes of this festival was the so-called Kruja Pact, declaring transnational solidarity in youth's struggle against autocrats.[48]

Like the graduates of earlier electoral revolutions, Azerbaijani civic activists became familiar with Sharp's work on nonviolent action. Maqam received a small grant from the Albert Einstein Institution to translate Sharp's book, *From Dictatorship to Democracy*, into the Azerbaijani language and disseminate it among local youth. Likewise, Nurullayev boasted familiarity with Sharp's work and personal contact with the author of the acclaimed book.[49] Even Isa Gambar ironically claimed reading Sharp's book every year to plan protest events in Azerbaijan.[50] Their exposure to Sharp's ideas, however, was insufficient to allow them to carry out an effective protest campaign.

The prevalence of social norms incompatible with democracy was an enormous obstacle to the adoption of innovative protest tactics in Azerbaijan. The veneration of age, albeit present in all post-communist states, appeared to be more pronounced in Azerbaijan, which undercut youth's defiance of the old opposition. As Ramin Hajili, leader of Dalga in 2005–06, pointed out, "Starting from the cradle, parents tell their children what they ought to do. In our society it is considered rude to argue with the elderly."[51] In addition, the dominant gender norms obstructed women's participation in the diffusion of nonviolent methods. For example, a young Serbian woman who shared her extensive NGO experience at a Baku-based workshop felt that older Azerbaijani men did not take seriously her advice about civil resistance.[52] Moreover, Western trainers reported difficulty in promoting independent thinking among local activists. A Dutch trainer, for example, observed the following phenomenon in Azerbaijan:

> [N]ext to the regime there are also other problems like ... the high level of temperament, the low level of discipline (at least in trainings) and the fact that people are used to a certain top-down structure. Sometimes I really notice that the people I work with who come from Azerbaijan would actually prefer me to tell them what to do and how to run their party or organization.[53]

47 Traynor, Ian. 2005. "Young Democracy Guerillas Join Forces." *Guardian*. June 5. www.guardian.co.uk/world/2005/jun/06/iantraynor.

48 The full text of the Kruja Pact is available on the website of Mjfat, www.mjaft.org/en/taf.php.

49 Author's interview with Razi Nurullayev, Baku, Azerbaijan, February 25, 2008.

50 Quoted from Bunce, Valerie, and Sharon Wolchik. 2011. *Defeating Authoritarian Leaders in Post-Communist Countries*, p. 177.

51 Author's interview with Ramin Hajili, Baku, Azerbaijan, February 21, 2008.

52 Author's interview with Tanja Azanjac, Belgrade, Serbia, February 7, 2008.

53 van der Velden, Zindi. 2011. "Dutch Party Assistance in Azerbaijan." M.S. thesis, University of Amsterdam, p. 52.

Notwithstanding these political and social constraints, the cross-national diffusion of ideas influenced the choice of antiregime symbols in Azerbaijan. Inspired by the example of Ukraine's Orange Revolution, the electoral bloc Azadlyq chose orange as its campaign color. Likewise, Yeni Fikir and Maqam adopted orange as a symbol of nonviolent resistance. Huseynov explained Maqam's logic behind this decision:

> We chose the orange color for the youth movement. It was an optimum choice. If we picked the green color, we would be accused of being Islamist fundamentalists. If we picked the blue color, we would be accused of being gay.[54]

In contrast, Yokh adopted green as the movement's color. The movement's press release provided the following justification for this choice:

> Green, which is a harbinger of spring, has a special place among colors. Ancient people viewed the green color as a symbol of water. Greenness brought by this year's spring will inspire our nation to say "Yox" ["No"] to all problems. Everything will be in green. This is the color of logic and high energy ... Every color is good. But green is a sign of forthcoming freedom and comfort.[55]

The next section examines in greater detail how the Azerbaijani youth movements engaged in civil resistance.

NONVIOLENT RESISTANCE AGAINST THE REGIME

Several youth movements were formed on the eve of the 2005 parliamentary elections. Azerbaijani youth demanded free and fair elections to propel democratic change. Yokh, for example, defined itself as "a nonviolent civil movement that seeks to bring about social and political changes by consolidating and activating most people in Azerbaijan, especially youth."[56] Like Kmara activists, movement participants also raised the issue of corruption in the education sector. Unlike Kmara, however, Azerbaijani youth refrained from poking fun at the incumbent president. Youth activists were convinced that a direct attack on Aliyev would trigger excessive political violence and immediately decimate the challenger organizations.

Recruitment

As in the preceding cases, movement leaders targeted the student population as a pool of potential movement participants. Yokh, for example, deliberately selected a neighborhood with a large concentration of universities to spray paint the movement's graffiti. According to the movement's leader, Razi

[54] Author's interview with Emin Huseynov, Baku, Azerbaijan, February 22, 2008.
[55] Yokh. 2005. "Color of YOX Movement Azerbaijan." Press release.
[56] Yokh. 2005. "Where Does Yox Stand?" Press release.

Nurullayev, this street action aimed to "boost the public spirit so that people will not fear their expression of dissent."[57] Youth activists also organized so-called leaflet rains on university grounds to propagate movement ideas and recruit new members. Yet the challenger organizations were unable to dispel the climate of fear in society. Out of concern about repression, students were often afraid to pick up movement leaflets strewn on the ground. In particular, the threat of expulsion from university and the fear of unemployment had a chilling effect on students.

Youth can see that those who work in state agencies drive expensive cars and wear fashionable clothes. And those who speak out against the government cannot find a job. Youth sees it and chooses the easier path, the easy life.[58]

A limitation of the recruitment campaigns was their focus on youth in the capital city. Yokh, for example, recruited only a handful of people in Ganja, Azerbaijan's second largest city. Compared with Yokh, Yeni Fikir made a greater effort to campaign in the provinces, but movement participants debated the utility of spreading into rural areas because Baku was considered the epicenter of political life. At the same time, rural youth appeared to be an easier target for recruitment than college-educated youth in the capital city.

In a way, it was easier for Yeni Fikir to recruit in the villages [than in the cities]. More people are unhappy with the current situation in the villages. The government does not provide sufficient funding for rural areas. Ninety percent of rural youth are unemployed or working on the father's farm. But with all due respect, rural youth are not well educated. So it is hard to deliver them such Western messages as democracy and human rights. They need a simpler message.[59]

An often-cited reason for the movements' focus on the capital city was lack of financial resources. The interviewed youth activists stated that they did not have money to travel to the regions.[60] Once recruited into the movement, many activists from the provinces could not afford to come to Baku to participate in protest events. The underdevelopment of the Internet infrastructure further compounded the cultivation of a nationwide network of activists.

Moreover, the dominant gender norms limited the scope of the recruitment campaigns. The prevailing view in Azerbaijani society was that politics was a man's domain. An opinion poll conducted in 2006 found that only 54 percent of respondents and in particular 45 percent of men would approve of their

[57] Quoted from Kerimova, U. 2005. "Aktivisty dvizhenia Yokh raspisali steny universitetov." DayAz. April 26. http://news.day.az/politics/23932.html.

[58] Author's interview with Ramin Hajili, Baku, Azerbaijan, February 21, 2008.

[59] Author's interview with Said Nuri (via Skype), October 17, 2014.

[60] Author's interview with Ramin Hajili, Baku, Azerbaijan, February 21, 2008; Said Nuri (via Skype), October 17, 2014.

daughter's decision to run for office.[61] Consistent with these views, only 10 percent of seats in the national parliament were held by women, according to the results of the 2000 parliamentary elections.[62] The public approval of women's participation in protests is likely to be even lower. Ukrainian youth activist Serhiy Taran, for example, made the following observation during his visit to Baku:

> When I was in the office of the Musavat Party, I noticed a photo of the protest rally. There was not a single woman in the picture. I asked them why it was the case. And they replied that it was uncommon for a woman to participate in politics or attend a rally.[63]

The youth movements championing the idea of democracy failed to break this gender stereotype. According to a Yeni Fikir activist, a few young women joined the youth movement, but they were hidden from the public eye to shield them from both state repression and family criticism.[64] All the movement spokespeople in 2005 were men. The 2007 election of Vafa Jafarova as Dalga's chair appears to be an isolated case of a young woman's rise to prominence within the social movement sector, whereas Lala Shevket, one of the founding members of the Movement of Democratic Reforms in the Soviet Union, turned 54 by the time of the 2005 election. Compared with Azerbaijan, Georgian young women assumed a more visible role in planning and implementing movement activities.

Another shortcoming of the recruitment campaigns was the movements' inability to enforce stringent procedures for screening new applicants. The youth movements were open to anybody who showed interest in their activities, which made them vulnerable to informants and provocateurs. The security services allegedly implanted regime collaborators into these youth organizations. According to Said Nuri, former vice-chairman of Yeni Fikir, the youth movement "had three governmental agents within the group who helped to prepare a provocation"[65] leading to the arrest of several youth activists in August–September 2005. In addition, the opposition political parties tried to keep track of developments inside the youth movements with the help of their informants.

[61] The question wording was, "Please indicate whether you would encourage your daughter to become engaged in politics as a candidate [for office]." $N = 1{,}400$. For more information on mass attitudes toward women and politics, see International Foundation for Electoral Systems. 2007. *Public Opinion in Azerbaijan 2006: Findings from a Public Opinion Survey*. Washington, DC: IFES, p. 34.

[62] Inter-Parliamentary Union. 2015. *Historical Archive of Parliamentary Election Results [database]*. www.ipu.org/parline-e/reports/2019_arc.htm.

[63] Author's interview with Serhiy Taran, Kyiv, Ukraine, April 28, 2008.

[64] Author's interview with Said Nuri (via Skype), October 17, 2014.

[65] Zamejz, Anna. 2008. "Baku Freedom Dreams Dashed, For Now." *Kyiv Post*. June 18. www.kyivpost.com/news/opinion/op_ed/detail/29121/print/.

Maqam wanted to recruit as many people as possible. We did not close our doors to anybody, though we knew that the opposition parties – the Musavat Party and the Popular Front – had sent their people into our youth movement. They wanted to keep an eye on us.[66]

The admission of young people associated with the opposition political parties compromised the public image of the youth movements as a politically independent force. For example, the participation of Ilkin Gambar, 17-year-old son of the leader of the Musavat Party, gave grounds to the rumors about Yokh's connections with the Musavat Party. Yokh activist Vugar Salamli described how Ilkin's membership affected the movement:

Because he was Isa Gambar's son, some people began to associate Yokh with the Musavat Party. His involvement in our movement became a problem for us and for his father. In fact, Ilkin was capable of making his own decisions. There were several members of the youth wing of the Musavat Party within Yokh. And Ilkin sometimes disagreed with them.[67]

Organizational Structure

The movement leaders declared their commitment to the development of a horizontal organizational structure, but hierarchical relations prevailed inside these democracy-oriented youth movements. As noted by Szrom, coordinating committees were created not to make horizontal decisions but to delegate tasks in a hierarchical manner.[68] For example, Yokh's decision-making procedures regarding a choice of the movement's symbols provide a stark contrast with internal deliberations in the Georgian youth movement. While Kmara activists discussed at great length a choice of the movement's symbol and used local talent to design it, Yokh leadership delegated the development of the movement's symbols to professional designers in the United States. Moreover, given the lack of consensus among the movement's leaders, Yokh opted for the use of two images as the movement's logos.

We liked the image of the person who shouted "No!" to dictatorship and urged people to join the democratic struggle. As the election campaign advanced, the person's hands were supposed to close forming the clenched fist. Another symbol was the big palm signifying the Stop sign. We thought that both symbols were good so we could not pick just one of them. We used both symbols in our print material.[69]

[66] Author's Interview with Emin Huseynov, Baku, Azerbaijan, February 22, 2008.

[67] Author's interview with Vugar Salamli, Baku, Azerbaijan, February 26, 2008.

[68] Szrom, Charlie. 2006. "Structuring for Success: How Pro-Democracy Student Groups Brought Down Dictators in the Recent "Color Revolutions." Senior honors thesis, Department of Political Science, Indiana University, p. 49.

[69] Author's interview with Razi Nurullayev, Baku, Azerbaijan, February 25, 2008.

The idea of unification put a strain on the youth movements. In July 2005, a faction of youth activists from Dalga, Maqam, and Yokh suggested uniting all the antiregime youth groups under the umbrella organization *Ary* ("Bees") to make a better use of available resources and jointly apply for Western grants. According to Ary's leader, Ruslan Asadov, youth activists would work as hard as bees to attain their goals.[70] Yet several leaders of the extisting youth movements opposed the idea of unification for various reasons. Some youth activists felt that competition for grant money was a flimsy basis for unification, while others viewed this merger as a surreptitious scheme to decimate all the youth movements. According to Nurullayev, inside proponents of the unification were nothing more than "contaminants in the movement":

> The "Yokh" Movement of Azerbaijan has found some contaminants in the movement and has cleared them. We were busy clearing the contaminants and that is why you did not hear from us so long. Some of them you know, especially the participants from Albania Activism Festival know them well – two persons who went there with me; Ilkin Gambar and Vugar Salamli. The first is the son of Musavat Party (one of the biggest opposition parties in Azerbaijan) leader. One day they came up with a proposal of uniting all of the youth movements, which is very good. But what was behind this is interesting. The idea was to destroy the "Yokh" Movement, which has become so popular and declared that it wishes to build a free and just society and does not support any political leader until the people of Azerbaijan express their will. Opposition parties think that this is not a good idea and Yokh should openly state who it is supporting. All of them want to get our support and if we talk in favor of one party, the others become our enemy. Azerbaijan's political landscape is very difficult and it is very difficult to survive. But we have survived and became even more persistent and firm.[71]

This press release is an illustration of bitter tensions within the opposition camp. Like opposition political parties, youth movements competed for scarce resources. Lack of genuine unity in the face of a common opponent weakened the capacity of the Azerbaijani youth movements to mobilize young people against the current regime. For comparison, youth activists within black and yellow Pora more effectively hushed their disagreements until the end of the Orange Revolution.

Tactics vis-à-vis Opponents

The Azerbaijani youth movements deployed such protest tactics as graffiti, the distribution of leaflets, and the organization of pickets during the election year. Given the relatively low cost, graffiti was the most commonly used method of nonviolent resistance. Yokh made a public appearance in spring 2005 by spray

[70] Miri, M. 2005. "Molodezhnye organizatsii objedinilis." *Zerkalo*. July 2005.

[71] Nurullayev, Razi. 2005. "Contaminants in Yox Movement Azerbaijan." Press release.

painting the movement's name throughout Baku, while Maqam and Yeni Fikir favored such one-word slogans as "Resign!" (*Estefah*) and "Freedom" (*Azadlyq*). In the context of the 2005 elections, Azadlyq referred to both a political demand and the opposition's electoral bloc. Over the course of the protest campaign, youth's deployment of nonviolent methods was modified to adjust to the increasing level of state repression. Since the distribution of print material in the street routinely resulted in arrests of movement participants, Azerbaijani youth activists began to stage so-called leaflet rains, tossing print material from rooftops or balconies. Furthermore, picketing was largely abandoned as a protest tactic due to prohibitively high fines for participation in an unsanctioned protest event.

Unlike earlier graduates of electoral revolutions, Azerbaijani youth adopted the hunger strike as a protest tactic. This method of nonviolent resistance has a long history in post-Soviet Azerbaijan: journalists, members of opposition political parties, and political prisoners frequently went on hunger strikes to draw public attention to their needs.[72] Similarly, youth activists organized several hunger strikes to demand the reinstatement of university students expelled for their affiliation with the youth movements. The first hunger strike lasted for ten days in the summer of 2005 and was "a huge success"[73] ending in the reinstatement of Yeni Fikir activist Namiq Feyziev as an undergraduate student at Azerbaijan State Pedagogical University.[74] A headline in the Russian-language daily *Zerkalo* declared "the first victory" for the youth movement.[75] But the university administration again expelled Feyziev, along with other youth activists, in November 2005. A longer hunger strike lasting 19 days seemingly resulted in another victory. Under the spotlight of international media and Western diplomats, the Minister of Education declared that Turan Aliyev and Feyziev would be allowed to continue their education. But university rectors insisted on their expulsion for unsatisfactory academic performance and disciplinary problems, so both expelled youth activists fled the country.[76]

72 See, for example, BBC. 1998. "Editors in Azerbaijan Threaten Hunger Strike." November 16. http://news.bbc.co.uk/2/hi/asia-pacific/215725.stm; *Caucasian Knot*. 2003. "Wives of Arrested Azerbaijan Oppositionists Going on Hunger Strike." December 1. http://eng.kavkaz-uzel.ru/articles/1588/; Human Rights Watch. 2004. "Azerbaijan: Media, the Presidential Elections, and the Aftermath." HRW Briefing Paper. August 4. P. 11; IFEX. 2003. "Arrested Editor Begins Hunger Strike, Other Journalists Join Him." December 2. www.ifex.org/azerbaijan/2003/12/02/arrested_editor_begins_hunger_strike/; Radio Free Europe/Radio Liberty. 2004. "Azerbaijani Opposition Activists Go on Hunger Strike." July 13. www.rferl.org/content/article/1053830.html.

73 Author's interview with Said Nuri (via Skype), October 17, 2014.

74 Muradova, Mina, and Rufat Abbasov. 2006. "Azerbaijani Hunger Strikers: Opposition of the Future?" EurasiaNet. January 30.

75 Bairamova, J. 2005. "Molodezh oderzhala pervuiu pobedu." *Zerkalo*. July 7.

76 Amirova, Leyla. 2006. "Azerbaijan: A Political Education." EurasiaNet. October 21. www.eurasianet.org/departments/insight/articles/pp102206.shtml.

Another seven-day hunger strike held on Bashirli's arrest ended without the release of the detained youth activist.[77] On the contrary, the police arrested hunger strike organizers. Overall, this method of nonviolent resistance produced mixed results.

Another distinguishing feature of nonviolent resistance in Azerbaijan was a shortfall of humor in street actions and campaign material. According to a Yeni Fikir activist, the creative use of humor was dismissed in favor of "organizational issues":

> We had internal discussions about the use of humor. But everyone does not have the same sense of humor. And most activists felt that we had to focus on organizational issues. We were mostly interested in having enough people in the street.[78]

Compared with previous youth movements, Azerbaijani youth activists also made little use of marketing techniques. The production of promotional materials such as T-shirts, stickers, and badges required access to financial resources that the youth movements lacked. The dearth of financial resources negatively affected not only the movements' tactics against the regime but also their relations with other civil society actors.

Tactics vis-à-vis Allies

As in preceding cases, the youth movements tried to enlist support of such influential allies as the mass media, opposition political parties, and the international donor community on the eve of the national elections. The youth movements received news coverage in publications of the opposition political parties, independent newspapers, and international media, but these media outlets had a relatively small readership in the country. For example, the largest opposition newspaper, *Yeni Musavat*, had a circulation of approximately 14,000.[79] Unlike Kmara, the Azerbaijani youth movements lacked access to television to spread their ideas within the local population. Instead, the youth movements attempted to reach the international community. Youth activists courted Western media with the use of English-language material. Yokh prepared English-language press releases, whereas Maqam and Yeni Fikir activists carried English-language posters at protest events. According to Huseynov,

77 Regnum. 2005. "Chleny molodezhnoi organizatsii Yeni Fikir prekratili golodovku." September 7. www.regnum.ru/news/polit/508499.html.

78 Author's interview with Said Nuri (via Skype), October 17, 2014.

79 Cornell, Svante, and Fariz Ismailzade. 2003. "Azerbaijan." In *Nations in Transit: Democratization in East-Central Europe and Eurasia*, eds. Adrian Karatnycky, Alexander Motyl, and Amanda Schnetzer. New York: Freedom House, pp. 100–22, p. 113.

Seventy percent of our slogans were written in Azerbaijani. Approximately one-third of our slogans were written in English so that international media could show them on TV without the need for translation.[80]

According to some analysts, however, the media coverage of protest events could not compensate for inherent weaknesses of the youth movements:

Youth movements made a lot of noise out of nothing. They sent out e-mails and prepared press releases. They called for free and fair elections, but their activities didn't go far beyond contacts with the media.[81]

A tactical misstep on the part of some youth movements was their failure to establish clear-cut independence from the opposition political parties. In particular, Ruslan Bashirli, 27-year-old leader of Yeni Fikir, was widely viewed as Ali Kerimli's protégé. These negative perceptions stemmed from the fact that APFP supplied Yeni Fikir with computer equipment and an office in same building as the APFP headquarters. The state-controlled media further fueled the public's negative attitudes by spreading allegations about a homosexual relationship between Bashirli and Kerimli. The interviewed youth activists attributed this overt acceptance of party support to lack of alternative choices:

No one else offered us a room. We did not have any other choice ... But our activists had different political preferences. Some Yeni Fikir activists, including me, favored APFP. Others supported the Musavat Party. Some activists did not like any political party at all.[82]

They organized their press conferences in the party's headquarters. They didn't have much choice. Either they could invite journalists to the party's office or they had to hold a press conference in the street.[83]

Another example of an overt connection between the youth movement and a political party was Nurullayev's decision to run for a seat in the national parliament without abandoning his role as a Yokh spokesperson.[84] This choice also weakened the movement's credentials as a politically neutral force.

Furthermore, the Azerbaijani youth movements did not see opportunities for in-kind support by local businessmen and sought assistance from the international donor community. The movement leaders blamed the West for lack of interest in funding their activities. Some Azerbaijani activists assumed that foreign governments were content with having Aliyev as the country's president as long as he guaranteed the safe transit of oil to his allies.

Without financing, politics is nothing. We contacted Freedom House, National Democratic Institute, other international organizations. But we did not get any grant.

[80] Author's interview with Emin Huseynov, Baku, Azerbaijan, February 22, 2008.
[81] Author's interview with Ilgar (pseudonym), Baku, Azerbaijan, February 26, 2008.
[82] Author's interview with Said Nuri (via Skype), October 17, 2014.
[83] Author's interview with Vugar Salamli, Baku, Azerbaijan, February 26, 2008.
[84] Nurullayev was a former deputy head of the Popular Front Party–Classic.

We didn't have any funds to have a GOTV campaign. The only grant we got was from the Netherlands. It was 1,000 euros, but it was nothing for a country of eight million people.[85]

Our financial situation was horrible. I cannot tell you how many times we slept on the chairs in our office a day prior to the protest event. We stayed up late to prepare everything for the protest event and it cost us a lot of money to commute home and come back the next morning, since most of us lived on the outskirts of the city ... We did not do any fundraising. Most people in Azerbaijan are poor, especially supporters of the political opposition. I cannot imagine anybody inside the government supporting Yeni Fikir.[86]

In sum, Azerbaijani youth activists cited lack of financial resources as a major obstacle to their execution of protest campaigns. Movement leaders underscored the detrimental effects of their meager funding on the movement's recruitment campaigns, protest tactics, and relations with their allies. But the underdevelopment of civil society was another formidable impediment to the success of challenger organizations.

STATE COUNTERMOVES

The frozen conflict provided a backdrop for nonviolent action in both Azerbaijan and Georgia. Compared with Shevardnadze, however, Aliyev more aggressively exploited the notion that the whole nation should rally around the incumbent president to settle a territorial dispute with the neighboring state. State-controlled media massaged the idea that everything else was secondary. Furthermore, the image of external enemy was invoked to taint the reputation of the political opposition.

In light of the dominant public discourse, state authorities discredited the youth movements by spreading allegations about Yeni Fikir's ties with the government of Armenia. For this purpose, the coercive apparatus targeted the movement's leader. According to several interviewed youth activists, Bashirli was lured into traveling to Tbilisi on the assumption that he would meet Georgian civic activists and learn about their struggle against the regime.[87] On his return to Baku, Bashirli was arrested on the suspicion of state treason. Osman Alimuradov, another Yeni Fikir member, allegedly tipped the police, but rumor had it that it was a well-planned operation by the Azerbaijani intelligence services.[88] Bashirli was framed as a participant in a coup d'état plotted by the Armenian intelligence services. In support of this claim,

[85] Author's interview with Razi Nurullayev, Baku, Azerbaijan, February 25, 2008.

[86] Author's interview with Said Nuri (via Skype), October 17, 2014.

[87] For a detailed account of the events, see Human Rights Watch. 2005. "Azerbaijan Parliamentary Elections 2005: Lessons Not Learned." Human Rights Watch Briefing Paper. October 31, pp. 17–21.

[88] Mirkadyrov, R. 2005. "Armianskaia verbovka ili zhe splanirovannaia operatsia?" *Zerkalo*. August 6.

the police allegedly confiscated three grenades and explosives in Yeni Fikir's office.[89] Furthermore, the state-controlled TV channels and humongous billboards in the capital city repeatedly showed footage capturing how drunken Bashirli had accepted US$2,000 from an alleged Armenian intelligence service officer. General Prosecutor Zakir Garalov reportedly decided to release a video recording of Bashirli's visit to Tbilisi so that "the Azerbaijani public could see with its own eyes the true face of the opposition and become fully convinced that they [opposition] are willing to collaborate with any political force, including the Armenian intelligence services, for the sake of coming to power."[90]

In response, movement participants denied any contact with the Armenian intelligence services. But youth activists were unable to salvage the reputation of their movements. The government's well-planned smear attack against a Yeni Fikir leader had detrimental effects on all the youth movements:

> We lost a lot of people after Ruslan's arrest. He discredited all the youth movements. The media turned all youth activists into some sort of degenerates without any morals. We couldn't recover from this black PR.[91]

Bashirli's arrest signaled what awaited other youth activists if they continued their engagement in civil resistance. Movement participants were summoned to police stations for the so-called informative interviews. They were advised to abandon nonviolent action or face the consequences. In addition to Bashirli, his deputies Said Nuri and Ramin Tagiyev were arrested and charged with plotting a coup d'état. Under Article 278 of the Criminal Code, Bashirli was sentenced to seven years in prison, Nuri five years, and Tagiyev four years.[92] According to youth activist Emin Milli, the punishment of a few youth activists, rather than mass violence, was the government's favored tactic:

> They don't organize mass killings ... They punish some people and let everyone else watch. To say, "This is what can happen to you."[93]

To bestow legitimacy on the government's actions, state authorities imitated the public outcry over youth's treacherous behavior. The government allegedly organized public rallies of angry citizens demanding a tough punishment for Bashirli and his accomplices. Taking a page from the opposition's playbook, the ruling party reportedly picketed the APFP headquarters. On August 6, for

[89] Giragosian, Richard. 2005. "Azerbaijan: Has Government Taken a Troubling Example from Andijon?" Radio Free Europe/Radio Liberty. September 22.

[90] DayAz. 2005. "Zakir Garalov: Ruslan Bashirli vedet sebia na sledstvii neiskrenne." August 8. http://news.day.az/politics/29168.html.

[91] Author's interview with Emin Huseynov, Baku, Azerbaijan, February 22, 2008.

[92] EurasiaNet. 2006. "Azerbaijani Youth Activists Trial Puts Spotlight on Human Rights." April 16. www.eurasianet.org/departments/civilsociety/articles/eav041706.shtml.

[93] Quoted from Barry, Ellen. 2011. "A Dissident Is Free from Jail, but His Punishment Is Not Over." *New York Times*. June 24. www.nytimes.com/2011/06/25/world/europe/25azerbaijan.html?_r=1&ref=azerbaijan.

example, more than 200 people descended on Azadlyq's building hurling eggs and tomatoes, which triggered a clash between APFP supporters and their opponents.[94] A related state countermove was the distribution of posters portraying Kerimli against the backdrop of the Armenian flag.[95] The state-controlled media insinuated that Bashirli acted on Kerimli's order, which damaged the party's reputation on the eve of the national elections.

Another negative outcome of Bashirli's arrest was a weakened position of international NGOs in Azerbaijani society. As seen in the notorious footage from Tbilisi, Bashirli blurted out that the National Democratic Institute (NDI) had provided assistance for Yeni Fikir to stage a revolution in Azerbaijan. In turn, NDI regional director for Eurasia Nelson Ledsky publicly denied NDI funding for the challenger organization.[96] This political scandal created problems for Western NGOs and diminished the likelihood of Western assistance for the Azerbaijani youth movements.

The state cutoff of the movements' access to resources also involved repression against movement sympathizers. The loss of employment was a common outcome of citizens' cooperation with the youth movements in opposition to the regime. Huseynov, for example, recalled how collaboration with the movement entailed a person's loss of job in the wake of a month-long police investigation:

> Once we did a leaflet rain from one of the highest buildings in Baku. Our friend worked in a bar on the top floor so our activists managed to escape without getting caught. In a month, the security services figured out who had helped us and fired the bar-tender.[97]

In particular, state authorities targeted university students as potential recruits into the regime-threatening youth movements. Unlike their counterparts in Georgia, most deans at Azerbaijani universities were expected to carry out ideological work with students and invite political conformists as guest speakers. Furthermore, the university administration reportedly collaborated with the security services to monitor student behavior. The threat of expulsion from university loomed large in Azerbaijan. Another common threat was the loss of employment or the loss of private business. Said Nuri, for example, was forced to terminate his co-ownership of an Internet café in Baku.[98]

The level of police violence against youth activists was also higher in Azerbaijan than in Georgia. Participants in protest events were ruthlessly beaten, so the opposition forces hailed as "good news" a police promise to

[94] Azer, P. 2005. "Noch by proderzhatsia, da den prostoiat." *Zerkalo*. August 9.

[95] *Baku Today*. 2005. "Posters Smear Azerbaijan Opposition." August 29. http://volodymyrcampaign.blogspot.com/2005/08/posters-smear-azerbaijan-opposition.html.

[96] Radio Free Europe/Radio Liberty. 2005. "NDI Denies Financing Azerbaijani Youth Group." *RFE/RL Newsline*. August 8. www.rferl.org/content/article/1143455.html.

[97] Author's interview with Emin Huseynov, Baku, Azerbaijan, February 22, 2008.

[98] Author's interview with Said Nuri (via Skype), October 17, 2014.

refrain from hitting protesters on the head.[99] In addition, the arbitrary detention and inhumane treatment of youth activists were common in Azerbaijan.[100] A Yeni Fikir spokesperson, for example, was arrested during his interview with local journalists, commenting on the picketing of the general prosecutor's office to demand an investigation into the violent beating of youth activists at a police station.[101]

In response, movement participants attempted to establish informal contacts with the police. Specifically, the distribution of flowers among police officers was meant to signal youth's commitment to nonviolent action. Yeni Fikir activists laid down flowers in front of police cordons, but the fear of purges within the coercive apparatus was so pervasive that the police officers refused to take them. Compared with the Georgian police, Azerbaijani police officers were more loyal to the incumbent. "Aliyev is a good president for them [the police]. On top of high wages, they are getting a lot of bribes. They can break the law, and they feel really powerful."[102]

State repression against the whole family became widespread in Azerbaijan. Reminiscent of the Soviet times, state authorities not only turned civic activists into social outcasts but also made their relatives targets of social exclusion. For example, an angry mob threw stones at Bashirli's parents,[103] his fiancé was pressured to cancel their engagement,[104] and his uncle was fired from the tax police for his kinship ties with the detained youth activist.[105] The government's targeting of family members significantly raised the stakes of youth engagement in civil resistance.

The coercive apparatus also drew lessons from the Orange Revolution and took preemptive action. To deprive regime opponents of certain resources, the government ordered the removal of orange-colored fabric and clothes from local stores. The police imposed fines on businesses that did not comply with the order and organized raids of local shopping centers to confiscate orange-colored merchandise.[106] In view of the tent city on Kyiv's Maidan, the incumbent government warned regime opponents against the occupation of

99 Abbasov, Rufat, and Mina Muradova. 2005. "A Change in Police Tactics and in Turnout for Baku Protests." EurasiaNet. October 23. www.eurasianet.org/departments/civilsociety/articles/eav102405.shtml.

100 Jayrun. 2005. "Politseiskie zaderzhali aktivistov molodezhnykh organizatsii." *Zerkalo*. September 2.

101 Teimurkhanly, F. 2005. "Starye metody protiv Yeni Fikir." *Zerkalo*. April 23.

102 Author's interview with Said Nuri (via Skype), October 17, 2014.

103 Radio Free Europe/Radio Liberty. 2005. "Arrested Activist's Father Alleges Harassment by Azerbaijani Authorities." *RFE/RL Newsline*. August 8. www.rferl.org/content/article/1143455.html.

104 Teimurhanly, F. 2005. "Zashchita Ruslana Bashirli polagaet, chto tot imel vstrechu s gruzinami po natsionalnosti." *Zerkalo*. August 9.

105 Guluzade, K. 2005. "Bashirliada: Den tretii." *Zerkalo*. August 10.

106 *MosNews*. 2005. "Orange Ban Continues." August 19. http://volodymyrcampaign.blogspot.com/2005/08/azerbaijan-orange-ban-continues.html.

the public space in Baku. In November 2005, Deputy Interior Minister Asker Alekperov stated, "Sit-down actions and pitched tents as were used in Ukraine during protests at that country's December 2004 presidential vote will not be allowed."[107] Four state-sanctioned rallies organized by the opposition political parties ended without police violence.[108] Once the opposition forces attempted to start a sit-in action and permanently occupy Qalaba Square, the police moved in and violently dispersed protesters.[109] Furthermore, the ruling party reclaimed the public space by celebrating its electoral victory with a public event in the square.

IRELI: FORWARD WITH THE PRESIDENT

The creation of the pro-regime youth movement Ireli was the government's response to the emergence of multiple youth movements in opposition to the regime. The movement's formation was unveiled by a group of six university students in August 2005, creating an illusion of a youth-led civic initiative.[110] According to Farhad Mammadov, one of Ireli's cofounders, the movement's main goal was to promote "modern development of Azerbaijan."[111] Ireli's central message, however, was that the young generation should move forward in line with the incumbent president. The movement's declaration mentioned the president 10 times, stating, for example, that Ireli members "want to become the most reliable allies of the president" and "will close ranks around our president who has channeled all his efforts into restoring the territorial integrity of our country."[112]

The size of the youth movement reportedly grew from a few hundred students in 2005 to 6,000 people in 2008, with representation at 20 universities and 12 high schools.[113] For comparison, the youth wing of the ruling party YAP boasted

[107] Muradova, Mina, and Rufat Abbasov. 2005. "Opposition Stages Protest for Election Corrections." EurasiaNet. November 9. www.eurasianet.org/azerbaijan/news/stages_20051109.html.

[108] Radio Free Europe/Radio Liberty. 2005. "Azerbaijani Opposition Convenes Rally in Baku." *RFE/RL Newsline*. November 14. www.rferl.org/content/article/1143519.html.

[109] Peuch, Jean-Christophe. 2005. "Baku Police Disperse Opposition Rally." Radio Free Europe/Radio Liberty. November 26. www.rferl.org/content/article/1063263.html.

[110] The list of Ireli cofounders includes Ziya Aliyev, Elnara Garibova, Elnur Mammadov, Farhad Mammadov, Jeyhun Osmanli, and Roya Talibova.

[111] Quoted from Guliyev, Iskender. 2007. "'Right of Choice': "We Want Azerbaijani Youth to Develop and Are Acting in this Direction." Demaz. August 16. www.demaz.org/cgi-bin/e-cms/vis/vis.pl?s=001&p=0056&n=001214&prfr=1&g=&prev=.

[112] Quoted from Yaqublu, Tofiq, and Rufat Garagyozli. 2007. "Monitoring of Youth Organizations of Azerbaijan (2006)." *III Era* 7: 79–92, p. 81. The Baku-based Center for Economic and Political Research FAR Centre published the magazine and reported the results from its project "Azerbaijani Students Abroad and at Home" in the August issue.

[113] Day. 2008. "V Azerbaidzhane raspushcheno obshcherespublikanskoe molodezhnoe dvizhenie Ireli." December 9. http://news.day.az/politics/139700.html; *Trend News*. 2008. "I Hope to See Founders of Irali Organization to Head New Projects: Department Head of Azerbaijani Presidential Administration." December 11. http://news-en.trend.az/politics/movements/1368113.html.

a membership of nearly 160,000 people nationwide.[114] Since the 1990s, YAP membership was an informal prerequisite for employment in the public sector. More recently, Ireli offered an alternative route for ambitious youth to pursue a career in the government. The state-sponsored youth movement, however, differed from the youth wings of the pro-government political parties. Compared with YAP, Ireli offered young people more opportunities for participation in a wide range of cultural or professionally rewarding activities. Ireli activists were also willing to carry out service projects, tackling such social problems as computer illiteracy and drug addiction among youth. The state sponsorship of the youth movement reflected an evolution of the government's approach to youth co-optation.

> The government realized that some young people couldn't be co-opted by using administrative or coercive methods. Ireli is loyal to the government, but it is closer to youth than youth wings of pro-government political parties.[115]

Notably, the case of Ireli illustrates the impact of the cross-national diffusion of ideas on state-sponsored mobilization of youth. While regime opponents drew inspiration from Ukraine's Pora, the ruling elite scrutinized the case of Russia's *Nashi* ("Ours"). The Russian youth movement was set up in the aftermath of the Orange Revolution to mobilize young people in support of the incumbent president.[116] To counteract a wave of the color revolutions, Nashi was open to cooperation with politically affinitive youth organizations in the post-Soviet region. In 2005, a few young Azerbaijanis went to Moscow to meet with Nashi activists.[117] The following year, three Ireli activists participated in the summer camp organized by Nashi activists on Lake Seliger, 220 miles northwest of Moscow.[118] The interviewed Ireli activist, however, pointed out how the Azerbaijani youth movement differed from its Russian counterpart:

> First, Ireli carries out a lot of community service projects in addition to political actions. Nashi focuses on political activities. Second, Nashi is used to fight against Western diplomats. We don't do such a thing. Third, Ireli has more independence in making its decisions. Fourth, they get much more money. We have normal relations with them, but not a permanent and deep cooperation.[119]

114 Yaqublu, Tofiq, and Rufat Garagyozli. 2007. "Monitoring of Youth Organizations of Azerbaijan (2006)," p. 89.
115 Author's interview with Vugar Salamli, Baku, Azerbaijan, February 26, 2008.
116 For an in-depth analysis of the movement, see Miinssen, Ivo. 2014. *The Quest for an Ideal Youth in Putin's Russia I: Back to Our Future! History, Modernity, and Patriotism, According to Nashi, 2005–2013*. Stuttgart, Germany: Ibidem Verlag.
117 Guliyev, Iskender. 2007. "'Right of Choice': "We Want Azerbaijani Youth to Develop and Are Acting in this Direction." www.demaz.org/cgi-bin/e-cms/vis/vis.pl?s=001&p=0056&n=001214&prfr=1&g=&prev=.
118 Author's interview with Leyla (pseudonym), Baku, Azerbaijan, February 2008.
119 Author's interview with Leyla (pseudonym), Baku, Azerbaijan, February 2008.

THE WATERMELON REVOLUTION?[120]

OSCE declared that the 2005 parliamentary election in Azerbaijan was marred with electoral irregularities. The OSCE election observation mission, for example, documented "a wide range of serious violations during the vote count at the polling stations and during the tabulation of results at constituency election commissions."[121] According to the initial official results, YAP headed by the incumbent president won 56 seats, and the main opposition political parties – the Musavat Party and the Popular Front of Azerbaijan – received a total of 6 seats in the 125-member national parliament.[122] The Central Election Commission also reported that the turnout rate was 42.2 percent, signaling mass withdrawal from electoral politics. Compared with the opposition forces in Georgia, the opposition political parties and youth movements convinced a smaller share of young voters to participate in the elections.

In the post-election period, leaders of the opposition political parties organized public rallies against vote rigging. According to some estimates, approximately 15,000 people participated in a rally held on November 9.[123] Almost 20,000 people joined another rally held on November 13.[124] Though some youth activists called for permanent occupation of the square and the installation of a tent city, leaders of the opposition political parties urged their orange-clad supporters to disperse after a state-sanctioned rally. The opposition's eventual attempt to set up a tent city was met with police violence. As an alternative method of civil resistance, Gambar suggested switching off the lights at home each night.[125]

Meanwhile, another wave of state repression engulfed the country.[126] Given an escalation in political violence, Maqam, Yeni Fikir, and Yokh self-dissolved. Some youth activists were arrested; others fled the country and sought political asylum in the West. In contrast, the pro-regime youth movement received a

[120] *Economist* used the term "Watermelon Revolution" to describe a possible scenario in the post-election period in Azerbaijan. See *Economist*. 2005. "A Watermelon Revolution: Azerbaijan and Democracy – Might Azerbaijan Be Next in Line for a Democratic Revolution?" June 4.

[121] OSCE. 2006. *Republic of Azerbaijan Parliamentary Elections (6 November 2005): OSCE/ODIHR Final Report*. February 1. Warsaw: Office for Democratic Institutions and Human Rights, p. 2.

[122] OSCE. 2006. *Republic of Azerbaijan Parliamentary Elections (6 November 2005): OSCE/ODIHR Final Report*, p. 30.

[123] Radio Free Europe/Radio Liberty. 2005. "Azerbaijani Opposition Convenes Protest Rally." *RFE/RL Newsline*. November 10. www.rferl.org/content/article/1143518.html.

[124] Radio Free Europe/Radio Liberty. 2005. "Azerbaijani Opposition Convenes Rally in Baku." *RFE/RL Newsline*. November 14. www.rferl.org/content/article/1143519.html.

[125] Ismayilov, Rovshan. 2005. "Azerbaijan: Election Results Finalized, But Tensions Simmer On." EurasiaNet. November 28. www.eurasianet.org/azerbaijan/news/final_20051128.html.

[126] For a recent overview of human rights violations, see Human Rights Watch. 2013. *Tightening the Screws: Azerbaijan's Crackdown on Civil Society and Dissent*. HRW Report. Retrieved from www.hrw.org/reports/2013/09/01/tightening-screws.

boost from the government. Ireli declared its transformation into a broad-based social movement on the eve of the 2008 presidential election,[127] and it actively campaigned for reelection of the incumbent president.

Despite the opposition's defeat, the 2005 election provided a critical push for the development of new youth organizations in the country. A few youth activists formed the youth movement *Ol!* ("Be!") in 2006, with the mission to foster the development of "independently thinking responsible youth."[128] More recently, Azerbaijani youth established the youth movement *Nida* ("Exclamation Mark") to propel democratic change in the country.[129] Azerbaijani youth activists also began to display a sense of humor in challenging the regime. A five-minute video clip posted on YouTube by Adnan Hajizada and Emin Milli in 2009 poked fun at government spending on imported donkeys. In turn, state authorities interpreted it as an insult to the president and imprisoned the "donkey bloggers."[130] Nonetheless, youth activists continue to experiment with new forms of resistance to the regime.

CONCLUSION

An analysis of interactions between the antiregime youth movements and the incumbent government provides an explanation for a low level of youth mobilization against the regime. Given the absence of a youth-led challenger organization in the years preceding the 2005 elections, youth activists lacked organizational skills to build a viable youth movement. By the same token, dominant social norms hampered the cross-national diffusion of nonviolent methods. Under these circumstances, the prior example of successful mass mobilization in the region was an insufficient condition for the execution of innovative nonviolent tactics in Azerbaijan.

Among organizational weaknesses of the Azerbaijani youth movements was their inability to build a nationwide network of youth activists based on a horizontal organizational structure, establish clear independence from the opposition political parties, and amicably resolve internal disputes. Had the Azerbaijani youth movements spread into the provinces, they would have mobilized a larger share of the youth population. The leakage of information

[127] Trend. 2008. "Na baze molodezhnogo dvizhenia Azerbaidzhana Ireli sozdano obshchestvennoe objedinenie." December 16. http://news.trend.az/index.shtml?show=news&newsid=1372720&lang=ru.

[128] *Ol! Azerbaijan Youth Movement Manifesto*. Retrieved from http://ol-az.blogspot.com/2006/06/ol-azerbaijan-youth-movement-manifesto.html.

[129] For an overview of the movement's activities, visit the website www.nidavh.org.

[130] Allnutt, Luke. 2010. "Azerbaijan's Donkey Bloggers Are Just the Beginning." Radio Free Europe/Radio Liberty. July 8. www.rferl.org/content/Azerbaijans_Donkey_Bloggers_Are_Just_The_Beginning/2094553.html; Gojayev, Vugar. 2009. "Azerbaijan: Donkey Bloggers Punished." *Index on Censorship*. November 25. www.indexoncensorship.org/2009/11/azerbaijan-donkey-bloggers-punished/.

regarding intramovement tensions into the public sphere also damaged the reputation of youth movements. In addition, Azerbaijani youth made little use of humor to overcome political apathy and fear in society. Most importantly, the youth movements were unable to generate a large-scale public backlash against state repression.

In turn, the government of Azerbaijan demonstrated the capacity to draw lessons from earlier episodes of contention in the region and suppress the level of civic activism among youth. The framing of Yeni Fikir activists as collaborators with the Armenian intelligence services was used effectively to discredit all the antiregime youth movements. By the same token, state authorities created a climate of fear by threatening students with expulsion from university, unemployment, or detention. Furthermore, the coercive apparatus struck against antiregime youth movements during the embryonic stages of their development. Finally, the government sponsored the establishment of a youth movement in support of the incumbent president. Using a combination of discursive strategies, channeling, and repression, the government prevented a breakdown of the authoritarian regime in the former Soviet republic.

More broadly, the analysis of civil resistance in Azerbaijan suggests that the presence of a robust civil society is necessary to provide a more favorable environment for the development of a viable youth movement. The severity of state repression alone does not fully explain organizational weaknesses of challenger organizations. Leaders of opposition political parties are also culpable of constraining the growth of the nascent youth organizations through their attempts to harness youth's energy to serve their own political interests. In addition, there appeared to be a limited number of organizationally viable NGOs that could forge a formidable alliance with nonviolent youth movements on the eve of the parliamentary elections.

9

Conclusion

The emergence of nonviolent youth movements has become a prominent feature of post-communist societies at the turn of the twenty-first century. The youth movement Otpor played a pivotal role in challenging the power of the incumbent president in war-torn Serbia. Inspired by Otpor's example, similar youth movements were formed throughout the post-Soviet region. As discussed in this book, youth activists in Azerbaijan, Belarus, Georgia, and Ukraine deployed novel protest tactics to demand free and fair elections. Youngsters concocted humorous street performances, distributed stickers with provocative slogans, and spray painted graffiti in defiance of the ruling elite. The youth movements, however, differed in the extent to which they were able to mobilize youth against the regime.

This book argues that tactical interactions between youth movements and incumbent governments influenced the level of youth mobilization. It is further argued that learning from prior civic campaigns both inside and outside the country shaped the development of protest tactics and state countermoves on the eve of national elections. The youth movements that built upon a national record of civil resistance and the experience of challenger organizations in a similar political setting developed more innovative tactics and more effectively offset state countermoves, which in turn increased their capacity to mobilize citizens against the regime. Concurrently, incumbents who drew lessons from previous episodes of contention and took preemptive action against the nascent youth movements were better positioned to contain the size of post-election protests.

This book contributes to the debate over the importance of agency and structure in explaining social movement outcomes. Some studies emphasize the significance of structural factors in determining the level of mass mobilization.[1] A structural account, however, is incomplete. Even challenger

[1] On this point, see Way, Lucan. 2008. "The Real Causes of the Color Revolutions." *Journal of Democracy* 19(3): 55–69.

organizations in repressive political regimes face a plethora of choices pertinent to their struggle against the government. Likewise, incumbents have a wide range of options on how to crush dissent. Given the possibility of strategic action on the part of social movements and their adversaries, it is necessary to consider the role of agency. Specifically, analysis of movement tactics and state countermoves can deepen our understanding of civil resistance in nondemocracies.

The empirical contribution of this book lies in analyzing state-movement interactions in five post-communist states: Azerbaijan, Belarus, Georgia, Serbia, and Ukraine. To date, there are few in-depth cross-national studies of youth movements in Eurasia. Though electoral revolutions have attracted a great deal of attention, the analysis of youth movements is rather limited in the literature. Youth movements are usually discussed as one of many civil society actors that had a bearing on electoral revolutions in the region. Instead, this book places youth movements at the center of empirical analysis. This study focuses on such youth movements as Kmara (Georgia), Maqam (Azerbaijan), Otpor (Serbia), Pora (Ukraine), Yeni Fikir (Azerbaijan), Yokh (Azerbaijan), and Zubr (Belarus). These youth movements had many similar characteristics, including the timing of mass mobilization, the focus on free and fair elections, and commitment to nonviolent action, but they differed in the extent to which they could mobilize young people against the regime. Within Eastern Europe, this study compares youth movements in Belarus and Ukraine. Another intraregional comparison includes Azerbaijani and Georgian youth movements in South Caucasus.

The success of the youth movements is here defined in terms of the level of antiregime mobilization, measured by the rates of electoral and nonelectoral political participation. Empirical evidence indicates that young people in Georgia, Serbia, and Ukraine participated in protest events at a higher rate than those in Azerbaijan and Belarus. In addition, public opinion data show that young voters in Georgia, Serbia, and Ukraine provided greater electoral support for the political opposition than their peers in Azerbaijan and Belarus. Youth voter turnout is found to be higher for the presidential elections in Belarus (2001), Serbia (2000), and Ukraine (2004) than for the parliamentary elections in Azerbaijan (2005) and Georgia (2003). Analysis of state-movement interactions explains, in part, these cross-country differences.

This book does not claim to explain the outcome of electoral revolutions in the post-communist region. A myriad of political, socioeconomic, and cultural factors accelerated the incumbent's defeat in some countries and strengthened his political longevity in others. The state of the national economy, for example, influenced the level of popular support for the incumbent. International actors also affected the chances of removing an autocrat from power.[2]

[2] On the role of international factors, see, for example, Mitchell, Lincoln. 2011. *Uncertain Democracy: U.S. Foreign Policy and Georgia's Rose Revolution*. Philadelphia: University of Pennsylvania Press; Petrov, Nikolai, and Andrei Ryabov. 2006. "Russia's Role in the Orange Revolution." In *Revolution in Orange: The Origins of Ukraine's Democratic Breakthrough*, eds.

The role of youth movements in bringing down an incumbent varied within the region. There is a near consensus in the academic and policymaking communities that Otpor was crucial to Milosevic's defeat.[3] Marek Kapusta, for example, states that "Otpor was absolutely critical and key in bringing about the change" in Serbia.[4] Most observers of post-Soviet politics also agree that Pora and, to a lesser extent, Kmara played a vital role in breaking political apathy and mobilizing citizens against the regime in Georgia and Ukraine.[5] As noted by Bunce and Wolchik, Pora "proved to be the critical actor in organizing mass protests in anticipation of the falsification of the first round of the presidential election."[6] In contrast, the youth movements in Azerbaijan and Belarus seemed to have a rather limited impact on the outcome of electoral revolutions. According to Shalayka and Mackevich, for example, Zubr's negative campaign "succeeded in instilling an atmosphere of denial," but it did not necessarily boost political participation during the 2001 presidential election.[7] Regardless of the degree of

Anders Aslund and Michael McFaul. Washington, DC: Carnegie Endowment for International Peace, pp. 145–64; Spoerri, Marlene. 2014. *Engineering Revolution: The Paradox of Democracy Promotion in Serbia*. Philadelphia: University of Pennsylvania Press.

[3] Bunce, Valerie, and Sharon Wolchik. 2006. "*Youth and Electoral Revolutions in Slovakia, Serbia, and Georgia.*" *SAIS Review* 26(2): 55–65; Bunce, Valerie, and Sharon Wolchik. 2007. "Youth and Postcommunist Electoral Revolutions: Never Trust Anyone over 30?" In *Reclaiming Democracy: Civil Society and Electoral Change in Central and Eastern Europe*, eds. Pavol Demes and Joerg Forbig. Washington, DC: German Marshall Fund, pp. 191–204; Carothers, Thomas. 2001. "Ousting Foreign Strongmen: Lessons from Serbia." Policy brief. Carnegie Endowment for International Peace, Washington, DC, p. 4; Cohen, Roger. 2000. "Who Really Brought Down Milosevic?" *New York Times*. November 26; Rosenberg, Tina. 2011. *Join the Club: How Peer Pressure Can Transform the World*. New York: Norton and William; Rubin, Joe. 2000. "The Kids Who Could Topple Milosevic." *Mother Jones*. September 26.

[4] Arias-King, Fredo. 2007. "Revolution Is Contagious: Interview with Marek Kapusta." *Demokratizatsiya: Journal of Post-Soviet Democratization* 15(1): 133–37, pp. 134–35.

[5] Angley, Robyn. 2010. "NGOs in Competitive Authoritarian States: The Role of Civic Groups in Georgia's Rose Revolution." Ph.D. dissertation, Boston University; Arias-King, Fredo. 2007. "Revolution Is Contagious: Interview with Marek Kapusta"; Demes, Pavol, and Joerg Forbig. 2006. "Pora – 'It's Time' for Democracy in Ukraine." In *Revolution in Orange: The Origins of Ukraine's Democratic Breakthrough*, eds. Anders Aslund and Michael McFaul. Washington, DC: Carnegie Endowment for International Peace, pp. 85–102; Demes, Pavol, and Joerg Forbig. 2007. "Civic Action and Democratic Power Shifts: On Strategies and Resources." In *Reclaiming Democracy: Civil Society and Electoral Change in Central and Eastern Europe*, eds. Pavol Demes and Joerg Forbig. Washington, DC: German Marshall Fund, pp. 155–74; Hash-Gonzalez, Kelli. 2013. *Popular Mobilization and Empowerment in Georgia's Rose Revolution*. Lanham, MD: Lexington Books; Mitchell, Lincoln. 2011. *Uncertain Democracy: U.S. Foreign Policy and Georgia's Rose Revolution*. Philadelphia: University of Pennsylvania Press.

[6] Bunce, Valerie, and Sharon Wolchik. 2007. "Youth and Postcommunist Electoral Revolutions: Never Trust Anyone over 30?" In *Reclaiming Democracy: Civil Society and Electoral Change in Central and Eastern Europe*, p. 196.

[7] Shalayka, Alaksandar, and Syarhey Mackevich. 2002. "Non-Governmental Organizations and the Presidential Election in Belarus in 2001: The First Steps Made, We Are Moving On." In *Belarus: The Third Sector: People, Culture, Language*, eds. Pawel Kazanecki and Marta Pejda. Warsaw, Poland: East European Democratic Center, pp. 82–88; see pp. 86–87.

the movements' impact on the outcome of electoral revolutions, youth activists accomplished a nontrivial task of displaying youthful opposition to the repressive political regime. According to Otpor activist Milja Jovanovic, even a small social movement can inflict a great deal of damage on the regime:

> We [Otpor members] saw ourselves as some kind of annoying insect that bites all around the body of the regime. Those were the proportions at the time – we were very, very small, and a large man stood before us. We stung him a couple of times, and those small insects grew larger and more numerous.[8]

Despite the short-term achievements of these youth movements, a close look at post-election developments casts doubt on their capacity to sustain a high level of youth civic engagement for an extensive period of time. Most youth movements discussed in this book self-dissolved at the end of the electoral revolutions. A high level of state repression took a heavy toll on civil society in Azerbaijan and Belarus, entailing self-dissolution of the youth movements. A somewhat different set of factors explains the fate of the youth movements in the aftermath of electoral revolutions in Georgia, Serbia, and Ukraine. One of the reasons for their demise was the emergence of internal divisions over the direction of the movement's development. Ukrainian youth activists, for example, debated whether the social movement should transform itself into a NGO or a political party to push for democratic reforms. Another reason for the movements' declining power arose from the fear of youth engagement in politics among members of the newly elected governments. A number of politicians who came to power in the wake of electoral revolutions vigorously opposed the emergence of a watchdog organization that could check their power and inhibit the persistence of corruption in the public sector. In addition, a few youth movement leaders accepted government jobs to push for reforms via institutional channels, which might have weakened the capacity of youth movements to implement novel protest campaigns. Furthermore, a slow pace of democratic reforms caused youth disillusionment with politics. Despite the disappearance of the above-mentioned youth movements from the political scene, their legacies laid the groundwork for the development of new youth-led civic initiatives in favor of democratic change.

The concluding chapter summarizes cross-country differences in movement tactics and state countermoves and points out the implications of these findings for the study of social movements and comparative democratization.

MOVEMENT TACTICS AND STATE COUNTERMOVES IN COMPARATIVE PERSPECTIVE

This book has examined movement tactics and state countermoves on the eve of national elections in five post-communist states: Azerbaijan, Belarus, Georgia,

[8] Quoted from Secor, Laura. 2000. "Rage against the Regime: Serbia Students Fight Milosevic." *Lingua Franca* 10(6). Retrieved from www.linguafranca.com/print/0009/otpor.html.

Serbia, and Ukraine. The Serbian youth movement Otpor is treated here as the initiator movement that engendered the rise of similar challenger organizations in the post-communist region. The paired comparison method is used to examine subsequent mobilization efforts. The study compares youth movements on the eve of presidential elections in Belarus and Ukraine due to cultural affinity and geographic proximity of the two East European states. Another paired comparison includes the Azerbaijani and Georgian youth movements that sought to mobilize youth on the eve of parliamentary elections in South Caucasus. In analyzing movement tactics, this study distinguishes recruitment tactics, tactics vis-à-vis allies, and tactics vis-à-vis opponents. The empirical analysis also singles out different forms of repression, including overt violence against youth activists and channeling, or state measures aimed at inhibiting the movement's access to resources. A cross-country comparison of movement tactics and state countermoves is summarized in this section.

Recruitment Tactics

This study finds cross-movement differences in the scope of recruitment campaigns. The Serbian youth movement proved to be successful in building a heterogeneous base of support and setting up its cells throughout the country. The paired comparison of Azerbaijani and Georgian youth movements registers a variation in the geographic dispersion of recruitment campaigns along the urban-rural divide. Faced with the difficulty of recruiting political novices in the capital city, Kmara launched a recruitment campaign targeting rural youth. In contrast, the recruitment campaigns of the Azerbaijani youth movements were mostly limited to Baku. The interviewed youth activists attributed a capital city bias in their recruitment campaigns to a lack of financial resources. In the paired comparison of Belarus and Ukraine, recruitment campaigns were affected by the country's linguistic divisions. Zubr positioned itself as an alternative to Malady Front, known for its emphasis on use of the Belarusian language, and targeted the Russian-speaking urban youth. Ukrainian activists, on the contrary, sought to downplay linguistic and regional differences to enlist support of youth from different parts of the country. This book suggests that casting a wider net and targeting different segments of the youth population are critical to boost a movement's growth.

One of the structural constraints on recruitment campaigns arose from the dominant gender norms in post-communist societies. Voluminous research shows that women, and in particular young women, face enormous political, economic, and cultural obstacles to gain access to power.[9] Opinion polls show

[9] For a thorough discussion of gender and politics in Eastern Europe, see Buckley, Mary, ed. 1997. *Post-Soviet Women: From the Baltic to Central Asia.* New York: Cambridge University Press; Gal, Susan, and Gail Kligman, eds. 2000. *Reproducing Gender: Politics, Publics, and Everyday Life after Socialism.* Princeton, NJ: Princeton University Press, 2000; Hankivsky, Olena, and

that politics is still seen as a male domain in Eurasia. The data from the third wave of the World Values Survey, for example, reveal that more than two-thirds of respondents in the former Soviet republics and half of respondents in Serbia agree with the statement, "Men make better political leaders than women."[10] Strikingly, the majority of 18–29-year-old respondents subscribed to this view in mid-1990s.[11] The barriers to women's participation in contentious politics are even higher than obstacles to women's representation in the national parliament. Given high odds of police violence, engagement in protest activity is often deemed inappropriate for women. Nonetheless, there are cross-country differences in the extent of women's involvement in civil resistance. Georgian women appear to be more actively engaged in protest activity than their counterparts in Azerbaijan.[12] At least, this study finds that the Georgian youth movement had a higher rate of women's representation in the movement's leadership positions than the Azerbaijani youth movements. Kmara also capitalized on the participation of female activists in protest events to signal the movement's commitment to nonviolent action and broaden the base of its support. In contrast, the sight of female protesters was uncommon in Azerbaijan. The gender gap was somewhat smaller in Belarus and Ukraine. Of the five countries, Serbia appears to have had the highest level of women's visibility in civil resistance. A group of Serbian women formed Otpor Mothers to underscore women's active involvement in civil resistance and demonstrate their solidarity with youthful protesters. In another symbolic act, Otpor female activist Milja Jovanovic, along with Branko Ilic, was selected to accept the 2000 MTV Award "Free Your Mind!" on behalf of the social movement. Overall,

Anastasya Salnykova, eds. 2012. *Gender, Politics, and Society in Ukraine*. Toronto: University of Toronto Press; Heyat, Farideh. 2002. *Azeri Women in Transition: Women in Soviet and Post-Soviet Azerbaijan*. New York: Routledge; Jaquette, Jane, and Sharon Wolchik, eds. 1998. *Women and Democracy in Latin America and Central and Eastern Europe*. Baltimore: John Hopkins University Press; Johnson, Janet Elise, and Jean Robinson, eds. 2006. *Living Gender after Communism*. Bloomington: Indiana University Press; Matland, Richard, and Kathleen Montgomery. 2003. *Women's Access to Political Power in Post-communist Europe*. New York: Oxford University Press; Rubchak, Marian, ed. 2011. *Mapping Difference: The Many Faces of Women in Contemporary Ukraine*. New York: Berghahn Books; Rueschemeyer, Marilyn. 2011. "Women's Participation in Postcommunist Politics." In *Central and East European Politics: From Communism to Democracy*, eds. Sharon Wolchik and Jane Leftwich Curry. Lanham, MD: Rowman & Littlefield, pp. 109–24.

[10] The third wave of the WVS was administered in Belarus, Georgia, Serbia, and Ukraine in September–December 1996 and in Azerbaijan in 1997. The percentage of respondents who agreed with the statement ranged from 79.1 percent in Georgia, to 71.5 percent in Azerbaijan, 70 percent in Belarus, 63.4 percent in Ukraine, and 55.9 percent in Serbia.

[11] According to the third wave of the WVS, 76.4 percent of 18–29-year-old respondents in Georgia, 71.9 percent in Azerbaijan, 66.3 percent in Belarus, 59.3 percent in Ukraine, and 49 percent in Serbia agreed with the above-mentioned statement.

[12] On women's contributions to democratization processes in Georgia, see, Tamuna Sabedashvili. 2007. *Gender and Democratization: The Case of Georgia 1991–2006*. Tbilisi, Georgia: Heinrich Boll Foundation.

these findings suggest that a high rate of female participation in civil resistance can bolster a movement's image as an inclusive organization and a champion of nonviolent action.

In addition, organizational structure influenced the effectiveness of recruitment tactics. This book finds cross-movement variations in the extent to which the challenger organizations instituted a horizontal organizational structure. Otpor is a prime example of a social movement that granted a great deal of autonomy to local cells and solicited input from movement participants. The Belarusian and Ukrainian youth movements subsequently sought to mimic Otpor's organizational structure, albeit with various degrees of success. From the comparative perspective, Kmara developed more inclusive decision-making procedures than Yokh. Georgian youth activists regularly discussed their prospective course of action and amicably resolved their differences over tactics. Though several Kmara members were charged with the responsibility to speak on behalf of the movement, they all delivered the same political message. In contrast, there was "a lot of drama" inside Yokh.[13] Razi Nurullayev designated himself as the sole spokesperson for the movement and publicly labeled a few prominent Yokh members as "contaminants," raising questions about the movement's capacity to unite young people against the regime. This study shows that the development of a hierarchical organizational structure has a negative impact on a movement's capacity to recruit and retain members.

Tactics vis-à-vis Allies

Comparative analysis reveals discernible differences in the movements' interactions with opposition political parties. Otpor succeeded in establishing itself as an independent challenger organization that could exert pressure on political parties and demand unification of the fragmented opposition. Within South Caucasus, Kmara gained greater organizational autonomy from the political opposition than most Azerbaijani youth movements. In particular, Yeni Fikir failed to distance itself from an opposition political party by openly accepting its assistance. The location of the movement's office in the same building as the party's headquarters, along with the perceived endorsement of the movement's leader by the party boss, tainted Yeni Fikir's reputation as an independent actor. In contrast, Pora achieved greater organizational autonomy from political parties by securing financial support from multiple sources and displaying a higher degree of discreetness in its dealings with the political opposition. What emerges from this study is that public perceptions of a youth movement as merely an appendix to a political party tend to diminish the movement's capacity to enlist popular support and recruit youngsters.

[13] Author's interview with Said Nuri (via Skype), October 17, 2014.

The level of the movements' cooperation with other challenger organizations and NGOs also differed across the countries. Otpor cooperated with a wide range of civil society actors within the framework of a GOTV campaign. Similarly, Georgian youth activists forged alliances with multiple civil society actors to press for political change. In Ukraine, black Pora and yellow Pora muted their differences to present a united front against the regime. However, interorganizational competition for resources seemed to have a debilitating effect on civil society in Azerbaijan and Belarus. As observed by Shalayka and Mackevich, Zubr "almost never coordinated its activities with other organizations" and considered other youth organizations primarily as its rivals.[14] A high level of the movement's cooperation with various civil society actors is necessary to strengthen the movement's position vis-à-vis the government.

Tactics vis-à-vis Opponents

This book demonstrates that some youth movements made a savvier choice of protest tactics than others. In particular, the case of Otpor vividly illustrates how innovative tactics can erode the strength of the regime. Remarkably, Serbian activists created a culture of resistance by deftly using a broad spectrum of marketing techniques. Otpor, for example, produced slick TV spots that promoted the youth movement as a brand in the marketplace of ideas. Notwithstanding state repression, participation in high-risk activism was depicted as a trendy youth lifestyle.

One of the main insights that emerges from this study is that the rootedness of nonviolent methods in the local history of civic activism tends to strengthen the movement's capacity to mobilize citizens against the regime. Ukrainian youth activists, for example, were able to draw a symbolic link between their struggle for political change and earlier episodes of contention by using the encampment as a method of nonviolent resistance. Previous protest campaigns held in the fall of 1990 and the winter of 2000 involved the occupation of Kyiv's main square and the installation of a tent city.[15] Building on this tradition of nonviolent resistance, civic activists mobilized thousands of ordinary citizens during the Orange Revolution. In contrast, the occupation of a trade union building by a few Zubr activists failed to jump-start a large-scale protest campaign in Belarus. The choice of a radical protest tactic might have alienated some movement sympathizers. Furthermore, structural disadvantages imposed

[14] Shalayka, Alaksandar, and Syarhey Mackievich. 2002. "Non-Governmental Organizations and the Presidential Election in Belarus in 2001: The First Steps Made, We Are Moving On." In *Belarus: The Third Sector: People, Culture, Language*, p. 86.

[15] On the symbolic importance of the Maidan, Kyiv's main square, see Otrishchenko, Natalia. 2015. "Beyond the Square: The Real and Symbolic Landscapes of the Euromaidan." In *Ukraine's Euromaidan*, eds. David Marples and Frederick Mills. Stuttgart, Germany: Ibidem-Verlag, pp. 147–62.

constraints on the effectiveness of protest tactics in a nondemocratic setting. Despite Zubr's efforts, the incumbent's popularity far exceeded mass support for a rather indecisive and uncharismatic candidate from the political opposition. Likewise, the Azerbaijani youth movements were unable to overcome structural constraints on civic engagement. The innovative use of leaflet rains, for example, was insufficient to break down a climate of fear in the former Soviet republic.

This book also finds cross-movement differences in the use of political humor. The use of humor was a potent weapon in Otpor's struggle against the regime. Otpor's street performances, for example, were brimming with political humor, lampooning the country's leader. At the other end of the spectrum, the Azerbaijani youth movements did not dare to ridicule the incumbent president out of fear of a draconian state response. Challenger organizations that did use political humor accentuated different attributes of the incumbent. Zubr members poked fun at Lukashenka's mental health, whereas Ukrainian activists dwelled on Yanukovych's criminal record. According to public opinion polls,[16] Zubr's emphasis on the president's alleged insanity seemed to cause less public outrage than Pora's focus on the politician's imprisonment on criminal charges. The deft use of humor is important because it can help challenger organizations overcome fear and political apathy in a repressive political regime.

A myriad of these cross-movement differences stem, in part, from variations in the capacity of movement participants to draw lessons from previous protest campaigns and adjust the adoption of innovative tactics to the local context. Notably, participation in the 1996–97 student protests informed the strategic thinking of Otpor leaders in 1998–2000. Serbian youth activists, for example, realized that the organization of short street performances was preferable to a daily march through the city. As adopters of Otpor's model of nonviolent resistance, the subsequent youth movements faced the task of aligning innovative protest tactics with local social norms and the domestic history of civic activism. The student hunger strike of 1990 and the Ukraine without Kuchma Movement of 2000–01 influenced the development of protest tactics by Ukrainian activists. Likewise, antigovernment protests in support of Rustavi-2 and the student campaign for institutional reforms at TSU informed Kmara's struggle for political change. In contrast, Azerbaijani youth activists lacked experience with organizing a protest campaign independent from opposition political parties, which negatively affected their capacity to craft savvy protest tactics.

[16] On the popularity of the incumbents in Belarus and Ukraine, see the Foundation "Democratic Initiatives" and Kyiv International Institute of Sociology. 2004. *Prezydentski vybory-2004: Reityngy ta prognozy* [press release]. Retrieved from http://dif.org.ua/ua/polls/2004_polls/prezii-ta-prognozi.htm; Independent Institute of Socio-Economic and Political Studies. 2001. *IISEPS Newsletter* (in Russian), September Issue. www.iiseps.org/arhiv.html.

State Countermoves

The discreditation of the youth movements through state-controlled media was a major state countermove in all the five countries. A recurrent government tactic was to invoke an image of an external enemy and frame rebellious youth as foreign agents. Azerbaijani state-controlled media claimed the opposition's collaboration with Armenia, a neighboring state with an unresolved territorial dispute. Likewise, some Georgian officials insinuated Kmara's ties with Russia. Similarly, incumbents in Belarus, Serbia, and Ukraine branded youth activists as pawns of the West in a CIA-sponsored plot to assume control over the region. Some governments, however, showed more sophistication than others in manufacturing the news. Specifically, compromising videos of youth activists were more persuasive than politically charged statements by government officials. The state-controlled media bombarded the Azerbaijani population with a video of a clandestine meeting between a Yeni Fikir leader and an alleged Armenian intelligence officer, which had a debilitating impact on all the youth movements in opposition to the regime. In contrast, a few Georgian officials who made questionable remarks about Russia's backing for Kmara failed to ruin the movement's reputation as a champion of democratic reforms. Similarly, news stories about the confiscation of explosives in Pora's office did not appear to be credible enough to convince the majority of Ukrainians that the youth movement was a terrorist organization. For comparison, media reports about Western funding for the Belarusian opposition seemed to be quite persuasive, damaging Zubr's public image as an independent actor. These findings suggest that the media framing of challenger organizations influences the level of mass mobilization against the regime.

The educational system was another common venue for state repression against the youth movements. The threat of expulsion from university hung like Damocles' sword over youth activists throughout the region. But harassment of university students occurred on a much larger scale in Azerbaijan and Belarus. According to numerous human rights reports,[17] dozens of politically active students were expelled from university in Belarus in the late 1990s and early 2000s. As in the Soviet times, denial of access to higher education and the subsequent denial of white-collar employment signified the government's treatment of critically thinking intelligentsia as social outcasts. Compared with Ukraine, Belarus had a smaller private sector, reducing prospects for any employment of regime opponents. Likewise, Azerbaijani youth activists faced higher obstacles to employment than their Georgian counterparts due to greater state control over the national economy. This comparative analysis indicates that a high level of coercion against

[17] Human Rights Watch. 1999. "Republic of Belarus: Violations of Academic Freedom." *HRW Report*. www.hrw.org/reports/1999/belarus/; Viasna Human Rights Center. 2002. *Obzor-khronika narushenii prav cheloveka v Belarusi v 2001 godu*. Minsk, Belarus: Viasna, pp. 153–82.

university students can suppress youth's engagement in protest activity, especially in countries with an underdeveloped private sector.

As discussed in this book, police violence against movement participants was routinely used to check the movement's growth. However, the detention of youth activists was more common in Azerbaijan and Belarus than in Georgia and Ukraine. A seven-hour detention of Kmara members for spray painting graffiti on the Ministry of Interior's building was a rare example of police action against the Georgian youth movement, whereas Azerbaijani youth activists were regularly detained and violently beaten for any public display of their opposition to the incumbent government. Moreover, the use of informants and provocateurs assumed different proportions in the selected states. Like the Soviet-era KGB, the security services in Azerbaijan and Belarus closely monitored student behavior at universities and systematically spied on regime-threatening youth organizations. The KGB of Belarus, for example, was notorious for its attempts to develop an extensive network of informants in Belarusian society. Based on their intelligence-gathering operations, the Belarusian security services carried out mass arrests of youth activists, whereas Azerbaijan's coercive apparatus preferred to target a few movement leaders to quell youth engagement in politics. In most cases, a high level of police violence tends to suppress mass mobilization against the regime. In Serbia, however, mass arrests and fingerprinting of Otpor members backfired, causing large-scale public outrage over state repression.

This book also detects cross-country variations in the timing of state repression. Incumbents in Georgia, Serbia, and Ukraine frequently acted in reaction to protest events organized by youth movements. By the time the Serbian government ordered mass arrests of movement participants, Otpor had firmly established itself as a nonviolent youth movement committed to political change. Likewise, an escalation in state repression against Pora occurred when the youth movement had already developed a nationwide network of activists and achieved name recognition in Ukrainian society. Furthermore, the president of Georgia dismissed the importance of the youth movement in destabilizing the political situation and did not issue an order for mass arrests of Kmara activists. In contrast, incumbents in Azerbaijan and Belarus adopted more preemptive strategies to suppress civic activism. State authorities in the two former Soviet republics hunted down the youth movements months in advance of national elections. The arrest of Yeni Fikir's leader, for example, occurred in August 2005, almost three months prior to election day. For comparison, a police raid on Pora's office occurred only two weeks prior to the first round of the presidential election. Preemptive state action can decimate a social movement during its early stages of development, while a belated response of the coercive apparatus can backfire and provide a youth movement with a greater opportunity for growth.

Furthermore, this study finds that incumbents addressed the issue of "diffusion-proofing" – obstruction of the cross-national diffusion of ideas – with various degrees of rigor.[18] The Serbian government inhibited the in-country interactions between domestic and international actors, but Otpor activists could travel to neighboring Hungary to meet various civil society actors and cultivate ties with influential allies. Since Milosevic's downfall, the governments of Azerbaijan and Belarus have placed greater obstacles to the diffusion of nonviolent methods of resistance than their counterparts in Georgia and Ukraine. In particular, the former imposed stiffer restrictions on the freedom of assembly and the freedom of movement. Yellow Pora, for example, managed to hold a summer camp for youth activists in the Crimea, with a few foreigners as guest speakers. In contrast, Belarusian civic activists had to travel outside the country to attend workshops on nonviolent action and faced harassment on their return. Likewise, a few veterans of earlier electoral revolutions could freely travel to Georgia, but they were deported from Azerbaijan on the eve of national elections. These findings show that incumbents who obstruct cross-national diffusion of ideas tend to be more effective at suppressing nonviolent action against the regime.

This book also shows that incumbents differed in their attempts to counteract a tide of civil resistance with the creation of managed civil society.[19] The incumbents in Georgia, Serbia, and Ukraine neglected the idea of establishing a nationwide youth movement in support of the current regime. Rather than setting up a novel youth organization, national leaders in those countries relied on youth wings of ruling political parties to drum up support for the regime. In contrast, the governments of Azerbaijan and Belarus opted for state sponsorship of regime-friendly youth movements. Interestingly, Lukashenka and Aliyev selected different models of youth co-optation. Lukashenka looked on the Soviet-era Komsomol as a template for building a regime-friendly youth movement in the former Soviet republic. Meanwhile, taking a cue from Putin's playbook, Aliyev modeled the youth movement Ireli on Russia's Nashi. A close look at these regime-friendly youth movements reveals the borrowing of tactics from the political opposition and the extensive use of positive incentives for compliant activism.

Finally, this book reveals variations in the movement's response to state repression. Specifically, the youth movements reacted differently to a smear campaign in state-controlled media. Otpor forcefully counteracted state propaganda, demonstrating the movement's rootedness in local communities and brushing away official allegations of Western funding. Likewise, Pora launched a public campaign *They Lie!*, naming and shaming media outlets for

[18] On the concept of diffusion-proofing, see Koesel, Karrie J. and Valerie Bunce. 2013. "Diffusion-Proofing: Russian and Chinese Responses to Waves of Popular Mobilizations against Authoritarian Rulers." *Perspectives on Politics* 11(3): 753–68.

[19] On the management of civil society as the government's survival strategy, see Robertson, Graeme. 2009. "Managing Society: Protest, Civil Society, and Regime in Putin's Russia." *Slavic Review* 68(3): 528–47.

serving as a mouthpiece of the ruling elite. Yet, Belarusian youth activists did not carry out a large public campaign to fend off the government's claims about the opposition's dependence on foreign grants. Similarly, the Azerbaijani youth movements were overwhelmed by state propaganda in the aftermath of Bashirli's arrest and did not win an information war. The analysis also suggests that a cookie-cutter approach to coping with police violence did not produce the same results in each case. Compared to the Ukrainian police, the Belarusian coercive apparatus was in a more privileged position, coming out as a beneficiary, rather than a victim, of the current regime. Under these circumstances, the distribution of flowers and sweets at police stations was insufficient to generate widespread security defections. In part, these findings indicate that structural conditions constrained the effectiveness of movement tactics directed at counteracting state repression.

In sum, this book uncovers discernible cross-country differences in movement tactics and state countermoves. Some youth movements adopted a more democratic organizational structure and designed a more inclusive recruitment strategy than others. Furthermore, some youth movements were savvier in their dealings with influential allies. In crafting tactics vis-à-vis their opponents, some youth activists better adjusted nonviolent methods of resistance to the local context and displayed a greater sense of humor. In turn, the incumbents differed in their choices of countermovement tactics and their timing of political violence. State authorities in Azerbaijan and Belarus deployed harsher repressive methods against regime opponents and took more preemptive action to curb civic activism. In particular, the governments in these former Soviet republics more forcefully blocked the cross-national diffusion of ideas and more systematically supported the development of regime-friendly youth organizations on the eve of national elections. These cross-country differences in movement tactics and state countermoves affected the level of mass mobilization against the regime in the selected states.

More broadly, this book demonstrates a distinct pattern of protests and repression in hybrid regimes. First, the organization of antigovernment protests is often scheduled for an election year. Challenger organizations in the selected states assumed that national elections would provide an opportune moment for mobilizing the populace against the regime. We are likely to observe a significant increase in protest activity during an election campaign in a hybrid regime. The level of mass mobilization might be especially high during competitive elections in which the political opposition has a great deal of popular support. Second, given the timing of mass mobilization, the conduct of free and fair elections is seen as a pivotal issue in hybrid regimes. As discussed in this book, youth movements in post-communist societies demanded state provision of electoral integrity and worked on a GOTV campaign to bring regime opponents to the polling station. Third, a distinct repertoire of contention prevails in hybrid regimes. Unlike challenger organizations in mature democracies, social movements in the selected states did not collect signatures for a petition, lobby their parliamentarians, or propagate their ideas on national TV channels. Compared with their counterparts in hardcore autocracies, however, youth movements had greater opportunities for the expression of their political grievances. As shown in this book, youth activists used the street as a venue for nonviolent action against the regime. Among protest tactics adopted by the youth movements in the early 2000s were the spray painting of graffiti, the distribution of stickers, and the organization of street performances. More recently, we can observe how social media has become a platform for civil resistance in nondemocracies.[20] Finally, the regime type influences patterns of state repression. Compared with dictators in totalitarian states, incumbents in hybrid regimes are more constrained in their use of political violence against their opponents. For example, the assassination of civic activists is quite rare in hybrid regimes. Rather than the deployment of overt repression, governments in hybrid regimes tend to impose a wide range of formal and informal constraints on the opposition's access to resources. Moreover, mimicking the opposition's tactics, incumbents might instigate elite-led mobilization in favor of the current regime. The government, for example, might sponsor the establishment of a regime-friendly youth movement to suppress youth engagement in civil resistance. Overall, this study reaffirms the importance of the regime type in analyzing state-movement interactions.

IMPLICATIONS

This book has shown how strategies pursued by social movements and incumbent governments affect the level of mass mobilization against the regime. On the one hand, the use of innovative protest tactics can boost the level of youth political participation. On the other hand, savvy state countermoves can suppress the level of civil resistance. History abounds with examples of antigovernment protests in repressive political regimes, wherein "the seemingly impossible ... became the seemingly inevitable."[21] The Rose Revolution in Georgia and the Orange Revolution in Ukraine, for example, would not have happened without strategic thinking, stamina, and courage displayed by a critical mass of people. Similarly, the Arab Spring is, to a large extent, a product of bold strategic action by civic activists. Egyptian youth, for example, developed innovative protest tactics and actively used social media to mobilize the population. A close examination of protest tactics and state countermoves is critical to explain the level of civil resistance in nondemocracies.

[20] See, for example, Diamond, Larry. 2010. "Liberation Technology." *Journal of Democracy* 21(3): 69–83; Howard, Philip. 2010. *The Digital Origins of Dictatorship and Democracy: Information Technology and Political Islam*. New York: Oxford University Press; Shirky, Clay. 2008. *Here Comes Everybody: The Power of Organizing without Organizations*. New York: Penguin.

[21] Beissinger, Mark. 2002. *Nationalist Mobilization and the Collapse of the Soviet State*. New York: Cambridge University Press, p. 8.

It should also be kept in mind that state-movement interactions are influenced by the political environment in which challenger organizations and state authorities are embedded. Unfavorable structural conditions can impose enormous constraints on civic engagement and thwart the effectiveness of novel protest tactics. In particular, tactical innovation on the part of youth movements might be insufficient to boost electoral participation if opposition political parties fail to nominate a viable presidential candidate. A youth-led push for democratic change can also be significantly weakened if various challenger organizations see themselves primarily as rivals rather than allies. In addition to the fragmented opposition, the severity of state repression might become an insurmountable impediment to the growth of a social movement.

Youth mobilization in Russia under Putin illustrates the relative importance of agency and structure in explaining social movement outcomes in an out-of-sample case. On the heels of the 2004 Orange Revolution, the youth movement *Oborona* ("Defense") was formed to press for free and fair elections in Russia.[22] The movement's leadership included members of the youth wings of the opposition political parties Union of Right Forces (*Soiuz pravykh sil* [SPS]) and Yabloko. According to some estimates, Oborona had approximately 1,000 activists[23] in the country with a total population of 143 million, of which 19.3 percent (27.7 million) were 18–29-year-old people.[24] Oborona's membership in Moscow was estimated to be 200 people, with as few as 20 active participants in movement activities.[25] Emulating Otpor, the Russian youth movement adopted Otpor's image of the clenched fist as a symbol of resistance and deployed nonviolent protest tactics against the regime. One of the first protest events organized by Oborona in April 2005 was titled "Enough of Putin."[26] Approximately 100 youth activists marched down Moscow's Tversky Boulevard carrying placards with such slogans as "Enough of Dictatorship," "Down with the Tsar," and "One, Two, Three, Putin Go." The movement's call for the incumbent's resignation, however, was in stark contrast to the political preferences of most Russians. Opinion polls showed that Putin's approval rating was consistently above 65 percent during his second presidential term, peaking at 86 percent in March 2008.[27] Furthermore, the challenger

[22] For an in-depth discussion of the movement's history, see Lyytikainen, Laura. 2014. "Performing Political Opposition in Russia: The Case of the Youth Movement Oborona." Ph.D. dissertation, University of Helsinki, Finland.

[23] Lyytikainen, Laura. 2013. "Gendered and Classed Activist Identity in the Russian Oppositional Youth Movement." *Sociological Review* 61: 499–524, p. 502.

[24] Russia's population statistics for the year 2005 are retrieved from US Census Bureau's International Database, www.census.gov/population/international/data/idb/informationGateway.php.

[25] Lyytikainen, Laura. 2013. "Gendered and Classed Activist Identity in the Russian Oppositional Youth Movement," p. 502.

[26] Savina, Ekaterina. 2005. "Studenty pereshli k Oborone." *Kommersant*. April 4. www.kommersant.ru/doc/560225.

[27] See, for example, the results of opinion polls conducted by the Levada Center, www.russiavotes.org/president/presidency_performance_trends.php#190.

organization failed to break through the information blockade and achieve name recognition in Russian society. When prompted to name Russian youth movements, merely 1 percent of polled Russians mentioned Oborona between 2005 and 2007.[28] For comparison, the regime-friendly youth movement Nashi was named by 26 percent of survey respondents in December 2007. The relatively low level of Oborona's popularity cannot be attributed solely to the severity of state repression.

The Russian government also drew lessons from the Orange Revolution and displayed "intensive innovation" in subverting regime-threatening civic activism.[29] The replacement of police detention with an arbitrary draft is an illustration of evolving coercive methods against regime opponents. Oborona leader Oleg Kozlovsky, for example, was sent to the barracks for nearly three months and released immediately after the conclusion of the 2008 presidential election.[30] The Kremlin's harnessing of the power of the Internet is another telling example of the government's adaptation to innovative protest tactics. Rather than bluntly blocking certain websites, the Russian government sponsored the production of state-sanctioned online content. An army of young Russians was reportedly employed to lambast the political opposition and steer online discussions in a certain direction with the help of inflammatory comments.[31] Another state countermove was the takeover of social network sites. LiveJournal, a popular platform for Russian bloggers, was bought by the Russian media company SUP, fueling concerns about increasing state censorship of online content.[32]

The emergence of the nationwide youth movement *Nashi* ("Ours") was a hallmark of the government's counter-revolutionary action.[33] The pro-regime

[28] The survey was based on a national representative sample. *N* = 1,600. For details, see Levada Center. 2008. "Patriotism and the Youth Movement Nashi." Press release. January 21. www.levada.ru/old/press/2008012101.html.

[29] On this point, see Robertson, Graeme. 2011. *The Politics of Protest in Hybrid Regimes: Managing Dissent in Post-Communist Russia*. New York: Cambridge University Press, p. 201.

[30] Kozlovsky, Oleg. 2008. "Putin's Gulag Stability." *Washington Post*. May 19. www.washingtonpost.com/wp-dyn/content/article/2008/05/18/AR2008051801911.html.

[31] For an overview of this practice, see Harrison, Virginia, and Alla Eshchenko. 2015. "Inside Russia's Pro-Putin Troll Factory." CNN. September 3. http://money.cnn.com/2015/09/03/news/russia-troll-factory-putin; Luhn, Alec. 2015. "Game of Trolls: The Hip Digi-Kids Helping Putin's Fight for Online Supremacy." *The Guardian*. August 18. www.theguardian.com/world/2015/aug/18/trolls-putin-russia-savchuk.

[32] Brown, Heidi. 2007. "Choking the Russian Voice." *Forbes*. December 4. www.forbes.com/2007/12/04/russia-blog-livejournal-tech-cz_hb_1204russianblog.html; Greenall, Robert. 2012. "LiveJournal: Russia's Unlikely Internet Giant." *BBC News*. March 2. www.bbc.com/news/magazine-17177053.

[33] On the movement's development, see Miinssen, Ivo. 2014. *The Quest for an Ideal Youth in Putin's Russia: I. Back to Our Future! History, Modernity, and Patriotism, According to Nashi, 2005–2013*. Stuttgart, Germany: Ibidem Verlag; Sperling, Valerie. 2012. "Nashi Devushki: Gender and Political Youth Activism in Putin's and Medvedev's Russia." *Post-Soviet Affairs* 28(2): 232–61.

youth movement was formed on the basis of Walking Together, another youth organization loyal to the regime.[34] According to the movement's leader, Vasily Yakemenko, the establishment of such a movement was initiated by various local youth organizations with the intent to set up an "antifascist" youth movement on the occasion of the sixtieth anniversary since Russia's victory in the Great Patriotic War.[35] The *Nashi Manifesto* declared that the movement's main objective was to make Russia a global leader in the twenty-first century by fostering patriotism among the young generation and supporting Putin's "modernization policies."[36] However, it was widely believed that Nashi was the brainchild of Deputy Chief of the Presidential Administration Vladislav Surkov.[37] The youth movement was supposed to act as a guardian of the current regime, luring youth away from the political opposition in the run-up to the 2008 presidential election.

Nashi organized a variety of public rallies, bringing thousands of youngsters to the capital city for a spectacular display of youthful support for the incumbent president. According to some estimates, as many as 60,000 people participated in Nashi's first public event, "Our Victory" (*Nasha pobeda*), held in May 2005.[38] As its predecessor, Walking Together, Nashi boisterously

[34] Walking Together was founded in 2000 with the government's tacit approval. The youth movement displayed support for the incumbent president and emphasized the importance of "spiritual education." The movement organized its first public rally in support of the incumbent president on November 7, 2000. Another large public rally, involving 10,000 movement participants, was held in May 2001 to celebrate the first anniversary of Putin's presidency. Youth activists also picketed Western embassies and publicly burned books by some Russian writers deemed as liberal. But the adoption of a strict disciplinary code, embroilment in a pornography scandal, and financial disputes led to the movement's decline and self-dissolution in 2007. On the movement's history, see Cecil, Clam. 2002. "Pro-Putin Cult Urges Return to Soviet 'Glory.'" *Telegraph*. January 27. www.telegraph.co.uk/news/worldnews/europe/russia/1382860/Pro-Putin-cult-urges-return-to-Soviet-glory.html; Corwin, Julie. 2005. "Analysis: Walking with Putin." Radio Free Europe/Radio Liberty. March 2. www.rferl.org/content/article/1057762.html; Myers, Steven Lee. 2003. "Russian Group Is Offering Values to Fill a Void." *New York Times*. February 16. www.nytimes.com/2003/02/16/world/russian-group-is-offering-values-to-fill-a-void.html?pagewanted=all&src=pm; Sborov, Afanasii. 2001. "Maika, pager, KGB." *Kommersant Vlast*. May 15. www.kommersant.ru/doc/264481; Shevchuk, Mikhail, and Dmitry Kamyshev. 2005. "Obyknovennyi Nashizm: Kreml sozdaet novoe molodezhnoe dvizhenie." *Kommersant*. February 21. www.kommersant.ru/doc/549170.

[35] Ryklin, Aleksandr. 2005. "Nashi poshli." *Ezhednevnyi zhurnal*. March 1. http://123.ejnew.org/?a=note&id=13498

[36] The full text of the manifesto was retrieved from www.nashi.su/manifest.

[37] See, for example, Barry, Ellen. 2011. "Architect of Russia's Political System under Putin Is Reassigned." *New York Times*. December 27. www.nytimes.com/2011/12/28/world/europe/putin-takes-another-swipe-at-russian-protesters.html?_r=0; *Spiegel*. 2005. "Interview with Kremlin Boss Vladislav Surkov: 'The West Doesn't Have to Love Us.'" June issue. www.spiegel.de/international/spiegel/spiegel-interview-with-kremlin-boss-vladislav-surkov-the-west-doesn-t-have-to-love-us-a-361236.html.

[38] *LentaRu*. 2005. "Desiatki tysiach chelovek vyshli na Leninskii prospect otprazdnovat Nashu Pobedu." May 15. https://lenta.ru/news/2005/05/15/nasha/.

marked each year of Putin's presidency. In March 2007, for example, more than 15,000 youngsters marched down Moscow streets, carrying posters with the slogan "Putin Generation, Forward!" and prompting citizens to send congratulatory SMS messages to the president.[39] In addition, Nashi celebrated Putin's fifty-fifth birthday by organizing a march of 10,000 members, placing more than 1,000 Russian flags on Moscow's tallest buildings, ordering prayers for the president's health in several Moscow churches, and making a giant birthday card on behalf of movement participants.[40]

Reminiscent of the Red Guards in the People's Republic of China, Nashi activists physically attacked regime enemies. Young Putinists reportedly sabotaged the work of liberal youth organizations through the use of informants and provocateurs. A Nashi activist, for instance, admitted that she received $1,100 per month for obtaining "videos and photos to compromise the opposition, data from their computers, and, as a separate track, the dispatch of provocateurs."[41] Apparently, the youth movement collaborated with the Russian security services to facilitate state surveillance of challenger organizations.

Moscow-based Western diplomats were another common target of Nashi activists. In winter 2006, for example, British Ambassador to Russia Tony Brenton was harassed by movement participants, demanding his apology for participation in a "fascist meeting" with representatives of Other Russia, a coalition of antiregime forces.[42] Nashi activists also systematically harassed US Ambassador to Russia Michael McFaul.[43] Nashi activists, for example, gathered in front of US embassy to videotape and hurl verbal abuse at opposition politicians and civic activists who attended a meeting with US diplomats in January 2012.[44] Another Nashi campaign targeted Estonian

[39] Azar, Ilia. 2007. "Zapishite telefon Putina" [Write down Putin's phone number]. *GazetaRu*. March 21. www.gazeta.ru/2007/03/20/oa_234398.shtml.

[40] *Moscow Times*. 2007. "Putin Party: A Birthday Farewell." October 8. www.themoscowtimes.com/news/article/putin-party-a-birthday-farewell/193813.html.

[41] Shachtman, Noah. 2009. "Kremlin Kids: We Launched the Estonian Cyber War." *Wired*. November 3. www.wired.com/2009/03/pro-kremlin-gro/.

[42] Blomfield, Adrian. 2006. "Envoy Demands Kremlin Calls Off Its Youth Gang." *Daily Telegraph*. December 13. www.telegraph.co.uk/news/worldnews/1536832/Envoy-demands-Kremlin-calls-off-its-youth-gang.html.

[43] *Daily Signal*. 2012. "From Russia with Hate: Anti-Americanism Rampant in Putin's Kremlin." April 23. http://dailysignal.com/2012/04/23/from-russia-with-hate-anti-americanism-rampant-in-putins-kremlin/; Elder, Miriam. 2012. "Russia's Treatment of US Ambassador a Reflection of Shaky Relations." *The Guardian*. April 5. www.theguardian.com/world/2012/apr/05/russia-us-ambassador-relations; Trenin, Dmitry. 2014. *The McFaul Experience*. Moscow: Carnegie Moscow Center. Retrieved from http://carnegie.ru/publications/?fa=54441.

[44] *Moscow Times*. 2012. "Opposition Leaders Brief McFaul." January 18. https://themoscowtimes.com/news/opposition-leaders-brief-mcfaul-11949; Saunders, Paul. 2012. "U.S. Ambassador's Rough Welcome in Moscow: Is the Reset Failing?" *The Atlantic*. January 23. www.theatlantic.com/international/archive/2012/01/us-ambassadors-rough-welcome-in-moscow-is-the-reset-failing/251808/.

diplomats in the aftermath of Estonia's decision to relocate a Soviet war memorial in the capital city of Tallinn.[45] In addition to picketing Estonia's embassy, movement participants launched a cyber attack against the Estonian government.

Nashi also endorsed censorship of cultural products and advocated a ban of Russian literature critical of the incumbent president. In a LiveJournal entry, for example, Nashi activist Natalia expressed outrage over the availability of Stanislav Belkovsky's book, *Vladimir Putin's Empire*, in a local bookstore. She wrote, "It is necessary to address the issue. Why are books written by traitors sold in bookstores?"[46]

Furthermore, Nashi performed "citizens' oversight over elections" so that "no anti-Russian forces could convince the electorate that voting was rigged," according to Sergei Belokonev, coordinator for Nashi's pilot project "Civic Oversight."[47] Nashi trained youth activists to observe the municipal elections and conduct an exit poll in Moscow in December 2005. The project "Our Elections" (*Nashi vybory*), allegedly separate from the youth movement, was extended to the whole of Russia during the 2007 parliamentary elections. Nashi activists participated in a voter mobilization campaign to boost youth's electoral support for the ruling party United Russia. For this GOTV campaign, youth activists adopted the slogan, "It's Time to Choose" (*Vremia vybirat*), and showed up at public rallies with ringing alarm clocks, resembling protest tactics previously used in Serbia. The movement's leadership also planned to bring 20,000 activists to Moscow during the 2008 presidential election so that they could occupy main public squares and reside in a government-sponsored tent city to prevent the repeat of the Ukrainian scenario during the Orange Revolution.[48]

Nashi has become one of the largest youth movements in Putin's Russia, with more than 100,000 members, within two years since its inception.[49] Thousands of young people participated in movement activities. Using Soviet-era vocabulary of military ranks, Nashi leaders bore the title of commissars.[50] To

45 Finn, Peter. 2007. "Protesters in Moscow Harass Estonian Envoy Over Statue." *Washington Post*. May 3. www.washingtonpost.com/wp-dyn/content/article/2007/05/02/AR2007050202547.html.

46 Natalia. 2007. "Eto knizhnyi fascism." December 12. http://notrestore.livejournal.com/210351.html.

47 Romancheva, Irina. 2007. "Nashi s budilnikami." *Vzgliad*. November 12. www.vz.ru/politics/2007/11/12/124052.html.

48 Kachurovskaya, Anna. 2007. "Paren iz 'Nashego' ozera." *Kommersant*. July 30. www.kommersant.ru/doc/790656.

49 Miller, Christopher. 2016. "'Girl Who Kissed Putin' Warns about Rise of Russian Nationalism." *Mashable*. January 6. http://mashable.com/2016/01/06/putin-drokova-russia-new-york/#eS5_mEad.qqP.

50 The commissar in the Red Army was responsible for ideological education of the military. Similarly, Nashi leaders were charged with the responsibility to provide ideological training of Russian youth.

provide ideological training for youth activists, Nashi annually held a summer camp on picturesque Lake Seliger. Testifying to the movement's numerical strength, the number of camp attendees increased from 3,000 people in 2005 to 10,000 in 2007.[51] As a recipient of state funding, the youth movement could implement a massive recruitment campaign and provide positive incentives for its members. Movement membership was promoted as a pathway to a future career in government.

Nashi's access to financial resources, however, cannot fully account for the movement's growth. The youth movement had a genuine following in Russia. Nashi commissar Masha Drokova, for example, recalled how school, as well as existing youth organizations, was "boring" for her, and Nashi provided a novel, appealing venue for becoming civically engaged.[52] Drokova became known for plastering a kiss on Putin's cheek at an award ceremony, idolizing the country's leader. Alissa, another Nashi commissar, also felt utmost admiration for Putin:

> We were in a black hole before him [Putin]. He made the Russian economy work again. We were no longer ashamed to feel a sense of national dignity. We demonstrated to the world that Russia is not and will not be a second-class country. We understood the importance of patriotic education for our youth.[53]

According to an Oborona activist, the movement's ideology had a sinister impact on youth's social identity:

> What is scary about Nashi is not its huge financing ... The worst part is they have this ideology that unfortunately they have begun to believe. You notice that their booklets have a lot in common with the Hitler Youth. And what you notice is their emphasis on social and political upward mobility ... So they have developed this idea that "we are the worthy youth, the rest are the unworthy, unchosen ones."[54]

A comparison of the two Russian youth movements demonstrates clear-cut differences in their level of youth mobilization. Notwithstanding its adoption of Otpor's innovative tactics, Oborona failed to win over a significant share of Russian youth. Nashi, on the contrary, attracted a large number of young people, skillfully borrowing the opposition's tactics and using them to serve the movement's political ends. The severity of state repression against Oborona provides a valid explanation for the movement's smaller size.

[51] The data were retrieved from Nashi's website, http://nashi.su/projects.

[52] Miller, Christopher. 2016. "'Girl Who Kissed Putin' Warns about Rise of Russian Nationalism."

[53] Quoted from Dzieciolowski, Zygmunt. 2008. "The Future's Ours: Russia's Youth Activists." *Open Democracy*. January 19. www.opendemocracy.net/article/the_future_s_ours_russia_s_youth_activists.

[54] Arias-King, Fredo. 2007. "A Revolution of the Mind: Interview with Yulia Malysheva." *Demokratizatsiya: Journal of Post-Soviet Democratization* 15(1): 117–28, pp. 121–22.

Nashi's popularity, however, cannot be reduced solely to the government's financial backing. Compared to Oborona, Nashi delivered a set of more appealing messages. In particular, Nashi's interpretation of patriotism seemed to resonate more strongly with the majority of Russian youth than Oborona's emphasis on political rights and civil liberties arising out of Western liberalism. The Kremlin's use of savvy countermoves also points to the importance of tactics in explaining the level of civil resistance in a nondemocratic setting.

In addition, this book demonstrates that national history of civic activism has far-reaching consequences for subsequent mobilization efforts. Otpor's civil resistance, for example, was influenced by prior protest campaigns during Milosevic's presidency. Likewise, contentious collective action during the Orange Revolution was informed by earlier protests in Ukraine. Since the confrontation between the ruling elite and regime opponents is an iterative process, social scientists need to place a specific episode of contention in the context of long-term national struggle for democracy. This long-term perspective will enable scholars to uncover the extent to which civic activists and their adversaries were able to draw lessons from earlier episodes of contention. A policy-relevant lesson is that long-term commitment to the development of civil society is necessary to bolster bottom-up mobilization for political change in nondemocracies. As advocated by Carothers in his critique of the transition paradigm, the international donor community should transcend its fixation on national elections and adopt a more comprehensive strategy for democracy promotion.[55] It might take civic activists years of experimentation with various protest tactics to build organizational skills and develop a fair share of expertise in nonviolent action. In the absence of a domestic history of civic activism, the blunt adoption of innovative ideas from abroad is unlikely to produce intended effects.

What emerges from this study is that young people can play an active role in facilitating democratization processes in the post-Soviet region. The youth movements established in Eastern Europe on the eve of national elections brought thousands of first-time voters to the polling stations and drew hundreds of apolitical youngsters into nonviolent struggle against the regime. Youth movements also contributed to the development of civil society in a nondemocratic setting. The emergence of youth-led challenger organizations provided an impetus for the development of various civic initiatives with a focus on the youth population. A general conclusion to be drawn from this study is that the political significance of youth should not be overlooked in comparative democratization literature.

[55] Carothers, Thomas. 2002. "The End of the Transition Paradigm." *Journal of Democracy* 13(1): 5–21.

To date, nearly two-thirds of the world's population lives in nondemocracies.[56] Challenger organizations in these regimes look on bottom-up mobilization as a mechanism for political change. This book provides insights into civil resistance in five post-communist states. The take-home message is that regime opponents need to display a great deal of resourcefulness to outwit the incumbent government and mobilize ordinary citizens in favor of democratic change.

[56] According to the *2017 Freedom in the World Report*, 61 percent of the world population currently live in political regimes classified as "partly free" or "unfree." For details, see https://freedomhouse.org/report/freedom-world/freedom-world-2017.

APPENDIX

List of Interviewees

AZERBAIJAN

Namiq Feyziev, Yeni Fikir member (via phone), October 27, 2014
Ramin Hajili, Dalga member, Baku, February 21, 2008
Emin Huseynov, Maqam member, Baku, February 22, 2008
Ilgar (pseudonym), International Republican Institute (Azerbaijan), Baku, February 26, 2008
Said Nuri, Yeni Fikir member (via Skype), October 17, 2014
Razi Nurullayev, Yokh member, Baku, February 25, 2008
Vugar Salamli, Yokh member, Baku, February 26, 2008
Leyla (pseudonym), Ireli member, Baku, February 25, 2008

BELARUS

Aleh, Zubr member, Minsk, March 15, 2008
Ales, Malady Front member (via Skype), January 29, 2012
Alexei, Zubr member (via Skype), January 25, 2013
Andrei, Zubr member (via Skype), December 19, 2012
Dzmitry, Zubr member (via Skype), January 21, 2013
Enira, Partnerstva NGO, Minsk, March 13, 2008
Iryna, Zubr member, Minsk, March 12, 2008
Maksim, Malady Front member, Kyiv, May 22, 2010
Uladzimir, Zubr member (via Skype), March 11, 2012

GEORGIA

Lali Chketia, project director, Georgian Young Lawyers' Association, Tbilisi, February 14, 2008
David Darchiashvili, executive director, Open Society–Georgia Foundation, Tbilisi, February 16, 2008

Nini Gogiberidze, Kmara member, Tbilisi, February 14, 2008
Giorgi Kandelaki, Kmara member, Belgrade, February 7, 2008
Ketevan Kobiashvili, Kmara member, Tbilisi, February 15, 2008
Gvantsa Liparteliani, Kmara member, Tbilisi, February 18, 2008
Gocha Lordkipanidze, Visiting Scholar, Columbia University, New York City, October 16, 2009
Giorgi Meladze, Kmara member, Belgrade, February 7, 2008
Akaki Minashvili, Kmara member, Tbilisi, February 17, 2008
Giorgi Nikoladze, Kmara member, Toronto, Canada, August 6, 2009
Levan Ramishvili, director of the Liberty Institute, Tbilisi, February 13, 2008

SERBIA

Dragan Ambrozic, music critic and program manager of Exit Festival Main Stage, Belgrade, February 2, 2008
Ivan Andric, Otpor member, Belgrade, January 28, 2008
Tanja Azanjac, program coordinator, NGO Civic Initiatives, Belgrade, February 7, 2008
Nenad Belcevic, Otpor member, Belgrade, February 8, 2008
Marko Blagojevic, program director, CeSID, Belgrade, February 6, 2008
Slobodan Djindovic, Otpor member, Belgrade, January 25, 2008
Ana Djordjevic, Otpor member, Belgrade, January 26, 2008
Slobodan Homen, Otpor member, Belgrade, February 7, 2008
Mladen Joksic, Otpor member, New York City, December 10, 2011
Nenad Konstantinovic, Otpor member, New York City, November 6, 2009
Stanko Lazendic, Otpor member, Novi Sad, January 24, 2008
Predrag Madzarevic, Otpor member, Kragujevac, February 4, 2008
Aleksandar Maric, Otpor member, Novi Sad, January 24, 2008
Ivan Marovic, Otpor member, Washington, DC, December 13, 2007,
Vladimir Pavlov, Otpor member, New York City, November 4, 2009
Srdja Popovic, Otpor member, Belgrade, January 23, 2008
Dejan Randic, Otpor member, Belgrade, January 30, 2008
Vesna Tomic, Otpor Mothers, Novi Sad, January 27, 2008

UKRAINE

Tetiana Boyko, Pora member, Kyiv, April 14, 2008
Andriy Kohut, Pora member, Kyiv, March 19, 2010
Ostap Kryvdyk, Pora member, Kyiv, April 16, 2008
Volodymyr Lesyk, Pora member, Kyiv, April 11, 2008
Nazar Matkivsky, Pora member, Kyiv, April 14, 2008
Dmytro Potekhin, coordinator of the civic campaign "I Know!" (*Ia znaiu!*), Kyiv, April 10, 2008

Olha Salo, Pora member, Kyiv, April 16, 2008
Taras Shamaida, coordinator of the youth campaign "Student Wave," Kyiv, April 14, 2008
Oleksandr Solontay, Pora member, leader of the Foundation of Regional Initiatives, Kyiv, April 11, 2008
Mykhailo Svystovych, Pora member, Kyiv, March 27, 2010
Serhiy Taran, Pora member, Kyiv, April 29, 2010
Oleksiy Tolkachov, Pora member, Kyiv, April 22, 2010
Yaryna Yasynevych, Pora member, Kyiv, April 16, 2010
Liubov Yeremycheva, Pora member, Kyiv, May 14, 2010
Andriy Yusov, Pora member, Kyiv, April 17, 2008
Oleksandra Vesnich, journalist and leader of a Sumy student protest, Sumy, March 19, 2008
Volodymyr Viatrovych, Pora member, Kyiv, March 2, 2010
Yaroslav Zen, Pora member, Kyiv, April 18, 2008
Yevhen Zolotariov, Pora member, Kyiv, March 30, 2010
Pavlo Zubiuk, Pora member, Kyiv, March 23, 2010

Index

Books in the Series (continued from p. ii)

Christian Davenport, *How Social Movements Die: Repression and Demobilization of the Republic of New Africa*
Christian Davenport, *Media Bias, Perspective, and State Repression*
Gerald F. Davis, Doug McAdam, W. Richard Scott, and Mayer N. Zald, *Social Movements and Organization Theory*
Donatella della Porta, *Clandestine Political Violence*
Donatella della Porta, *Where Did the Revolution Go?: Contentious Politics and the Quality of Democracy*
Mario Diani, *The Cement of Civil Society: Studying Networks in Localities*
Todd A. Eisenstadt, *Politics, Identity, and Mexico's Indigenous Rights Movements*
Daniel Q. Gillion, *The Political Power of Protest: Minority Activism and Shifts in Public Policy*
Jack A. Goldstone, editor, *States, Parties, and Social Movements*
Jennifer Hadden, *Networks in Contention: The Divisive Politics of Climate Change*
Michael T. Heaney and Fabio Rojas, *Party in the Street: The Antiwar Movement and the Democratic Party after 9/11*
Tamara Kay, *NAFTA and the Politics of Labor Transnationalism*
Neil Ketchley, *Egypt in a Time of Revolution: Contentious Politics and the Arab Spring*
Joseph Luders, *The Civil Rights Movement and the Logic of Social Change*
Doug McAdam and Hilary Boudet, *Putting Social Movements in Their Place: Explaining Opposition to Energy Projects in the United States, 2000–2005*
Doug McAdam, Sidney Tarrow, and Charles Tilly, *Dynamics of Contention*
Holly J. McCammon, *The U.S. Women's Jury Movements and Strategic Adaptation: A More Just Verdict*
Sharon Nepstad, *Religion and War Resistance and the Plowshares Movement*
Olena Nikolayenko, *Youth Movements and Elections in Eastern Europe*
Kevin J. O'Brien and Lianjiang Li, *Rightful Resistance in Rural China*
Silvia Pedraza, *Political Disaffection in Cuba's Revolution and Exodus*
Héctor Perla Jr., *Sandinista Nicaragua's Resistance to US Coercion*
Eduardo Silva, *Challenging Neoliberalism in Latin America*
Erica S. Simmons, *Meaningful Resistance: Market Reforms and the Roots of Social Protest in Latin America*
Sarah Soule, *Contention and Corporate Social Responsibility*
Sherrill Stroschein, *Ethnic Struggle, Coexistence, and Democratization in Eastern Europe*
Yang Su, *Collective Killings in Rural China during the Cultural Revolution*
Sidney Tarrow, *The Language of Contention: Revolutions in Words, 1688–2012*
Sidney Tarrow, *The New Transnational Activism*
Wayne P. Te Brake, *Religious War and Religious Peace in Early Modern Europe*
Ralph A. Thaxton Jr., *Catastrophe and Contention in Rural China: Mao's Great Leap Forward Famine and the Origins of Righteous Resistance in Da Fo Village*
Ralph A. Thaxton Jr., *Force and Contention in Contemporary China: Memory and Resistance in the Long Shadow of the Catastrophic Past*
Charles Tilly, *Contention and Democracy in Europe, 1650–2000*
Charles Tilly, *Contentious Performances*

Charles Tilly, *The Politics of Collective Violence*
Marisa von Bülow, *Building Transnational Networks: Civil Society and the Politics of Trade in the Americas*
Lesley J. Wood, *Direct Action, Deliberation, and Diffusion: Collective Action after the WTO Protests in Seattle*
Stuart A. Wright, *Patriots, Politics, and the Oklahoma City Bombing*
Deborah Yashar, *Contesting Citizenship in Latin America: The Rise of Indigenous Movements and the Postliberal Challenge*
Andrew Yeo, *Activists, Alliances, and Anti-U.S. Base Protests*